Overview

Introduction

Britain is relatively small in area yet remarkably diverse, with landscapes ranging from sea-cliffs and rocky offshore islands, to the massifs of the Scottish Highland, the low fenland of East Anglia, and the gentle wooded coombes of the south-west. The long, intricate coastline includes many fine estuaries with their associated mudflats and coastal marshes, several of which are internationally famous for the wildlife they support.

Although much of lowland Britain is intensively farmed, to the general detriment of the wildlife (at least in the arable areas), there are still many regions with rich natural or semi-natural habitats, such as ancient woodland, moorland, and, perhaps most importantly, lowland heath. In only a short distance one can experience windswept hills with alpine flowers and mountain birds, lowland woodland, or open saltmarsh and estuary alive with the calls of waders and wildfowl. Nowhere in Britain is far from the coast, and the sea is one of the dominating features affecting the climate and wildlife of these islands. No other European area has such a varied coastline, nor so much marine wetland habitat to offer.

Geography

Britain is a country of rolling hills rather than high mountains. Nevertheless, even our modest 'mountains' dominate the landscape in many places, notably in central and west Scotland. This is partly because, although the altitudes reached are not great by European standards (the highest, Ben Nevis, reaching a mere 1343 m), many of the ranges rear up close to the sea, starting from a low base level. It is only parts of Scotland and Wales that are truly mountainous, with high hills and plateaux dominating the overall landscape. The Cairngorms Massif is the highest range, and has its own very characteristic fauna and flora. The most notable ranges in Wales are Snowdonia and the Brecon Beacons, and the Lake District in the north-west of England has scenery recalling parts of Scotland, although its particular concentration of meres and hills is unique.

In England, the high ground is mainly to be found along the backbone range of the Pennine Hills, which extend from Derbyshire north to the Scottish Borders. Other more isolated areas of high ground include the moors of Bodmin, Exmoor, and Dartmoor in the south-west, the Mendips and Cotswolds, the North and South Downs, the Chilterns, and the North York Moors.

Elsewhere Britain is a landscape of undulating, mostly farmed country, with pasture and grazing land concentrated in the damper west, and arable cereal and other crops in the more intensely farmed midlands and south-east. Woodland generally increases towards the west, too, and East Anglia is the region with the fewest trees and the least woodland cover, although Kent and Sussex retain the highest concentrations of ancient woodland.

The geology of Britain is complicated, with outcroppings of many different types of igneous and metamorphic rocks, such as granites, schists, and gneiss, and sedimentary rocks such as limestone, chalk, and sandstones. As a generalization and simplification one can say that the harder rocks (which usually underlie acidic soils) tend to be in the uplands of the north and

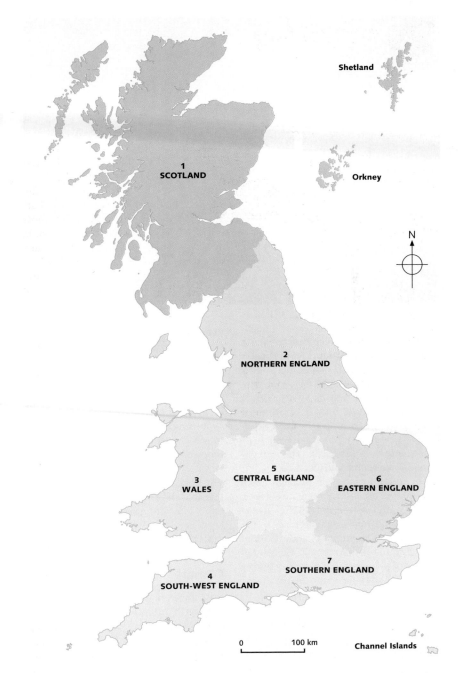

west, while the lower land of the south and east sits generally on softer, sedimentary rocks (many of which are calcareous, producing alkaline soils). Superimposed on this picture are soils formed elsewhere, but deposited by glacial action, examples being the sandy soils of the Breckland and areas overlain by boulder clay.

Heath, New Forest

Upland Britain lies mainly to the north and west of a line running from the Exe Estuary in Devon, along the Bristol Channel, to the lower Trent Valley, reaching the North Sea coast at the North York Moors. The natural history of Britain is influenced very strongly by this difference in topography, but also of course by other factors, notably soil type and climate (both regional and local).

The upland mountainous areas with high rainfall are mostly on neutral rocks, with a neutral or acid soil developed over them. Acid-loving vegetation tends therefore to be prominent in upland sites, and in boggy habitats in the high rainfall regions of the north and west. Interesting exceptions provide some of the finest flower-hunting areas on outcrops of calcareous rock on upland sites, such as at Ben Lawers or in Upper Teesdale, and on the limestone pavements in certain parts of the Pennines.

Other areas with acid soils include those developed over sandstone or pockets of heathland, where leaching has impoverished the surface soil by removing minerals. Lowland heathland occurs mainly in Dorset, Hampshire, Surrey, and in parts of East Anglia. Here the plants tend to include heather and relatives, and there is a very characteristic assemblage of both animals and plants, with several rarities. In eastern, central, and southeast England, the soils are often lime-rich, especially along the chalk and limestone ridges of the North and South Downs, the Chilterns, and the Cotswolds. The flora again reflects the geology, with flower-rich chalk grassland a cherished habitat in southern England. Chalk grassland is also an excellent habitat for butterflies and other invertebrates.

Climate

Britain's climate is strongly influenced by the North Atlantic Drift, which swings warm water up towards the coast from further south in the Atlantic. This means that the climate here is milder than one might expect from latitude alone. The seas around our shores also vary relatively little in temperature between winter and summer, so that the effect of the prevailing westerly and south-westerly winds is to warm the land in winter and cool it in summer. On average, the summers are cooler and wetter than those further east, and the winters, which are also wetter, are considerably warmer. The average temperature difference between winter and summer is only about 11°C in eastern England, for example.

The combination of equable temperature and a long growing season favours tree growth and woodland development, and trees can grow almost everywhere in Britain, at least potentially. The only dry-land sites which are probably naturally treeless are the extreme mountain tops and very exposed offshore islands and coasts.

The western and northern regions have the highest rainfall, being exposed to the regular series of westerly depressions which characterize the climate. Since much of the high ground is also in the north and west, the rain clouds tend to form there and drop much of their precipitation first in these areas, whilst the land further east gains some protection by being in a rain shadow. This combination of geology and climate also results generally in poorer, thinner soils in the north and west, contrasting with more fertile, deeper soils in the south and east. The high rainfall feeds many upland streams, and a fine network of rivers, ponds, and lakes, adding to the variety of habitats.

Even though the climate is mild compared with more Continental regions, the winters can occasionally be fierce, and in some highland regions snow lies almost throughout the year. Many species, particularly some birds, cannot survive such rigours and have evolved strategies for escaping when times are tough. Many insect-eating birds, such as swallows, martins, swifts, and most warblers migrate south in the autumn, to richer feeding grounds in southern Europe or Africa. There is also a big autumn and winter influx, particularly of waders and wildfowl, which flee their largely frozen northern breeding grounds and gather on coastal and inland wetlands where food is abundant. Britain has some of the finest wetland habitats in Europe, and the estuaries in particular are vital for many thousands of ducks, geese, swans, and shorebirds.

Vegetation and habitats

It is doubtful whether any of the habitats we see today are natural in the sense that they are unaltered by human influence, with the possible exception of the high mountaintops, inaccessible rocks and cliffs, both inland and at the coast, and some mudflats and saltmarshes. Elsewhere, the wildlife refuges we seek to preserve are mainly semi-natural, a product of centuries of close interaction with people and their ways of life. Such habitats range from established ancient woodland (most of which is or has been managed in one form or another, often for centuries) through to lowland heath and chalk grassland. Many of our richest and most interesting habitats rely upon regular management to keep them in their most diverse state. Examples include heath, water meadow, machair, upland heather moor, chalk grassland, traditional hay meadows, and coppiced ancient woodland.

The Industrial Revolution not only accelerated destruction of natural habitats, but also initiated a phase of pollution, still a major problem today. Waste gases from industry and cars cause acidification of some habitats, particularly upland lakes, lowering the range of species. At the same time, nitrates and minerals from fertilizers find their way into rivers, streams, and lakes, also causing reduced diversity and occasional destructive algal blooms. The use of pesticides, several of which had unforeseen and dramatic effects on wildlife, caused crashes in raptor populations, thankfully now largely reversed. Naturally wet habitats, such as the once extensive fens of East Anglia, were systematically drained to provide yet more fertile soil for planting crops. Today this habitat has almost entirely gone, with just a very few remnants left to remind us what it must have been like, although welcome and ambitious schemes are now underway to reverse this trend.

There is a growing awareness that straightforwardly economic land-use and conservation are not incompatible, but can be of benefit to each other. Indeed, there is also an increasing realization of the dangers of over-intensive farming procedures; these tendencies may result eventually in the reintroduction of more wildlife-friendly procedures. Although it is clearly still important to retain and protect certain types of site and habitat from the more directly damaging influences of people, conservation today must retain to some extent an element of land-use, especially in a densely populated country such as Britain. Nevertheless, many pressures on the environment remain, and we cannot afford to be complacent. Some raw statistics bring home the extent of habitat loss: about 40% of ancient woodland and lowland heath, 50% of lowland fens and mires, and 95% of lowland neutral grassland lost since 1945, internationally significant estuaries threatened by development, and countless Sites of Special Scientific Interest (SSSIs) destroyed or damaged.

Nor are urban sites without their wildlife value, and it is often surprising how quickly species appear when new reserves are created, even in built-up areas (for example the London Wetland Centre). With the increased popularity of ecological gardening, we can all do our bit to help local wildlife. Many urban sites, including gardens, are attractive to wildlife, and garden ponds are soon colonized by invertebrates such as water beetles, water boatmen, and dragonflies, and by vertebrates such as newts and frogs. Some birds formerly associated with wilder habitats, such as green woodpecker, jay, magpie, and sparrowhawk, are being seen more and more in our gardens. Classic urban butterflies are the three whites (large, small, and green-veined), orange tip, red admiral, peacock, small tortoiseshell, meadow brown, wall, holly blue, and sometimes speckled wood, common blue, and large and small skippers.

Woodland

'Wildwood' is a term used to describe the original woodland cover before the impact of people and domesticated animals. True wildwood almost certainly no longer exists in Britain (although arguably patches remain in some parts of Continental Europe) and Britain is one of Europe's least wooded countries, having lost 50% of its ancient woodland since the 1930s. This despite the fact that woodland is the potential natural climax vegetation over much of the country (including most upland and hill country, as well as non-waterlogged lowland sites). Wildwood persisted for millennia after the most recent ice age (which ended about 12 000 BC), but is now just an ancient memory in the romantic imagination.

Woodland has been felled, managed, replanted, or used in a variety of ways for many centuries, giving rise eventually to the pattern we see today. Even in Medieval times there was probably very little natural woodland left, and the countryside has been worked hard for thousands of years. Perhaps surprisingly, the main concentration of ancient woodland today is in the south-east of England, in Sussex and Kent, where the soils are particularly rich and deep. There are very few large stretches of ancient woodland, but instead we find a patchwork of mostly rather small woods, dotted over the countryside, and ancient woodland covers only about 2% of the land. What we now detect in these ancient woodland remnants are merely echoes of the wildwood, a sort of watermark in the parchment of woodland left by tell-tale combinations of indicator species, meaningful only to the seasoned naturalist or expert botanist. Such plants include (in different regions) small-leaved lime, midland hawthorn, spindle, and oxlip. Relict ancient woods are therefore well worth preserving (and visiting), not only for their fascinating wildlife but also for the link they provide with history; the historical ecologist can 'read' such places for an insight into the past.

The original wildwood of Britain displayed much regional variation, some of which may still be detected to this day. Broadly speaking, central and southern England were dominated by small-leaved lime, with elm, ash, oak, and hazel; western and northern England and southern Scotland were the province of oak and hazel; birch was the main tree of northern Scotland, and Scots pine dominated in the Highland of Scotland. Ash and beech are now much more common than originally. Oliver Rackham estimates that by 500 BC about half of England's wildwoods had disappeared, and by the time of the Romans the woodland cover may well have been similar to what we see today. Domesday Book (1086) records information about woodland, and analysis of this indicates that the woodland cover then was as low as 15%, which is less than that of France today. Some of the largest wooded areas then (as now) were in the Weald, the Chilterns, and Forest of Dean, and probably in Wales. Scotland was already mainly moorland and farmland, with few areas of extensive woodland.

Woodlands were very often used to provide a renewable source of wood for fuel and timber, and were managed by traditional methods such as coppicing. Such management used to be much more widespread when people relied on a crop of natural wood for poles and branches. Coppicing consists of cutting back to stumps certain species, such as ash, field maple, and hazel. These then regenerate and produce a regular crop of fairly straight poles, which can be harvested. Occasional tall 'standard' trees are left to develop fully, and these, too, are felled from time to time to give bulkier timber. Coppicing is a form of exploiting the woods without destroying them. It also allows a wide range of woodland animals and plants to flourish, because there is more variety of habitat in a coppiced wood. Many woodland plants and animals became adapted to such management regimes, and today woodland reserves (such as Hayley Wood, Cambridgeshire) are often retained

Loch Daven, Aberdeenshire

in these semi-natural states specifically for the benefit of the wildlife.

Most ancient woodland was (and is) broadleaf, with the exception of some native Scots pine communities in Scotland, and the main species involved are oaks, limes, ash, elm, and hazel, with beech and hornbeam mainly in the south and east. Aspen, birch, sallow, field maple, holly, and alder are all native species which colonized (or re-colonized) Britain after the retreat of the ice. Sycamore, introduced in the late sixteenth century, and sweet chestnut, a Roman import, have established themselves widely, and, in the case of sycamore, aggressively. Many conservationists disapprove of invasive aliens, often on the grounds that they diminish the 'natural' species-richness of a given site. This may sometimes be true, as in the case of rhododendron, which shades out other species in acid woodland; but introductions have also enriched our natural history, and one should not dismiss all introduced species as uninteresting. Indeed, invasion may itself be considered a natural process, albeit one often aided by people.

The biggest losses of woodland came after the Second World War, when many woods were felled to make way for farmland. A serious programme of tree planting also began, but this was a commercial enterprise, too, mainly using alien conifers as a fast-growing crop of 'softwood'. Thankfully, this trend has been halted in recent decades and broadleaved woods are now being cared for and recreated, reversing many years of gradual loss, partly through the efforts of the Woodland Trust, the Forestry Commission, and many other conservation bodies.

The major tree dominants – oaks, ash, lime, and elms – probably formed a mixed tree-layer in much of the original lowland 'wildwood'. In the north, ash plays a much more dominant role in damp woods on calcareous soils. Birch is another very common tree; it tends to prefer sandy, acid soils and is usually found mixed with other species, such as oaks or Scots pine. In Scotland in particular, birch may form fairly pure woods, especially at reasonably high altitudes, but there are relatively few such remnants remaining. Further south, birch woods also occur as a mosaic in lowland heathland. Beech woods occur in some parts, particularly on shallower soils in the south, such as on the crests of chalk and limestone outcrops like the Downs and Chilterns.

Wet soils, especially along river valleys, typically develop alder woods. Examples of these can be seen in and around the Norfolk Broads, where the soils are very swampy and other trees find it hard to survive. One rather special type of wet scrub woodland is known as carr. Carr develops in fenland and represents a stage in succession from sedge and grass-dominated fen to wet and damp woodland. Fen carr tends to be dominated by shrubs such as sallow, buckthorn and alder buckthorn, and fine examples can be seen in areas such as the Norfolk Broads, and at reserves like Wicken Fen.

Typical woodland birds include tits, warblers, woodpeckers, flycatchers, wren, thrushes, owls, and sparrowhawk, and rarer species such as red kite and honey buzzard. Deciduous woodlands also provide safe homes for badgers, foxes, squirrels, mice, voles, and shrews.

Characteristic butterflies of mature broadleaved woodland are brimstone, speckled wood, silver-washed fritillary, white admiral, purple emperor, and purple, white-letter, and black hairstreaks. Duke of Burgundy, and heath,

Beadlet anemone *Actinea equina*

Easton Broad, Suffolk

both pearl-bordereds, high brown, and dark green fritillaries, are typical of cleared and regrowing woods, while wood white and large, dingy, and grizzled skippers are more likely to inhabit woodland glades and rides.

The only truly native coniferous (evergreen) woodlands in Britain and Ireland are the remaining patches of Caledonian Scots pine forest in Scotland. Several remnants of these fine communities are now carefully protected, but threatened in many places through overgrazing by deer. Scots pine also forms woods elsewhere, as for example on sandy, well-drained soils in the heathlands of southern and eastern England, but these are mostly planted or semi-natural.

Large tracts of countryside, especially in the hill country of the north and west, have been steadily planted with coniferous trees, usually with species of spruce, and particularly with the North American sitka spruce. These trees grow well on 'poor' soils and rapidly give a crop of timber, being usually felled by rotation.

Plantations such as these are not without their own wildlife interest, but they certainly have a less diverse fauna and flora than the native, mostly broadleaf, woods they have replaced. Furthermore, they have also been implicated in channelling and concentrating the effects of acid rain. Fortunately, the move now amongst foresters is back towards a mixed planting strategy, using broadleaved species as well.

The most rewarding coniferous woods for the visiting naturalist are those mature forests in which the trees regenerate naturally, and which also include open areas and clearings. Here light penetrates, a rich ground flora can develop, and scrubby stands of pioneer birch often intermingle. These contrast with the dark ranks of exotic spruce, all destined to be felled together, with little or no natural regeneration allowed.

Special birds and mammals of coniferous woodland include long-eared owl, goshawk, capercaillie, black grouse, coal tit, crested tit, goldcrest, firecrest, redpoll, crossbill, siskin, pine marten, and red squirrel. In felled or

Crested tit *Parus cristatus*

newly planted sites, nightjar, woodlark, and hen harrier may breed.

Lowland heath

This habitat is one of our most prominent, and also one of Europe's most threatened, with the remnants that remain being of major international importance. Heaths are the product of human (or animal) interference with the processes of nature, although they consist almost entirely of wild, mostly native, species. Heaths return quickly to woodland (usually birch and oak), via various stages of scrub, if the traditional methods used to create and preserve them are withdrawn. Thousands of years ago, most of the areas of lowland heath were covered by woodland. Heaths were gradually created in place of much of this woodland, until, in Anglo-Saxon times, heath covered large tracts of England and lowland Scotland. In their heyday in the Middle Ages, lowland heaths were used in a variety of ways – as grazing land, cut for fuel (mainly gorse and heather), or for rabbit warrens (the latter notably in Breckland). Although lowland heath recovers well after fire, burning was probably not the main tool of traditional heathland management, but bracken was burned to provide a source of potash (for making glass and soap). For the last three or four hundred years, though, lowland heath has been in retreat, and more than

40% of Britain's lowland heath has been lost since 1950, with only scattered fragments remaining. At the Continental level, Britain's lowland heath is very significant, with some 20% of Europe's total being in the UK. The best lowland heath sites are now to be found mainly in Hampshire, Dorset, and Surrey, and in the Breckland of East Anglia.

The main dominant plants of these habitats are heather and heaths, with gorse, broom, and bracken often quite abundant, and flowers such as tormentil and heath bedstraw. Birds of heathland include tree pipit, yellowhammer, wren, stonechat, and whinchat, as well as local or rare species such as hobby, nightjar, woodlark, stone curlew, and Dartford warbler. Lowland heaths are also Britain's last main refuge for the rare smooth snake and sand lizard, where they occur along with more common reptiles such as adder and viviparous lizard, and some heaths have colonies of the threatened natterjack. Butterflies of lowland heath and acid grassland include small copper, grayling, small heath, and silver-studded blue.

Grassland

Like heath, grassland mostly occupies land that was once forested. By the time of the Domesday Book (1086) about a quarter of the country was probably grassland of one sort or another, and the great expanses of chalk downland we know today already existed.

There are two main types of grassland: pasture, which is used for and maintained by regular grazing, and meadow,

Wren *Troglodytes troglodytes*

which is managed as a hay crop. These differ in their composition, and there are many variants according to the soil type, degree of dampness, and precise management regime. Typical plants of pasture are buttercups, thistles, and yarrow, while meadows have a different set, with species such as salad burnet, meadowsweet, oxeye daisy, bird's-foot-trefoil, meadow saxifrage, meadow-rue, and common sorrel. Some grassland species are more characteristic of woodland grassland, such as open glades or rides within woods. Examples of these are self-heal, bugle, and ragged-robin. Chalk and limestone grassland is a very rich habitat, and many of our butterflies depend upon it, especially on warm, south-facing

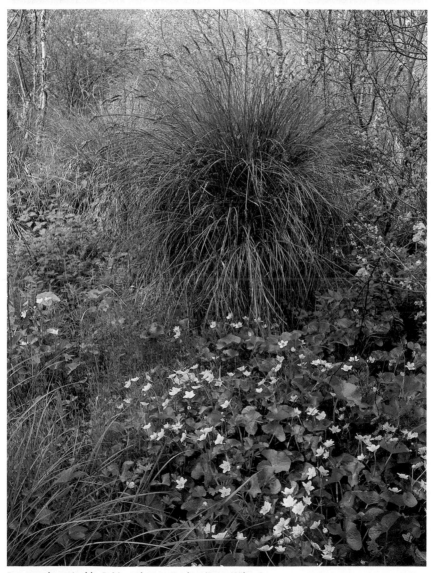

Bog, marsh-marigolds *Caltha palustris*, Borders (Peter Wilson)

slopes. These include most of the skippers (with Lulworth and silver-spotted restricted to this habitat), several blues, including small, chalk-hill, and Adonis, and marbled white. On damp grassland one may find orange tip, and marsh and small pearl-bordered fritillaries.

Grassland is a habitat under multiple threat from farming, building development and, in recent years, major road-building programmes as well. Some of the most interesting types of grassland for the naturalist are undoubtedly the unimproved chalk downland and sheep pastures, where traditional grazing regimes maintain a close-cropped sward with a rich and fascinating flora, including many beautiful flowers such as horseshoe vetch, common rock-rose, a whole range of orchids, and the rare pasqueflower.

Birds associated with open fields, pasture, and farmland in general are skylark, kestrel, grey partridge, lapwing, jackdaw, rook, and little and barn owls, as well as rarer species such as stone curlew, cirl bunting, quail, and Montagu's harrier.

Hay meadows are another wildlife-rich habitat, but one sadly much diminished. Unsprayed hay meadows, with a regular, but not too frequent regime of cutting, have many beautiful flowers and also provide nesting opportunities for birds, including lapwing and the rare corncrake. Some of the best are now found in the machair habitats of the west of Scotland.

Wet lowland grasslands are rapidly disappearing as a wildlife habitat, mainly because of drainage schemes and changes to the water table. Many birds depend on these grasslands for breeding or as a feeding ground. These include yellow wagtail, garganey, pintail, pochard, ruff, black-tailed godwit, curlew, barn owl, and harriers. In winter, flooded grassland attracts large numbers of wildfowl and waders such as Bewick's and whooper swans, Brent, bean and white-fronted geese, pintail, shoveler, wigeon, gadwall, teal, pochard, shelduck, redshank, golden plover, and black-tailed godwit. Important areas of lowland grassland pasture can be found, for example, in the Broads of East Anglia, on the Ouse Washes, at Pennington and Keyhaven Marshes, and on the Somerset Levels. Typical flowers of wet meadows include marsh-marigold, meadowsweet, yellow iris, ragged-Robin, marsh-orchids, and the rare fritillary.

Coastal habitats

Britain is superbly well endowed with rocky coasts and islands, from the isolated and daunting fastness of remote St Kilda to the crumbly chalky cliffs of southern and eastern Britain. These habitats contain some of our most important wildlife, particularly the thriving colonies of seabirds, some of which are huge. Sheltered rocky coves also provide a haven for seals.

Over 60% of the world's gannets (more than 160 000 pairs) breed on the rocky islands and cliffs around the coasts of Britain and Ireland, as well as about a third of all storm petrels (about 20 000 pairs) and about a fifth of the world's razorbills (about 145 000 pairs). Other notable species associated with these habitats are Manx shearwater, Leach's petrel, fulmar, shag, cormorant, kittiwake, guillemot, puffin, black guillemot, great

Fritillary *Fritillaria meleagris*

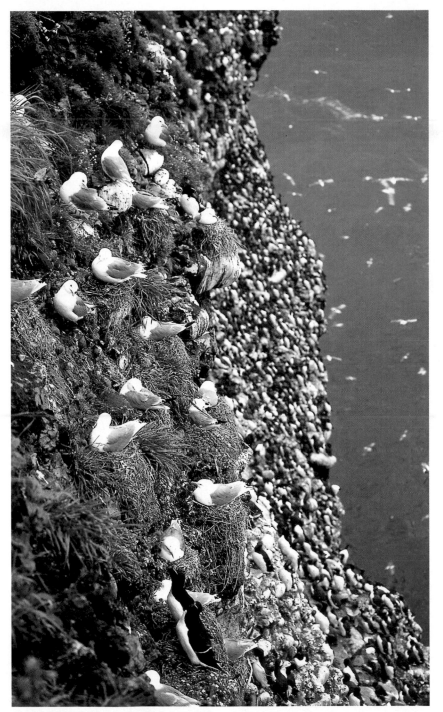

Kittiwakes *Rissa tridactyla*, Fowlsheugh (Peter Wilson) (see p. 48)

Caledonian pine forest: ❶ (Scots pine) *Pinus sylvestris* ❷ Osprey *Pandion haliaetus* ❸ Crested tit *Parus cristatus* ❹ Northern emerald dragonfly *Somatochlora arctica* ❺ Capercaillie *Tetrao urogallus* ❻ Red Squirrel *Sciurus vulgaris* ❼ Twinflower *Linnaea borealis*

Reedbed: ❶ Marsh harrier *Circus aeruginosus* ❷ (Common reed) *Phragmites australis* ❸ Bearded tit *Panurus biarmicus* ❹ Yellow iris *Iris pseudacorus* ❺ Bittern *Botaurus stellaris* ❻ Southern marsh orchid *Dactylorhiza praetermissa* ❼ Grass snake *Natrix natrix*

Lowland heath: ❶ Hobby *Falco subbuteo*
❷ Stonechat *Saxicola torquata* ❸ (Gorse) *Ulex europaeus* ❹ Dartford warbler *Sylvia undata*
❺ Keeled skimmer *Orthetrum coerulescens* (male)
❻ Smooth snake *Coronella austriaca* ❼ Silver-studded blue *Plebejus argus* ❽ Bell heather *Erica cinerea*

Rocky coast/cliffs: ❶ Peregrine *Falco peregrinus*
❷ Fulmar *Fulmarus glacialis* ❸ Kittiwake (adult perching and juvenile flying) *Rissa tridactyla*
❹ Guillemot *Uria aalge* ❺ Viper's-bugloss *Echium vulgare* ❻ Thrift *Armeria maritima*

skua, Arctic, Sandwich, and roseate terns, rock dove, golden eagle, white-tailed eagle, peregrine, chough, and rock pipit.

On seabird cliffs, heavily manured by droppings, certain characteristic plants can be found, often growing luxuriantly. Examples are tree-mallow, sea beet, sea campion, scentless mayweed, common chickweed, red campion, cow parsley, and angelica. Salt-tolerant species of cliffs in general include thrift, rock samphire, sea-spurrey, sea aster, and sea spleen-wort. In the north, this is the habitat of Scots lovage and roseroot.

Sand dunes are fairly common around our coasts, and they form wherever light sand accumulates in exposed sites under the influence of regular strong winds. On such coasts, the wind is constantly building up new dunes, which develop roughly at right angles to the prevailing wind direction. Amongst the first colonists of new dunes are marram, sand couch, lyme-grass, and sand sedge, with plants such as sea rocket and sea sandwort growing on the nearby strand. As the dunes stabilize, other plants such as sea-holly, sea bindweed, common ragwort, and rosebay willowherb join the community, and (mainly in the west) the delicate dune pansy. In still older dunes, mosses are common in the ground-layer and the number of other species rises to include flowers such as white clover, restharrow, bird's-foot-trefoil, wild thyme, and viper's-bugloss. The natural

Sea sandwort *Honkenya peploides*

succession from this stage, seen in many places, is towards scrub, with woody plants such as sea buckthorn, wild privet, elder, and blackthorn.

Many dune habitats have wet hollows between and to the landward side of the dunes themselves, known as dune slacks. These can be very rich for both plants and animals and often have fine displays of orchids, as well as being good for butterflies, with grayling, wall, small heath, dark green fritillary, and small and common blue typical species of dune grassland. Pools in dune slacks are also a favoured breeding site of the natterjack.

Estuaries and mudflats act as magnets to the large flocks of migrating waders and wildfowl which stop over every year from northern Europe, Iceland, and Siberia. There are about 170 estuaries around the coasts of Britain and Ireland, and many birds depend upon them for winter survival. Because the estuaries have a wide tidal range, large areas of food-rich mud are regularly exposed, offering easy pickings to the birds. In addition, the mild oceanic climate of the region and the relatively salty water means that they very rarely freeze over. Many estuaries support good growths of eelgrasses and also the green seaweed *Enteromorpha*. These are the staple diet of several wildfowl, in particular Brent geese and wigeon, which flock in their thousands to favoured sites.

Slightly firmer soils on saltmarshes are the habitat of the succulent glassworts, with annual sea-blite and sea aster

Storm petrel *Hydrobates pelagicus* (Mike Lane)

appearing to the landward. The vigorous common cord-grass also spreads rapidly over muddy saltmarshes in many areas, and sea-purslane often covers wide areas in somewhat drier sites. Higher up the marsh are species such as sea-lavenders, sea wormwood, thrift, and sea-milkwort.

Birds of these habitats include wildfowl such as white-fronted, barnacle, pink-footed, and Brent geese, whooper and Bewick's swans, wigeon, mallard, and pintail, terns, gulls, and waders like dunlin, knot, redshank, oystercatcher, ringed, golden, and grey plovers, bar-tailed and black-tailed godwits, turnstone, curlew, and whimbrel.

Wetlands

The high and usually regular rainfall, the varied landscape, and the geology all combine to create a great range of wetlands throughout Britain. In upland regions, mountain streams and rivers surge over their rocky beds, providing homes to birds such as dipper and grey wagtail, and their damp rocks create a fern enthusiast's paradise. At the other extreme are the slow rivers of the lowlands, meandering through their fertile floodplains. Such habitats, with their pools and reedbeds, have a rich flora and also attract many birds, particularly wildfowl and other waterbirds such as great crested and little grebes, mallard, tufted duck, moorhen, coot, and grey heron. The clear, chalk streams of southern England are the haunt of kingfishers, and, where the natural vegetation is allowed to flourish, they also attract otters and water voles, as well as many invertebrates such as damselflies and mayflies, many of which provide food for healthy populations of trout and other fish. The nutrient-poor (oligotrophic) lakes of upland and northern Britain represent a rather special habitat with a small number of specialized plants and other wildlife. This is the habitat of the pretty water lobelia and quillwort. There are also characteristic breeding birds here, including common sandpiper, red-throated diver, red-breasted merganser, and goosander, and some rather rarer species such as black-throated diver, goldeneye, and common scoter. By contrast, nutrient-rich (eutrophic) lakes are very fertile, having a good supply of minerals and organic matter. These are commonest in lowland sites, mainly in southern and eastern Britain, especially where the rocks are calcareous. The Cheshire and Shropshire meres are examples of natural nutrient-rich lakes, but many artificial lakes, gravel pits, and reservoirs also fall into this category. Such lakes tend to have well-grown, often reed-fringed margins with abundant water plants and bank vegetation. They also support healthy populations of insects and birds, and in winter they attract migrant waterfowl.

Peatlands, which include upland bogs as well as lowland bogs and fens, are a notable feature of the landscape, a direct result of our wet Atlantic climate, although most have been lost to drainage or peat extraction. As with heaths, Britain has a major responsibility on a European scale for the conservation, protection, and management of these most precious and delicate of environments.

Wet peat habitats are known collectively as mires, and may be subdivided into (a) nutrient-poor acid bogs and (b) nutrient-rich, generally alkaline fens (though intermediates exist). In the north and west, lowland peatlands cover large stretches of the landscape, clothing the lower slopes of hills with blanket bog. Valley bogs and fens tend to be found in lowland sites. All peatlands have a very special assemblage of characteristic species, including the fascinating insectivorous sundews and butterworts. In England, especially in the south-east, lowland fen still clings on in pockets, representing a habitat that was previously much more widespread. Lowland fens often have associated reedbeds with their own characteristic birds, amongst them some rather rare species including bittern, marsh harrier, water rail, spotted crake, bearded tit, and reed, sedge, Savi's, and Cetti's warblers. Classic fenland butterflies are brimstone, large copper (now sadly extinct), and swallowtail (now local and rare).

Uplands

Much of upland Britain is clothed in moorland, a kind of high-level heath developed on acid, peaty soil. Moorland is usually an artificial community in that much of it is carefully managed, largely for rearing red grouse or deer. If left to its own devices, much upland heather moor would probably revert, perhaps only quite slowly, to birch or oak woodland, and most of the region is potentially capable of supporting woodland as a climax community. Upland moors are best-developed on hills and mountains in areas of high rainfall or humidity, such as in the major mountain ranges of Scotland and Wales, and in the three major upland areas of south-west England (Bodmin Moor, Exmoor, and Dartmoor). These moors are usually above about 300 m, and upland heath, upland grassland, and the coastal northern heaths of northern Scotland, Orkney, and Shetland form the largest semi-natural habitat in Britain. Typical plants of the high moors are heather, bell heather, bilberry, and cross-leaved heath. These bushy species are often accompanied by purple moor-grass, mat-grass, and the vigorous and invasive fern bracken. In wetter areas, shrubs like bog bilberry appear, along with cottongrasses and rushes. In very wet sites, bog-mosses proliferate, and these peaty communities also support the insectivorous sundews and butterworts.

Moorland and mountain birds include golden eagle, merlin, hen harrier, peregrine, raven, golden plover, curlew, dotterel, dunlin, purple sandpiper, red grouse, ptarmigan, red-throated diver, ring ouzel, wheatear, snow bunting, shore lark, and twite. The importance of the uplands in the European context may be seen in the proportions of the western European population represented by the numbers breeding here: about 10% of hen harriers, 20% of golden eagles, and over 90% of merlins and golden plovers.

Typical mammals of upland sites are field vole, mountain hare, red deer, and wildcat (the latter mainly in Scotland). The characteristic butterflies of upland grassland and moorland are small and large heaths, green-veined white, mountain ringlet, Scotch argus, green hairstreak, and small pearl-bordered and dark green fritillaries.

The natural history of Britain

Britain's wildlife is rather impoverished when compared with that of many other countries in Europe – for example there are only about 2500 native wild plant species, compared with over twice this number in France. This large difference is mainly explained by the ice ages, which wiped out the earlier vegetation covering much of what we now call northern Europe. Of course the ice also covered, and denuded, regions of high ground elsewhere, such as the Alps, but these areas were quickly recolonized from the large pool of species in the adjacent lowlands, or from other protected sites. The native flora we now have is largely a re-immigrant one, but whole groups of plants (including magnolias and plane trees) that we know from fossil remains once grew in northern Europe never succeeded in returning until some were introduced into gardens.

The fauna of the region is also relatively poor compared with that of the Continent, especially in those groups

Wildcat *Felis silvestris*

which are unable to fly, such as mammals (other than bats), reptiles, and amphibians. For example, there are 45 species of amphibian and 85 non-marine reptiles in Europe, but only 6 of each are native to Britain. Only about 75 mammals are found here out of more than 170 in Europe as a whole: 44%. For birds, however, the British list of about 255 is about 60% of the European total of about 430 species. Birds are very mobile, and most species can overcome the physical barrier of the Channel and other stretches of sea with ease (indeed migrants do so regularly). In addition, the very varied habitats, augmented by the long coastline with its rocky islands, provide arguably the greatest potential for birds of any European country.

Britain has internationally significant numbers of several rare bird species, including golden eagle, merlin, and corncrake, and peregrines are now increasing around our coasts, using rocky inland crags, and even tall city buildings, as nest sites. Other species with their main or major populations here are red-throated diver, Manx shearwater, storm and Leach's petrels, gannet, red grouse, curlew, great skua, Sandwich, Arctic, roseate, and little terns, guillemot, razorbill, twite, and Scottish crossbill.

Whilst there have been worrying losses amongst our wildlife, for example many birds of arable farmland such as skylark and grey partridge, there are encouraging signs, too, with record numbers of corncrakes breeding in their strongholds of Orkney, the Western Isles and Inner Hebrides, and choughs returning to Cornwall in 2001, after more than 30 years. Stone curlews and red kites are also showing significant increases, at about 250 and 430 breeding pairs, respectively, and Dartford warblers have returned to several former haunts, such as the coastal heaths of Suffolk. Hobbies have extended their range considerably, ospreys are now breeding again in England (in the Lake District and at Rutland Water) for the first time for 150 years, and white-tailed eagles are grad-

Corncrake *Crex crex* (Mike Lane)

ually spreading on the west coast and islands of Scotland. One of our most secretive birds of prey, the honey buzzard, has also spread in recent years, most notably into some of the coniferous plantations of Wales. Experiments are underway to reintroduce beavers using Norwegian stock, and these large, harmless rodents may soon begin grazing selected wetland sites. Wild boar once roamed the forests, and have now established themselves anew, following escapes from specialist farms, especially in Dorset, East Sussex, and Kent. There is some evidence that their rooting increases plant diversity. Meanwhile, the British otter population is recovering well, which may benefit water voles that have been hard hit by introduced American mink. The large blue butterfly may now be seen at a handful of sites in the south-west, following successful reintroductions.

Access and route-finding

Compared with those of many other countries, Britain's wild places and wildlife are not difficult to observe. There is a multitude of reserves of differing status and size, administered by a range of different organizations, most of which may be visited without difficulty. In addition, it is possible to roam through vast tracts of countryside, using a network of footpaths, tracks, and rights of way of various kinds. There are moves under way to increase access to the countryside still further, with the 'right to roam' enshrined in law. Nevertheless, private land with no access does exist, and any notices denying entry should be respected. Some of these areas are in private hands, and others are owned, for example, by the Ministry of Defence and may even be dangerous to enter. Ironically perhaps, the MoD properties, such as those in the Breckland or Salisbury Plain, are actually splendid nature reserves in their own right, whose natural inhabitants are only occasionally disturbed by military exercises.

Certain precautions should always be taken when in the countryside, partly for your own safety and that of others, and partly so as to minimize disturbance to wildlife or livestock. Rights of way and footpaths are clearly marked on the latest maps and should be followed where possible, and the basic tenets of the country code adhered to. It is advisable not to walk alone in hill or mountain country, and in any case to inform someone of your route and estimated location and time of arrival.

Always plan your trip carefully, taking full advantage of any detailed maps and published information. Many reserves stock useful leaflets, site maps, and other information which help explain features of the wildlife and indicate routes, footpaths, and tracks. In coastal sites always pay full attention to signs and notices giving information about safe paths, and especially to the times of low and high tides. Always respect other restrictions, such as fenced-off areas of shingle, which may protect rare nesting birds or easily damaged vegetation.

Protective clothing is essential, particularly in the winter months and when visiting exposed sites, such as hills, or coasts, and estuaries. Cold, wet weather, especially when combined with a strong wind, can quickly chill, even if the thermometer reading is not unduly low! By contrast, it is also surprisingly easy to get sun- and wind-burnt when out walking in the open. For extended hill walks take an anorak and gloves, with a spare jumper and socks, and dry trousers if possible. Shorts may be comfortable in good weather, but it is wise to have dry and warm clothes handy. Take sufficient food and drink and eat little and often, a tactic which keeps up energy levels most efficiently. A good, supportive pair of walking boots is desirable when walking over rough or wet ground. Some people prefer lighter footwear, however, which is fine as long as the soles give an adequate grip – test them on wet, sloping grass first. For very wet areas, 'gumboots' are really the only sensible choice.

Always take a good map when out walking for a long period in relatively wild country, travel in pairs or small groups whenever possible, and be sure to tell someone else where you are going. You should also take a compass, a first-aid kit, a loud whistle, and a portable torch plus spare battery. If caught in a thunderstorm, avoid exposed positions such as hilltops or ridges.

A recent development is the availability of portable position-finders which integrate information from satellites to give a reading of location. These are now being produced at prices affordable to the individual and will doubtless become essential items for the serious naturalist, field researcher, or hill-walker.

Good, portable field guides are also useful to take out into the field, as is a handy notebook and pencil. The further reading section at the end of this book lists some recommended guides. For the birdwatcher, a pair of binoculars is essential (preferably 8× magnification, or possibly 10×), and the range available is now very wide. Many binoculars can focus very close, and this is helpful when observing insects such as butterflies and dragonflies. Most really keen birdwatchers use a telescope as well, especially for waders on estuaries, or for sea-watching.

Always take care to follow the guidelines for visiting a particular site. Sometimes a permit is required from the controlling body or owner. In other cases there is easy and open access. Always follow public footpaths when these are marked (they are clearly shown on the Ordnance Survey Landranger maps). Watch out for, and respect, restrictions imposed by landowners, especially in upland moorland. Above all, perhaps the best advice for the naturalist is to keep quiet, to move slowly, and to watch carefully; you will see a lot more that way.

There are three main categories of rights of way in Britain: public footpaths, bridleways, and byways. Public footpaths may be used freely by walkers only, bridleways are for use on horseback, but also by walkers and cyclists, and byways (which are usually old roads) by any traffic. Other normally accessible areas are public parks, commons, country parks and picnic sites, most beaches, towpaths, National Parks, and many of the nature reserves and other protected areas, including Forestry Commission woods.

Maps

The Ordnance Survey (OS) publishes a number of types of map, some designed for the tourist or hill-walker. The main series are:

Travelmaster 1:250 000 (1 cm = 2.5 km). A series of nine maps covering the whole of Britain, showing routes and tourist information.

Landranger 1:50 000 (1 cm = 500 m). A series of 204 maps covering the whole of Britain, giving National Grid co-ordinates, tourist information, and rights of way (not Scotland).

Explorer, Outdoor Leisure, and Pathfinder 1:25 000 (1 cm = 250 m). These are all larger-scale maps for investigating an area more thoroughly, and have much more detail of footpaths and beauty spots, for walking and exploring. The Outdoor Leisure series features National Parks and Areas of Outstanding Natural Beauty. The newer Explorer series is gradually replacing the earlier Pathfinder series.

There are also even more detailed maps, at 1:15 000 (1 cm = 150 m), used for example for walking and orienteering. Unless otherwise stated, the references to OS maps in the text refer to the Landranger series.

Grid references

We have provided grid references for many of the described or listed sites as these provide the simplest method of location, and, with a little practice, are easy to use.

The two-letter code indicates the 100-km square on the National Grid. After each letter code are either four or six figures. In a four-figure reference, the first two figures refer to the vertical grid-lines (known as 'eastings'), and the second two figures to the horizontal grid-lines (known as 'northings'). In a six-figure (more precise) reference, the first three figures refer to the vertical grid-lines, and the second three figures to the horizontal grid-lines. Thus a four-figure grid reference defines a 1-km grid square, and a six-figure grid reference a 100-m grid square. Where six-figure references are given in the text, this usually pinpoints the entrance or centre of a site, or a convenient car park.

Codes

The Country Code

- Enjoy the countryside and respect its life and work.
- Guard against all risk of fire. Do not leave litter, lighted cigarettes or matches.
- Respect other people's property.
- Keep dogs under close control, if necessary on a lead.
- Keep to public footpaths and other rights of way.

- Use gates and stiles to cross fences, hedges, and walls; fasten all gates.
- Avoid damage to fences, gates, and walls.
- Leave livestock, crops, and machinery alone.
- Take your litter home.
- Help to keep all water clean.
- Protect wildlife, plants, and trees.
- Take special care on country roads; when walking on country roads, keep to the right (thus facing the oncoming traffic) and in single file.
- Drive slowly and safely.
- Make no unnecessary noise.

The Seashore Code

- Leave seaweed attached to rocks – it can take years to grow and provides vital shelter and food for animals.
- Replace rocks and seaweed carefully.
- Take photos, not living things, and always put animals back where you found them.
- Only take home empty shells.
- Take your litter home – it can harm wildlife and it looks ugly.
- Try not to disturb the wildlife.
- Check the tide times and take extra care near rocks or cliffs.

Birdwatchers' Code of Conduct

- Protect habitats; its habitat is vital to a bird.
- Keep disturbance to a minimum. No birds should be disturbed from the nest in case opportunities for predators to take eggs or young are increased. In very cold weather disturbance to birds may cause them to use vital energy at a time when food is difficult to find.
- *Rare breeding birds.* If you discover a rare bird breeding and feel that protection is necessary, inform the appropriate Royal Society for the Protection of Birds Regional Office, or the Species Protection Department at the Society's headquarters. Otherwise it is best in almost all circumstances to keep the record strictly secret in order to avoid disturbance by other birdwatchers and attacks by egg-collectors. Never visit known sites of rare breeding birds unless they are adequately protected. Disturbance at or near the nest of species listed on the First Schedule of the Wildlife and Countryside Act 1981 is a criminal offence.
- Rare migrants or vagrants must not be harassed. If you discover one, consider the circumstances carefully before telling anyone. Will an influx of birdwatchers disturb the bird or others in the vicinity? Will the habitat be damaged? Will problems be caused with the landowner?
- Behave abroad as you would at home. This code should be firmly adhered to when abroad (whatever the local laws). Well-behaved birdwatchers can be important ambassadors for bird protection.

Nature conservation in Britain

Although Britain is relatively heavily populated, and its natural habitats largely destroyed or altered, nevertheless the conservation movement here is perhaps stronger and longer-established than anywhere else. Britain has a long and admirable history of nature conservation, and boasts an impressive network of reserves and other protected areas.

Britain has more than 200 National Nature Reserves, covering in total in excess of 80 500 ha. There are also about 600 Local Nature Reserves protecting about 29 000 ha, established by local planning authorities. A thriving system of Wildlife Trusts administers about 2000 reserves in a wide range of habitats and many of these can be visited with ease (for details contact your local Trust – see Appendix). The RSPB has about 160 reserves, mostly with free access to members (non-members pay a fee), and the Woodland Trust has a growing number of woodland sites, now standing at over 1110.

Key wildlife organizations

Britain has many organizations concerned with nature conservation, and the major ones are listed in the Appendix. Here we present a little more detail about some of the more prominent bodies, most of which administer reserves. The initials after the names are abbreviations used in the site descriptions.

English Nature (EN)

Advises the Government on nature conservation, selects and manages National Nature Reserves, and identifies Sites of Special Scientific Interest.

National Trust (NT)

Founded in 1895, and cares for over 248 000 ha of beautiful countryside in England, Wales, and Northern Ireland, plus almost 600 miles of outstanding coastline and more than 200 buildings and gardens of outstanding interest and importance. The NT owns 26 National Nature Reserves and 466 Sites of Special Scientific Interest. As most of these properties are held in perpetuity their future protection is secure, and the vast majority are open for visitors. It is a registered charity and completely independent of government, therefore relying heavily on the generosity of its members (now numbering over 2.6 million) and other supporters. The National Trust for Scotland (NTS) plays a similar role north of the border.

Royal Society for the Protection of Birds (RSPB)

Europe's largest wildlife conservation charity and the UK partner of BirdLife International, supported by over one million members, and with over 160 nature reserves (many featured in this book), covering in total more than 275 000 ha.

Wildlife Trusts (WT)

Over 2300 sites in the UK are cared for as nature reserves by 46 WTs. Together, they cover 60 000 ha (an area slightly larger than the Isle of Man) and include habitats of all types, from woods and meadows to mountains and moorlands, and from ponds and rivers to cliffs and beaches. Many are provided with information centres, leaflets, and signs. Most of these nature reserves are open to the public, and the reader should find out more about the reserves by contacting their local WT, some of which are on-line (see Appendix).

Woodland Trust (WdT)

Owns over 1110 sites, covering more than 17 700 ha, most open to the public, with free access. This is the UK's leading charity dedicated solely to the protection of native woodland. Woodland is the natural vegetation of much of Britain and therefore the WdT is vital to nature conservation in Britain. Since the 1930s about half of our ancient broadleaved woodland has disappeared and the WdT is doing its bit to reverse this sad decline. In addition to acquiring and managing existing woods, it is also creating new woodland.

Designated sites

The abbreviations below are those used in the text.

Areas of Outstanding Natural Beauty (AONB)

These are designated by the Countryside Agency and the Countryside Council for Wales. National Scenic Areas are the Scottish equivalent, designated by Scottish Natural Heritage.

National Parks (NP)

These are large areas of particular landscape and wildlife value. There are 12 in England and Wales, with one more approved but not yet formalized:

- Brecon Beacons NP
- Dartmoor NP
- Exmoor NP
- Lake District NP
- New Forest NP
- Norfolk Broads NP
- North York Moors NP
- Northumberland NP
- Peak District NP
- Pembrokeshire Coast NP
- Snowdonia NP
- South Downs NP status approved
- Yorkshire Dales NP

Plans have also been drawn up for Scotland's first NP, which will be centred on Loch Lomond and the Trossachs, stretching from the Firth of Clyde to Tyndrum. A second Scottish NP is likely to be in the Cairngorms.

National Nature Reserves (NNR)

These are reserves established to protect the most important wildlife habitats and geology in Britain. Many are visitable nature reserves (some requiring a permit), but some are research sites. There are currently more than 200.

Special Areas of Conservation (SAC)

These are part of the Habitats Directive and aim to protect rare habitats and species across Europe, in a network known as Natura 2000.

Sites of Special Scientific Interest (SSSI)

Areas of land notified for their special natural history or other scientific interest, by EN, Countryside Council for Wales, and Scottish Natural Heritage. There are about 23 000 owners and occupiers of over 4000 SSSIs in England, about 60% of which are privately owned or managed. The remaining 40% are managed by public bodies (such as the Forestry Commission, Ministry of Defence, or Crown Estate). Owners of SSSIs are legally obliged not to damage them, although in practice many have been harmed or lost. Recent legislation promises to give SSSIs better protection.

Local Nature Reserves (LNR)

These are sites with wildlife or geological features that are of particular value locally, which give people special opportunities to study and learn about them or simply enjoy and have contact with nature. There are over 600 LNRs in England, ranging from windswept coastal headlands, ancient woodlands, and flower-rich meadows to former inner city railways, long abandoned landfill sites, and industrial areas. In total they cover over 29 000 ha.

Wildlife law in Britain

As well as the special regulations that apply to designated sites such as NPs, NRs, and SSSIs, several hundred species of animals and plants in Britain are strictly protected by law. There is also extensive and comprehensive national and international legislation to protect wild species and their habitats. This is continually reinforced, and special licences are needed to work with protected species, not all of which are rare.

Wild flowers should not be picked. It is illegal to uproot any wild plant without permission, and many species are further protected from being picked or having their seeds gathered. All wild plants have some protection under the laws of the United Kingdom and the Republic of Ireland. Under the Wildlife and Countryside Act 1981, which covers Britain, it is illegal to uproot any wild plant (including fungi, algae, and lichens) without permission from the landowner or occupier. Similar general protection covers all plants in Northern Ireland, under the Wildlife (Northern Ireland) Order 1985. It is also an offence to uproot plants for commercial purposes without authorization.

Most birds are protected, and it is generally illegal to take, injure, or kill any wild bird, or to destroy the nest or eggs of any species. Many of our native mammals are also protected, including the badger, despite being abundant, and all bats, as are invertebrates such as many butterflies, dragonflies, and crickets.

The Countryside Agency, which succeeded the Countryside Commission in 1999, is the body responsible for advising government and taking action on issues relating to the social, economic, and environmental well-being of the English countryside. It designates NPs and AONBs, as well as generally promoting an understanding of the countryside. The new Countryside and Rights of Way Act 2000 (CroW) will give the public greater access to open country (mainly mountain, moorland, heath, and downland), supported by a series of new maps, though it will not come into force until 2005. This act also improves conditions for wildlife by strengthening the protection of individual species and of SSSIs.

A note about the layout of the book

In Wales and England the sites are arranged by county, and in Scotland by region.

Scotland

Introduction

Think of Scotland, and some who live beyond the country will immediately picture heather-cloaked glens under misty mountains, perhaps with a red deer stag somewhere in the frame. The image is more than romantic whimsy. You can find places where such a combination of landscape and wildlife exists, and the thrill of that mixture easily transcends the cliché.

But to equate the country, in all its gloriously sea-girdled, wood-softened, farm- and town-sprinkled variety with one type of scene is to miss one of Scotland's key assets for a wildlife enthusiast. There is variety here by the county-load, so much that relatively short journeys can often produce large contrasts in the local scene.

Travel north, for example, from the rolling hills that heave their rounded shoulders up at the border with England, and it doesn't take long to drop down into the utterly different lowlands of the central plain. Home to the majority of the Scottish population in and around the cities of Glasgow and Edinburgh, this is also an area drained and watered by rivers such as the Clyde whose valleys have wildlife diversity in abundance.

To the east lie the soft coasts of Fife, Angus, and Aberdeen, with their sand dunes, beaches, and low cliffs. To the north-west is the Atlantic seaboard, deeply indented by fjord-like sea lochs and fringed by hundreds of islands. Or travel to the inner Highland heartland in the area of the Cairngorms NP, where the climate is more continental, with cold winters and (sometimes) hot summers, and where more nationally scarce species breed than almost anywhere in Scotland. Ancient pine and birch woodlands, lochs, rivers, and heaths all lie close to the towns and villages here, where the largest continuous expanses of mountain ground in Britain and Ireland stretch above in huge plateaux. Travel further north, and the strange-shaped hills of Torridon and Assynt beckon, or the vast, sodden flatlands of the Flow Country – home to a tundra-like community of plants, birds, and insects, and arguably one of the finest blanket bog areas on the planet.

Pushing on again, and the island groups at the outer fringes offer a richness of marine life above and below the waves hard to match elsewhere in northwest Europe. Seabird colonies and grey seal breeding stations, channels hunted by different kinds of dolphins and whales, beetles, bees, and butterflies: all of these are in and around the islands of Orkney, Shetland, and the Outer Hebrides.

For Scotland as a whole, certain broad-brush features give an impression of its value for wildlife. The coast, at 11 800 km, is much longer than the land would suggest. So the influence of the sea is pervasive, whether in the weather that rolls in along western lochs and waters the peatlands, or in the North Sea chills which carry snow to the core of the Grampian Mountains.

Red deer *Cervus elaphus* (Mike Lane)

Opposite page: Dee Valley, Cairngorms (see p. 41)

Scotland

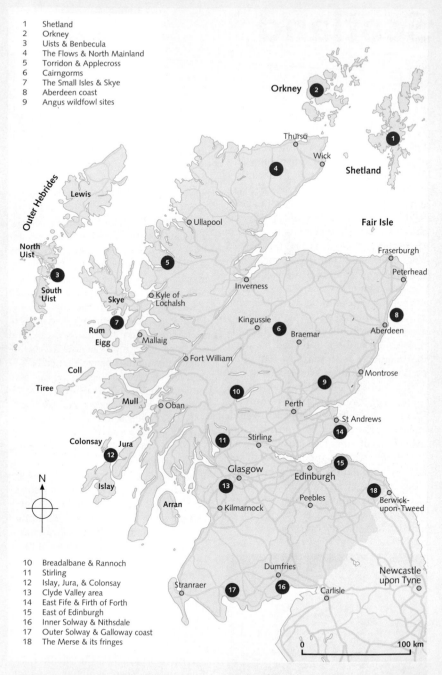

1   Shetland
2   Orkney
3   Uists & Benbecula
4   The Flows & North Mainland
5   Torridon & Applecross
6   Cairngorms
7   The Small Isles & Skye
8   Aberdeen coast
9   Angus wildfowl sites

Orkney

Shetland

Fair Isle

Thurso
Wick

Outer Hebrides

Lewis

Ullapool

North Uist

Fraserburgh
Peterhead

South Uist

Inverness

Skye

Kyle of Lochalsh

Kingussie

Braemar

Aberdeen

Rum
Eigg   Mallaig

Fort William

Coll

Tiree

Mull

Oban

Montrose

Perth

Colonsay   Jura

Stirling

St Andrews

N

Islay

Glasgow

Edinburgh

Peebles

Berwick-upon-Tweed

Arran

Kilmarnock

10   Breadalbane & Rannoch
11   Stirling
12   Islay, Jura, & Colonsay
13   Clyde Valley area
14   East Fife & Firth of Forth
15   East of Edinburgh
16   Inner Solway & Nithsdale
17   Outer Solway & Galloway coast
18   The Merse & its fringes

Dumfries

Newcastle upon Tyne

Stranraer

Carlisle

0   100 km

Polar air masses play a part in this winter transport, and can also help to shape communities of Scottish wildlife: it is a chilling thought, perhaps, that Edinburgh sits closer to the Arctic than to the Mediterranean. And in Shetland, northern outpost of the kingdom, Bergen in western Norway is much nearer than Scotland's capital.

Overall, the climate is mainly oceanic, with prevailing winds from the Atlantic blowing moisture-laden but mild air in from the west. This influence is seen to advantage in the many ferns, mosses, liverworts, and lichens that thrive here, including in the native oak woodlands of the west. So rich are these damp woods in different species of such vegetation that they merit, without exaggeration, the title of Britain's temperate rainforest. Aside from the lush greenery of the woods, sweeps of seasonal colour can also come from this Atlantic link, whether in the banks of gorse in coastal areas, sheets of bluebells in summer woods, or the

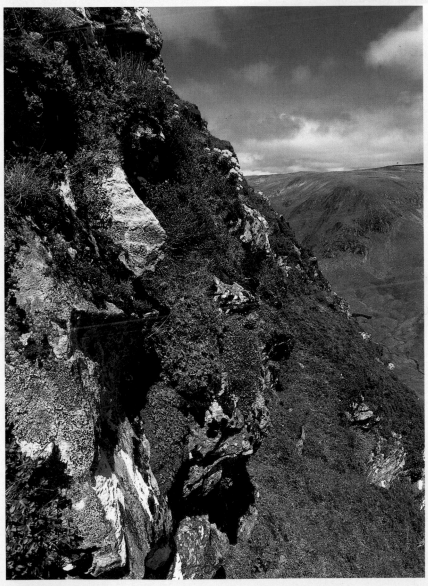

Caenlochan (see p. 44)

Scotland

purpling of heather over heathlands managed as grouse moors.

Connections to the Continent are here, too, through birds, plants, and insects with arctic, alpine, and boreal affinities, such as some of the rarer flora of lime-enriched mountains, or native pine wood splendours such as twinflower and the timberman beetle. Even for those mountain flowers that also occur in England and Wales, the majority of the UK population is usually in Scotland.

Add to those international links the foundation of a wide range of other species which occur more widely in Britain, and you build a picture of some of the attractions Scotland can hold for a traveller with an eye for wildlife. If you still hanker for heather and peat and associated fauna, don't worry – more than one-third of the land surface is covered in moorland and blanket bog, and the bulk of the British red deer population still roams here. In the conifer plantations the introduced sika deer also thrives, occasionally interbreeding with the native red deer where their ranges overlap.

Shetland and Orkney

SITE
1 Shetland

Set in wind- and current-churned waters some 160 km clear of John o'Groats, the hundred islands of the Shetland group are a half-way house between Britain and western Norway.

Among a range of interesting plants, birds, and animals here, the community of seabirds breeding in Shetland is perhaps of greatest importance, with a range of species unmatched elsewhere in northern Europe. Largest of all the isles here is the 'Mainland', the location of Shetland's capital Lerwick, and home to the bulk of the human population.

First landfall from the south on Mainland is Sumburgh Head reserve (RSPB; HU 405100), near the principal airport. The cliffs here have easily viewable breeding puffins, guillemots, razorbills, fulmars, and kittiwakes. This is also the best place in Shetland to spot killer whales and other cetaceans in summer. The small quarries in the vicinity and the areas around Sumburgh Hotel are worth checking for migrant passerines in spring and autumn.

Only a short distance north, the Lochs of Spiggie (RSPB), Hillwell (HU 3716), and surrounding marshland are the best places for wintering wildfowl in Shetland. Up to 400 whooper swans gather here in late autumn, plus tufted duck, pochard, and goldeneye. In summer the boggy areas and farmland around the lochs are home to a variety of breeding waders.

The small island of Mousa (HU 4623) is worth visiting on an evening boat trip from nearby Sandwick in summer. Hundreds of Arctic terns, and a mixture of fulmars, black guillemots, shags, and eiders breed here. The island's star attraction is the storm petrels which breed in the walls of the Iron

Storm petrel *Hydrobates pelagicus*

Age broch (circular stone tower) – itself the finest surviving anywhere.

East of Lerwick and just clear of the island of Bressay the NNR of the island of Noss (HU 5440) is easily accessible by boat in summer. A ramp of heathland, rich in sedges and grasses, leads up to huge sandstone cliffs, weathered into a swiss-cheese of nooks, hollows, and ledges by the action of wind and waves. Thousands of pairs of gannets and kittiwakes breed here, while great and Arctic skuas and great black-backed gulls patrol the air above.

Away from Mainland, Shetland has an abundance of wildlife riches. Fetlar – site of a brief occupation by breeding snowy owls in 1967–75, still boasts almost all of Britain's breeding red-necked phalarope –

best seen at the Loch of Funzie (HU 656900) in the south of the island. It also has an outstanding mix of other breeding waders, including whimbrel.

Hermaness NNR (HP 613149), at the northern tip of Unst, holds the largest puffin colony in Shetland, estimated at about 50 000 pairs. Cliffs in the 980-ha reserve rise to 170 m. The scatter of jagged stacks and skerries offshore includes Muckle Flugga and Out Stack, the northernmost point in Britain. Other breeding seabirds here include gannets (some of which can be seen at fairly close range), fulmar, gulls, auks, Arctic skuas, and several hundred pairs of great skuas.

Not far south of Hermaness, the Keen of Hamar NNR (HP 6409) supports a unique community of plants on its serpentine rock debris, including the Unst endemic, Shetland mouse-ear.

Fair Isle (NTS; HZ 2070), home to a thriving population of about 70 people, is the site of perhaps the most famous bird observatory in Britain, if not in Europe. Some 34 species of birds breed on the island – including some 100 000 pairs of seabirds and a Fair Isle subspecies of wren – but more than 350 species (mostly migrants) have been recorded here, including many national rarities.

SITE 2 Orkney

An archipelago just north of the Scottish mainland, but with its own unique character.

A mere 10 km of sea separates Orkney's southernmost point from the mainland at Duncansby Head near John o'Groats. But the 27 principal islands (20 of them inhabited, plus dozens of islets or 'holms') are utterly different from the moors, bogs, and cliffs of Caithness.

Old red sandstone – a legacy of sediments in long-vanished Lake Orcadie –

provides the geological framework for much of Orkney. So soils, in general, are much more fertile here than over the acid rocks of Shetland to the north.

Many of the pastures are prime grazings for beef cattle and dairy herds. Where rough or marshy ground adjoins these, and owners have been cautious in fertilizer and spray use, there is also

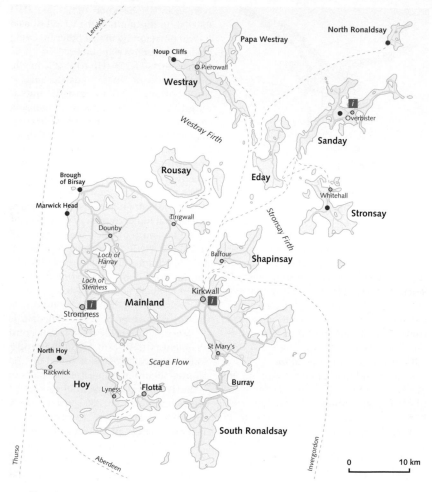

excellent breeding, feeding, and wintering territory for wading birds and starlings. Rank vegetation flanking fields is also a haven for the Orkney vole, a species which, oddly, is found only here and on Guernsey – though widespread in mainland central Europe (common vole).

A trip across many islands in the group can be enlivened by sections where flocks of curlews and lapwing, with sprinklings of redshank and snipe, add spice to the sights and sounds. First port of call for visitors from the south is 'Mainland', largest island in the group and site of the two principal towns, Kirkwall and Stromness. Mainland is linked by road to

several other islands by the 'Churchill Barriers' – causeways built in part over block ships sunk to restrict submarine access to Scapa Flow in the Second World War. So you can travel from Kirkwall to South Ronaldsay without using a ferry.

The area to the north of Stromness offers a particularly good variety of wildlife viewing opportunities. The Loch of Stenness (HY 2812) and Loch of Harray (HY 2919), close to the most famous chambered cairn and stone circles in Orkney, have various species of duck breeding along their margins, nesting mute swans and internationally important numbers of wintering wildfowl,

Heather *Calluna vulgaris*

have a range from salt through to freshwater conditions, adding to plant variety. This includes several species of pondweed and the rare spiral tasselweed.

Cliffs on the coast near the Neolithic village of Skara Brae, a few miles away, have superb ledges for breeding seabirds at the Marwick Head reserve (RSPB; HY 2224). Tens of thousands of guillemots and thousands of kittiwakes are highlights here. North again a short distance, the Brough of Birsay (HY 2328) provides the best seawatching opportunities on Mainland, with passages of Manx and sooty shearwaters and different species of skuas in the autumn.

Heathland above sea-cliffs in Orkney has become scarce in many parts, and is always worth a close look. The mix of plants in these maritime heaths may be dominated by crowberry, with abundant kidney vetch and bird's-foot-trefoil. Spring squill and sea campion can be spectacular, but the real gem of the Orcadian coastal heaths is the tiny

including wigeon, pochard, scaup and goldeneye. Harray holds a big coot flock (unusual in northern Scotland). An intriguing feature of the lochs is that they

A selection of other important sites

Shetland

Kergord (HU 395542): mixed woodland with goldcrest; good for migrants.

Tresta Voe (HU 3652): inlet with divers, sea ducks, and grebes.

Orkney

Birsay Moors (HY 346247): heather moorland with hen harrier, merlin, great and arctic skuas, and red-throated diver.

Copinsay (HY 610010): sea-cliffs with auks, kittiwake, and raven.

Cottescarth and Rendell Moss (HY 360200): heather moorland with hen harrier and merlin.

Hobbister (HY 396070): moorland, cliffs, and saltmarsh with hen harrier, merlin, red-throated diver, eider, and merganser.

North Hill, Papa Westray (HY 496538): sea-cliffs and coastal heath with auks, arctic tern, and arctic skua.

The Loons (HY 246242): marshland with gulls, waders, and Greenland white-fronted geese.

Trumland (HY 427276): hen harrier, merlin, great and arctic skuas, red-throated diver, and common gull.

Scottish primrose – found only here and along the north mainland of Scotland.

Inland, moors where heather and heaths hold sway among the moor-grass can be good hunting areas for several kinds of birds of prey. Orkney is a British stronghold for both hen harrier and merlin, and also has healthy numbers of peregrines, kestrels, and short-eared owls.

Away from Mainland, a superb system of ferries and short-hop air routes allows good access to many of the other large islands. But repeated visits to Orkney would be needed to do justice to these. Some highlights include: the huge sandy beaches, muddy inlets, and dunes of Sanday (great for wintering waders); Noup Cliffs (RSPB; HY 3950) seabird colonies and the swathes of maritime heath on Westray; grey seals offshore and at breeding stations in the Firth and coastal waters west of Stronsay; the bird observatory island of North Ronaldsay, where the eponymous rare-breed sheep chomp seaweed along the shore; and sparse trees and classic cliff scenery of North Hoy (RSPB; HY 223034), where the moors are home to large numbers of breeding great and Arctic skuas and great black-backed gulls. Because of the exposed conditions, heath communities including bearberry (normally found over 1000 m on the Scottish mainland) descend to around 100 m on Hoy.

Western Isles

SITE
3 Uists and Benbecula

A chain of islands stretching north and south beyond the shallow lagoon of the Sound of Harris.

Huge expanses of bare rock, shapely hills, and glorious beaches are a feature of the scene of Harris, swathes of blanket bog and dramatic headlands some aspects of Lewis. To the south, the islands of North Uist and South Uist are different again. Some of the finest flower-rich grasslands in Britain and Ireland and largest concentrations of breeding waders in Europe are here, where the Atlantic pounds the western shores. Seen from the air, North Uist is like a flooded moonscape, seeming more water than land, its surface studded with a myriad small pools and larger

Puffin *Fratercula arctica*

Scotland

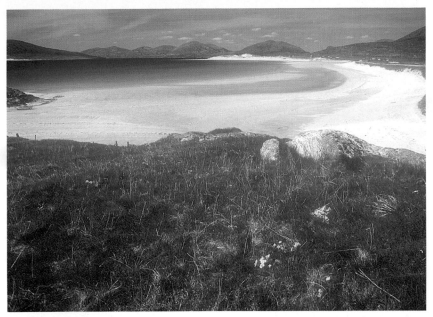

View (Peter Wilson)

lochans. White and yellow flowers of water-lilies contrast with these peat-brown waters in summer, while a mix of low-growing native trees, especially willows, birch, hazel, and rowan, can thrive on small islands away from sheep-bite.

The Balranald reserve (RSPB; NF 7070) can give an introduction to machair – the Gaelic word for the sandy, grass-covered, flowery plain at the ocean rim of some of the western Highland and islands. Lime-rich sand, blown from the shore to the peatlands beyond, supports a profusion of plants. Set within a core of red fescue, clovers, bird's-foot-trefoil, yarrow, lady's bedstraw, daisy, and rib-wort plantain, you may look for meadow crane's-bill, meadow-rue, wild carrot, and several orchids. Among the latter, the Hebridean machair specialities include the subspecies of common spotted- and early marsh-orchids, and the western marsh-orchid.

Machair systems have a patchwork of interweaving habitats, some dry, some wet, and support a rich insect and bird

community in the greenswards, marshes, and cultivated ground. Dunes provide the first area near the beach for snails such as *Hellicella itala* and *Cochlicella acuta* (also found throughout the machair) and for the dune snail. Warm conditions here also favour butterflies such as meadow brown, common blue, small tortoise-shell, and grayling, and various moths (common rustic and dark arches are widespread).

Bumblebees thrive here on dry machair (with machair now a stronghold for the declining *Bombus distinguendus*) and the numbers of breeding dunlin, ringed plover, redshank, snipe, oyster-catcher, and lapwing can be huge. Machair is also the UK stronghold for breeding corncrakes. Uncultivated areas at Baleshare and Kirkibost have a particularly high diversity of birds and plants.

In South Uist, Loch Druidibeg NNR (NF 7937) holds extremes of scenery and wildlife. To the west are several kilometres of sandy beaches, backed by machair. East, heather moorland and

Scotland

Balranald (Peter Wilson)

rough grassland – the domain of golden eagles, red grouse, and recently introduced red deer – stretch to the summit of Heda (606 m). Freshwater lochs (including the reserve's namesake) are home to Britain's largest breeding population of greylag geese. Corncrake, corn bunting, and twite breed in and near the cultivated fields.

Almost cradled by the western sweep of North Uist, the Monach Islands (NF 6462) are major rookeries for grey seals (often seen inshore around the other islands), and wintering ground for barnacle and white-fronted geese.

Tens of kilometres farther west, the islands of the St Kilda NNR (NA 1000) form the most important area for marine wildlife – both above and below the waves – in Britain and Ireland. Tantalizing on the horizon on a clear day, St Kilda is tricky to reach. Specialist commercial boat tour charters and work parties

organized by the NTS allow some tourists to visit. The lucky few who get there can be rewarded by views of the largest colony of gannets in the north Atlantic, huge puffinries, fulmars by the thousand on dizzying sea-cliffs, and the expertly crafted drystone walls and storage structures built by former inhabitants. Waters all around here are a major feeding and migration route for cetaceans. Minke whales are commonest, but pilot, fin, and humpbacked have also been seen, while blue whales travel unseen, but sometimes heard on underwater microphones, at great depths nearby.

Also in the region

Monach Islands (NF 6463): machair, grey seal, barnacle, and white-fronted geese.

Highland

SITE
4 The Flows and the North Mainland

These huge peatlands of Caithness and Sutherland are unique in Europe, and rank as some of the finest blanket bogs anywhere.

Also known as the 'Flow Country', these bog-moss-cloaked flatlands and their pools hold tundra-like mixtures of breeding birds and other creatures. Beyond them, along Scotland's north mainland coast, sweeping sandy bays, rocky headlands, lime-rich coastal grasslands, and tall cliffs flank the turbulent waters of the Pentland Firth.

Bogs are not hard to find in the interior of Caithness and Sutherland. But perhaps the most straightforward way to get ready access to a representative chunk of classic Flow Country is through the RSPB's massive Forsinard reserve (NC 891425), where the society manages over 8000 ha of peatland (a further area of nearly 4000 ha at

Mountain avens *Dryas octopetala*

Blar nam Faoileag in Caithness is also under RSPB care). Set in Strathhalladale, with the A897 road running through its core, Forsinard has a rolling landscape studded with thousands of pools.

The Flow Country came to prominence in the 1980s because of ill-conceived forests on the bogs which threatened an array of breeding birds unique in Britain (more than half the EU's greenshank breed here, for example). Forsinard holds many of these breeding bird species, including black-throated divers, common scoter, wigeon, teal, hen harrier, golden plover, dunlin, and greenshank. Other typical birds of the Flows include Arctic skua and merlin. Otters use the river, and red deer roam the mosses and low hills.

Dunlin *Calidris alpina* (Mike Powles)

Scotland

Taken as a whole, these northern bog-lands hold a range of highly specialized invertebrates in the pools or 'dubh lochans' and their surrounds. Communities are less diverse than further south, but what they lack in variety they often make up for through the presence of arctic-alpine relicts. The beetle *Oreodytes alpinus* is one of those; first discovered alive in Britain when it was found in the Flows in 1985, this beetle was previously known only as a sub-fossil from glacial deposits. Ten species of dragonfly recorded include the azure hawker, and more numerous golden-ringed dragonflies, four-spotted chasers, highland darters, and various damselflies. Northern eggar and emperor moths and large heath butterflies are widespread.

At Munsary, a Plantlife reserve includes a mire with a rich array of bogland plants, including bearberry and small cranberry. Bog-mosses are the builders of the Flows, and Munsary has a good variety, including *Sphagnum papillosum* and *S. tenellum*.

Beside Dunnet Head (ND 2076) – the northernmost promontory in mainland Britain – the broad sandy arc of Dunnet Bay stretches for 3 km to the south of the sandstone cliffs. From the shore over a high ridge of dunes there is a great variety of plants (230 species have been recorded here), including several orchids, Scottish primrose, and Baltic rush. Butterflies include meadow brown, common blue, and dark green fritillary.

The headland itself has Scottish prim-rose and spring squill in maritime heath along the cliff-tops, and alpine saw-wort on the cliffs themselves. There is an excellent seabird colony beneath the lighthouse. Fulmar, kittiwake, guillemot, razorbill, black guillemot, puffin, and rock dove breed around the cliffs, with twite and the occasional great skua on the moors behind.

On the outskirts of Durness village, limestone grassland near the shore has abundant mountain avens, and a wide

Flow country

Handa

Scotland

area is also one of the last mainland strongholds for corncrake.

Beyond Durness and Balnakeil, Faraid Head (NC 390705) has breeding seabirds which include a puffin colony. Some 18 km from Durness is Cape Wrath (NC 2675) – north-westernmost point in Britain, with the cliffs of Clo Mor (NC 3272) (at 300 m, the highest sea-cliffs in mainland Britain) about 6.5 km to the east. The cliffs have large seabird colonies, with thousands of puffins, kittiwakes, razorbills, and fulmars, but access can be difficult and great care is needed above the sheer drops. Other cliff-nesting species here include peregrine and rock dove, with red grouse and the occasional ptarmigan inland.

More accessible major seabird colonies are on Handa Island (SWT; NC 138480) close to Tarbet and Scourie, 25 km or so to the south-west of Durness. This holds the largest guillemot colony in Britain and Ireland, a major razorbill colony, an expanding puffinry, and Arctic and great skuas. The cliff flora includes Scots lovage, thrift, rose-root, and sea campion. Offshore, seawatching can give the chance of seeing minke whale, white-beaked dolphin, common porpoise, and other cetaceans.

range of other flowering plants including a mixture of orchids, alpine bistort, yellow saxifrage, and hoary whitlowgrass. Scottish primrose does well here in low grassland with blown shell sand. This

SITE
5 Torridon and Applecross

A wild, mountainous landscape on Scotland's western mainland.

Between Lochcarron in the south and Gruinard Bay in the north, huge, angular mountains of quartz and sandstone dominate the scene, rising above hill ground where red deer roam and the westernmost relics of Caledonian pine wood cling to the heathy slopes. At the heart of this area lies Beinn Eighe (NG 960600). The first NNR to be designated in Britain, Beinn Eighe has since been awarded many more accolades in recognition of its ecological importance. Biosphere Reserve, Council of Europe Diploma site, and part of a larger Special Area of Conservation, this is a

Scotland

Redstart *Phoenicurus phoenicurus* (Mike Powles)

place where the scale of the scenery matches the breadth of its awards.

The reserve includes a vast area of 48 square kilometres, stretching from lochside to mountaintop. Most of it is covered in open heathland, bare rock, wet grassland, and bogs, with prime woodland areas on some slopes and gorges. Its backbone is a cluster of rugged peaks, ridges, and scree-covered slopes between Loch Maree and Glen Torridon. Inside and close to the reserve there are seven high peaks, whose summit ridges glisten white with quartzite – the legacy of sand build-up in a long vanished ocean. Within ground managed by the NTS sits the magnificent amphitheatre of Coire Mhic Fhearchair, rated by many as the finest corrie in Scotland. In places, older Torridonian sandstone has been pushed over the younger quartzite by major upheavals of the Earth's crust. This reversal of the usual bedding sequence led to Beinn Eighe's designation as a Geological Conservation Review site of international significance.

Characteristic north-western mountain plants grow among the crags, including Wilson's filmy-fern, sea spleenwort, three-leaved rush, and spiked wood-rush. Scarcer species include rock whitlowgrass and black spleenwort, and there is a particularly rich growth of 'Atlantic' mosses and liverworts reflecting the pervading oceanic influence here, in the crevices of

more shady crags. Northern prongwort (a liverwort) grows at its only British location at Beinn Eighe, representing 75% of the known world population.

Above the treeline at about 400 m, there are different kinds of dwarf shrub heaths. One type includes dwarf juniper, heather, and bearberry, while slightly higher up the mountains, additional species such as crowberry, trailing azalea, and least willow add greater variety to the ground-hugging shrubs.

Star attraction among Beinn Eighe's vegetation is undoubtedly the woodland, which grows below 300 m close to Loch Maree and includes the finest surviving western pine-wood tracts in Britain. Some of the 'granny' pines here are more than 350 years old. A nature trail runs through the largest pine-wood area at Coille na Glas Leitre (Wood of the Grey Slope) and three other small sections of woodland have survived on the steep sides of river gorges. Unusually for a Caledonian pine wood, heather, ivy and rowan grow among the pines, and unlike the eastern pinewoods there is very little juniper here. Flowers include serrated and chickweed wintergreen and creeping lady's-tresses, with abundant moss growth. Areas of birch hold a typical spring broadleaved flora including wood anemone, wood-sorrel, primrose, and bluebell.

Birds include crossbill, siskin, great spotted woodpecker, spotted flycatcher, redstart, sparrowhawk, and buzzard (with a chance of golden eagle high over the crags). In summer, golden-ringed dragonflies patrol the burn banks, and locally breeding hawkers include azure hawker.

Black-throated diver *Gavia arctica*

More ancient woodland survivors can be enjoyed from a distance by looking out from the shores of Loch Maree – one of the most scenic inland waters in Scotland – to 40 small islands where oaks grow in close proximity to pines.

At the coast near Poolewe, the gardens of Inverewe (NTS) give beautiful views out over the sheltered waters of Loch Ewe. It is worth keeping a lookout around the loch for shorebirds on the coastal rocks and saltings and for both red- and black- throated divers, while the substantial tree groves and ornamentally planted slopes of the gardens provide good opportunities for seeing a range of local woodland birds. Further south, at Sheildaig, is the western-most pine wood of all, notable for its range of mosses and liverworts, and long-estab-lished oak woodland. Between here and the Inner Sound across to Raasay and Skye, the Applecross Peninsula gives great opportunities for exploration of wild ground in a virtually roadless area.

Scotland

6 Cairngorms

The largest expanse of ground over 900 m in Britain.

Ice, snow, wind, and water have shaped the granites of the central Cairngorms (named for the mountain massif at its core), and moulded the plant and animal communities that live there to yield par-allels with the Arctic.

But there is also much more to the region than mountains. Rivers, wetlands, pinewoods, and heaths are as much a part of the natural scene here as towering crags and late-lying snowfields. It is this variety which has prompted the designa-tion of many places of natural heritage interest here, including SSSIs, the largest NNR in Britain, and the forthcoming Cairngorms NP.

Of the two principal rivers in the area – the Spey and the Dee – the Spey has a richer flora, and is one of the least polluted and modified river systems in Britain. Insh Marshes (RSPB; NH 775998), flanking the Spey between Kingussie and Insh, is the largest expanse of flood-plain mires in northern Britain. Huge beds of estuarine sedge feature here, within a mosaic of habi-tats that includes poor fen, reedbed, swamp, willow carr, wet grassland, and ditches. The site also has the very rare string sedge, and

Ptarmigan *Lagopus mutus*

about 150 moss species. The marshes are important breeding grounds for several species of wading birds, including wood sandpiper. Goldeneye breed here, and in winter flocks of up to 200 whooper swans gather in the floodplains, and hen harriers roost in the reedbeds. Eight species of fish live in the reserve, including Arctic char. The butterflies include pearl-bordered fritillary and there are over 200 species of moth,

including the confusingly named Kentish glory and Rannoch sprawler, both local and endangered. Strathspey also boasts a rare hoverfly (*Hammerschmidtia ferruginea*), only known from two other locations.

Further downriver, there is a range of interesting lochs in the valley of the Spey, including Loch Garten (RSPB; NH 975180), famous for the pinewoods where the recolonization of Scotland by ospreys

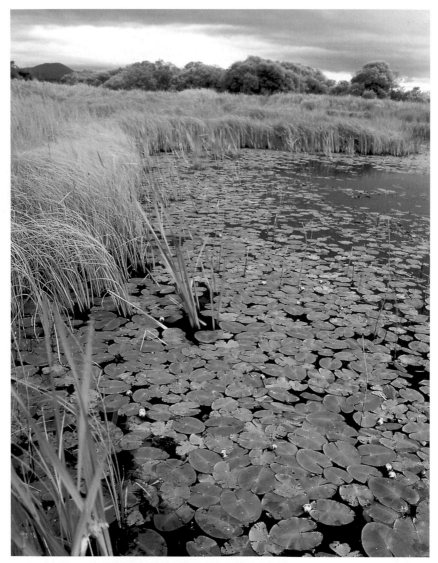

Least water-lily *Nuphar pumila*, Insh marshes

Scotland

Loch Avon

began in the 1950s and which is now the site of an RSPB Visitor Centre. Together, lower ground flanking the mountains in both Strathspey and Deeside hold the largest remaining stands of 'Caledonian' forest anywhere. Dominated by pine and different species of birch, these old woods also have a large range of other native trees and shrubs. There are large stands of juniper, and the understorey is thick with mosses, blacberry (bilberry), cowberry, heather, bell heather, and heath plants.

There are good places to see the structure of the surviving pinewoods at Glenmore (NH 9810) near Aviemore, where massive clearance of exotic conifers in the 1990s paved the way for native tree cover to expand, and Glen Tanar (NO 4897) on Deeside. Other interesting Caledonian remnants are on the Mar Lodge Estate owned by the NTS. The road between here and Braemar is often good for viewing red deer. Beside the town, the Morrone Birkwood NNR (NO 1390) – reminiscent of a montane Norwegian birch wood in structure – is rich in lichens and invertebrates.

Pine-dominated woods in this area are home to Scottish crossbills, crested tits, and dwindling numbers of capercaillie and black grouse. Pine martens, wildcats, and red squirrels are thinly scattered but widespread, and there are large numbers of red deer in the woods and on the hill grazings beyond.

Heather-dominated moors managed for grouse shooting are a particular feature of Deeside. As well as being prime sites for seeing red grouse, these are also good areas for mountain hares, short-eared owls and various birds of prey including merlin and peregrine.

Above 750 m, alpine dwarf shrubs, including bearberry, crowberry, least willow, and trailing azalea appear commonly in the heather carpets. In areas with prolonged snow cover, dwarf shrub heath communities give way to snowbed plant mixtures, stiff sedge, and mat grass, with alpine lady's-mantle in snow hollows.

Fell-fields with thin vegetation covering large expanses of ice-shattered stone and frost-heaved ground are a feature of some of the high plateaux in the mountains. Reaching these usually involves a long walk in from places at the base of the hills, although views of the plateaux (with restricted access) can be had from the funicular at Cairngorm.

Lake in Rothiemurchus pine forest

The high tops are home to scarce breeding birds, including dotterel and snow bunting. The mainly acid rocks of the central Cairngorms do not generally support luxuriant alpine plant communities, but towards the flanks of the massif, where granite changes to schistose or even limestone, there is a striking increase in the richness of the flora. The finest place for arctic-alpine plants is Caenlochan NNR (NO 2278), at the head of Glen Clova and Glen Isla. Here, cliff ledges can have lush growth of various saxifrages, rushes, roseroot, and red campion. There are patches of sub-arctic willow scrub elsewhere while spring sandwort, thrift and scurvygrasses grow on serpentine screes. Rare species to be found in the area include the very local alpine blue-sowthistle and twinflower, and least water-lily thrives in many of the upland lochans. On the plateau above the downhill skiing areas fell-fields fuzzed with woolly fringe-moss and stiff sedge are home to ptarmigan and dotterel.

SITE 7 The Small Isles and Skye

Rum, Eigg, Muck, and Canna form a glorious cluster of contrasting island scenes in the waters to the south of Skye. Each is utterly different from the other.

The closest to the mainland is Eigg (NM 4686), given prominence in recent years through a community-linked buy-out by a partnership involving local residents, the SWT, and the Highland Council. The towering lump of the Sgurr Ridge – the largest exposed mass of pitchstone in Britain – dominates the Eigg skyline. A

Puffin *Fratercula arctica* (Mike Powles)

walk to the summit and along part of the ridge can be rewarded with views of swarms of basalt columns poking through the heathland surface. Eigg's wildlife value lies in the variety of different habitats contained within a relatively small area of a few thousand hectares. Manx shearwater, black guillemot, red-throated diver, golden eagle, and raven all breed here. Orchid-rich grassland areas behind beaches and along road-sides are a colourful summer feature. Low-growing native woodlands, dominated by hazel and ash and festooned with lichens, are a feature of many places skirting Eigg's higher ground. Estate policy woodlands in the Kildonan area have taller trees, which shelter some of the island's thriving buzzard population as well as a mixture of smaller birds. Beaches include the Singing Sands, at the north of the Cleadale crofting area, where the quartzite grains squeak underfoot. Otters live along much of the coast, and shelduck and waders are common at Kildonan Bay.

Canna (NG 2605), and the bridge-linked island of Sanday are the western-most of the Small Isles, usually hidden from view on the mainland behind the lofty peaks of Rum. Owned by the NTS, Canna's western cliffs have the largest variety of breeding seabirds in the group, including puffins, razorbills, and Manx shearwaters. Native hazel scrub with rowan is interspersed with sycamore and other introduced trees.

Muck (NG 4279) is a little gem of an island, with a sheltered harbour and cheerful ambience, even on a dull day. Skylarks, meadow pipits, and wheatears dot the grasslands, with seabirds (including puffins) breeding along the coast and greylag geese present year-round as breeding and migrant visitors. A subspecies of field vole is unique to the island.

Rum (NG 3797) is a giant among small islands, rising to 812 m at the summit of Askival – one of a cluster of peaks over 500 m high in the south-east corner of the island. Managed as an NNR since 1957 when it was purchased for the nation from the Bullough family, Rum has been used as an outdoor laboratory ever since. Long-running studies of red deer, pioneering native tree restoration programmes, and reintroduction of the white-tailed eagle as a Scottish breeder have been part of this. There are now over 20 breeding pairs of white-tailed eagles in western Scotland.

Around the main settlement and harbour at Kinloch, estate policy woodlands with a mixture of beech, sycamore, and other trees are home to a mixed community of tits, thrushes, and other small birds. Beyond, much of Rum is covered in rough grassland grazed by the island's pony herd, highland cattle, feral goats and

Alpine lady's-mantle *Alchemilla alpina*

Scotland

Eigg and Rum

red deer. This provides a good hunting area for peregrine, merlin and the occasional white-tailed eagle. Other breeding birds include golden eagle, eider, and red-throated diver.

In lime-rich areas, the plants include mountain avens, alpine saxifrage, alpine meadow-grass, and alpine penny-cress. Rum has a rich insect fauna, including 19 species of butterfly. Among the breeding seabirds, a huge colony of Manx shearwaters high in the hills is of international significance – but evident to most visitors mainly through gatherings of birds offshore.

Deeply indented by sea lochs, and topped by the jagged ridges of the Cuillin Hills (NG 4522) and the lumpen mass of the Red Hills, Skye is a large and varied island. The underlying rocks and the landforms support a wide range of contrasting plant communities. Woodland, dominated by hazel and birch, is commonest in the low-lying areas of Sleat and

Kyleakin, over generally acid gneiss and sandstone. But at the Coille Thocabhaig reserve at Ord (NG 6212), ash thrives on Durness limestone outcrops, with a varied mix of mosses, liverworts, lichens, and ferns in the ground vegetation.

Jurassic limestone cliffs on the mountain Blaven (927 m) have luxuriant cover of tall herbs, including roseroot, globe-flower, and saxifrages. In the Suardal area, south of Broadford, there is some fissured limestone pavement, and mountain avens and some other arctic-alpines grow down to sea level. The basalt escarpment of the Trotternish Ridge has abundant yellow saxifrage and alpine lady's-mantle, with birds including ring ouzel, ptarmigan, raven, and golden eagle. White-tailed eagles are now recolonizing Skye and there is a viewing facility in Portree. The Storr Ridge (NG 4854) is famous as the site of Iceland-purslane at one of its only British localities – the other being on Mull.

A selection of other important sites in the region

Abernethy Forest Reserve (NH 981184): pinewoods, loch; osprey centre, crested tit, capercaillie, crossbill, red squirrel.

Ben More Coigach (NC 075065): moorland, bog, loch; upland birds.

Loch Fleet (NH 794965): marsh, dunes, shingle, woodland; seabirds.

Loch Ruthven (NH 638281): loch, woodland; Slavonian grebe, peregrine, hen harrier, osprey.

Grampian and Tayside

SITE
8 Aberdeen coast

Contrasting coasts stretching to the north and south of Aberdeen: soft, sandy shores predominate to the north, sandstone cliffs and hard shores to the south.

Some 20 km north of Aberdeen, close to Newburgh, the narrow twisting estuary of the river Ythan meets the sea (NJ 997252). Mudflats, mussel beds, and sands are a feature of this SSSI. Stretching for about 8 km, 6.5 km of which are tidal, the average width from bank to bank here is only 300 m. This, and the proximity of Aberdeen University's Culterty Field Station, mean that the Ythan has fair claim to the title of most studied British estuary. Mudflats close to where the Tarty Burn enters the river provide good feeding areas for curlew, ringed plover, bar-tailed godwit, knot, and golden and grey plover in different seasons, while mussel beds in the middle reaches of the estuary are good for oystercatcher and turnstone.

Stretching north from the estuary is Forvie NNR (NK 020275), a huge expanse of sand dunes, coastal heath, grassy cliffs,

Ythan Estuary (Peter Wilson)

and saltmarsh. Forvie is home to some 1500 Sandwich terns (the largest Scottish colony), plus breeding Arctic, common, and little terns, and eiders. Some 14 species of butterfly have been recorded here, including small pearl-bordered and dark green fritillaries. Green-veined white and small heath are the commonest, most widespread butterflies on the reserve. Six-spot burnets along the cliff-top paths are among the day-flying moths which can be seen in summer. The wide range of habitats at Forvie supports a diverse flora, with the coastal vegetation and low dune heath (good places to look for orchids) considered the best of their kind in northern Scotland.

Prime wildfowl site in this part of north-east Scotland is the Loch of Strathbeg SSSI (RSPB; NK 057581). This large, shallow loch, roughly midway between Peterhead and Fraserburgh, is separated from the North Sea by an area of sand dunes. The reserve covers more than 1000 ha of open water, marsh, dunes, farmland, and woodland. Strathbeg is of prime importance for wintering wildfowl, particularly greylag

and pink-footed geese, whooper swans, and large numbers of ducks (including tufted, wigeon, mallard, pochard, teal, goldeneye, red-breasted merganser, and goosander). A small flock of barnacle geese also overwinters. In summer, breeding duck include shelduck, tufted, and eider. Water rails live in the marshland areas, and sedge warbler and reed bunting nest in the reedbeds. Sandwich and common terns breed on a nearby island.

South of Stonehaven, the cliffs of the Fowlsheugh reserve (RSPB; NO 880796) hold one of the largest seabird colonies in mainland Britain. About 65 000 individual guillemots (the second-largest colony in Britain and Ireland) and around 60 000 pairs of kittiwakes are the peak breeding season attractions, plus some 8000 razor-bills (also a huge colony). A few thousand herring gulls and fulmars and a smattering of puffins and shags also breed.

St Cyrus NNR (NO 743635) just north of Montrose has a 4-km curve of golden sand backed by a narrow coastal plain and inland cliffs. The few hundred metres from shore to cliff hold contrasting

Loch of Strathbeg (Peter Wilson)

Scotland

habitats, including dune, dune-pasture, and sun-warmed rock ledges, all of which contribute to the wide variety of plants and insects here. Several of some 350 species of flowering plants and ferns in the reserve are at their northernmost limit in Britain. One of these is clustered bellflower. This grows on the grassy dune-pastures, together with more abundant maiden pink, meadow sax-ifrage, purple milk-vetch, and bloody crane's-bill. The plants below the cliffs include marjoram and carline thistle. The inland cliffs hold the core of the botanical interest, with some 200 higher plants recorded, including Nottingham catchfly, knotted clover, rough clover, common rock-rose, and wild liquorice, as well as more common species includ-ing red campions, bluebells, primroses, and cowslips.

Razorbill *Alca torda*

Over 200 species of moth have been recorded here. Six-spot burnet, fox moth, and cinnabar are among the more conspic-uous of these (either as adults or larvae). There is also a large colony of breeding terns (Arctic, common, Sandwich, and little) and colonies of eider and fulmar.

SITE
9 # Angus wildfowl sites

Lochs and an estuary of international importance.

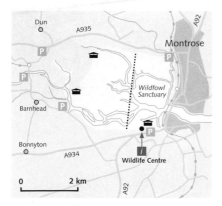

North of the Sidlaw Hills which overlook Dundee, and close to the Grampian Mountains, a swathe of fertile farmland holds a chain of wildfowl-rich lochs. To seaward, the finest enclosed river basin along the east coast of Scotland forms an estuary of international importance for migrating geese and swans.

The rich grazings of Strathmore are one of the traditional touch-down and winter-ing areas for Icelandic-breeding pinkfeet and greylag geese. The Loch of Lintrathen reserve (SWT; NO 278550) in the foothills of the Braes of Angus west of Kirriemuir is particularly favoured by greylags. Several thousand may come in to roost here from late autumn onwards after feeding on stubble, potato fields, or grassland on sur-rounding farms.

Lintrathen was created in the nineteenth century by damming the Melgam Water and now provides a water supply for Dundee and Angus. Its food-rich water is popular with waterbirds year round, includ-ing the great crested grebes, ducks, and grey herons which use it in summer.

Scotland

Just to the west of Kirriemuir, the Loch of Kinnordy reserve (RSPB; NO 361539) has a mixture of open water, mires, and fens surrounded by farmland. This is one of the best places in Scotland to see black-necked grebes. They nest among floating islands of bogbean and cowbane in the middle of a large colony of black-headed gulls. The loch is also visited by ospreys in the summer, and by goosander, goldeneye, and whooper swans in winter.

Several kinds of fen flank the loch, including patches dominated by common reed. Willow scrub gives cover for sedge warblers and reed buntings, and waders including snipe, curlew, and redshank breed in drier marshy areas. More than 4000 pinkfeet can join a few hundred grey-lags and a variety of duck here in winter.

East of Forfar, reedbeds and woodland also fringe Balgavies Loch reserve (SWT; NO 534508) in the Upper Lunan Valley. Fringed by reedbeds and with a large fen to the west, there is also one of the few surviving oakwoods in Angus on higher ground here. Wintering wildfowl include large numbers of grey geese, wigeon, shoveler, pochard, goldeneye, and goosander. In summer, great crested grebes and several duck species are among the breeding birds.

The waters of Balgavies once supported an eel fishery, based on traps set at the outflow here and at nearby Rescobie Loch. Perch, pike, and trout in the loch provide food for cormorants, grey herons, and otters that use the area. Both tufted loosestrife and coralroot orchid grow in the sedge-rich fens, while yellow water-lily and amphibious bistort cover large areas of water. Cowbane is at its northern limit here.

Where the river South Esk flows down to meet the sea, the broad estuary of the Montrose Basin (SWT; NO 690580) pushes its mudflats to the edges of the town that gives it its name. More than 1000 ha of tidal basin and surrounding land has been run as a LNR since 1981. Calls of eider duck and waders mix with the sea breezes here for much of the year. The major

Montrose Basin (Peter Wilson)

Yellow water-lily *Nuphar lutea*

landowner is the SWT, which operates a year-round ranger service, based in an attractive visitor centre near the southern shore of the basin. Ten other landowners are also involved, including the NTS.

There is traditional wildfowling at Montrose, administered through a permit system, but also with a sanctuary area. Up to 30 000 pink-footed geese and greylags roost on the basin in winter – with October usually a peak month. This is also a nationally important site for moulting mute swans and a migratory stop-over or winter home for many kinds of waders, including knot, redshank, bar-tailed godwit, curlew, turnstone, ringed plover, whimbrel, and greenshank. The basin provides a haven for many kinds of ducks, including (in addition to the ubiquitous eiders), wigeon, shelduck, mallard, teal, goosander, red-breasted merganser, and pintail. A flock of pintail, unusual in this part of Scotland, favours the north-west corner at high tide.

SITE 10 Breadalbane and Rannoch

A picturesque landscape of lochs, moorlands, hills, forests, and mountainous terrain.

At the geographical heart of Scotland, with scenic Loch Tay at their core, the lands of Breadalbane between Aberfeldy and Tyndrum hold landscape and wildlife glories in their woods, lochs, and hills. To the north, the lochan-pocked moorland, old Caledonian forest remnant, and mountain ground of Rannoch give a feel of starker wilds.

Between Killin and Kenmore, Loch Tay – famed for its beauty and its salmon – stretches for some 22 km. Dominating the view to the north of the loch is Perthshire's highest mountain, Ben Lawers (NTS; NN 6138). Due to the 'Tay overfold' the schists at high levels of the mountain are much older than the Loch Tay limestone, which outcrops some 1000 m below.

Partly because of the mineral-rich schists, this is one of the classic sites in Britain for arctic-alpine willow scrub – now very scarce elsewhere. Ben Lawers has the largest known population of mountain willow in the UK. This has

Woolly willow *Salix lanata*

Scotland

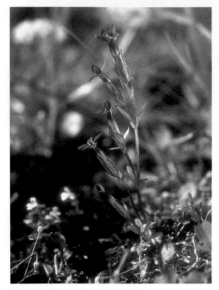

Alpine gentian *Gentiana nivalis*

associated with high altitude tall herb communities or alpine grassland.

Ben Lawers has the country's most extensive high-level alpine calcareous grassland. The main type, dominated by moss campion, occurs on the open hill. Another community, where mountain avens mixes with moss campion, is mainly on crags. On broad, moist ledges, inaccessible to sheep, tall herbs such as globeflower and red campion, great wood-rush, wild angelica, hogweed, and wood crane's-bill thrive.

A wide range of characteristic arctic-alpine flowering plants grow at Ben Lawers, and many rare ones, such as cyphel, sibbaldia, mountain pansy, alpine forget-me-not, alpine fleabane, alpine gentian, and rock speedwell. The birds include raven, ring ouzel, red grouse, ptarmigan, dipper, and curlew.

developed on crags and rock ledges on steep, rocky slopes that are difficult for grazing animals to reach. Other willows restricted to crags and ledges here include downy, dark-leaved, and net-leaved willows. There are also scattered individual woolly willow plants, often

Not far from the north end of Loch Tay, beside the hamlets of Keltneyburn and Coshieville, the Keltneyburn reserve (SWT; NN 767508) includes a steep, wooded gorge and adjacent gently sloping meadowland. Here, more than 200 different plants have been recorded on Balchroich Meadow, including greater

Ledges, Ben Lawers

Rannoch Moor

butterfly, fragrant, and small white orchids. An old curling pond attracts common red and emerald damselflies and hawker and black darter dragonflies.

Both here and on neighbouring hills, the most notable butterfly is the mountain ringlet (found only in a few colonies in the Lake District and in the central Highland – especially Breadalbane). Small heath is also fairly common up to around 750 m.

North of Glen Lyon, the shapely pointed mountain of Schiehallion (John Muir Trust) looks north and west over Loch Rannoch to the sweep of Rannoch Moor beyond. Near the base of the quartzite-dominated mountain, Scottish asphodel grows in low grassland in a small outcrop of limestone.

Flanking the southern shore of Loch Rannoch is the largest surviving native pine wood in Perthshire (the other is at Glen Lyon). Unlike the pinewoods in Deeside and Strathspey, there is a great deal of birch in the Black Wood of Rannoch (FC; NN 5956), intermixed with Scots pine and with pure stands of pine or birch. Scarce plants here include coralroot orchid and serrated wintergreen, with lesser twayblade, intermediate wintergreen, and chickweed wintergreen more common. Scottish crossbill and capercaillie are among the breeding birds.

Timberman beetles live in pine logs and stumps here, while the old, hoary birches of Rannoch (thick with mosses and lichens) are home to the rare, spring-emerging Rannoch sprawler moth. Another rare woodland moth – the Rannoch looper, also takes its name from the area, as does the Rannoch-rush. Blanket bog in Rannoch Moor (NN 4053) is now the only British location for this plant.

The mix of bogland, lochs with tree-clad islets, heathy and rocky knolls, and small valleys, set at some 330 m above sea level and stretching wide over a glacier-scoured granite basin, gives the moor a wild and challenging aspect. A long hike here could be rewarded with the sight of a golden eagle or osprey, the calls of grouse and curlew – or just the squelch of bog-moss.

Scotland

Close to Kinross lies one of Britain's best wildfowl sites: Loch Leven. This large lake is best investigated from Vane Farm (RSPB; NT 160993), on the south shore. This well-appointed reserve has an obser- vation centre, and a trail with hides through woodland, moorland, flooded grassland, and lakeside. The wintering wildfowl include 20 000 pink-footed geese, and whooper swans.

A selection of other important sites in the region

Culbin Sands (NH 900580): saltmarsh, dunes; seabirds, waders, wildfowl.

Cullaloe (NT 188877): loch, scrub, woodland; wildfowl, waders.

Killiecrankie (NN 907627): birchwood, moorland; buzzard, crossbill, black grouse, peregrine, raven.

Lein, Spey Bay (NJ 325657): coastal, shingle; waders, wildfowl, seabirds.

Loch of the Lowes (NO 042435): loch, woodland; viewable breeding osprey, wildfowl, woodland birds.

Longhaven Cliffs (NK 116394): auks, kittiwake.

Seaton Cliffs (NO 667416): seabirds.

Central and Strathclyde

SITE
11 Stirling

A characterful region of mountains, a huge raised bog, and abundant woodland.

Sliced across by the Highland Boundary Fault, the Stirling region has the allure of a borderland, where you can travel from lowland to highland and back again in the course of a single day. Although not far north of Glasgow (Scotland's largest city), it is a green lung close to the nation's industrial and commercial heartlands.

Loch Lomond, whose southern shores are just a few kilometres north of the urban areas of Dumbarton and Alexandria, has the largest surface area of any body of freshwa-

Four-spotted chaser *Libellula quadrimaculata*

Scotland

ter in Britain. A great variety of fish make this a prime spot for anglers. Salmon and sea trout come up the river Leven to the southern reaches of the loch, mingling with brown and rainbow trout, pike, perch, roach, chub, and dace. The relatively rare powan, a whitefish found only in a handful of British waters, also lives here, while the river Endrick feeding the loch is of European importance for its river lamprey population.

The patchwork of swamp, lagoons, fen, and willow carr to the south of the Endrick is rich in aquatic plants, with mats of bogbean, nodding bur-marigold and cowbane, and yellow and purple-loosestrife in the swamp. Wintering wildfowl here include a mixture of ducks and swans and a small number of Greenland white-fronted geese. Five oak-clad islands in the loch also lie within Loch Lomond NNR. The largest of these, Inchcailloch, has a nature trail through sessile oak woodland.

Ben Lomond, which rises from the east shore of the loch to a height of 974 m, offers straightforward walking (thousands ascend it every year). Wildlife interest is limited (meadow pipits and the odd grouse are par

Loch Lomond (Peter Wilson)

for the course), but the rewards come in the potentially huge views in every direction. Further up this shore, the Inversnaid reserve (RSPB; NN 340088) has fine broadleaved woods with rich communities of bryophytes and lichens, and a breeding bird fauna typical of western oak wood, including buzzard, wood warbler, pied flycatcher, and tree pipit. There are also blackcock in the area. In spring there are displays of bluebell, lesser celandine, primrose, wood-sorrel, ramsons, wood anemone, sanicle, and woodruff.

Beyond the loch and its varied surrounds, a further area of mountain and woods is also at the heart of the new Loch Lomond and Trossachs NP (the first area in Scotland to receive this designation). A large part of the greater Trossachs, which runs from Loch Lomond to Callander, Thornhill, Doune, and Strathyre, is covered by woodland of different kinds. Much of this woodland is within the Queen Elizabeth Forest Park – a mix of commercial conifer plantations and semi-natural and ancient woodland owned by the Forestry Commission, which includes the forests of Loch Ard, Achray, and Strathyre.

Bogbean *Menyanthes trifoliata*

Scotland

A network of waymarked trails gives easy access through many of these areas.

Some of the most varied woodlands are around Aberfoyle and Loch Ard, where red squirrel and roe deer are among the resident mammals which live amongst mixed stands of birch, spruce, larch, and other trees, including some juniper. Oakwoods in the area include the long established Fairy Knowe wood near Aberfoyle.

Close to Aberfoyle, the Lake of Menteith (NN 583009), the only body of freshwater in Scotland to be called a lake, sits at the north-west edge of Flanders Moss NNR (NS 645973). Once part of an even larger system of Forth Valley boglands which stretched from here to beyond Stirling, what remains is the largest intact raised bog in Britain. Bog-building *Sphagnum* mosses of many species are of prime importance to the area, whose flora includes white beak-sedge, cranberry, bog-rosemary, and the nationally rare Labrador-tea (possibly an introduction).

More common bog plants include heather and cross-leaved heath in drier areas, and bog myrtle, bog asphodel, and sundews in damper parts. Larvae of a local population of Rannoch brindled beauty moth feed on bog myrtle and heaths here. Four-spotted chasers are among the dragonflies and damselflies which breed in the bog pools. Adders breed here, and Flanders Moss is unusual in having a low-ground population of mountain hares. In winter, it is an important feeding and roosting site for geese – especially pinkfeet – and hen harriers.

12 Islay, Jura, and Colonsay

SITE

Islands that guard the Atlantic approaches to Argyll, with huge goose flocks, herds of red deer, and clean, quiet beaches among their many natural attractions.

At the southern end of the Inner Hebrides, about 19 km from the mainland, sits Islay, greenest of the Hebrides, with a near frost-free climate thanks to the influence of the Gulf Stream. Rugged upland with low summits, small valleys, lochans, and woods takes up much of its north-east portion. To the west, a wide range of moors, with bays and headlands to seaward, is almost severed from the rest of the island by two large sea lochs – famous for their wintering wildfowl. In the south, a low range of hills is flanked by a gloriously indented coast between Port Ellen and Claggain Bay, sandy flatlands between Laggan and Kintra, and rounded off by the fine cliffs edging the Oa.

This degree of landscape variety within a modest-sized island of just under 62 000 ha is enough to indicate the potential for wildlife diversity. But there are added bonuses, not least in the sheer size of the goose populations which winter here,

Golden eagle *Aquila chrysaetos*

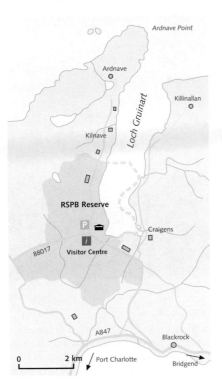

redshank, and knot, with one of the largest scaup flocks in Britain offshore in winter.

Aside from geese, Islay is also very much associated in birdwatchers' minds with the chough. The Rinns peninsula is now one of the best places to look for choughs, both in and around derelict buildings and in the major dune areas at Machir Bay (NR 2064) and Ardnave (NR 2874), where they forage for grubs in short turf and cowpats. The island also has breeding corncrake. Sea-holly (uncommon in Scotland) grows along the southern shore of the Rinns, and butterflies in the area include large and small whites, green hairstreak, small copper, dark green and marsh fritillaries, and large heath.

It is worth looking out for signs of otters along any part of Islay's long coastline. Emphasizing the proximity to Ireland, the brown hares here are of the Irish race, while the subspecies of both common shrew and field vole are unique to the island.

Only a narrow stretch of water separates Islay from Jura to the north-east, but the two islands are utterly different in character. Blanket bog, peaty soil, and rock dominate the scene below the highest points of the three-peaked 'Paps'. Along the west coast, and several kilometres from the island's one road, there are more arches, caves, and raised beaches than in any other similar-sized stretch in Scotland. North, between Jura and the satellite island of Scarba, runs the Corryvreckan, the most formidable tide-race whirlpool in Britain. No wonder many consider Jura to be the wildest of the inner isles. Several thousand red deer live here (even feeding along the tideline in places) and there are also some feral goats. The island has a particularly large number of adders.

In gentle contrast to the elemental wilds of Jura, Colonsay to the north-west is blessed with sandy bays and the sheltered, wooded Vale of Kiloran. An oddity of the Colonsay woods is the Australian landhopper, an introduced crustacean which lives among leaf litter (and may

and the variety of different birds of prey and owls that breed.

Some 30 000 barnacle geese can come to Islay from east Greenland each autumn, with first arrivals in late September and early October. These join several thousand Greenland white-fronted geese (also an important part of the world population) and make particular use of the areas around the two large sea lochs. Much of the inner half of Loch Gruinart (NR 2867) and the pastures to the south of the loch are managed as an RSPB reserve, where good, car-based goose viewing is possible from lay-bys off the road at the southern end. In spring and summer the fields which provide winter goose grazings are busy with breeding waders, including abundant lapwing, snipe, and redshank. A short distance further south, the tidal sandflats at the head of Loch Indaal (NR 3261) have an excellent range of feeding waders in most seasons, including curlew, oystercatcher, bar-tailed godwit, dunlin,

Islay (Mike Lane)

have come here in pots of ornamental plants or trees shipped by collectors to add to Colonsay's woodland gardens). Purple hairstreak butterflies live among the oaks of Coille Mhor – the island's ancient coastal woodland.

Loch Fada has a range of breeding waterbirds, with reed bunting and sedge warbler in the dense reedbeds, and skylark, lapwing, and snipe in surrounding fields. In winter, it is used by wintering ducks and geese and migrating whooper swans. Between Colonsay and the tidally separated island of Oronsay, the large coastal flats of the Strand are excellent for a variety of feeding waders outside the

breeding season. Cliff areas on Colonsay hold thousands of breeding guillemots, razorbills, fulmars, and gulls (including many kittiwakes).

To the north lies Mull, easily accessible by ferry from Oban. The west coast is wild and rocky with fjord-like inlets, while the east has a gentler aspect. Golden eagles breed on the island, and a special plant here is Iceland-purslane found (in Britain) only here and in Skye. To the west of Mull are Coll and Tiree. Tiree in particular is good for birds, with wintering barnacle and white-fronted geese, and breeding twites and corncrakes, while Coll holds about a tenth of the national corncrake population.

SITE 13 Clyde Valley area

Deep river valleys south and south-west of Glasgow, holding choice remnants of ancient woodlands.

Beside the World Heritage Site at New Lanark (designated for its importance as a mill and factory community in the early years of the Industrial Revolution) the

river Clyde tumbles down a spectacular gorge. Cut by glacial meltwater, this has a series of dramatic waterfalls over sections of harder rock.

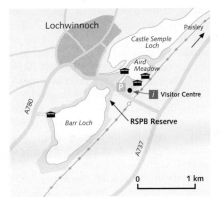

The Falls of Clyde reserve (SWT; NS 882425) covers both sides of the river here, and includes steep cliffs, wooded slopes, and the falls of Dundaff Linn, Cora Linn, and Bonnington Linn. The largest of these, Cora Linn, has a 28-m drop and is an awesome sight in full flow. Wordsworth and Coleridge, and the artists J. M. W. Turner and Jacob More all visited here to savour the landscape romance of the scene. Sadly, water abstraction for a nearby power station now tames the grandeur for much of the year. Steep ledges provide root-holds for purple saxifrage, butterwort, ferns, and mosses. A mosaic of woodland, part natural, part planted, fringes the gorge. Current management is gradually replacing conifer plantations on the reserve with birch, oak, ash, and other natives. Beneath the deciduous trees there is a good ground flora, including bluebell, wood anemone, dog's mercury, wood vetch, and common cow-wheat, with wood avens and marsh-marigold in damper areas. The river is used by dipper, grey wagtail, grey heron, and kingfisher. Birds of prey include breeding peregrine (viewable from a hide) and sparrowhawk. Otters live along the banks, and the woods beyond support badgers (the SWT provides organized watches), foxes, roe deer, bats, and red squirrels. Invertebrates include many kinds of ground beetle and 12 species of butterfly, including ringlet, meadow brown, orange tip, and green-veined white.

On the outskirts of the towns of Lanark and Carluke, three different woodlands form the Clyde Valley Woodlands NNR (NS 9045). These have the most extensive area of river valley ash–elm woodlands in Scotland, with a ground flora which includes some southern species such as herb-Paris and pendulous sedge. Ash, wych elm, and oak are dominant in the canopy, with alder, hazel, rowan, and birch forming a dense understorey. Wood anemone, ramsons, dog's mercury, wood-sorrel, bluebell, and primrose give a spring floral splash, while plants on wetter gorge-side slopes include alternate-leaved golden-saxifrage and rough horsetail.

Local topography has made these woods inaccessible for timber extraction in the past, and the large amount of dead wood here supports rich communities of fungi and wood-boring invertebrates. Tawny owls, great spotted woodpeckers, redstarts, and treecreepers also benefit from the old timber, while the wider breeding bird fauna also includes wood warblers.

Close to where the river Nethan flows down to meet the Clyde, there is further variation on the ravine–woodland theme at the SWT's two Nethan Gorge reserves (NS 820466; NS 801442). Unusual aspects here include slope alder wood, and scattered

Common butterwort *Pinguicula vulgaris*

clearings with wet, herb-rich meadows which hold stands of wood club-rush. Seepage from lime-rich outcrops produces wet, base-rich growing conditions, and the ground flora (in addition to a good range of usual native woodland flowers) includes giant bellflower, broad-leaved helleborine, and wood melick.

Just east of Lochwinnoch village, the main road from Largs to Paisley divides Lochwinnoch reserve (RSPB; NS 358582) into two. The northern part, Aird Meadow, has an area of shallow open water surrounded by varied marshland (including beds of reed canary-grass and sedges), willow scrub, and some mature woodland. To the south-west lies the larger, deeper Barr and to the north (outside the reserve) the even larger Castle Semple Loch.

Lochwinnoch is one of the main Scottish breeding sites for great crested grebes (an uncommon nester elsewhere); it also has a colony of black-headed gulls and is a major site for other breeding and wintering wildfowl. These include mallard, teal, shoveler, pochard, tufted duck, moorhen, and coot.

This is also a good spot for grasshopper warblers. Barr Loch is used as a roost by a few hundred greylag geese and moderate numbers of whooper swans, and goldeneye and goosander are generally present. Plants along the edge of the marsh include meadowsweet, valerian, and purple-loosestrife.

Nestling to the east of the Kintyre Peninsula is the island of Arran, which may be reached by regular ferry from Ardrossan. The highest point is the granite peak of Goatfell (874 m) with its corries and hanging valleys. The birds here echo those of the Highland: raven, peregrine, ring ouzel, and golden plover, with even a population of ptarmigan and the occasional golden eagle. Arran also has a healthy population of nightjars. The plants on Arran include heath milkwort, heath spotted-orchid, starry saxifrage, mountain sorrel, northern buckler-fern, and two rare service-tree species: *Sorbus arranensis* and *S. pseudofennica*. The wet heaths and moorland are particularly noteworthy for their dragonflies, which include highland darter and four-spotted chaser.

A selection of other important sites in the region

Ayr Gorge Woodlands (NS 457249): woodland with riverside birds.

Barons Haugh (NS 755552): woods, marsh, river; warblers, waders, wildfowl.

Cambus Pools (NS 846937): wetland; wildfowl, waders, migrants.

Gartmorn Dam (NS 912940): woodland, wetland, farmland; wildfowl, kingfisher, water rail.

Hogganfield Park (Glasgow): loch, woodland; wildfowl.

Knockshinnock Lagoons (NS 776113): lagoons, woodland; waders and wildfowl.

Machrihanish Seabird Observatory (NR 628209): rocky shore, upland; peregrine, twite, golden eagle, seabirds.

Fife and Lothian

East Fife and Firth of Forth

A large dune and forest system, enclosed estuary, beaches, low cliffs, and headlands, with one of eastern Britain's finest seabird colonies a few kilometres offshore.

Shaped like a terrier's head facing out to the North Sea, the peninsula-cum-kingdom of Fife sits between the firths of Forth and Tay. The Eden, northernmost of the two principal rivers of Fife, flows eastwards through Strathmiglo and Cupar to meet the sea just north of St Andrews. Designated as an LNR, the Eden Estuary (NO 485195) has a rich mix of invertebrates, such as lugworms and gastropods, in its tidal muds. Together with estuarine vegetation, these provide year-round food for may kinds of birds, with the estuary having prime importance for passage and wintering wildfowl and waders.

Large numbers of shelduck and red-breasted merganser can gather here, with sometimes nationally significant flocks of scaup, common and velvet scoter, and

Marram *Ammophila arenaria*

eider offshore. Redshank, oystercatcher, dunlin, and knot blend with grey plover and black-tailed godwit (two of the reserve's wader highlights) in winter, while sanderlings can be numerous near the estuary mouth. Sandbanks between Shelly Point and the river mouth are also favourite haul-outs for common seals.

Between the Eden and the outer part of the Tay Estuary, Tentsmuir Forest (FC) covers 1500 ha of sandy land out to the coast. Planted mainly with Scots and Corsican

Common stork's-bill *Erodium cicutarium*

Scotland

Redshank *Tringa totanus* **(Mike Lane)**

pine, the woodlands have red squirrels and (by Scottish standards) a good variety of bats, including common pipistrelle, brown long-eared, and Natterer's. Paths give easy access through the forest, including to where the trees give way to sand dunes at the east in Tentsmuir Point NNR (FC/SNH; NO 5027).

This is one of the few actively growing dune systems in Scotland, as can be seen at the western end of the reserve, where a line of concrete anti-tank blocks (installed close to the sea in the early 1940s) is now several hundred metres inland. Maps and aerial photographs have shown that,

between 1812 and the present, the reserve shoreline has advanced by more than 1 km (much of this in the last few decades). The Tentsmuir dunes are a good place to see contrasts in colonizing vegetation from the beach to inland, and between dune tops and hollows (slacks) behind them.

Sea rocket forms on the embryo dunes, with lyme-grass and marram stabilizing them. Sea sandwort grows on open areas or sandy shingle, common stork's-bill is widespread, and grass-of-Parnassus grows in damp hollows. Common and seaside centaury, purple milk-vetch, and coralroot orchid are among the hundreds of flowering plant species here, while the dunes and grassy areas have a wide variety of butterflies and moths. Grayling can be abundant, and there are good numbers of small copper, dark green fritillary, and ringlet. Offshore, the Abertay Sands are used by flocks of waders and roosting geese and as a haul-out for both common and grey seals.

Near Crail, at the easternmost tip of Fife, there are two SWT reserve areas close to the sea. The Kilminning Coast, which stretches for about 1 km and

Tentsmuir Point (Peter Wilson)

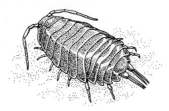

Sea-slater *Ligia oceanica*

includes the area between the present shoreline and the top of a former raised beach, is particularly rich in lichens and algae. Saltmarsh at the head of many tiny bays grades into freshwater fen in places, giving an unusual mix of maritime and marsh plants, including sea arrowgrass, northern marsh-orchid, sea-milkwort, and ragged-Robin.

Close by, Fife Ness Muir (NO 633090) has been planted with a wide range of shrubs and trees to give shelter and food to migrant birds and butterflies in spring and autumn. Small paths allow visitors to move quietly around the reserve at these seasons. Migrant birds recorded include 17 species of warbler.

Eight kilometres out to sea from the east Fife coast lies the Isle of May NNR (SNH), the largest of the Forth islands. Cliffs along its western side hold thousands of pairs of breeding guillemots, razorbills, fulmars, shags, and kittiwakes. Grassy areas above the cliffs and along much of the 1.5-km length at the east side are home to a still expanding colony of more than 20 000 pairs of puffins. There is also a large population of many hundreds of nesting eiders, and both common and Arctic terns breed.

A bird observatory, housed in the 'Low Light' former lighthouse-keeper's cottage, has operated here since the 1930s, with more than 240 species now recorded on the island, including national rarities. Grey seals breed here in the autumn.

Scotland

SITE 15 East of Edinburgh

Sweeps of wader-thronged estuary, cliffs loud with seabirds, old woods in steep, narrow gorges, and breezy moorland, all within easy reach of Edinburgh.

Between the Firth of Forth and the Lammermuir Hills, a swathe of varied countryside sits between Edinburgh and the North Sea – close to Scotland's capital, yet utterly different.

Some 26 km east of the centre of Edinburgh, where the Peffer Burn runs down to meet the sea, Aberlady Bay LNR (NT 4681) spreads wide beside Aberlady village. This is one of the best-known birdwatching sites in Scotland, but the sheer variety of habitats means that Aberlady Bay is designated as an SSSI on botanical and geological grounds, in addition to its ornithological value.

Mudflats, mussel beds, intertidal sand, and saltmarsh are bordered by dunes, calcareous grassland, freshwater marsh, pools, scrub, and woodland, with the close-mown swards of five golf courses nearby and the food-rich waters of the Forth beyond. Plant communities here show the full succession from mudflat through saltmarsh and dune to dune scrub and grassland.

All three species of eelgrass grow in the bay, and there are some unusual saltmarsh mosses here. In some parts of the moss-and-lichen-rich fixed dunes, autumn gentians, grass-of-Parnassus, burnet rose, and moonwort grow, with 15 species of sedge in the dune slacks and good aquatic plant growth in the Marl Loch.

Aberlady has year-round birds, with over 250 species having been seen here. In winter, pink-footed goose numbers peak in early November (with 15 000 or more recorded) and a flock of whooper swans roosts. Wigeon, mallard, teal, shelduck, and goldeneye are common in the bay, with flocks of eider, long-tailed duck, and scoters in the sea beyond. In spring, passage and arrival to breed of passerines and waders gives daily variations to local

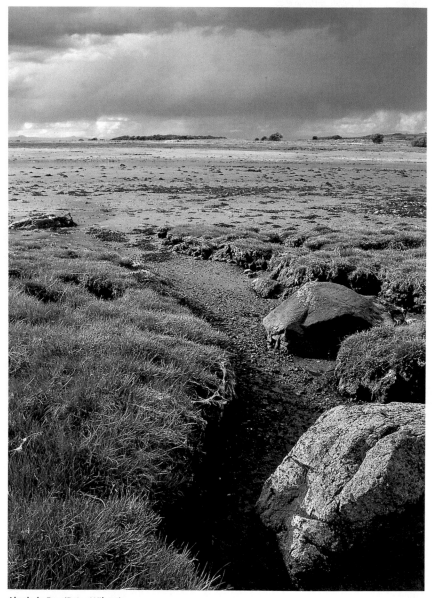

Aberlady Bay (Peter Wilson)

Scotland

Gannets *Morus bassanus*, Bass Rock (Mike Lane)

bird life, while the autumn wader passage can be particularly impressive.

More than 50 bird species breed here, including sedge warblers and reed buntings in the marsh, redpolls, bullfinches, and blackcaps in sea buckthorn spinneys, and ringed plovers, eiders, and shelducks along the shore and among the dunes. About 1500 species of beetle, a large number of flies and moths, and 13 species of butterfly have been recorded at Aberlady.

Not far from the town of North Berwick, the Bass Rock (NT 602873) has an impressive colony of thousands of gannets plus a mixture of other breeding seabirds including guillemots, razorbills, kittiwakes, and shags. Much of the rocky coast from Gullane, past North Berwick to Tyninghame, is good for purple sandpipers and turnstones in winter, with the possibility of divers offshore.

Inland, near the headwaters of the Tyne, the small, steep-sided glen of Linn Dean (SWT; NT 468594) sits at the top of Soutra Hill. The largest common rock-rose population in the Lothians grows on a south-fac-

ing bank here, thanks to base-rich water seepage along the slopes, while the grassy slope opposite has several stands of juniper. Deeper, damper parts of the dean have a wealth of mosses and liverworts. Northern brown argus butterflies breed on the sunny, south-facing slopes.

At Woodall Dean (SWT; NT 680728), on the edge of the Lammermuir Hills south of Dunbar, large woodland dominated by sessile oaks (with surprisingly little evidence of hybrids) grows on the steep slopes of three burns. Breeding birds include redstarts and occasional wood warblers. The shrub layer includes rowan, holly, elder, hazel, and hawthorn. On damper slopes beyond the wood there are wall lettuce, giant bellflower, maidenhair spleenwort, and golden-saxifrage, with marsh thistle, common spotted-orchid, and meadowsweet on flushed soils. Old deciduous trees by the Brunt are one of the most regular sites in the Lothians for marsh tits, which reach their northern limit in Britain here.

The Lammermuirs themselves, peppered with the remains of Iron Age hill forts along their north-east facing fringe, are mainly covered in rough grassland. Cleft by small glens which hold fast-running streams, this is territory for grey wagtail, dipper, common sandpiper, and ring ouzel in summer, with red grouse on the heathier ground and the chance of a variety of birds of prey, including merlin, hen harrier, and peregrine.

A selection of other important sites in the region

Bawsinch and Duddingston Loch (NT 003631): marsh, loch, scrub; wildfowl.

Cameron Reservoir (NO 478115): wildfowl.

Scotland

Dumfries, Galloway, and Borders

SITE
16 Inner Solway and Nithsdale

Muddy twists and coastal flats that provide some of the finest British havens for wildfowl; rocky grassland, and established woodland sheltering a choice blend of birds and plants.

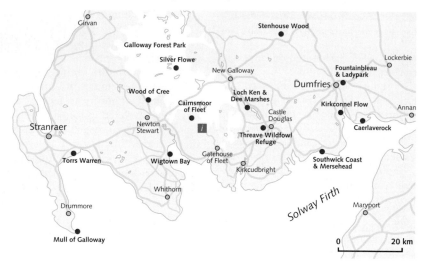

A prime site for wildfowl along the whole of the Solway – north or south – is the 5500-ha Caerlaverock NNR, which stretches between the estuaries of the river Nith to the west and Lochar Water to the east. Within this, the Wildfowl and Wetland Trust's reserve (NY 051656), with its network of observation hides and towers linked by carefully screened approaches, gives the best opportunities for relaxed viewing.

Key to Caerlaverock's popularity with wildfowl, and a distinctive feature of different parts of the Solway, are the flat salt-marsh grazings above high water, known locally as 'the Merse'. In winter these become the feeding and roosting places for huge numbers of barnacle, pink-footed, and greylag geese, and wigeon. The barnacle geese are Caerlaverock's glory, and a real conservation success. The entire breeding population from Spitzbergen winters here.

Scotland

Mainly whooper swans *Cygnus cygnus*, Caerlaverock

Thanks to carefully regulated wildfowling on the Solway, and good breeding success in the high Arctic, numbers have grown from a low ebb of 400 or so in the mid-1940s to the current level of around 25 000 birds, often peaking in mid-November.

Pink-footed geese are more numerous later, between January and March. Other wildfowl include, mallard, pintail, and teal, with smaller numbers of shoveler and several hundred shelduck by late winter. There are also hundreds of whooper swans, dozens of mute swans, and some Bewick's swans. Thousands of waders, including, golden plover, godwits, curlew, dunlin, knot, and oystercatcher pass through here or stay between autumn and spring.

In addition to its wildfowl splendours, Caerlaverock is a notable breeding site for natterjacks. The entire Scottish population of this rare amphibian lives between Southwick and Annan. Flooded pools, created during construction of coastal banks on the margins of the saltmarsh, give ideal habitat for them.

Around 8 km south of Dumfries, Kirkconnel Flow NNR is a good example of a coastal raised mire. Like other coastal mosses it sits beside estuarine flats, and is flat and poorly drained. Flora and fauna on this wooded bog include cranberry and bog-rosemary, scarce invertebrates, and adder.

Over and seaward of the landmark hill Criffel (569 m) from Kirkconnel, the Southwick Coast reserve (SWT) sits between the A710 and the sea. Slopes up to the road are cloaked with ancient oak woodland with hazel and holly in the understorey, with smaller open areas of lime-rich grassland. These banks have good populations of common rock-rose and bloody crane's-bill. At the base of the cliff there is a patch of marshy ground where water figwort grows. Beyond this marshy area and the Southwick Water is the local merse, cut with creeks and gullies and supporting beds of reeds, sea club-rush, and common sea-lavender. The most prominent landscape features here are a natural arch: 'The Needle's Eye', and a rock pillar: 'Lot's Wife'. These ancient geological curios sit in the middle of the marsh, but were formed through erosion by waves at a time when sea levels were higher than they are now. The Mersehead reserve lies nearby (RSPB; NY 9356), protecting saltmarsh and mudflats which

Scotland

Shelduck *Tadorna tadorna*

attract waders and wildfowl, including barnacle and pink-footed geese.

Flanking the Shinnel Water (a tributary of the Nith), north-west of Dumfries, the mixed deciduous woodland of the Stenhouse Wood reserve (SWT; NX 795930) grows on fairly lime-rich soil. Ash, wych elm, and oak are the main tree species, with formerly coppiced hazel and ash seedlings, hawthorn, and rowan. Moss growth on both living and dead wood is lush, and the varied ground flora includes dog's mercury, ramsons, bluebell, and bugle, plus a colony of toothwort (parasitic on hazel and other trees).

At the very edge of Dumfries a site which was a loch in late medieval times is now heavily wooded at the Fountainbleau and Ladypark reserve (SWT; NX 986772). Birch covers much of the site, with alder and willow in damper areas. Swampy ground is mainly covered with bottle sedge and patches of marsh violet, marsh cinquefoil, marsh pennywort, and bog-bean. There is a small breeding population of willow tits here, occasional breeding pied flycatchers, and willow warbler, sedge warbler, and reed bunting – observable from a duck-boarded nature trail.

SITE 17 Outer Solway and the Galloway coast

A coastline and high uplands offering richly varying habitats.

There are many contrasts between the western coastline of the Solway and the soft shores of the inner part of the Firth. There are cliffs and raised beaches, and also many broad bays, sheltered sandy shores, and stretches of gently sloping shingle. Inland, marshes, bogs, ancient woods, and recent plantations add variety to the highest uplands in southern Scotland.

Thanks to a hydroelectric dam across the river Dee north of Castle Douglas, a shallow-sided loch system, bordered by marshland, woods, and meadows, now snakes down the river valley for more than 14 km. When water levels fall, extensive mudflats can be revealed, especially along the south-western shore.

The Loch Ken and River Dee Marshes reserve (RSPB; NX 699684) forms part of this linear wetland which, with its areas of swamp, fen, grassland, and carr woodland, is one of the best examples of a semi-natural freshwater system in north-west Europe. Five separate areas, including marsh, meadow, and broadleaved woodland, are managed by the RSPB here.

In autumn and winter more than 300 Greenland white-fronted geese (one of the biggest concentrations in the country) roost and feed in the valley, together with more than 800 greylags, scores of whooper swans, and a mixture of other wildfowl. These include pintail, wigeon, teal, mallard, goosander, and goldeneye. Hen

Scotland

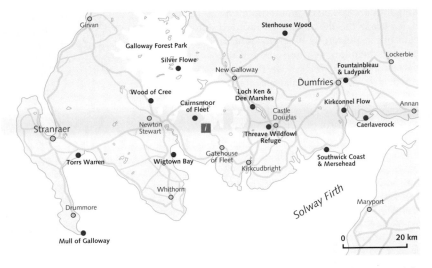

harriers, peregrines, and merlin may also be spotted here. The wetland complex supports nationally rare aquatic plants and invertebrates. In summer, rough grasslands on the valley sides have abundant meadowsweet, valerian, and marsh cinquefoil, with stands of spignel, saw-wort, and wood bitter-vetch. Mature oak woods hold breeding redstarts and pied flycatchers, and the RSPB reserve is also the Scottish stronghold for willow tits. Around one-fifth of the red squirrels in Scotland live in Dumfries and Galloway, including here, and otters also use the area. Close by, the Threave Wildfowl Refuge (NTS; NX 7463), at Threave Castle on the outskirts of Castle Douglas, also provides good feeding grounds for wildfowl using the Ken–Dee system.

Covering a huge swathe of the Galloway Hills, the Biosphere Reserve of Cairnsmore of Fleet/Merrick Kells/Silver Flowe includes areas of the Galloway Forest Park, several SSSIs, and two NNRs within its sweep. Cairnsmore of Fleet (NX 5266) is a granite massif which has the most extensive open moorland in Galloway and areas of montane grassland and dwarf shrub heath. Breeding raptors include golden eagle, merlin, and hen harrier; red grouse and black grouse use the moors and their fringes, and there is a population of feral goats.

Merrick Kells includes Merrick, Scotland's highest summit outside the Highland (NX 4386), and has blanket bog, montane acid grassland, wet heath, and mires, set within Galloway's largest remaining unafforested area. At the Silver Flowe NNR (NX 4782), 19 km north-east of Newton Stewart, there is one of the least disturbed mire systems in Western Europe. The patterns of pools and hummocks here are one of high landscape and scientific value, and this is a breeding site for the rare azure hawker dragonfly.

The Galloway Forest Park includes huge conifer plantations, moorland, lochs, and high uplands within its vast area. Quiet toll drives give access away from the main roads. Stroan Loch, near the southern end of the Raider's Road Forest Drive is one of the park's good

Goldeneye *Bucephala clangula* (Mike Lane)

Scotland

dragonfly lochs. Red deer and mountain hares graze the hills and there are red squirrels in the forests. A variety of birds of prey, including hen harriers and the occasional golden eagle, use the area, which also has good populations of barn owls and crossbills.

The Wood of Cree reserve (RSPB; NX 382708), 5 km north of Newton Stewart, holds the largest remaining ancient woodland in southern Scotland. Sessile oaks, with former coppice of birch, ash, hazel, rowan, and willow grow here. Redstart, pied flycatcher, garden warbler, and willow tit are some of the abundant breeding birds, while butterflies include Scotch argus and purple hairstreak. The reserve is part of an ambitious project to expand and link semi-natural Galloway woodlands along a 40-km stretch from Loch Trool to the sea. Migrating fish which swim up the river Cree from the sea include Scotland's only surviving spawning population of sparling or smelt, a species once much more common and eaten as a delicacy.

Wigtown Bay LNR (NX 438547) has extensive merse, with abundant thrift, sea-milkwort, sea aster, and the local rarity, lax-flowered sea-lavender. As many as 7000 pink-footed geese may gather here.

Spring squill *Scilla verna*

Further west, plants in the Torrs Warren to Luce Bay sand dune system include a rich lichen flora, lesser twayblade, shepherd's cress, and coralroot orchid.

At the Mull of Galloway (RSPB; NX 156304), Scotland's southernmost point, impressive cliffs have abundant spring squill and purple milk-vetch in the cliff-top turf, Scots lovage at its southern British limit, and a Mediterranean plant – small restharrow – at its northern limit. Nesting seabirds include fulmar, cormorant, shag, kittiwake, guillemot, razorbill, and black guillemot.

SITE 18 The Merse and its fringes

Rich woodlands and outstanding coastal scenery.

Between the southern rim of the Lammermuir Hills and the wide curve of the Tweed, the fertile lowlands of the Merse hold rich woodlands along burns and riversides and in the parklands of its great estates. To seaward

Foxglove
Digitalis purpurea

St Abb's Head

is some of the finest coastal scenery in southern Scotland.

St Abb's Head NNR (NTS/SWT; NT 914688) has a wild, indented coastline, with steep cliffs up to 100 m high, rocky promontories, cliff-top grasslands, and an artificial freshwater loch. The volcanic rocks of the head itself are flanked by older sedimentary rocks which form the sloping cliffs, often with shingle beaches below. Large numbers of seabirds breed here, including big populations of kittiwakes and guillemots with smaller numbers of razorbills, shags, fulmars, and a few puffins.

Common scurvygrass, thrift, and sea campion are widespread along the cliffs, together with common rock-rose, spring sandwort, and kidney vetch by the lighthouse road, and roseroot and Scots lovage in places. Swathes of purple milk-vetch, mixed with primrose, thrift, and early purple orchid, give colour splashes around the cliff-top.

Butterflies regularly seen here include small copper, common blue, northern brown argus, and grayling, as well as larger day-flying moths such as yellow shell, silver Y, and six-spot burnet. Offshore, a stretch of nearly 9 km of

coastline from Pettico Wick to Eyemouth is administered as the St Abbs Marine Reserve (SWT and local committee; NT 919674), where cold-water species such as wolf fish, lumpfish, and the *Bolocera* anemone live around their southern limit. Underwater scenery here can be as impressive as that above the waves, with tunnels, caves, gullies, and arches.

Above Pease Bay east of Cockburnspath, the native woodland remnant of Pease Dean (NT 790705) – all that survives of the once extensive Penmansheil Woods) – cloaks a steep-sided, Y-shaped valley. In the upper part, sessile oaks thrive on acidic soil, above a ground layer of great wood-rush, honeysuckle, foxglove, hard-fern, and wavy hair-grass. On richer soils, ash, elm, and sycamore grow above dog's mercury and ramsons. The wood is notable for its locally rare mosses and liverworts, and the breeding birds include marsh tit and the occasional lesser whitethroat.

Just outside the town of Duns, two artificial lochs within a former glacial meltwater channel between Duns Law and Hare Law form the core of an SWT reserve within the Duns Castle estate (NT 778550). The shallow Hen Pool is fringed

Scotland

Pease Dean (Peter Wilson)

with yellow iris, rushes, and bulrush, with yellow water-lilies on its surface. Mute swan, mallard, moorhen, and other waterbirds breed here, and pochard and goosander visit in winter. Vegetation in the smaller Lower Mill Pond, which once provided power for the estate's sawmill, includes greater spearwort. In the surrounding mixed woodland there are great spotted and green woodpeckers, jay, pied flycatcher, and redstart, and the ground flora includes abundant bluebells and ramsons, while the rides and glades benefit a wide range of butterflies and moths.

Very close to the border with England and less than 2 km north-east of Coldstream, the private estate of The Hirsel (NT 8341), seat of the Douglas-Home family, has one of the highest breeding-bird diversities in south-east Scotland. Central to this variety are the estate policy woodlands, and the shallow Hirsel Lake created in a damp hollow in the late eighteenth century and now one of the largest inland waters in the region. Leet Water – a small tributary of the Tweed – winds among wet pasture to the east. Breeding birds include a variety of wildfowl and woodland birds. Unusually

for Scotland, both marsh tit and hawfinch breed at The Hirsel.

Immediately west of Gordon village, Gordon Moss (SWT; NT 635425) is the surviving remnant of a much larger mire. Birch wood and scrub containing six species of willow grow with alder and aspen over a carpet of mosses, grasses, and ferns. On the bog surface there are stems and branches thick with lichens. Springs of mineral-rich water boost plant diversity. Six species of orchid including coralroot and lesser but-

A selection of other important sites in the region

Bemersyde Moss (NT 614340): marsh and loch; black-headed gull, grasshopper warbler, black-necked grebe.

Carstramon Wood (NT 592605): oakwoods; woodland birds and flowers.

Yetholm Loch (NT 803279): marsh and loch; wildfowl, including wintering pink-footed geese and whooper swan.

terfly, plus common wintergreen, moon-wort and greater spearwort grow here.

More than 200 species of moth have been recorded at Gordon Moss, including some with a limited distribution in Scotland. These include small chocolate tip, miller, northern drab, powdered Quaker, and beautiful carpet. Pearl-bordered fritillaries and ringlets are common among the 16 species of butterfly.

Northern England

Introduction

This area encompasses a wide variety of scenery, from the rather sparsely populated uplands of Northumberland and Durham, to the scenic Lake District, through the rolling dales and moors of Yorkshire, south to the gentler countryside of Nottinghamshire with its remnants of Sherwood Forest.

The Cheviots are the northernmost range of hills in England, lying along the Scottish border and rising to 816 m at The Cheviot. Here deep valleys cut into the rolling, sheep-strewn uplands developed largely over granite rocks. It is great rambling country and much of the landscape is protected by the Northumberland NP. A little further south lie the impressive Roman remains of Hadrian's Wall.

The Lake District, to the west, is a distillation of British landscapes, with coastal, mountain, and lake habitats aplenty, and is justifiably famous as a tourist destination. It also has a rich and varied wildlife, with many reserves and other protected sites to visit. The dome of old rocks is drained by a radial series of rivers and lakes, and the classic effects of glaciation, such as hanging valleys, corries, and waterfalls, are very much in evidence. Some of the lakes here, like Windermere, result from damming behind morainic barriers.

The central spine of this region is formed by the Pennine Hills, a series of dissected plateaux stretching from the upper Tyne southwards to the Derbyshire Peak District. Although much of this hill country is over 300 m, the Pennines are lower than the Highlands of Scotland or the high hills of the Lake District, or Snowdonia in Wales. The Pennines reach their highest point in Cross Fell (893 m) in the northern, broadest block, where the hard Millstone Grit is a feature of the geology. The karst-like country of the central block is drained mainly by the Ouse and its tributaries. Whernside (736 m) is the highest point here. The Pennines are broadest in the north and central regions, with the southern section (south of the upper Aire Valley) being markedly narrower, though broadening again in Derbyshire, where there are further areas of karst-like country. Limestone pavement is well represented in Northern England and is one of our rarest habitats, with an unusual flora.

As in most of Britain, the coast has its wildlife interest too, and there is considerable variety in this region. The western coasts have some of the finest dune formations, as well as extensive mudflats and estuaries, while the eastern coast tends to feature rocky coves and headlands, with a number of impressive bird-cliffs such as those around Flamborough Head.

Opposite page: **Scar Close NNR** (see p. 110)

Northern England

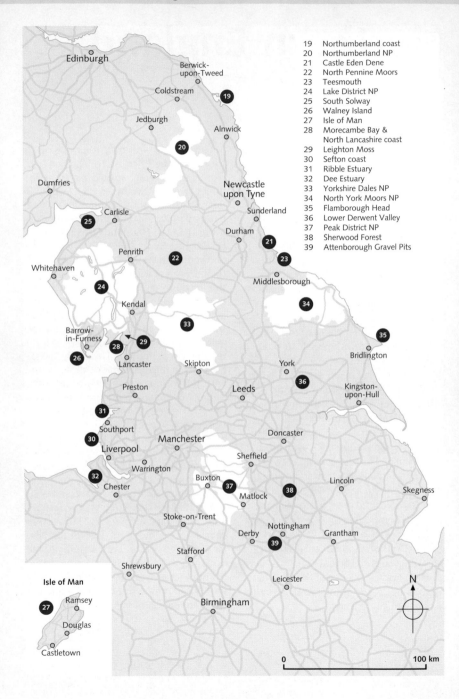

19   Northumberland coast
20   Northumberland NP
21   Castle Eden Dene
22   North Pennine Moors
23   Teesmouth
24   Lake District NP
25   South Solway
26   Walney Island
27   Isle of Man
28   Morecambe Bay &
      North Lancashire coast
29   Leighton Moss
30   Sefton coast
31   Ribble Estuary
32   Dee Estuary
33   Yorkshire Dales NP
34   North York Moors NP
35   Flamborough Head
36   Lower Derwent Valley
37   Peak District NP
38   Sherwood Forest
39   Attenborough Gravel Pits

Northumberland and Tyne and Wear

SITE 19 Northumberland coast

Wild and unspoilt coast with offshore islands holding large colonies of seabirds.

Some 12 km south of Berwick-upon-Tweed lies Holy Island, with its famous Priory of Lindisfarne. The Farne Islands are about 8 km further south, and this whole stretch of coast, from Berwick south to Druridge Bay just north of Ashington, forms the North Northumberland Heritage Coast, a marvellous area with outstanding coastal habitats.

Holy Island is connected to the adjacent mainland by a causeway, flooded at high tide. Lindisfarne NNR (EN/NT; NU 100420, OS 75) is centred upon Holy Island and covers over 3500 ha of dunes, grassland, saltmarsh, and mudflats. The site is also of great ornithological interest, with huge numbers (up to 50 000) of wintering wildfowl – notably whooper swans and the world's largest concentrations of pale-bellied Brent geese, this being the main wintering site in Britain for this race, which breeds in Spitzbergen. Waders are frequent, too, with large numbers of bar-tailed godwits and grey plover in particular. There are birdwatching hides, a nature trail, and interpretation boards.

This is one of the best birdwatching sites in the north-east, especially for wildfowl and waders in autumn and winter. Red-throated diver and Slavonian grebe are fairly common in the sea, and black-throated diver and red-necked grebe are also possible. In addition to the Brent geese, there are greylags, sometimes with pink-footed and bean goose as well, and the occasional Bewick's swan. Regular ducks include wigeon, shelduck, teal, eider, common and sometimes velvet scoters, long-tailed duck, and scaup. Raptors such as hen harrier, short-eared owl, peregrine, and merlin are all frequent visitors in the winter. There are dunlin,

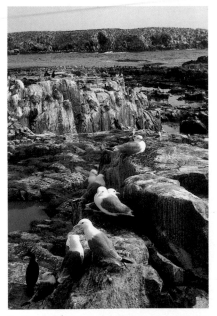

Nesting kittiwakes on the Farnes

Lindisfarne

knot, and bar-tailed godwit aplenty, with rarer species fairly likely, too, including purple sandpiper and greenshank.

Holy Island Harbour, at the south of the island, is a good spot for winter sea-watching, with red-necked and Slavonian grebes, long-tailed duck, and velvet scoter, and possibly black-throated and great northern divers. Inland, at Felham Flats, some 2000 pale-bellied Brent geese and up to 15 000 wigeon gather. Nearby Budle Bay often yields snow buntings and shore larks, and is good for waders and geese, while the dunes at Ross Back are well worth investigating.

Holy Island's calcareous dunes have a rich flora, with grass-of-Parnassus, and 10 species of orchids, such as the dune helleborine, and several rare bryophytes. Below the castle (itself worth a detour) grow thrift, biting stonecrop, and sea campion. Lindisfarne also has a small colony of common seals. Grayling and dark green fritillary butterflies also breed amongst the dunes.

The Farne Islands, opposite Bamburgh (with its impressive castle) may be reached by regular boat trips (April–September) from Seahouses, weather permitting, with landings on Inner Farne and Staple Island. It thus takes a little effort to reach these wonderful islands, but for the keen naturalist it is well worth it. This collection of some 25 small islands is protected as the Farne Islands NNR (NT; NU 230370, OS 75). The low, rocky islands are a haven for breeding seabirds, protected from mainland predators and human disturbance. There are few offshore islands in eastern Britain, which increases their importance.

During the breeding season, in May and June, the islands are noisy with calls of thousands of birds. The cliffs and rocks have 6000 pairs of kittiwake and 16 000 pairs of guillemot, and four species of tern nest on the islands – the rare roseate as well as common, Arctic, and Sandwich. Here the commonest tern is in fact the Arctic, with 3000 pairs. Note that the terns may be aggressive when breeding and

Northern England

Eider *Somateria mollissima*

regularly dive-bomb visitors, sometimes making painful contact!

Other breeders are puffin (30 000 pairs), shags (about 2000 pairs), and eider (about 1200 pairs). Many of the birds here are quite approachable, and surprisingly tame, especially the shags and kittiwakes, perhaps because they have been so well protected for so long. The shores here are also an ideal habitat for rock pipits. In autumn, the Farne Islands host one of Britain's largest breeding colonies of grey seals, with around 4000 individuals at present.

Probably the most notable plants are sea campion, and the introduced alien fiddleneck.

Out to sea, there are good numbers of gannets soaring and fishing in the area, as well as passage movements of Manx and sooty shearwaters. In the winter, scoters, long-tailed ducks, and divers are frequent.

Other sites nearby

Alnmouth (NT; NU 241094) is a good area of saltmarsh, sand dunes, grassland, and mudflats. Marram, lymegrass, lesser meadow-rue, purple milk-vetch, bloody crane's-bill, and eyebright grow here, with biting and white stonecrop on drier ground. The flats are important for waders.

Arnold Memorial Reserve (WT; NU 255197, OS 81), close to Craster, is a small reserve with a quarry and mixed woodland. It is a magnet for migrant birds, regularly turning up wryneck, bluethroat, red-breasted flycatcher, and icterine and barred warblers.

Beadnell Bay to Embleton Bay (OS 75). Some 14 km north-east of Alnwick, this is a lovely stretch of coast owned largely by the NT (Embleton Links (NT); NU 243240). Beautiful beaches, with extensive dune systems, grazing, and pools. The dune flora includes burnet rose, bloody crane's-bill, restharrow, harebell, tufted centaury, and butterwort. Black-headed gulls breed in the area, along with common, Arctic, sandwich, little, and sometimes roseate terns. Autumn seawatching for skuas and shearwaters. **Dunstanburgh Castle** (NT; NU 258220). These fourteenth-century ruins dominate the southern end of Embleton Bay, but it is the cliffs here which have the natural history interest. This is a great seabird site, with some 700 pairs of kittiwake, fulmars, shags, and breeding eider ducks. The grassland is rich in flowers, with purple milk-vetch, spring squill, wild thyme, and bloody crane's-bill.

Coquet Island (RSPB; NU 2965), near Amble, has over 3000 pairs of puffins and a colony of eider ducks, but is best known for its terns – mainly Sandwich, Arctic, and common, but with a sprinkling of the rare roseate tern. This site has over half of the UK population of roseates.

Hauxley (WT; NU 285023, OS 81; 32 ha), just south of Amble, is a fine coastal reserve created from an old open-cast coal mine. It is a notable spot for seabirds, including roseate terns.

Northern England

20 Northumberland National Park

Upland expanses of moorland, with pockets of woodland and extensive conifer plantations.

The Northumberland NP encompasses some 1049 square kilometres of hill country in the very north of England, its north-eastern edge following the Scottish border and the Cheviot Hills, and stretching south to Hadrian's Wall, in the vicinity of Haltwhistle. On the western side are the extensive plantations of Border Forest Park, centred on the huge reservoir of Kielder Water.

The main habitats are the woodlands and farms of the valleys, with rocky streams, and the open upland grassland and moorland of the higher areas, in places topped by crags and cliffs which reach their highest point at The Cheviot (815 m). The vast brooding plantation of Kielder Forest dominates the western flank of the park, but there are also scattered natural deciduous woods in some of the valleys – oak on drier sites, and alder in wetter places. The upland heather moors are mainly managed for grouse and, although much of the park is

Brown hare *Lepus europaeus* (Robert Dickson)

private land, rights of way and footpaths abound. The Pennine Way long-distance path runs the length of the park, passing along part of Hadrian's Wall before turning sharply northwards at the famous fort of Housesteads, through Bellingham and further north, eventually to follow the Scottish border towards The Cheviot and beyond.

Curlew, golden plover, and red grouse are common on the hills, with blackcock, short-eared owl, and merlin occurring in some of the heather moorland. Another typical upland bird is the wheatear, which often chooses a drystone wall in which to nest. Mammals of the park include roe deer, fox, badger, brown hare, rabbit, otter, and red squirrel.

Hadrian's Wall near Haltwhistle is well worth visiting, and the experience of walking along part of the Roman wall unforgettable. The lochs in this area attract good numbers of wildfowl in the winter. Grindon Lough (NY 806675), just south of the wall, has whooper swans, bean, pink-footed, and greylag geese, and is easily watched from the road. Greenlee Lough NNR (NY 767697, OS 87; 57 ha) protects the largest of these lakes. It shows a good example of a natural succession from open water to woodland, with reedbeds and poor fen in between. Greenlee tends to have more whoopers. Crag Lough (NY 7767) is probably the best for seeing the typical vegetation of these border loughs. Here carr-like scrub grades into swampy fen vegetation dominated by reed and sedges. Flowers here include marsh-marigold, marsh cinquefoil, bogbean, ragged-Robin, skullcap,

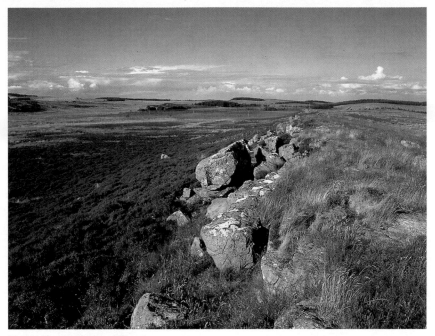

Muckle Moss NNR (Peter Wilson)

and marsh lousewort. Nearby Muckle Moss NNR (NY 799668, OS 86; 169 ha) is valley bog with rare bog-mosses; access is by permission only. Gowk Bank NNR (NY 679739, OS 86; 15 ha), some 5 km north of the wall, protects upland meadow and grassland, and has a rich flora.

Right at the heart of the Northumberland NP is the river Coquet, which rises high in the Cheviot Hills, then winds its way eastwards through the park before meandering out towards the sea at Amble. This pretty valley is well worth investigating, and its upper reaches give a good general impression of the park as a whole. The clear waters have dipper and grey wagtail, and oystercatchers and common sandpipers appreciate its shingle banks. The riverside woods have redstart and pied flycatcher, while in the upper moorland section there are whinchat, ring ouzel, and curlew. Harbottle Crags (WT; NT 9305) lies in this valley, just west of Harbottle village. It has a typical mix of heather moorland and upland grassland, managed by regular cutting and burning. An interesting feature of

this reserve is the cliffs and crags which jut out above the moorland. These provide good sites for taller clumps of heather, with bilberry, crowberry, and cowberry. Black and red grouse can both be seen, as can ring ouzels, wheatears and whinchats, short-eared owls, kestrels, and sometimes merlins. Goosanders and whooper swans visit the lough in winter. The moths include northern eggar, fox, and emperor. The lough in this reserve has a quaking bog (*Schwingmoor*) developed at its eastern end and there are cottongrasses, sundew, and cranberry. Cragside (NT; NU 073022) is close to the Coquet, near Rothbury, near the eastern edge of the NP. This fine house has a landscaped estate with planted conifers. There are red squirrels, roe deer, woodcock, sparrowhawk, tree pipit, pied flycatcher, wood warbler, and siskin.

Kielder Water (NY 6888) and Forest on the south-western end of the NP. This is Britain's largest reservoir, and lies amid extensive conifer plantations. The road skirting the southern side is well supplied with car parks, and there are visitor centres at both ends of the lake, as well as a raptor viewpoint just south of Kielder (NY 635910) from which goshawks may sometimes be seen, as may hen harriers, buzzards, or a passing osprey. Other birds to watch out for here are crossbills and tree pipits in or near the forest, and great crested grebe, goldeneye, goosander, and common sandpiper on the reservoir.

Kershope Forest (NY 521808) lies on the border with Cumbria and also with Scotland, on the western flank of Border Forest Park. This is a good site for birds of prey, particularly buzzard, kestrel, and sparrowhawk, but there is also the chance of barn owl, raven, merlin, and goshawk. Other birds breeding in the forest are redstart, crossbill, siskin, and grasshopper warbler. There are red grouse and hen harriers on the nearby moorland, and common sandpipers and goosander along the rivers.

A selection of other important sites in the county

Big Waters (NZ 227734, OS 88), just north of Newcastle, is a lake surrounded by birch, alder, and carr, and one of the best northern sites for butterflies and dragonflies, including banded demoiselle. Great crested and little grebes breed, as do common tern.

Bolam Lake (NZ 080819) is good for woodland birds, and also roe deer and red squirrels.

Briarwood Banks (WT; NY 791620, OS 86/7; 19 ha) is one of the best ancient woods in the county, with ash, oak, birch, and alder. Wood warbler, pied flycatcher, and red squirrels.

The Leas and **Marsden Rock** (NT; NZ 388665). Cliffs near South Shields with big seabird colonies: 4000 pairs of kittiwakes, fulmar, herring and lesser black-backed gulls, cormorants. Good for seawatching, too; also purple sandpipers on rocks in winter, with occasional snow and Lapland buntings.

Washington (WWT; NZ 3156), between Washington and Sunderland, has good wildfowl, waders and woodland birds.

Durham and Cleveland

SITE
21 Castle Eden Dene

Sheltered mixed woodland, with a rich flora; one of the largest and least disturbed woods in the north-east of England.

Castle Eden Dene NNR (NZ 435397, OS 93; 221 ha) is on the south side of Peterlee, east of the A19. There is a car park at the main entrance, and disabled access to the gardens and buffer zone. It lies in the valley of the Castle Eden Burn and its tributaries as they carve their way through a boulder clay and limestone plateau, creating a romantic fairytale landscape of caves, hollows, and pools. There are steep,

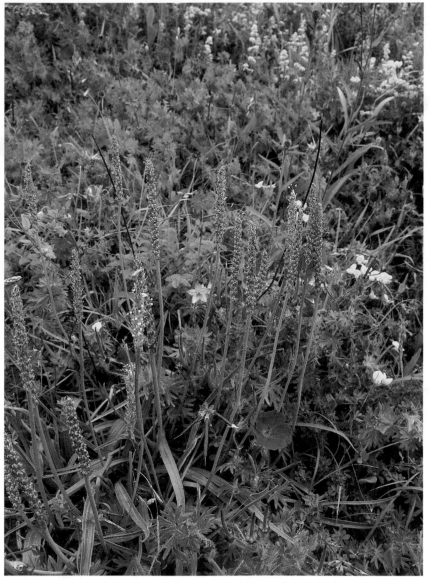

Limestone grassland with bloody cranesbill *Geranium sanguineum* (Peter Wilson)

wooded banks and some spectacular limestone cliffs and gorges. The burn itself flows seasonally, disappearing into the limestone rock in summer.

The rich flora here includes meadow, bloody and wood crane's-bills, and fly and bird's-nest orchids. The invertebrate fauna is also of great interest. A butterfly speciality here is the very local northern brown argus. Some 300 invertebrate species are listed as being important, nationally, regionally, or locally.

The almost 20 km of footpaths allow exploration of the varied habitats. Most of this reserve is heavily wooded, with a mixed community of ash, wych elm, oak, and sycamore, and a sprinkling of more recently introduced trees. There are also large patches of yew, and an unusual dry plateau alder wood. The limestone grassland towards the coast is particularly rich, with species such as bloody crane's-bill, rock-rose, bird's-foot-trefoil, common spotted- and fragrant orchids, rough hawkbit, and the grass Yorkshire-fog. This site was famous as a locality for the lady's-slipper (orchid), now one of Britain's rarest flowers.

Most typical woodland birds occur and many passage migrants have been record-ed, especially at the coast, and red squirrels may still be spotted.

At Eden Denemouth the river reaches the sea at a sandy beach affected by colliery tipping. Seawatching here may reveal divers and scoters in winter, with snow buntings regular on the shore.

About 7 km north lies Hawthorn Dene, Seaham (NZ 4245, OS 88), an impressive coastal wooded ravine, good for migrant birds. Seawatching from the coast nearby can also be rewarding, especially for divers and grebes. Little gulls are regular.

SITE 22 North Pennine Moors

Wild moorland, some managed for red grouse, with pasture and hay meadows in the east-draining valleys of the Tees and Wear.

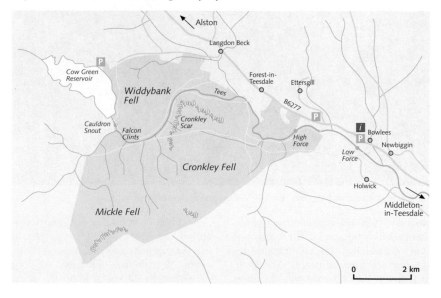

One element of the unique flora, the shrubby cinquefoil, was first recorded in 1671 as new to science 'on the south bank of the River Tees' by the famous naturalist

Red grouse *Lagopus lagopus scoticus* (Mike Lane)

John Ray. Ever since Ray's time Teesdale has been one of the most famous botanical hunting-grounds in Britain. In 1965, a long political battle was fought in a vain attempt to prevent the construction of a reservoir on the Upper Tees above the waterfall of Cauldron Snout. The botanical objectors lost, and the Cow Green reservoir was constructed.

These moors offer a dramatic, wild landscape, with breeding upland birds such as curlew, snipe, lapwing, red grouse, golden plover, and dunlin. These hills are also the haunt of merlins, whose favoured prey, the meadow pipit, is common here. In some areas blackcock may be still be found and ring ouzels nest amongst the crags. In the grassy meadows there are breeding lapwing, snipe, redshank, oystercatcher, curlew, and yellow wagtails, while the rivers and streams hold common sandpiper and dippers.

The most famous of the Teesdale flowers is the spring gentian, whose blue flowers stud parts of the grazed limestone areas. But there are several other rarities too: hoary rock-rose, Teesdale violet, hoary whitlowgrass, alpine forget-me-not, dwarf milkwort, and mountain avens. In the wetter sites, for example around the flushes, one finds alpine bartsia, hairy stonecrop, Scottish asphodel, bird's-eye primrose, early marsh-orchid and Teesdale sandwort, the latter at its

only British locality. Flowers of the hay meadows include melancholy thistle, marsh-marigold, mountain pansy, wood crane's-bill, pignut, and northern marsh- and lesser butterfly-orchids.

Two species of lady's-mantle, *Alchemilla acutiloba* and *A. monticola*, are not uncommon in the hay meadows and roadside verges, but are very rare elsewhere in Britain. They grow together with other lady's-mantle species in assemblages which resemble the Scandinavian rather than the British flora.

Moor House–Upper Teesdale NNR amalgamates two previously separate NNRs, around the headwaters of the river Tees, and amounts to nearly 7400 ha. Upper Teesdale NNR (NY 815308, OS 92) is one of the most famous of all British reserves, covering almost 3500 ha on the eastern flank of the Pennines. The renowned Pennine Way long-distance footpath runs through the reserve, which therefore receives a steady stream of hill-walkers, especially in summer, despite its relative remoteness.

Alpine bartsia *Bartsia alpina*

Northern England

Northern England

The underlying geology is very unusual and partly explains the rich flora here. There is a mixture of limestone, a volcanic rock known as sill, and, most importantly, a derived form of limestone called sugar limestone, which has a granular structure (hence the name) and whose soils favour the special Teesdale flora.

Some of the scenery is quite dramatic, with impressive waterfalls at Cauldron Snout and High Force, and lines of cliffs by the river Tees at Cronkley Scar and Falcon Clints. The Cow Green reservoir abuts on to the nature reserve along its eastern edge.

The most important areas botanically are Cronkley and Widdybank Fells, for their limestone floras, and the unimproved hay meadows around the farms lower down. A 125-ha natural juniper grove adds to the interest of the site. The moorland on the Durham–Yorkshire border produces the rare marsh saxifrage, and wood stitchwort is more common in the lowland parts of county Durham than anywhere else in Britain.

Cronkley Fell (NY 8628) can be reached by following the Pennine Way up from Holwick, or by following the river upstream from Dale Chapel. The plants of the sugar limestone here are a mixture of arctic-alpines, some of them rare, and more usual southern species, and include wild thyme, spring sandwort, and northern bedstraw. Alongside the river there are splendid stands of juniper and also, in places, shrubby cinquefoil. The hay meadows in this area (at their best in late June) are very fine and unimproved, with a large array of flowers, including several species of lady's-mantle, yellow-rattle, great burnet, marsh-orchid, ragged-Robin, melancholy thistle, and globeflower.

Widdybank Fell (NY 8328) is a marvellous upland site, with hundreds of breeding waders – lapwing, oystercatcher, curlew, golden plover, snipe, and redshank – goosander, common sandpiper, and grey wagtail along the rivers, and ring ouzel and twite. Nearby Langdon Beck makes a good centre. This scenic spot has a pleasant hotel, and also boasts the highest youth hostel in England. The area has England's largest black grouse lek, and there are buzzards, ravens,

Low Force

Northern England

Spring gentian *Gentiana verna*

peregrines, and merlins in the vicinity. Amongst the botanical specialities are spring gentian, Teesdale violet, Scottish asphodel, and Teesdale sandwort. Other flowers include alpine penny-cress and spring sandwort.

Moor House NNR (NY 7729) lies further up the Tees valley, towards the highest point of the Pennines at Cross Fell (893 m). Here there is splendid blanket bog (one of the finest in the region) and an alpine flora on the rocky outcrops.

Bowlees Visitor Centre (WT; NY 907282, OS 93) is close to the Bowlees Beck, a tributary of the Tees near Newbiggin. The centre has displays explaining the wildlife of the area, and a series of footpaths give access to a variety of habitats nearby. A short walk leads to the waterfall of Low Force, and a 3-km walk along the Pennine Way brings one to the even more impres-

sive High Force (NY 8828), which carries the dark, peaty water of the Tees in a broad cascade through a gorge into a deep pool below. The woods here and around the visitor centre hold redstart, wood warbler, pied flycatcher, and tree pipit, and some also have red squirrels. The intrepid walker can follow the Pennine Way west into the heart of Upper Teesdale and beyond to distant Alston and Hadrian's Wall.

Hannah's Meadow (WT; NY 933186, OS 93) is a reserve with traditionally managed hay meadows, a few kilometres south of Middleton. This SSSI is a wonderful place to witness the diversity of flowers which accompany such unimproved fields – species such as globeflower, ragged-Robin, wood crane's-bill, adder's-tongue, and moonwort.

The rock-strewn rapids and pools of the Tees between Eggleston and Cotherstone attract common sandpipers, dippers, and goosanders, and the adjacent woods have woodpeckers, nuthatches, redstarts, pied flycatchers, and wood warblers, with tree pipits in the more open sites.

There are car parks at Cow Green, High Force, Hanging Shaw, and Bowlees.

The North Pennines have recently received European Union Special Protection Area status, covering nearly 150 000 ha from Hexham, Northumberland to Harrogate, North Yorkshire.

SITE 23 Teesmouth

A wildlife haven ringed by urban and industrial developments; a vital stopover for migrant birds.

Teesmouth NNR (NZ 534282; 355 ha) is a splendid coastal site with habitats including intertidal mud- and sandflats, sand dune systems, saltmarsh, and grazing marsh. It lies close to industrial sites and

major centres of population between Middlesbrough and Hartlepool, but is nevertheless of great wildlife importance.

The sand dunes and saltmarshes here have good plant communities, with some

Northern England

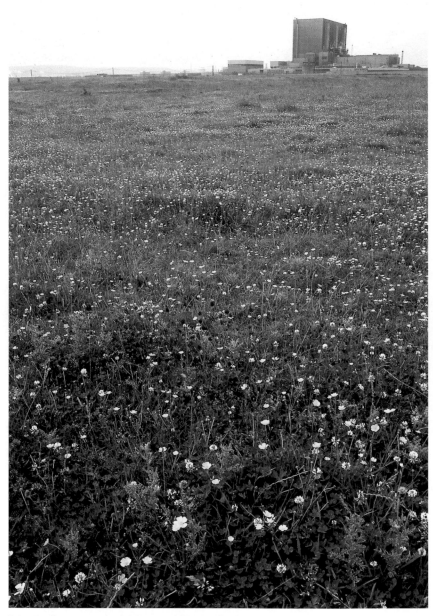

Extensive flowery grassland at Teesmouth (Peter Wilson)

nationally rare species (notably rush-leaved fescue, stiff saltmarsh-grass, and brackish water-crowfoot) alongside more familiar coastal plants. The dunes around Seaton Sands have purple milk-vetch and bloody crane's-bill, with areas of sea buckthorn scrub. In the dune slacks there are fine displays of marsh-orchids.

As a roosting and feeding station for wildfowl and waders, Teesmouth is internationally significant. Large numbers of waders such as knot, redshank, and ringed plover gather here, along with high concentrations of shelduck. In late summer there are passage terns and skuas, and wintering birds include twite, snow and Lapland buntings, peregrine, merlin, grebes, and divers. The areas of reedbed are increasingly attractive to bit-terns, water rails, and bearded tits, and get the occasional spotted crake.

The invertebrates are also of interest and include the rare lyme-grass moth. The reserve is also the site of the only regular breeding colony of common seals on the north-east coast of England, with grey seals also regular visitors.

Teesmouth is about 6 km south of Hartlepool. There are car parks, observation hides, leaflets, and interpretive panels. Hartlepool itself is worth visiting, especially for its passing seabirds in late summer and autumn, or for passage migrants in spring and autumn. North-east winds bring shearwaters, gannets, and skuas quite close to shore, and rare gulls such as glaucous, Iceland, and Mediterranean turn up at the fish quay.

A selection of other important sites in the county

Derwent Gorge and Muggleswick Woods NNR (NZ 056490, OS 87; 71 ha) is woodland south-west of Consett.

Hamsterley Forest (NZ 067300) is a fine upland, wooded valley in the upper catchment of the river Wear. Mixed woodland, with redstart, tree pipit, siskin, and crossbill, and on the nearby moorland ring ouzel, red grouse, and whinchat. Winter hen harriers and peregrine.

Low Barns (WT; NZ 160315, OS 93; 50 ha) is a good wetland (and woodland) reserve close to the river Wear. Kingfisher, redstart, pied flycatcher.

Moor House Woods (NT; NZ 305460) lie close to Durham, in the Wear Valley.

These mixed oak woods also contain beech and hornbeam – unusual so far north. Bluebells, wood avens, and sanicle grow on the woodland floor.

Roseberry Topping (NT; NZ 575126) has woodland and moorland and rises to 322 m. The woods have green woodpecker, tree pipit, wood warbler, redstart, and pied flycatcher, and there are red grouse on the managed heather moor.

Saltburn Gill SSSI (WT; NZ 674205, OS 94; 21 ha): a steep-sided, fern-rich, wooded valley.

Thrislington NNR (NZ 324325, OS 88; 24 ha) has the best magnesian limestone grassland in Britain.

Northern England

Cumbria and Isle of Man

SITE
24 Lake District National Park

One of Britain's finest NPs, with a beautiful landscape of mountains, sheltered valleys, and lakes, and a plethora of nature reserves. Covers 2292 square kilometres.

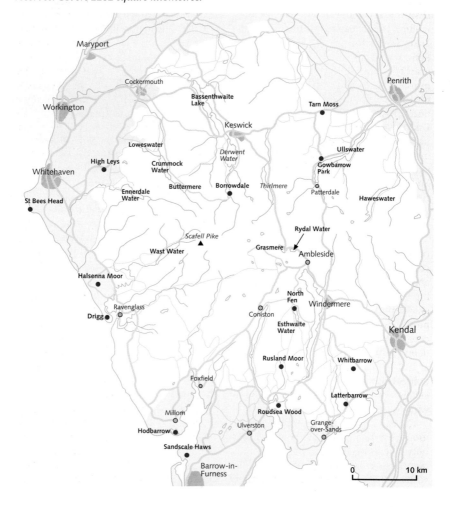

The Lake District is a marvellous area, and feels almost like a separate miniature country, contrasting as it does so markedly from the landscapes nearby. It is compact and accessible, yet also wild and diverse, combining England's highest mountains (peaking at Scafell Pike, 977 m) and moorland with deep, sheltered, often wooded valleys, meadows, and beautiful lakes, the latter usually known here as meres. Though visited by hordes of tourists and ramblers, most people restrict their activities to a handful of 'honeypot' sites, so it is easy to escape the crowds, especially if you don't mind hill-walking, when the rewards of stupendous views can be well worth the effort. More than a quarter of the Lake District is NT land.

From the natural history viewpoint, the Lakes share some of their species with the Pennine moors, but also with the even grander, though less compact hills and mountains of Scotland. Many upland birds, such as buzzard, peregrine, raven, and ring ouzel, are found in the Lake District, and even golden eagles are gradually beginning to regard the region as an extension of the Highland to the north, with at least one pair regularly breeding here – the only English locality. Mountain ringlet butterflies frequent the high ground; the Lake District is the only area where this species is found in England.

Gouging by ice-sheets during glaciations was responsible for the dramatic scenery of the Lake District, and these hills abound with classic features such as hanging valleys, corries, moraines, and other glacial phenomena. The lakes themselves mostly radiate outwards from the central core of higher ground, and many are very deep (Wastwater being the deepest of all at 78.5 m). They tend to have fringing vegetation of reeds and tall flowers, notably yellow loosestrife, with floating patches of white water-lily in the shallows.

The hills of the Lake District have a good mountain flora and fauna, although with only relatively few rarities. Amongst plants, those few include alpine catchfly, with a small population in a rather secret

**Pearl-bordered fritillary *Clossiana euphrosyne*
(David Element)**

locality. Another remarkable Lake District rarity can, however, be publicized with safety: on the vertiginous screes above Wastwater, and around the Pillar high level track can be found the only mountain populations in Britain and Ireland of shrubby cinquefoil, otherwise confined to Teesdale and the Burren (Ireland). The tops of the Lake District mountains offer a typical wind-swept flora, including dwarf willow, a miniature tree. Several of the smaller lakes and tarns provide a good habitat for water lobelia and quillwort.

Although the weather can be glorious, this is a high-rainfall area, so be prepared with waterproof clothing.

With such a rich and varied region, we can only pick out a selection of sites which repay visiting, and the possibilities for the keen naturalist and hill-walker here are unlimited.

Windermere is one of the most popular and accessible of the lakes; it is narrow and very scenic, stretching some 16 km in the south-east of the NP. Windermere itself is an excellent centre, with information about the many sites and trails which abound in the district. Winter brings many wildfowl to the lake, notably pochard, tufted duck, and goldeneye. Brockhole (NY 3901) is the visitor centre for the NP (open daily from late March to early November) and should be visited early for the information provided, useful in planning outings. However, it is worth a visit in its own right as well. It is an attractive spot, with a frontage onto Windermere. Look out for nuthatch, pied flycatcher, and buzzards overhead. The forests between Windermere and Esthwaite Water on the opposite shore, such as Claife Heights (SD 382976), have coniferous plantations and mixed deciduous stands, and are the haunt of red squirrels. The alders and willows close to the lake attract siskins in the winter. This site has acid pools, with interesting species such as golden-ringed dragonfly, white-faced darter, and downy emerald. Cunsey Beck (SD 374938) which flows from Esthwaite Water to Windermere is another good dragonfly site, with golden-ringed dragonfly and beautiful demoiselle. North Fen NNR (SD 358977, OS 97; 2 ha) protects a patch of vegetation around the inflow at the north end of Esthwaite Water, with reedbeds, fen, and woodland.

Rydal Water (NY 3606) is easily reached and well worth a stop. A footpath circles the lake, passing woodland, and taking in the rich fen vegetation between Rydal Water and Grasmere.

Roudsea Wood and Mosses NNR (SD 332824, OS 96/7) is also in the south of the region, protecting some 475 ha of varied terrain close to the head of Morecambe Bay, with woodland, salt-marsh, fen, and bog. A footpath passes through the reserve, although a permit is

required to visit some areas. There are few sites which offer such a range of habitats within a short distance, and the wildlife of Roudsea is correspondingly rich. The woodland on the limestone ridge has yew, small-leaved lime, wild service-tree, and field maple, and a rich herb-layer featuring tutsan, lily-of-the-valley, herb-Paris, early purple orchid, and others. Closer to the bay, the woodland lies on acid soil and is dominated by both native oaks, with species such as wood-sorrel, bluebell, yellow pimpernel, and wild daffodil. The fen has royal fern, yellow iris, marsh pennywort, and wild angelica, and the sedge-rich acid bog in the north has all three sundews, cranberry, bog-rose-mary, crowberry, bog asphodel, and white beak-sedge. Breeding birds include hobby, short-eared owl, kestrel, curlew, snipe, wood warbler, and redstart. This is still a good site for red squirrels, perhaps because it is somewhat isolated from major tracts of woodland, and common dormice breed here at the northern edge of their range. Butterflies do very well here, with high brown, dark green, and both pearl-bordered fritillaries, and large heath, all noteworthy. The dragonflies include black darter, four-spotted chaser, and southern hawker.

Whitbarrow NNR (WT; SD 452885, OS 97) is about 8 km south-east of Windermere, near Witherslack Hall. A footpath leads through ash–hazel woods and limestone pavement, and the rich flora includes hoary rock-rose, fly orchid, and buckler-ferns. It also has fine butter-flies: Duke of Burgundy, northern brown argus, grayling, and small pearl-bor-dered, high brown, and silver-washed fritillaries. Nearby Latterbarrow (WT; SD 440828, OS 97; 4 ha) is a small reserve with a remarkably rich flora: woodland, grassland, and some limestone pave-ment, with cowslips, early purple orchid, rock-rose, and wild thyme. The reserve also harbours high brown and pearl-bor-dered fritillaries, and grayling.

The Duddon Estuary, on the southern edge of the NP, north of Barrow-in-

White water-lily *Nymphaea alba*

Purple saxifrage *Saxifraga oppositifolia*

Furness, has some good sites. One such is Sandscale Haws (NT; SD 190750) which has tall, chalky dunes with an interesting flora. Ten species of orchid are known from here, with bloody crane's-bill, sea-kale, and the rather local yellow-vetch. The insects include mining bees, wasps, and two rare moths: shore wainscot and coastal dart. This is also a breeding site for natterjacks. The estuary is popular with birders, too, being an important site for wildfowl and waders, and for hunting birds of prey in winter. Wader-watching from the shore just south of Foxfield can be most productive, especially on an incoming tide. Hodbarrow (RSPB; SD 1778) near Millom is also on the Duddon Estuary. The lagoon attracts red-breasted mergansers, and this is a good site for divers, grebes, and sea ducks (notably scaup) in winter. Sandwich, common, and little terns nest, and there is a colony of natterjacks.

At Ravenglass, three of the Lake District rivers converge at a narrow estuary. These are the Esk, Mite, and Irt, the latter draining Wastwater on its way down from the central peaks of Great Gable and Scafell Pike. Here there are dunes, saltmarsh, and mudflats, with the nearby reserves of Drigg and Eskmeals Dunes. Banks of sea buckthorn grow amongst the dunes. This area is also excellent for ducks, waders, and seabirds. The mudflats of the Irt Estuary are feeding grounds for a variety of waders, including green sandpiper, spotted redshank, greenshank, grey plover, and whimbrel. This reserve boasts all six native amphibians, with colonies of common frog, common toad, and natterjack, as well as great crested (warty), palmate, and smooth newts. Adders also breed here.

The flowers include Portland spurge, sea spurge, and sea bindweed amongst the dunes, and glasswort, common sea-lavender, and sea-purslane in the saltmarsh, with the uncommon Isle of Man cabbage on the shingle.

Wastwater (NY 1606) has a very different feel and aspect. This lake is deep, and its waters are acidic. Although relatively lifeless, they are nevertheless home to a special fish, the Arctic char. The shores of this lake are also rather lifeless, being mainly steep and formed from unstable scree. To the intrepid botanist, however, they are worth inspecting for mountain species such as purple saxifrage and alpine lady's-mantle.

Buttermere and Ennerdale (NT; NY 1815) cover 3588 ha of hillsides and common land, farmland, and woodland, as well as the lakes of Buttermere, Crummock Water, and Loweswater, and the shore of Ennerdale Water. Remnants of ancient sessile oak woodland cling here and there to the slopes, as at Long and Nether How Woods, and Ghyll Wood. The woods close to Loweswater are particularly fine. Typical birds here are buzzard, sparrowhawk, tawny owl, and pied flycatcher. Along with the inevitable mallards and coots there are great crested grebes, goldeneye, and red-breasted mergansers on the lakes. The hillside of Fleetwith, near Honister Pass (NY 216134, OS 89) is one of the best sites in England for mountain ringlet, which may be seen in sunny weather during the first 3 weeks of July.

Borrowdale Woods (NT; NY 258147). Borrowdale is one of the prettiest and most wooded of all the Lake District valleys and the NT owns about 75% of the

woodland here. Sessile oak is the dominant woodland tree, with ash, birch, rowan, and alder, the composition varying subtly with aspect, soil, and drainage. In this moist climate the epiphytes flourish and trunks are clothed with a wide range of mosses, liverworts, and ferns. The woodland flowers here include herb-Robert, alpine enchanter's-nightshade, and small cow-wheat. The bird life is typical for such woods, with redstarts, pied flycatchers, and wood warblers. Some of the woods also have populations of red squirrels, and there are pine martens in the Dale Head area (NY 2215).

Bassenthwaite Lake (Bassenthwaite NNR; NY 2031) is the fourth largest of the lakes, with about 70 bird species breeding and thousands of duck in winter, and whooper swans. It is also home to the rare fish, the vendace. The southern edge has a large area of mire and reedbeds. Ospreys are regular visitors here, and in 2001 they started breeding at Thornthwaite Forest where there is a public viewpoint at Dodd Wood on the eastern side of the lake. It is fervently hoped that this will be the van-

Roudsea Wood

View of Skiddaw

guard of a natural recolonization (see also Rutland Water, p. 245).

Ullswater (OS 90) provides a good flavour of the Lake District and offers a range of typical habitats with good walks, especially on the southern shore. There are parking spots at Patterdale and Sandwick and paths leading through the woods and along the shore. Expect upland birds such as ring ouzel, peregrine, and wheatear, with woodpeckers, goldcrest, and redstarts in the woods. In addition to the indigenous trees, many exotics were planted around the lake, such as copper beech and the majestic Wellingtonias.

Gowbarrow Park (NT; NY 4020) contains the fine waterfall of Aira Force, the spray from which creates a constantly damp microclimate promoting luxuriant growth of mosses, liverworts, and ferns. Glencoyne Wood (NT; NY 3819) lies at the southern end of Ullswater. This oak wood has a good display of daffodils in spring.

Haweswater (RSPB; NY 4814) is a somewhat remote region, where there is the chance that you might see one of England's very few golden eagles hunting over the hills near the lake. They now breed regularly in this area. The woods here have wood warblers, tree pipits, and woodcocks, and this is still a stronghold for the red squirrel.

Some Lake District NNRs

Great Asby Scar (NY 648103, OS 90; 166 ha): limestone pavement and grassland, with rare plants.

High Leys (NY 064181, OS 89; 9 ha): unimproved meadows.

Halsenna Moor (NY 066007, OS 89; 24 ha): raised bog, with carr and wet and dry heath, near Seascale.

Rusland Moss (SD 334886, OS 97; 24 ha): marsh, bog, carr, and wet and dry heath. Royal fern. Heronry.

Tarn Moss (NY 400275, OS 90; 16 ha): raised bog and fen.

SITE
25 South Solway

Southern shore of the Solway Firth, with a range of peatlands, England's best remaining active lowland bogs.

South Solway Mosses NNR (NY 235604, OS 96) consists of three large, raised bogs – a rare habitat – Glasson Moss, Wedholme Flow, and Bowness Common. Although all have been affected by cutting and drainage, these remnants are a good example of a threatened habitat. Birch scrub is invading around the drying edges and the water levels are maintained at a high level to counteract this. Glasson Moss is the best preserved, and is actively growing with a carpet of bog-mosses, including the rather striking orange-coloured *Sphagnum pulchrum*. Drumburgh Moss NNR (WT; NY 256590, OS 85; 90 ha), south of Drumburgh, is one of the best peatbogs in England. The bog has more than a dozen species of bog-moss, and the adjacent drier spots have tussocks of purple moor-grass and heather. Curlew and redshank nest on the reserve, and adders may often be seen. The insects include large heath butterfly, and emperor and drinker moths.

Curlew *Numenius arquata* (Mike Lane)

Thornhill Moss and Meadows NNR (NY 174485, OS 85) is a valley mire some 10 km to the south-west, near Abbeytown. It has a range of mire types, ranging from acid bog through to poor and rich fen, and a good growth of bog myrtle.

The south Solway also offers a number of good birdwatching sites. The inner Solway, between Rockcliffe on the river Eden and Port Carlisle, is quite productive, especially Burgh and Rockcliffe Marshes, with good numbers of wintering ducks and geese. Further west lies Morecambe Bay, with Grune Point near Skinburness being a good vantage point. Wildfowl here include pink-footed and barnacle geese, shelduck, wigeon, teal, pintail, shoveler, eider, long-tailed, duck and scaup. The waders feature often huge flocks of golden plover, along with both godwits, knot, sanderling, whimbrel, greenshank and turnstone. Campfield Marsh (RSPB; NY 207620), about 5 km west of Bowness-on-Solway, has open water, grassland, and saltmarsh, in addition to views over the estuary. At high tide, the wader roost here can be very impressive, with large numbers of knot, grey plover, oystercatcher, and godwits. In winter, pink-footed and barnacle geese, peregrine, merlin, and barn owl are regular, and in spring there is good seawatching, with skuas, grebes, and divers a speciality.

SITE 26 Walney Island

Famous birdwatching site at the western end of Morecambe Bay.

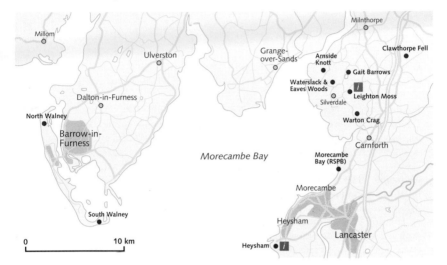

Walney Island hangs from the southern tip of the bulge of the Lake District, close to Barrow-in-Furness. It is a narrow strip of land some 12 km long, and has a permanent road link with Barrow. Walney has long been known as a prime seabird site, and its dunes, shingle, and salt-marshes also support a fine coastal flora.

North Walney NNR (SD 177724, OS 96; 144 ha) is a varied reserve at the north end of Walney Island. There are tidal mudflats, shingle, dunes, dune slacks, heath, and saltmarsh, with 360 species of

Whimbrel *Numenius phaeopus* (Mike Lane)

plants being known from the dune slacks alone. There is a large wader roost, and natterjacks also breed.

At the southern tip is South Walney (RSPB/WT; SD 215620, OS 96; 130 ha) with its bird observatory. Migrant birds are funnelled through Walney and this reserve has the longest list of migrants in the county. Rarities are regularly recorded here, with such species as red-breasted flycatcher, firecrest, and black redstart. More exotic species turn up, too, such as dowitcher, buff-breasted sandpiper, Richard's pipit, and barred and yellow-browed warblers. Other frequent passage birds are curlew, green, wood, and common sandpipers, osprey, whimbrel, greenshank, spotted redshank, terns, and wheatear. Seawatching is very good from near the observatory, especially in May and June when gannets, skuas, shearwaters, kittiwakes, auks, and scoters may be spotted. South Walney also has a large gull colony, with 20 000 lesser black-backed, 10 000 herring, and about 100 pairs of great black-backed, as well as the most southerly breeding colony of eider ducks, numbering some 600 pairs. Other breeding birds here are shelduck, ringed plover, and oystercatcher. In late summer, onshore winds sometimes bring storm petrels into the nearby waters. Merlins and peregrines feature in winter, as do short-eared owls. The shingle flowers include sea beet, sea bindweed, sea campion, sea spurge, sea-holly, yellow horned-poppy, and thrift, with heather, cross-leaved heath, tormentil, gorse, and bracken in the drier sites.

A selection of other important sites in the county

Clawthorpe Fell NNR (SD 537786, OS 97; 14 ha): limestone pavement.

Finglandrigg Woods NNR (NY 275568, OS 85; 65 ha), west of Carlisle, is a mixed woodland, with heath, bog, and acid grassland. Red squirrels.

Geltsdale (RSPB; NY 606556) in the northern Pennines is high moorland, with woodland in the valleys of the Gelt and Irthing. The moors have red grouse, curlew, golden plover, and ring ouzel, and the woods redstart, pied fly-catcher, and wood warbler. Tindale Tarn has whooper swans in winter.

Park Wood NNR (SD 565778, OS 97; 15 ha) is a good ash wood, with a rich flora.

Smardale Gill NNR (WT; NY 739083, OS 91). This old railway line is known for its butterflies. It is one of only two English sites for Scotch argus. Also northern brown argus, dingy skipper, and dark green fritillary. Birds include wood warbler, pied flycatcher, and redstart, and there are red squirrels.

St Bee's Head (RSPB; NX 962118): sandstone cliffs with seabird colonies.

27 Isle of Man

An island wildlife refuge midway between Ireland and Britain.

Although seldom in the itinerary of mainland naturalists, the Isle of Man has much to offer, with its impressive scenery and dramatic rocky coasts. The coasts have flowers such as sea-holly, sea bindweed, and spring squill, and the Calf of Man supports large numbers of breeding seabirds, including Manx Shearwaters. The Isle of Man even has one very special plant named after it, the Isle of Man Cabbage, that grows on sea-cliffs especially on the west coast from Lancashire to Ayrshire, and which is endemic to Britain. Perhaps the best bird symbol of the island is the chough, the beautiful red-billed crow relative, which breeds here at one of its last strongholds, liking the combination of cliffs and rough, traditional pasture. The Manx hills are a favoured breeding ground for hen harriers and the island has an amazing 10% of the entire British population of these graceful birds of prey.

Ayres Visitor Centre (WT; NX 435038) is near the northern tip of the island. The shingle here has an unusual lichen–

Isle of Man (Val Williams)

heath community and the flora generally is rich, with orchids, including the rare dense-flowered orchid at its only British site. The birds include Arctic, common, and little terns, oystercatcher, ringed plover, and shelduck.

One of the best reserves is Ballaugh Curragh, between Ballaugh and Sulby. This is a mixed area with bog, willow, and birch woodland and rich hay meadows. The breeding birds include water rail, curlew, occasional corncrake, woodcock, and grasshopper warbler, while in winter it is host to one of western Europe's largest communal roosts of hen harriers (100 in most years). These are best watched from the tower hide at Close Sartfield (WT; SC 358956). Whooper swans are regular to the meadows and fields in the area. The plants include royal fern, bogbean, bog myrtle, marsh cinquefoil, yellow iris, and bladderwort, with ragged-Robin, devil's-bit scabious, and common and heath spotted-orchids. This site also boasts one of Britain's few feral populations of the exotic red-necked wallaby, courtesy of escapes from a nearby wildlife park.

Cooildarry (WT; SC 314901), near Kirk Michael, is a mixed wood with natural-ized holm oaks. The spring flowers are impressive, with ramsons, wood anemones, primroses, and bluebells.

Scarlett Visitor Centre (WT; SC 258664) is just south of Castletown in the south of the island. The highlight here is a columnar basalt stack, and the maritime heath vege-tation includes a fine show of spring squill, the blue contrasting with the pink of thrift. A rare orthopteran, the lesser mottled grasshopper is found here at its only British site, where it was discovered in 1962.

The Calf of Man (which has a famous bird observatory) lies just off the south-west tip of the main island, and may be

Hen harrier *Circus cyaneus* (male)

reached by boat (April–August) from Port Erin (SC 192689) or Port St Mary. The breeding birds include peregrine, raven, chough, hen harrier, storm petrel, and Manx shearwater. Many rare birds are recorded each year on migration. This is a breeding site for grey seals, and sea-watchers may be rewarded by the sight of porpoises or dolphins, or perhaps even a basking shark.

A selection of other important sites

Cronk y Bing (NX 381017): dunes, grassland; terns, gulls, divers.

Dalby Mountain (SC 233769): heath; hen harrier, red grouse.

Lancashire, Merseyside, and Greater Manchester

SITE
28 Morecambe Bay and North Lancashire coast

Huge expanse of water with tidal inlets. World famous for its wildfowl and waders. Limestone coastal habitats.

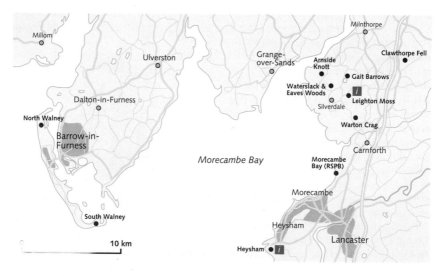

Morecambe Bay is a large inlet, fringed by shallow estuaries, between the bulk of the Lake District to the north and Lancashire to the south. Its main wildlife value lies in the many rich sandy and muddy feeding grounds revealed by the shifting tides and welcomed by millions of birds, especially wildfowl and waders.

Morecambe Bay reserve (RSPB; SD 468666), between Morecambe and Carnforth at Hest Bank, is a famous site for winter wildfowl and waders. The best season to visit (for birds) is September through to April, when the various creeks and mudflats are host to large numbers of migrants. Specialities here are Slavonian grebe and long-tailed duck, along with eider, goldeneye, red-breasted merganser, common scoter, and scaup. The jetty sometimes has a Mediterranean gull.

Heysham NR (SD 407599, OS 97/102) at the southern edge of Morecambe Bay is a prime site for seabirds, especially in the autumn. A footpath leads down to the shore, and there is also a hide. The waders are attracted partly by the warm water issuing from the power station (the latter sometimes has black redstart). This is particularly recommended for gulls and terns, with little and Mediterranean gulls regular, and the occasional black tern and Sabine's gull. Onshore autumn winds can bring in ocean species such as Leach's petrel.

The north Lancashire coast has rather a special character, with several remarkable outcroppings of limestone pavement, an unusual habitat with a rich flora. Most of these sites are between Carnforth and the Kent Estuary, the latter lying just across the county boundary in neighbouring Cumbria.

One of the finest of these reserves is Gait Barrows NNR (SD 480772, OS 97; 106 ha), which protects some of the best limestone pavement and woodland in the country. Limestone pavement is pockmarked with holes, channels, and gulleys (or grikes) in which the soil accumulates, creating a natural rock garden of great botanical value. Some recorded figures

Grass-of-Parnassus *Parnassia palustris*

may help to indicate its richness: about 475 flowering plants and ferns, 180 bryophytes, over 1000 fungi, 1150 lichens, 100 species of bird, 20 mammals, 29 butterflies, and 400 moths. Special flowers of the limestone pavement here are dark red helleborine, angular Solomon's-seal, bloody crane's-bill, and pale St John's-wort, with lily-of-the-valley in the woods. In the damp gulleys there are ferns like rustyback, hart's-tongue, and hard shield-fern. On the wet meadows the plants include fragrant and northern marsh-orchids, bird's-eye primrose, butterwort, and grass-of-Parnassus. Many of the species found growing here, such as spindle, dogwood, and small-leaved lime, are at their northernmost limit in the country. Around the lake, Little Hawes Water, there is an alder carr woodland with fen vegetation. The lake has bird interest as well, with bittern and water rail both nesting, and occasional visits from marsh harriers and migrating ospreys. This is one of the best sites for the rare high brown fritillary, other notable butterflies being both pearl-bordered fritillaries, northern brown argus, Scotch argus, and Duke of Burgundy. Access is by permit only to the pavement, but public foot-

Morecambe Bay

paths cross the reserve. There is another good limestone pavement reserve at Hutton Roof Crags (SD 5578), about 10 km east, near Burton-in-Kendal.

Arnside Knott NT (SD 453774, OS 97). This reserve, which is just in Cumbria, lies on the south side of the Kent Estuary. It has woodland and scrub, and limestone pavement, sloping down to saltmarsh. There are several species of orchid and many butterflies, including high brown fritillary, northern brown argus, Scotch argus (one of only two English sites), and grayling. Glow-

worms are also found here, and the mammals include roe deer and red squirrels. Nearby Waterslack and Eaves Woods (NT; SD 465758) are of mixed oak on fertile limestone and have a very rich flora, with small-leaved lime, juniper, wild servicetree, larch, wych elm, Scots pine, and wild cherry in the tree layers, and herb-Paris, angular Solomon's-seal, lily-of-the-valley, mezereon, and yellow star-of-Bethlehem in the ground flora. Woodcock, sparrowhawk, green woodpecker, and wood warbler also occur here, as do red squirrels.

SITE 29 Leighton Moss

One of the region's best coastal reserves, with the largest expanse of reedbed in north-west England.

Leighton Moss (RSPB; SD 478751, OS 97; 130 ha), at Silverdale near Carnforth, is one of the society's star reserves. It has a variety of habitats, dominated by the very

extensive reedbeds. The edges of the fen are wooded, and there is also a small area of heath. At the seaward side the land slopes down towards a saltmarsh with

Northern England

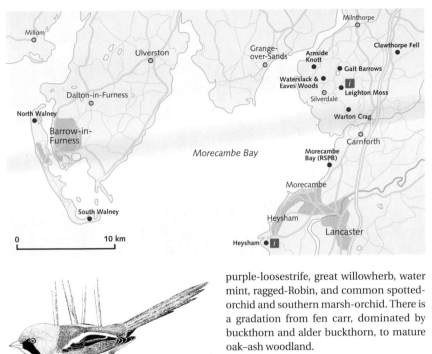

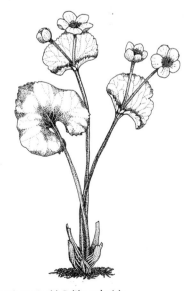

Bearded tit *Panurus biarmicus*

purple-loosestrife, great willowherb, water mint, ragged-Robin, and common spotted-orchid and southern marsh-orchid. There is a gradation from fen carr, dominated by buckthorn and alder buckthorn, to mature oak–ash woodland.

In addition to more common butterflies such as peacock, small tortoiseshell, orange tip and small copper, there are also pearl-bordered, small pearl-bordered, and

views out over Morecambe Bay. The reserve has recently been extended to Silverdale Moss, which includes some fine limestone woodland.

The reserve has a special claim to fame as the main stronghold of the bittern, with around 20% of the national population found here. Bearded tits also breed in the reedbeds, as do water rail, the rare spotted crake, and marsh harrier, and buzzards and sparrowhawks breed on the reserve. In 2001, avocets started breeding here – the first in north-west England. Winter brings in large number of waders and wildfowl.

Tussocks of tufted sedge dominate part of the fen towards the northern end, with flowers such as marsh-marigold, meadowsweet,

Marsh-marigold *Caltha palustris*

Leighton Moss

high brown fritillaries, and a rich moth fauna, with hawkmoths a feature. The woods have red squirrels, and the mere attracts otters. There are five hides, four of which have wheelchair access.

Close to Leighton Moss is Warton Crag (WT; SD 493728, OS 97; 35 ha), an area of woodland, scrub, and limestone grassland.

The flowers here include several orchids and there is a rich butterfly fauna – 33 species recorded, notably both pearl-bordered fritillaries, grayling, and northern brown argus. High brown fritillary occurs in good numbers, at one of the best sites in Britain for this endangered species. Both red and grey squirrels may be seen.

SITE
30 Sefton coast

Coastal sites with extensive dunes, between the estuaries of the Ribble and Mersey.

The gently curving coast around Formby is dominated by extensive dune systems, which together cover more than 2000 ha, making this the largest dune complex in Britain, and one of the best sites for wildlife in north-west England. There are several reserves of note here, all offering protection to these rather fragile habitats: Ainsdale Sand Dunes, Formby Point, and Cabin Hill,

and the local reserves of Ainsdale and Birkdale and at Ravenmeols. The foreshore and dunes have Ramsar status, and part of the site is a Special Protection Area for birds.

There is no better place to witness the full range of coastal sandy habitats, from shore through dunelets and larger, shifting dunes to fixed dunes and dune heath, and finally to coastal scrub and woodland, and the special

Northern England

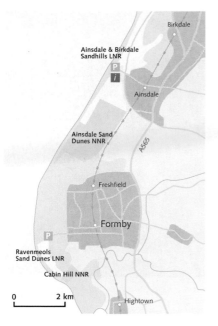

Natterjack *Bufo calamita*

habitat of dune slacks. Some special species of the dune slacks are: round-leaved wintergreen, flat-sedge, early marsh-orchid, and marsh helleborine. The list of special plants is a long one, and includes northern species such as variegated horsetail, northern marsh-orchid, and grass-of-Parnassus, alongside southern species such as lesser centaury, southern marsh-orchid, ploughman's-spikenard, and yellow bartsia. Amongst the rarities here are dune helleborine, Isle of Man cabbage, Baltic rush, sharp club-rush, and early sand-grass. The dunes also have rare mosses and liverworts.

Butterflies are here in great variety, with 23 species: dark green fritillary and grayling are both common, and the dragonflies include ruddy darter, broad-bodied chaser, and emperor. There are many other special insects as well – notably two local sand wasps (*Podalonia affinis* and *Psen littoralis*), a mining bee (*Colletes cunicularius*), and the rare heath tiger beetle.

A star mammal is the red squirrel, this being one of only a few mainland English sites where this charming species may easily be spotted – there is a good population in the pine plantations.

Reptiles and amphibians are well represented, with sand lizard at its most northerly site now numbering about 300, great crested newt (breeding in ponds at Ainsdale Sand Dunes NNR and numbering several hundred), and natterjack, at one of its major strongholds, with numbers probably topping 2000.

Ainsdale Sand Dunes NNR (SD 288102, OS 108; 492 ha) preserves the finest lime-rich sand dunes on the north-west coast. The other main habitats here are dune slacks and woodland, the latter mainly introduced conifers. These dunes are botanically some of the richest in Britain, and also some of the most extensive: about 10 km long and 1.5 km wide. All stages of dune succession are visible here, from shifting young dunes through to stable dunes with a developed tree cover of alder and willow scrub. In places, the younger dunes have a very rich flora, with grass-of-Parnassus, and orchids such as early marsh-orchid, bee orchid, pyramidal orchid, marsh helleborine, green-flowered helleborine, and the rare dune helleborine. Ainsdale is the most northerly known locality for the nationally

Red squirrel *Sciurus vulgaris* (Mike Lane)

Rest-harrow (*Ononis repens*) and Curtis's pansy (*Viola tricolor* ssp *curtisii*) on the dunes

rare sand lizard, and also holds one of the largest colonies of natterjacks. The planted Scots and Corsican pines have populations of red squirrels which are sometimes quite easy to spot. The patches of sea buckthorn attract migrant birds in the autumn and thrushes in the winter. The insects include dark green fritillary and oak eggar moth, as well as sand wasps and emperor dragonfly. Ainsdale and Birkdale Sandhills LNR lies adjacent to the NNR, and has a comparable range of species.

Cabin Hill NNR (SD 283050, OS 108; 28 ha), south-west of Formby, has a similar dune-slack fauna, and a colony of natterjacks, along with reintroduced sand lizards.

The dunes at Formby (NT; SD 275080) are another breeding site for natterjack, and sand lizard. Shelduck nest in the dunes amongst the marram. The sandy grassland has harebell, yellow-rattle, restharrow, wild parsnip, maiden pink, yellow-wort, and Portland and sea spurge.

<small>SITE</small> 31 Ribble Estuary

Narrow estuary with extensive mud- and sandflats, and big expanses of saltmarsh.

The river Ribble flows through Preston and enters the sea as a narrow estuary before broadening into the open sea between Lytham St Anne's and Southport. On either side, but especially on the south bank, the estuary is lined by extensive mudflats and

saltmarsh, offering some of Britain's best feeding grounds for waders and wildfowl.

In fact, the Ribble Marshes NNR (SD 390240, OS 102/108; 4112 ha) is the most important site in the whole of the country for wintering wildfowl, which assemble here in their hundreds of thousands. This reserve encompasses about half of the estuary, and includes one of the largest areas of saltmarsh in England, in addition to considerable expanses of sand- and mudflats. Managed grazing keeps the marsh vegetation short for the benefit of the wildfowl, notably the large numbers of wigeon and pink-footed geese which assemble here each winter.

The saltmarshes also support many breeding birds, key species being black-headed, herring gulls, and lesser black-backed gulls, common terns and redshanks, skylarks, meadow pipits, and linnets.

There are also both whooper and Bewick's swans feeding on these marshes during the winter. In addition to the geese, look out over the sea for red-throated diver, red-breasted merganser, goldeneye, and common and velvet scoter. The waders are very impressive, with up to 70 000 knot, in addition to more usual species such as redshank, dunlin, sanderling, and golden plover, and the estuary also attracts large numbers of bar-tailed and black-tailed

Oystercatcher *Haematopus ostralegus* (Mike Lane)

godwits. A seawatch can be rewarding for the birdwatcher, especially after north-westerly gales, with the chance of sooty as well as Manx shearwater, Leach's petrel, kittiwakes, and little gulls. Raptors are often about in the winter.

North Ribble Marshes (SD 434283, OS 102) lie south of Freckleton and Warton and may be viewed from a footpath skirting the shore. This gives good opportunities to spot the waders and wildfowl, including wild swans and black-tailed godwits. This site also has the rather curious reputation of being

A selection of other important sites in the county

Cuerdon Valley Park (WT; SD 565238, OS 102; 240 ha), just south of Preston, is a river valley with woods, grassland, and ponds.

Darwen Moor, south of Blackburn, is good for moorland birds including red grouse, and autumn migrants. Nearby Roddlesworth Woods (SD 662521, OS Pathfinder 689) and reservoirs is a good site for birds, with pied flycatcher, red-start, tree pipit, and wood warbler, and short-eared owl on the nearby moorland.

Martin Mere (WWT; SD 430144, OS 108; 152 ha), east of Southport, is a superb site for wildfowl, with pink-footed geese peaking at 27 500, and whooper and Bewick's swans.

Marton Mere Blackpool (BC; SD 345352; 39 ha) may have bittern and Cetti's war-bler, and rare gulls.

Mere Sands Wood SSSI (WT; SD 447157, OS 108; 42 ha), has lakes and woodland, with rich flora and good birds. Also red squirrels.

Pennington Flash Country Park (SD 6499), near Leigh, is a fine wetland reserve.

Seaforth NR (WT), near Bootle at the mouth of the Mersey, is excellent for sea-watching and for rare gulls.

one of the best places to see water pipits, which are usually about in March, along with rock pipits.

There are car parks at Lytham, and on the Marshside coastal road. Access is mainly by public footpath.

Marshside (RSPB; SD 355202; 110 ha) lies just north of Southport, in the southwest of the Ribble Estuary. This reserve gives good views over the wet grassland, from a hide or from the roadside. Key winter species here are pink-footed geese, black-tailed godwits, and wigeon. High-water wader roosts gather here, with concentrations of dunlin, knot, black-tailed godwit, oystercatcher, and grey plover.

St Anne's Dunes, near Blackpool Airport, is a small dune system with a fine flora, including many orchids, such as bee orchid, early marsh-orchid, and marsh helleborine. This site also provides good opportunities for seawatching.

Cheshire (and Wirral, Merseyside)

SITE
32 Dee Estuary

Some of the finest coastal marshes, mudflats, and sands, with spectacular gatherings of waders.

Gayton Sands (RSPB; SJ 274789) on the western side of the Wirral is a great place to see coastal birds, especially waders, which sometimes congregate here in huge numbers. The best time for a visit is around high tide (consult tide tables). As the water advances, the birds move closer and closer to the shore as they are concentrated onto a smaller and smaller stretch of sand and mud. A track follows the sea wall north to Gayton, and this makes a pleasant walk alongside the open expanse of the estuary. In winter there is often a hen harrier roost near the car park, short-eared owls regularly hunt over the marshes, and there are occasional merlin and peregrine. Pintails and shelducks are a particular feature of Gayton.

Hilbre Island (OS 108), near West Kirby, is reached by a walk (about an hour) across tidal sands in the Dee Estuary (check tide tables carefully). This is a well-known spot for seabirds, especially in the autumn when unusual species turn up, including Leach's petrel, pomarine and long-tailed skuas, and glaucous, Iceland, Mediterranean, and Sabine's gulls. Waders gather here in often huge numbers to roost at high tides. There is also a colony of grey seals. Hilbre has interesting plants,

Shelduck *Tadorna tadorna* (Mike Lane)

too, such as sea spleenwort, western gorse, and rock sea-lavender.

Red Rocks Marsh SSSI (WT; SJ 206880, OS 108; 4 ha) lies opposite Hilbre Island. The habitats consist of dunes, with slacks behind them, as well as a freshwater marsh and reedbeds, adjacent to a golf course. The rich flora includes species such as parsley-piert, wild asparagus, and sea club-rush. It is also noted for its colony of natterjacks. The waders are varied, with bar-tailed godwit, turnstone, grey plover, sanderling, and knot. In spring, terns pass through and Slavonian grebes are regular. Seawatching from the tip of the Wirral is worthwhile, especially after north-westerly autumn gales, as rare seabirds such as Leach's petrel and skuas may be driven into the coastal waters. Scaup, long-tailed duck, common scoter, and red-breasted merganser are all pretty frequent in winter.

Heswall Shore is a good vantage point from which to view the estuary. This is the site of the largest redshank roost in the country, and good passage waders and winter wildfowl.

A selection of other important sites in the county

Alderley Edge (NT; SJ 860776): wooded escarpment on a former copper mining area; mixed woodland with many birds, including redstart.

Black Lake SSSI (SJ 537709, OS 117). Part of Delamere Forest, this is an acid lake with fringing bog vegetation and a rich fauna of dragonflies, with white-faced and black darters. Woodland birds here include siskin and pied flycatcher.

Fiddlers Ferry (SJ 552853; 81 ha), near Widnes, has woodland, grassland, and lagoons. Good birds, including waders and many rare migrants.

Lyme Park (NT; SJ 965825) lies on the rim of the Pennines. This is a large, old, deer park with herds of fallow and red deer.

Moore NR (SJ 577854; 75 ha): wetland and woodland with hides and nature trails; rare gulls and waders are regular.

Rivacre Valley LNR (SJ 384778, OS 117). This local reserve with scrub, grassland and woodland, with adjacent ponds and stream is a fine site for butterflies and dragonflies, with purple and white-letter hairstreak, ruddy darter, broad-bodied chaser and emperor dragonfly.

Rostherne Mere NNR (EN; SJ 744843, OS 118; 152 ha) is a large mere, with woodland and willow, wet pasture, reedbeds, and open water. Roosting site for ducks, cormorants, and gulls.

Sandbach Flashes (WT; SJ 728608): fresh and brackish water with reedbeds, saltmarsh, and carr; waders and wildfowl.

The Quinta (WT; SJ 801671, OS 129; 15 ha) is a woodland, partly planted, with old meadows and a rich flora.

Wirral Way (SJ 238835, OS 107/8) is a footpath along a disused railway. It has dingy skipper and purple and white-letter hairstreaks.

Wybunbury Moss NNR (SJ 698502, OS 118; 17 ha) is a remarkable floating bog (*Schwingmoor*).

Yorkshire and Humberside

SITE
33 Yorkshire Dales National Park

Beautiful upland country, cut by many attractive, sheltered valleys, and containing a wealth of wildlife sites.

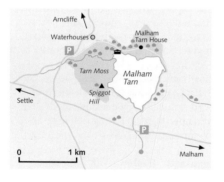

The Yorkshire Dales NP covers 1769 square kilometres in the northern Pennines, between Skipton in the south and Richmond in the north-east, and is centred around the village of Hawes in upper Wensleydale. The region is a favourite with walkers, and the famous Pennine Way long-distance path passes right through the heart of the park. It contains some grand scenery, with high limestone and millstone grit peaks, upland grassland, limestone pavement, and heather moor, contrasting with gentle valleys such as Ribblesdale, Airedale, and Wharfedale, which drain south, and Wensleydale and Swaledale, draining east, all with their characteristic network of drystone walls. The highest hills are mostly towards the western side of the park and include Pen-y-Ghent

(693 m), Ingleborough (723 m), and Whernside (736 m). In some places, such as at Malham Cove and Gordale Scar, there are impressive limestone cliffs. The park has about half of Britain's limestone pavement, a rather rare habitat, and the porous rocks have been channelled into a huge complex of cave systems and underground rivers, streams, and potholes. Recent surveys show that it also supports the highest population of breeding curlews in England.

Ingleborough NNR (SD 767764, OS 97; 698 ha), near Ingleton, protects the finest limestone 'karst' landscape in Britain, with limestone pavement (notably at Scar Close NNR). There are also areas of limestone and acidic grassland, heather moor, bog, and pasture, and pockets of woodland, such as the ash woods of Colt Park Wood and Ling Gill, both NNRs. There are no car-parking facilities on the reserve, although they are available at Chapel-Le-Dale, Ribblehead, and Horton-in-Ribblesdale. Public access is limited to footpaths, entry to elsewhere on the reserve being by permit only, available from the local English Nature office in Leyburn. Ling Gill NNR is a flower-rich ash wood on a rocky site, where woodland flowers such as wood anemone and primrose rub shoulders with northern and upland species such as mountain pansy, globe-flower, baneberry, and mossy saxifrage. Colt Park Wood is rooted in limestone pavement and consists of stunted ash trees with gnarled hazel, bird cherry, and hawthorn; its flora includes alpine cinquefoil. Souther Scales reserve (WT), just to the north of Ingleborough itself, has splendid limestone pavement, with ash, hazel, and hawthorn scrub, and fern-rich grikes with green spleenwort, herb-Robert, dog's mercury, herb-Paris, and baneberry.

More accessible is Grass Wood (WT), near Grassington in Wharfedale. This ash wood has a fine flora, including lily-of-the-valley, burnet rose, and mountain melick. Scoska Wood NNR (SD 913725, OS 98; 10 ha) is another rich ash wood with baneberry and patches of limestone grassland.

Hudswell Woods (NT), just to the west of Richmond, is a fine natural oak wood alongside the beautiful river Swale. It is excellent for woodland birds, with treecreeper, nuthatch, and all three woodpeckers, and the chance of buzzard. Northern specialities are pied flycatcher, redstart, and wood warbler, and the river has grey wagtail, dipper, and common sandpiper.

Malham Tarn NNR (NT; SD 890668, OS 98; 137 ha), about 9 km east of Settle, is one of the star sites of the NP. It is internationally famous for its special animal and plant life, and includes the famous Field Centre. The habitats here are varied, with lake, fen, limestone pavement, grassland, scree, woodland, and cliffs. Notable flowers of the reserve include bird's-eye primrose, mountain pansy, cranberry, cloudberry, and bog-rosemary, and green spleenwort also grows in the area. Access is by road and footpath from the village of Malham, but note that a permit is required away from the nature trails or footpaths. Malham is a botanist's paradise, and the tarn surroundings have a rich flora of peatland species, some growing in alkaline fen conditions, others in the more acid

raised bogs nearby. Bottle sedge colonizes the open water, and there are many other sedge species in the fen vegetation, along with flowers such as bogbean, marsh cinquefoil, and valerian. Dwarf milkwort is an uncommon species found growing here, and other interesting flowers in the reserve include alpine bartsia, alpine cinquefoil, mountain avens, hoary whitlowgrass, and northern bedstraw. Upland birds abound, with curlew, golden plover, red grouse, wheatear, and ring ouzel on the high ground, while the lake and streams have common sandpipers and dippers. Redstarts may be seen in the woods, and peregrines and merlins may sometimes be spotted in the area. The curving cliffs of Malham Cove and the impressive gorge of Gordale Scar lie just to the south of the reserve.

Gouthwaite Reservoir (SE 124698, OS 99) lies in Nidderdale, some 18 km west of Ripon, in an AONB just to the east of the park. The wooded hills here are a good site for raptors, with buzzard, peregrine, hen harrier, and red kite, the latter from the northern introduced population. Osprey are occasional on passage and golden eagles have also been seen, although rarely.

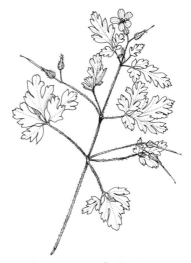

Herb-Robert *Geranium robertianum*

SITE
34 North York Moors National Park

Superb scenery with rolling moorland and partly wooded valleys, clear streams and rivers, and a stunning coastline of cliffs, headlands and sandy coves.

Chickweed wintergreen
Trientalis europaea

The North York Moors NP occupies an area of upland to the north and west of Scarborough, stretching west almost to Thirsk and north to the border with Cleveland. It covers nearly 144 000 ha, and includes valleys such as Bransdale and Rosedale in the south-west of the park, and Eskdale in the north. The gentle landscape of the river valleys contrasts with the rather bleak open plateaux of the hills, which reach a maximum height of 454 m (Urra Moor) in the north-west. The Cleveland Way track runs from Helmsley in the south through the Hambleton Hills, around the western and northern side of the park before reaching the sea at Saltburn-by-the-sea, then turning south along the coast through Whitby to Scarborough. In the north, the drainage is mainly to the river Esk, which runs roughly west to east, to Whitby, while the southern hills have a series of more or less parallel valleys, notably (from west to east) Ryedale, Bransdale, Farndale, Rosedale, Newton Dale, and the upper Derwent, all draining ultimately southwards into the Derwent.

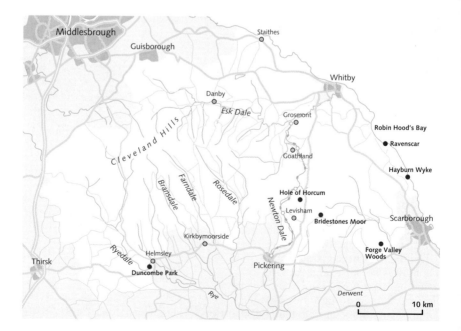

Northern England

Wild daffodils *Narcissus pseudonarcissus*, Farndale (Peter Wilson)

The hills, which comprise the largest expanse of heather in England, have flowers such as bell heather and bilberry, crowberry, cowberry, and cloudberry in some places. On the boggy areas, there are cottongrasses, cranberry, bog myrtle, and a wide range of sedges. Other plants of the damp sites are globeflower, grass-of-Parnassus, and bird's-eye primrose.

Duncombe Park NNR (SE 607828, OS 109; 103 ha), near Helmsley, has ancient broadleaved woodland (mainly oaks, elm, ash, and beech) and pasture alongside the river Rye, with shingle and sandbanks, and rich grassland. The breeding birds include all three woodpeckers, wood warbler, and pied flycatcher. The impressive house here may also be visited. Nearby are the splendid ruins of the Cistercian abbey of Rievaulx, and the NT terrace and temples behind.

Farndale (SE 673953), north of Kirkbymoorside, is a central southern valley with all the atmosphere of the moors. The river Dove is famous for its wild daffodils, which flower in profusion along the river banks each spring, along with golden-saxifrage, sweet cicely, primroses, and red campion.

Levisham Moor NPA (SE 8594), about 10 km north of Pickering, is set right in the heart of the NP and offers splendid walks through typical scenery. A visit can be combined with a journey on the North York Moors Railway, which operates old carriages pulled by steam between Pickering and Grosmont, stopping at Levisham and Goathland. There is also a convenient car park near the famous Hole of Horcum. The latter is a spectacular amphitheatre-like basin through which the Levisham Beck flows. The main habitats here are heather moor, cliffs, woodland, plantation, pasture, and bog. The reserve is famous for certain arctic-alpine plants such as chickweed wintergreen, dwarf cornel, and bearberry. The pastures have species such as pignut, adder's-tongue, betony, and fragrant and small white orchids. The moorland birds here include merlin, golden plover, red grouse, curlew, and snipe, with dippers on the streams.

A little to the east of Levisham is Bridestones Moor (NT; SE 8791; 120 ha) – typical moorland country, with patches of woodland (oak, ash, larch, birch, and rowan), bog, rocks, and grassland. The 'bridestones' themselves are Jurassic outcrops of sandstone.

The coastline of the park stretches from just north of the picturesque village of Staithes to just north of Scarborough, through Whitby, which makes a good centre for visitors. The NT sites of Ravenscar (NZ 980025) and Hayburn Wyke (TA 0297) lie between Scarborough and the scenic Robin Hood's Bay (NZ 9505). The latter has a fine platform coast with rock pools, below fossil-rich cliffs with many ammonites. Ravenscar has a good coastal flora with adder's-tongue, grass-of-Parnassus, and wild angelica. The cliffs are much eroded and unstable, so take care. At Ravenscar the rocks are also very rich in fossils, and some even have dinosaur footprints. Hayburn Wyke, a little to the south, is a pretty bay with mixed woodland.

Forge Valley Woods NNR (SE 9986; 63 ha), about 7 km west of Scarborough, is a fine example of relatively unspoiled woodland within the NP.

35 Flamborough Head

One of the top birdwatching sites on the east coast, especially during spring and autumn, known mainly for its seabirds and migrants.

The impressive chalk cliffs of Flamborough Head rise to 120 m, and jut out into the North Sea where the rolling hills of the Yorkshire Wolds come to an abrupt end, between Filey Bay and Bridlington. An ancient earthwork known as Danes Dyke crosses the headland between the villages of Bempton and Flamborough. This feature, dating from the Iron Age, has a nature trail with car park just off the B1255.

Gannet *Morus bassanus*

Flamborough Head itself is a prime site for watching seabirds, especially those passing in coastal waters during spring and autumn migrations. The lighthouse is easily reached from a car park and this area gives a commanding view out to sea (telescope essential). Between August and October, auks, skuas, petrels, terns, and shearwaters are pretty regular, and one may also spot relative rarities such as little auk and sooty, Cory's, and great shearwater.

Just inland from the lighthouse on the south of the head there is an area known as Old Fall and New Fall. Here the hedgerows and bushes hold migrant birds, especially after easterly winds. Another good spot for such migrants is South Landing, reached from a road south of Flamborough village. Yellow-browed warbler and firecrest are often encountered here, with bluethroat and wryneck also possible.

Nearby Bempton Cliffs (RSPB; TA 197738, OS 101) can be reached from the B1229

Flamborough Head (Peter Wilson)

(Flamborough to Filey). This cliff-top reserve is at its most interesting between May and July when seabird breeding is at its height. There is a car park on the cliff road from Bempton and an information centre, from where visitors can walk to the main viewpoints. **Please be very careful, especially with children – these cliffs (which rise to over 120 m) are very dangerous, and the barriers should not be crossed!**

Bempton is most famous for its colony of gannets, and other seabirds. In fact, this Grade 1 SSSI is England's largest

Fulmars *Fulmarus glacialis*

seabird breeding colony and the long stretch of cliffs provide a home to over 200 000 pairs, the main species concerned being guillemots (about 30 000), razorbills

Other sites nearby

Filey Brigg Bird Observatory (TA 1382) is a magnet for migrant birds, with rarities always possible. As well as the Brigg itself, the area includes a number of sites with trees or scrub: Arndale Ravine, Top Scrub, Long Hedge, and Church Ravine – all worth checking for migrants, especially in the autumn. Redstart and pied flycatcher are regular, with the chance of barred, icterine, and yellow-browed warblers, firecrest, and red-backed shrike. All four skuas may be spotted passing the Brigg in the autumn. Filey Dams (WT; TA 106807) is a wetland reserve with smooth and great crested newts.

(7500), kittiwakes (at least 75 000 pairs), puffins (6000 pairs), gannets (about 2500 pairs), and fulmars (about 800 pairs). About 20 pairs of shags breed amongst the boulders at the cliff-base. Other birds to watch out for are rock pipits, rock doves and, with luck, peregrine.

A cliff-top walk leads all the way from Bempton to North Landing, which is just west of Flamborough Head. The cliffs are also a good vantage point for seawatching, and, in late summer and autumn, terns can often be seen moving south, sometimes accompanied (and harried) by Arctic skuas. Under certain conditions a sea-watch might reveal Manx shearwaters, scoters, great skuas, and even sooty shearwaters, but these are usually seen well offshore, so a good telescope is essential.

Though less easy to see than the birds, there are mammals here, too: brown hares, stoats, weasels, fox, and badger around the grassy hilltops, and occasionally grey seals and common porpoises offshore.

Plants include thrift, scurvygrass, greater knapweed, and pyramidal orchid, and the butterflies common blue, small copper, and meadow brown.

SITE 36 Lower Derwent Valley

Floodplain habitats in the valley of the Derwent, with exceptionally rich wet meadows that are ideal for flowers and wetland birds.

The Lower Derwent Valley NNR covers 415 ha and includes parts of three SSSIs, and now also has Special Protection Area and Ramsar site status. Much of it is flood meadow, but there are also sections of pasture and some woodland. It includes the well-known reserve of Wheldrake Ings (WT; 'Ings' coming from the Viking term for a riverside meadow). The wetter areas are mainly grazed in summer, and the drier parts are managed mostly as hay meadows. Each autumn, the floodplain is usually inundated, and the valley becomes a large sheet of shallow water, rather like the washes of East Anglia, before gradually drying out again the following spring. There are car parks in the villages of Newton and North Duffield, which are about 1.5 km from the reserve.

The hay meadows are very rich in species, with flowers such as mead-

Ragged-Robin
Lychnis flos-cuculi

owsweet, ragged-Robin, great burnet, sneezewort, common valerian, and narrow-leaved water-dropwort (the latter a national rarity). Other flowers of the reserve are cowslip, marsh-marigold, fairy flax, marsh stitchwort, marsh valerian, adder's-tongue and green-winged orchid, and the interesting bulbs field garlic, wild onion, and sand leek.

Northern England

Siskin *Carduelis spinus* (Mike Lane)

In the wetter sites there are reed sweet grass, reed canary-grass, and bladder sedge, with marsh stitchwort and tubular water-dropwort, while brown, carnation, and greater and lesser pond sedges grow in the slightly less wet sites, along with meadow and tall fescues, and marsh and meadow foxtails. The ditches also have a rich flora, with water-violet, mare's-tail, greater water-parsnip, and flat-stalked pondweed.

Birds find the habitats here provide an unusually beneficial combination of feeding grounds (wet, rich mud, water, and pools in various stages of drying out) and breeding sites (hay meadow, ditches, riverside vegetation, carr). The result is that the numbers of wetland birds breeding here are quite remarkable, with snipe, lapwing, and redshank in their hundreds, as well as curlew, water rail, garganey, shoveler, gadwall, and other ducks. Black-necked grebes, ruff, and black-tailed godwits also breed, although in small numbers.

The flooded grasslands bring in large numbers of wintering wildfowl and waders, with up to 5000 teal, 10 000 wigeon, 2000 pochard, 5000 golden plover, and Bewick's swans. Barn owls breed here, and regularly patrol the meadows and ditches, and the mammals include brown hares and otters.

There are 15 species of dragonfly, including red-eyed damselfly at its most northern British site.

Wheldrake Ings NNR/SSSI (WT; SE 703440, OS 105) is an area of pasture and hay meadows fringing the river Derwent. This is one of the best sites in the region for wintering wildfowl, and also for breeding waterbirds in summer. Up to 200 Bewick's swans are regular here in winter and in spring the breeding redshank, lapwing, and snipe may be joined by passage black-tailed godwits and ruff. Autumn waders include green and wood sandpiper and spotted redshank. It also boasts a fine array of insects – purple hairstreak, ringlet, and small skipper, and banded demoiselle, red-eyed damselfly, hairy dragonfly, and broad-bodied chaser.

Fairburn Ings (RSPB; SE 450275) is a mixed wetland reserve with open water, reedbeds, wet woodland, and marsh. It has a good system of hides and boardwalks. The site is famous for its moulting flock of some 300 mute swans in July and roosting herd of about 100 whooper swans in winter; ruff and greenshank are regular migrants. The flora includes yellow iris, skullcap, and celery-leaved buttercup. In autumn, large numbers of swallows and sand martins seek out a safe roost in the reeds, while the alders attract redpolls and siskins. Little gulls, and terns including black, may be present on passage, and glaucous gulls are regularly seen in winter.

Barn owl *Tyto alba*

Other sites nearby

Blacktoft Sands (RSPB; SE 843232, OS 106), at the confluence of the rivers Ouse and Trent, is a fine reserve with six hides giving good views over the lagoons, reedbeds, and estuary. Marsh harrier, short-eared owl, bearded tit, avocet, and autumn passage waders. Pink-footed geese on the estuary in winter; hen harriers around the reedbeds, and occasional merlin.

Crowle Moor (WT, OS 112) is part of the Humberside Peatlands NNR and a good place to find heathland and wetland birds, with water rail, teal, and long-eared owl. Nightjar and tree pipit breed, as do all three woodpeckers and

willow tit. Hobbies feed on the abundant dragonflies. Adders and grass snakes are both common here.

Far Ings (WT; TNC OS 112). This is a wetland reserve with extensive reedbeds and lagoons alongside the Humber Estuary. Hides give good viewing of the birds, which include marsh harrier, water rail, bearded tit, and common tern.

Skipwith Common (WT; SE 6637), near Selby, has woodland, heath, marsh, and open water. The flowers include sundew, bog pimpernel, broad-leaved helleborine, and spotted-orchids.

A selection of other important sites in the county

Brockadale (WT; SE 499176, OS 111; 37 ha): wooded valley with good flora.

Burton Riggs (WT; TA 032832, OS 101; 15 ha), near Scarborough, has old gravel pits, with orchids, good birds, and common and great crested newts.

Carlton Marsh LNR (SE 379103; 80 ha), near Barnsley, is a wetland with reedbeds.

Coatham Marsh (WT; NZ 586427; 54 ha), near Redcar, has good birds.

Fountains Abbey (NT; SE 2769), near Ripon, is a fine ruined Cistercian abbey set in an old park landscape with aged trees. Good for woodland birds, including hawfinch, and insects, including white-letter and purple hairstreak. All the British newts have been found in the ponds here.

Hardcastle Crags (NT; SD 973302; 175 ha). Mixed woods on a rocky site near

Hebden Bridge. The spring bluebells are impressive. Alongside more usual woodland and upland birds there are ring ouzel, and both red and grey squirrels.

Hornsea Mere (RSPB; TA 1947), the largest natural lake in Yorkshire, is a superb birding site, with wetland birds, including a varied range of migrants.

Old Moor Wetland Reserve, near Barnsley, is a diverse wetland, very good for wildfowl and waders; regular whooper swans and goosander in winter.

Potteric Carr (WT; SE 589007; 130 ha). Wetland with varied bird life.

Spurn Head NNR (WT; TA 4215). Shingle spit with bird observatory. Good coastal flora, seabirds, and migrants.

Stoneycliffe Wood (WT), Wakefield. Mixed woodland with rich flora.

Thorne Moors NNR (SE 7215; 73 ha). Part of the largest remaining lowland peatland in England. Bog-mosses, cottongrass, cranberry, bog-rosemary, round-leaved sundew. Also good invertebrates, with large heath, and 17 species of dragonfly. Nightjar and nightingale breed, the latter at its most northerly in Britain. Winter brings hen harriers, short-eared owls, and merlins.

Tophill Low NR (TA 071482; 110 ha). Reservoirs, woodland, scrub, grassland; wildfowl and waders.

Upper Don Valley and Winscar Reservoir (OS 110). The Trans-Pennine Trail runs from Penistone along the valley, following the river Don. Birds of this area include red grouse, golden plover, curlew, ring ouzel, wheatear, whinchat, siskin, redpoll, peregrine, merlin, kestrel, short-eared and long-eared owls, and goshawk.

Worsbrough Country Park (SE 345034; 60 ha): reedbeds, open water, carr; wildfowl include ruddy duck.

Derbyshire

SITE 37 Peak District National Park

Britain's first NP, with scenery grading from high, open moorland, to sheltered valleys with woods and flower-rich grassland.

Dog's mercury *Mercurialis perennis*

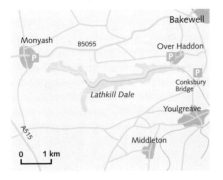

The Peak District NP, at 1438 square kilometres, covers a large part of the southern Pennines, from just south of Huddersfield in the north to Ashbourne in the south. Most of it lies in Derbyshire, but in the north and east it overlaps into Yorkshire, in the north and west into Lancashire and Cheshire, and in the south-west into Staffordshire. It was the first park to be designated, as early as 1950. It is much visited, lying as it does between Manchester and Sheffield, and close to several highly populated areas, and visitors are often surprised by how quickly one enters the delightful rural uplands of the Peak

Miller's Dale (Peter Wilson)

District from either of these cities. Convention divides the park into two parts: the North (or Dark) Peak, which is mainly dominated by acid soils overlying millstone grit, and the South (or White) Peak, where the soils are influenced mainly by the large area of carboniferous limestone.

The Dark Peak is well named, and takes its character from the heather-clad moorlands which dominate much of the landscape here, in a region strongly influenced by sheep farming and grouse moors. Although it includes much private land, most parts of the park are accessible by footpath, and the southern part of the Pennine Way starts here (at Edale).

The terrain reaches its highest point of just over 630 m at Kinder Scout (SK 048869), and there are a number of other high hills, notably Bleaklow (628 m) and Black Hill (582 m), which lie further north. Here the vegetation is mostly acid upland grassland, heather moor, and eroded blanket bogs, or peat hags. The Kinder–Bleaklow uplands are easily accessible from the A57 Sheffield–Glossop road. This area, which is crossed by the Pennine Way, has one of the best blanket bogs in the country. Hardly any bog is actively growing now, however, and erosion has cut through the layers of peat to the hard millstone grit rocks beneath. Bilberry, crowberry, and cowberry grow on the moors, and in some places cloudberry, here towards its southern limit. Moorland birds include curlew, ring ouzel, red grouse, golden plover, and the occasional peregrine, hen harrier, or merlin.

Several of the valleys of the Dark Peak have been flooded to create reservoirs. The largest are Ladybower, Derwent, and Howden Reservoirs which lie in a string in the upper Derwent valley, about 15 km west of Sheffield. These attract birds such as red-breasted merganser and common sandpiper, as well as wintering goosander and goldeneye. The margins have been well landscaped, with adjacent plantations of broadleaved as well as coniferous trees, where goshawks, crossbills, and a few red squirrels breed. The hillsides are home to mountain hares, weasels, and foxes, with upland birds including red grouse, golden plover, curlew, ring ouzel, and wheatear.

The NT looks after over 12% of the Peak District NP. The Hope Woodlands (NT) preserve mainly moorland near Kinder Scout, and there are also Trust lands at nearby Edale and Mam Tor, and at the Derwent and Howden Moors. The Derwent Estate (NT; SK 1994), on the borders of Derbyshire and Yorkshire, forms part of the High Peak area. Here cotton-grass waves over large areas, with heather and purple moor-grass. There are mountain hares, too, which turn a patchy white and brown in winter, as well as emperor and fox moths, which feed on the heather. The breeding birds include dunlin, golden plover, curlew, snipe, and red grouse.

Padley Woods (NT; SK 2480) is dominated by sessile oak, with birch, ash, alder, and rowan, and with wood-sorrel, wavy hair-grass, bilberry, ferns, and climbing corydalis. It is bird-rich, with all three woodpeckers, tawny owl, hawfinch, redstart, and pied flycatcher.

Burrs Wood (WdT; SK 305755, OS 119; 13 ha), near Unthank, is a sessile oak wood with some large and quite ancient coppiced stools.

The southern Peak District, or White Peak, is somewhat gentler in aspect than the northern part, and is characterized by a series of valleys (dales) cutting down into the mainly limestone rock. These typically hold clear streams (some of the purest in Britain), whose flow varies enormously with the rainfall and water table, occasionally drying up, and quite often turning fairly rapidly into torrents, or even flooding over into the adjacent meadows.

Here the soils of the lower valleys and farmland are mostly calcareous, and the flora reflects this difference. The valley sides sometimes have semi-natural woodlands, mainly dominated by ash, and there are some fine sites on exposed rocks and scree slopes with a rich flora. The fields margins are marked by picturesque drystone walls.

The rocky grassland in many of these dales is of great botanical interest, especially on the slightly steeper gradients, which escape intense grazing. The White Peak lies at a transition point between northern and southern plants, and the richness of the flora is reflected in the presence of upland, lowland, northern, and southern species. Perhaps the most famous of plants here is the lovely Jacob's-ladder, which grows wild in certain valleys, often in some profusion, preferring damp or shady sites. This special flower is only found wild elsewhere in Britain in the Yorkshire Dales and at a single site in Northumberland, although it is widely planted, and occasional garden escapes occur. The Peak District also holds good numbers of that attractive northern species the mountain pansy, in both its yellow and purple forms. Another equally pretty flower is bloody crane's-bill, which has deep purple-red flowers (though not really blood-red) up to 3 cm across. Though more widespread elsewhere, it is nevertheless typical of these dales. Other local species here are spring cinquefoil and Nottingham catchfly, and also basil thyme, melancholy thistle, dropwort, globeflower, and fragrant orchid. More common flowers such as bird's-foot-trefoil, marjoram, rockrose, wild thyme, globeflower, and salad burnet add to the display, and these communities make a wonderful sight in spring and early summer. The rockier sites have mossy saxifrage, dark red helleborine, spring sandwort, and western polypody, among others. In spring there are good displays of cowslips and early purple orchids.

Scattered amongst the limestone grassland are pockets of woodland, some of it

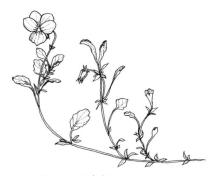

Mountain pansy *Viola lutea*

Monsal Dale

ancient. Woodland flowers to search for here include wood melick, yellow archangel, lily-of-the-valley, and mezereon, the latter a protected rarity.

The butterflies include dingy skipper, brown argus, and dark green fritillary, and slow worms can also be found.

The cliffs echo to the calls of jackdaws, which breed here in profusion, and dippers and grey wagtails are common along the streams and river. Redstarts and wood warblers also breed in these woods.

Lathkill Dale (SK 200664, OS 119) is one of the best-known and most visited of the Derbyshire dales, and one of five to be protected in the NNR, the others being Biggin, Cressbrook, Hay, and Long and Monk's. Public access is from Over Haddon village or from the road just east of Monyash. Lathkill is a pretty valley with a clear stream and makes an excellent (if sometimes rather too-popular) walk, with the chance to see many typical species. This reserve consists of woodland and limestone grassland in a beautiful valley setting. It also has one of

the finest natural ash woods, with woodland shrubs including hazel, whitebeam, bird cherry, guelder-rose, rowan, wych elm, field maple, hawthorn, and dogwood. On the woodland floor grow such species as lily-of-the-valley, dog's mercury, and red campion, and even the rare mezereon. The grassland here is very rich, especially on southerly aspects, and the clear waters of the river have brown trout and bullhead, with dippers and grey wagtails usually in evidence.

A number of dales lie between Buxton and Bakewell. Monk's Dale (SK 1473) is a peaceful site, rich in flowers, with scree and flush communities as well as grassland. Chee and Miller's Dale (WT; SK 1473) has nice woods with whitebeam and yew in a somewhat steep site. Cressbrook Dale (EN; SK 1774) is very rich, with lily-of-the-valley, bloody crane's-bill, Nottingham catchfly, dwarf thistle, and spring sandwort. Monsal Dale (SK 1872) is a scenic spot where an impressive disused railway viaduct spans the river valley. Some of the steep slopes here carry ash-dominated woods.

Northern England

Dovedale (NT; SK 1453) lies right on the border between Derbyshire and Staffordshire, some 10 km north of Ashbourne. It is a wonderful reserve, distilling the full flavour of the White Peak, with the clear river Dove running alongside limestone cliffs, wooded thickets, and open, flower-rich grassland. Special plants here include Nottingham catchfly, dwarf thistle, dropwort, northern bedstraw, and greater burnet-saxifrage. Grey wagtails and dippers inhabit the streams and the invertebrates include northern brown argus and glow-worms. The woods are mostly dominated by ash, with oaks, beech, whitebeam, and rowan, and they are home to many woodland birds, including buzzard, wood warbler, redstart, kingfisher, dipper, and grey wagtail. The grassland and the nearby cliffs and rocky areas are rich in species, including Nottingham catchfly, orpine, mossy saxifrage, dark-red helleborine, and spring sandwort. Amongst the butterflies found here are dingy and grizzled skipper, brown argus, and green and white-letter hairstreaks.

A little further west, in Staffordshire, lies the Manifold Valley (NT; SK 1054), with a similar mix of habitats. The plants here include mezereon, Jacob's-ladder, greater butterfly and green-winged orchids, and sweet cicely.

Gratton and Long Dale (EN), near Matlock, has woodland, scrub, calcareous and acid grassland, and mining spoil heaps, all with their distinctive floras. The spoil heaps have unusual species including alpine penny-cress and spring sandwort.

Derwentside (WT; SK 316556) and Cromford Canal SSSI (WT; SK 348519), near Matlock, has flower-rich canal-side meadows and woods, with wild daffodils and flowering-rush. A good site for water voles.

Ogston Reservoir (Severn Trent Water; SK 3861) on the edge of the Peak District is probably best known for its gulls – with a large winter roost and regular sightings of rarer species including Mediterranean, glaucous, and Iceland. Ospreys may be seen on spring passage. It is easily accessible and has three car parks and a public hide. The adjacent reserve of Carr Wood (WT) has a heronry.

No visitor to the Peak District should fail to see the splendid estate of Chatsworth, some 5 km north-west of Bakewell. As well as the imposing house, the grounds make a fine nature reserve, with a good collection of trees and approachable herds of fallow and red deer. Another marvellous property is the beautifully preserved ancient manor of Haddon Hall, overlooking the river Wye.

A selection of other important sites in the county

Calke Abbey (NT; SK 368227). Much of the estate surrounding the abbey consists of old parkland – pasture with old trees. A good site for woodpeckers, nuthatch, treecreeper, and spotted flycatcher. The ancient trees support a rich insect fauna, while the acid grassland has tormentil, harebell, sheep's sorrel, and heath bedstraw.

Foremark Reservoir (SK 3324), just south of Derby in the Trent Valley, is the largest expanse of open water in the area. Access is via car parks and

footpath on the eastern shore. Summer birds here include great crested grebe, grey heron, cormorant, buzzard, and sparrowhawk. In winter, rarities such as divers, velvet scoter, eider, and little auk may turn up, alongside more regular species like goldeneye, smew, goosander, and red-necked grebe.

Hilton Reserve SSSI (WT; SK 249315, OS 128; 29 ha), near Derby, has gravel pits with good flora, bird life, and smooth and great crested newts.

Nottinghamshire

SITE
38 Sherwood Forest

Remnants of a once extensive forest, with ancient relict oaks.

For many people, the name Sherwood Forest conjures up vast expanses of dense woodland in which Robin Hood and his folk used to hide to escape the law and from which they raided the rich. It is doubtful whether the famous outlaw actually operated in this area, although likely that it was the haunt of robbers, as were many similar places elsewhere. However, Sherwood Forest was once much more extensive and most probably managed as a hunting forest, with forest interspersed with patches of heath and grassland, covering an area which stretched from Nottingham northwards to Worksop. Nowadays only small remnants remain, such as the woods of Sherwood Forest Country Park, Clumber Park, and Treswell Wood.

Sherwood Forest Country Park (SK 625675) is near Ollerton, and a very popular site. It contains hundreds of ancient oaks, most famously one called the Major Oak, and many of these are gnarled, hollow, and stag-headed. These, some of the largest in the country, provide vital

Major Oak (Peter Wilson)

habitats for a range of invertebrates and associated birds, and are probably up to 600 years old. Some 1500 species of beetle are known here, and there are also several rare spiders. Noctule bats are frequently seen hunting around these trees and over the adjacent grassland.

Clumber Park (NT; SK 6475) lies just south of Worksop and is a large site at the northern edge of the area. It covers about 1500 ha and is well visited, being so close to several large towns and cites. Remnants of ancient woodland persist in the form of venerable oaks and beeches, which have a rich insect fauna. A striking feature is the magnificent double avenue of lime trees. Woodland birds are well represented, with nightingale at one of its most northerly sites, woodcock, woodpeckers, long-eared owl, redstart, and hawfinch. Patches of heath have nightjar, tree pipit, grasshopper warbler, and woodlark, and a large lake has good wildfowl, including breeding gadwall. The grassland, which is acid, has the pretty wavy hair-grass, with small-flowered crane's-bill, while gorse and bell heather are prominent on the heaths. In the centre of the park is a large serpentine lake with Canada geese and assorted other wildfowl in winter.

Treswell Wood SSSI (WT; SK 762798, OS 120; 48 ha), near Retford, lies further east. It is one of the finest mixed oak woods in the county, and is truly ancient, getting a mention in Domesday. Wych elm and wild service-tree grow here, as do herb-Paris, dog's mercury, and early purple orchid, with marsh-marigold and yellow iris in wet patches. This wood is a site for speckled bush-cricket, which is mainly a southern species.

Duke's Wood (WT; SK 677603, OS 120; 8 ha), near Newark, is a mixed wood, with oak, ash, hazel, birch, wild privet, dogwood, and guelder-rose. Primroses, bluebells, and wood anemones are prominent in spring, and nightingales sometimes breed here at onc of their most northerly sites.

SITE 39 Attenborough Gravel Pits

A fine riverside wetland site close to a conurbation.

Attenborough Gravel Pits (WT; SK 513342, OS 129; 146 ha) lies about 8 km south-west of Nottingham. It is a splendid group of flooded gravel pits between the river Trent and the railway line, and also includes a small wood, reedbeds, and scrub. This reserve is a good spot for wetland and marsh birds, and probably best visited in spring or summer. The breeding birds include garden, reed, sedge, and sometimes grasshopper warblers, great crested grebe, common tern, little ringed plover, kingfisher, and sand

Migrant hawker *Aeshna mixta*

martin. Hobbies are often seen hunting dragonflies or hirundines. In the winter, large numbers of wildfowl visit, with shoveler and wigeon in addition to mallard and teal, with cormorants and occasional sea ducks. Black terns are regular visitors on passage, as are many waders.

The wet meadows and marshes have a plethora of plants, with reeds, flowering-rush, water-plantain, bulrush, bur-reeds, arrowhead, marsh-marigold, hemp-agrimony, yellow iris, purple-loosestrife, water mint, and ragged-Robin, while the water plants include water-starwort, spiked and whorled water-milfoil, and horned, fennel, curled, and lesser pondweeds. In the old meadows and grassland there are great burnet, meadow saxifrage, yellow-rattle, salad burnet, kidney vetch, and common centaury, among others. The patches of carr have alder and the following species of willow: almond, crack, goat, grey, osier, purple, and white.

The insects include four-spotted chaser and southern and migrant hawkers among the dragonflies, and this is also a site for two rather local diving beetles (*Dytiscus marginalis* and *D. circumcinctus*), aggressive predators who even include tadpoles and small fish in their diet.

A selection of other important sites in the county

Bunny Old Wood (WT; SK 579283, OS 129; 16 ha), near Nottingham, is an ancient wood with good flora, birds, and insects (including white-letter hairstreak).

Colwick Country Park (SK 600391), Nottingham, has lakes which attract good winter wildfowl.

Wales

Wales

Introduction

Wales is much the smallest of the three mainland countries making up the United Kingdom – barely larger than south-west England or East Anglia. However, it makes up in variety for what it lacks in size, and is a wonderfully varied and unspoilt region.

Its landscape and ecology are dominated by mountains and the coast. Mountains or high hills are the defining characteristic of the interior; the Snowdon Massif (entirely within the Snowdonia NP) dominates the north of the country, and includes the highest mountain in England or Wales – Snowdon itself, at 1085 m. Just to the south lies Cadair Idris, close to the coast near Dolgellau, then a broad band of mountains runs southwards through the country, known collectively as the Cambrian Mountains and including ranges such as the Rhinog Hills. In the south, the Brecon Beacons are the most southerly significant mountains in the UK, while to the east of them lie the Black Mountains, and to the west, in Pembrokeshire, the Preseli Mountains.

Wales is essentially a broad peninsula, surrounded by coast on three sides. In places the coast is deeply indented, especially in the south-west, and there are many offshore islands such as Anglesey (with its own offshore islands), Bardsey, Ramsey, Skomer, Skokholm, and Caldey.

Coedydd Maentwrog (see p. 139)

Previous page: **Rheidol Valley** (see p. 151)

Wales

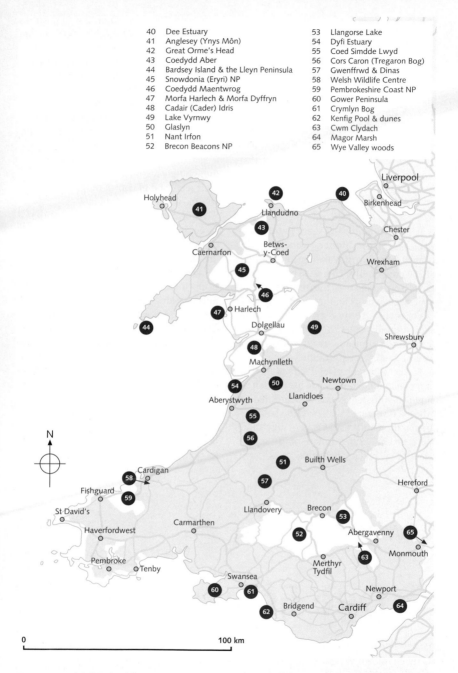

40	Dee Estuary	53	Llangorse Lake
41	Anglesey (Ynys Môn)	54	Dyfi Estuary
42	Great Orme's Head	55	Coed Simdde Lwyd
43	Coedydd Aber	56	Cors Caron (Tregaron Bog)
44	Bardsey Island & the Lleyn Peninsula	57	Gwenffrwd & Dinas
45	Snowdonia (Eryri) NP	58	Welsh Wildlife Centre
46	Coedydd Maentwrog	59	Pembrokeshire Coast NP
47	Morfa Harlech & Morfa Dyffryn	60	Gower Peninsula
48	Cadair (Cader) Idris	61	Crymlyn Bog
49	Lake Vyrnwy	62	Kenfig Pool & dunes
50	Glaslyn	63	Cwm Clydach
51	Nant Irfon	64	Magor Marsh
52	Brecon Beacons NP	65	Wye Valley woods

Consequently, the total length of coast is enormous, with a great variety of habitats, including some of the best sand dunes in Britain, saltmarshes, high cliffs of many different rocks, rocky foreshore, mudflats, and others. Many of the finest seabird colonies in southern Britain are here, especially on the offshore islands,

Wales

and there are rich displays of coastal flowers, including rarities, in places such as Pembrokeshire, and on the Gower and Lleyn peninsulas.

The climate of Wales is Atlantic and montane, or – to put it another way – wet! It lies open to the arrival of depressions from the south-west, which deposit large quantities of rain on the first high land they reach, and many higher parts of Wales have an annual rainfall of 200 cm or more. There are rain-shadow areas to the east of the mountains, of course, such as in Radnorshire, and some of the more easterly coastal areas are not exceptionally wet, though the general impression is of a luxuriant vegetation, well watered throughout the year.

Purple-loosestrife
Lythrum salicaria

This combination of high rainfall and hilly or mountainous countryside means that the land is dominated by pastoral farming and forestry. Compared with, say, lowland East Anglia, the countryside is generally much more diverse and intimate, with smaller fields, many hedges, hedgerow trees, patch-

es of woodland, and unimproved pastures and damp areas. Arable fields of any size are rare. Broadly speaking, this means that many generalist countryside species are more common here than further east: yellowhammers, whitethroats, dunnocks, song thrushes, purple-loosestrife, yellow iris, and so on are all frequent in the general countryside. To a certain extent, this means that the reserves are less crucial – not being islands in a sea of intensively used countryside – though they are often the best examples of their type, and of course they are managed specifically for conservation.

For the naturalist, Wales is a wonderful place to visit. Apart from the generally unspoilt nature of the countryside, there are major wetlands such as Cors Caron, superb sites for birds in winter such as the Burry inlet and the Dyfi Estuary, marvellous displays of coastal flowers almost all around the coast, some of the best sand-dune and dune-slack complexes in Britain, such as at Kenfig and Gower, and the seabird colonies already mentioned, on the offshore islands. It is also a good place to find many northerly species at their southern limit, such as water lobelia, purple saxifrage, roseroot, and large heath, yet often not far from strongly southern species such as small red and southern damselflies, yellow centaury, and least restharrow.

Clwyd

SITE
40 Dee Estuary

A major bird site in winter, wholly protected as an SSSI, with scattered nature reserves along its shores. See also p. 108.

The river Dee reaches the Irish Sea to the north-west of Chester, forming a vast linear estuary squeezed between Wales and the Wirral peninsula. There are huge areas of saltmarshes, mudflats, sand, and silt exposed at low tide, which become a feeding ground for tens of thousands of birds in winter. Estuaries are remarkably

Common cockles *Cerastoderma edule*

productive ecosystems, and many invertebrates occur in the mud in high densities: common cockles, ragworms, the amphipod crustacean *Corophium volutator*, Baltic tellin, and various other shells and worms occur in tens or hundreds of thousands per cubic metre. These support enormous numbers of waders such as oystercatchers, godwits, knot, dunlin, and sanderling – 26 species of waders have been recorded here over the years. There may also be huge numbers of wildfowl, such as pintail, shelduck, mallard, teal, and various sea ducks in winter. Such numbers of birds naturally attract predators, and peregrines, merlin, hen harriers, and short-eared owls may often be seen working the saltmarshes and mudflats. In summer there is less activity, though there are breeding shelduck, lapwing, oystercatchers, and common terns.

Access to the estuary is not very easy on the Welsh side, though there are several reserves where viewing is possible. The RSPB has a reserve at the Point of Air (SH 125847), where there are parking, guided walks, and a hide. There is a reserve at Connah's Quay power station (sign-posted from the A548). Flint Castle (SJ 247734) has a car park and access to a good viewpoint on the foreshore. In general the best time to see the birds in winter is towards high tide, as they are pushed off the mudflats by the rising tide.

South of the estuary, there are two accessible sites which are worth a visit. Marford (SJ 357560) is an attractive sheltered reserve in an old quarry, particularly rich in flowers and butterflies. It lies about 4 km north-east of Wrexham, just off the B5445. In the hills south-west of Denbigh, there is a reservoir called Llyn Brenig; the northern end (SH 970580) is managed as a reserve called Gors Maen Llwyd, with heather-clad hills, boggy areas, and the lake margins. It is a good locale for breeding birds, passage migrants, upland flowers, and insects such as emperor moths.

A selection of other important sites in the county

Ceiriog Valley (SJ 136347): moorland, river, woodland; red and black grouse, hen harrier, merlin, short-eared owl, pied flycatcher, kingfisher, dipper.

Loggerheads Country Park (SJ 198626): woodland and river; pied flycatcher, hawfinch, crossbill, dipper.

Wales

Gwynedd

SITE
41 Anglesey (Ynys Môn)

The largest Welsh island, boasting spectacular coastline and dozens of nature reserves and sites of special interest.

Although only some 30 km across, the island of Anglesey has a marvellous spectrum of nature reserves and other protected sites. Despite being connected to the mainland of Wales by good direct roads, it still retains the feel of an unspoilt island.

The coast is its greatest glory. It is all scheduled as an area of outstanding natural beauty, and within it there are a number of special sites. Working clockwise from the Menai Bridge, the first site is Newborough Warren and Forest. This is a very large site, of which 1550 ha are an NNR, comprising one of the finest sand-dune systems in the country, a large tract of planted forest, and vast expanses of mudflats and saltmarsh extending into Malltraeth Sands to the west. It is a fine area for birds at any time of year; in winter, the intertidal stretches attract huge numbers of waders and wildfowl, including internationally important numbers of pintail, and good numbers of wigeon and shelduck, amongst others. In spring, there are breeding curlew, oyster-catchers, shelduck, cormorant, ringed plover, redshank, and many more, though not in especially large numbers. There is also a large raven roost here, attracting up to 2000 birds. It is a noted plant site, with about 560 species recorded, including uncommon flowers such as grass-of-Parnassus, round-leaved wintergreen, dune helleborine, dune pansy, and small adder's-tongue. It is also well known as a classic site for insects and other invertebrates; the broad sandy rides in the forest are especially good. Ynys Llanddwyn is noted for its bees and wasps, the rare medicinal leech occurs in some ponds, and dark green fritillaries are widespread.

Ravens *Corvus corax*

North-westwards from here, the whole coast is of interest, though the next major site is the South Stack reserve on Holy Island (RSPB; SH 207821). This is a lovely place, with high sea-cliffs backed by maritime heath that is a blaze of purple and gold in late summer. It is primarily a bird site, with breeding chough (resident all year), guillemot, razorbill, puffin, shag, fulmar, kittiwake, and peregrine. The rare spotted rock-rose occurs in one of its few UK localities. There is also a small population of the maritime subspecies of field fleawort, at its only world locality! The heathland here also supports the largest colony of silver-studded blue butterflies in Wales. There is a good information centre in Ellin's Tower (RSPB; well signposted), open daily from Easter to mid-September.

On the north coast, towards Cemaes, Cemlyn (WT; SH 337932) is well worth a visit. The reserve itself covers 25 ha of fine habitat, though the surrounding areas (including the land bordering the nuclear power station at Wylfa, to the east) are also good. Within the reserve, there is a large brackish lagoon held back by a shingle beach, with the aid of a sluice system to control water levels. The lagoon itself is a noted bird site, and has been managed as a bird sanctuary for over 60 years; in summer, there may be hundreds of pairs of terns, particularly of common, Arctic, and Sandwich, with occasional roseates. The terns can be watched from the shingle ridge opposite the islands, from where the breeding colonies can be clearly seen, with the adults plying to and fro across the shingle to the sea. Other breeding birds include ringed plover, oystercatcher, shelduck, grasshopper warbler, and reed bunting. In winter, there may be good numbers of wildfowl. The shingle ridge is a lovely example of a storm beach, with a fine mixture of specialized flowers. The displays of sea-kale are as good as anywhere, together with yellow horned-poppy, sea campion, thrift, sea-milkwort, sheep's-bit, and small quantities of autumn lady's-tresses in the more stable parts. Within the lagoon, there is a good range of brackish water invertebrates including prawns, shore crabs, and bivalve molluscs, with typical lagoon fishes such as grey mullet.

The inland sites of Anglesey are less spectacular, but of great interest. In the north-east of the island, inland from

Sea-kale *Crambe maritima* on the shingle at Cemlyn

Wales

Common tern *Sterna hirundo* **(Peter Wilson)**

Benllech, there is a series of nationally important fens, rather similar to those in Norfolk. The most accessible is Cors Goch reserve (WT; SH 497813), with boardwalks and footpaths. The fen lies in the bed of a former lake, fed with lime-rich water, and is particularly noted for its plants, including narrow-leaved marsh-orchid, green-winged orchid, bog asphodel, and marsh gentian. It also has

breeding curlew, redshank, and snipe, and an impressive list of insects. Cors Erddreiniog NNR (SS 470820) is the largest of the fens, but can only be visited by permit from the CCW; it has a similar range of species, though more extensive. Cors Bodeilio NNR (SS 500775) has a footpath across it.

South-eastwards from Cemlyn, there are two well-established reservoirs with good birdwatching facilities. Llyn Alaw has an information centre and hides, west of Llanerchymedd. Llyn Cefni lies just north-west of Llangefni, by the B5111, where there is a picnic site and hides.

About 3 km south of Caegeilliog, there is a small reserve known as Valley Lakes (RSPB; SH 306770), with a nature trail and good views of wildfowl on the reed-fringed lakes.

There is a countryside centre at Aberffraw, which provides information and organizes walks and displays.

SITE

42 Great Orme's Head

A mixture of sites along the north Gwynedd coast between Llandudno and Bangor.

Great Orme's Head (SH 7683) is a large limestone headland projecting north-west into

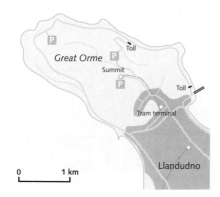

Conway bay from Llandudno. It is mainly managed as an LNR by the Borough Council, and retains a surprising air of wildness, thanks to its size and rugged nature. It has long been recognized as a special botanical site, with a fascinating mixture of southern, northern, and maritime species. Wild cotoneaster occurs here at, perhaps, its only native locality, together with uncommon limestone species such as hoary rock-rose and white horehound, amongst a mass of more widespread species. Another speciality here (and on a number of other limestone cliffs in Wales) is the western subspecies of spiked speedwell, which is abundant in places. It is also considered to be nationally important for lepidoptera, with endemic dwarf subspecies of silver-studded blue and grayling both occurring, as well as several scarce moths. Other insects of interest include glow-worms, and a number of uncommon beetles. The WT runs a small reserve on the south-west side of the head.

At Conway, clearly sign-posted from the A55, is a new RSPB reserve that has been created since the road tunnel was built. Lagoons, islands, reedbeds, and wet grass-land combine to produce an exciting and developing reserve, with easy access and several hides. There is also a good shop and information centre, open all year.

Along the coast of Conway Bay, between Llanfairfechan and Bangor, there is a series of four nature reserves which pro-vide excellent access to the shoreline and views of the vast mudflats known as Traeth Lafan. The whole area is particularly good for birds in winter.

Working westwards from Llanfairfechan, the reserves are Glan y Môr Elias (SH 667745) with saltmarsh and lagoons; Morfa Madryn (SH 662740) with marshy grassland and a series of pools with hides; Morfa Aber (SH 648732), which has saltmarsh edge, brackish pools, and damp grassland, with easy parking and a hide; and finally The Spinnies (SH 613271) which, though small, has an excellent reputation for the range of birds that it attracts.

SITE 43 Coedydd Aber

Woodland NNR in a deep north-facing valley, with a fine waterfall at Aber Falls.
Grid ref: SH 665715; OS 115 or Outdoor Leisure 17.

Although this lovely reserve lies just within the Snowdonia NP (see p. 138), it is treated separately as it is right on the edge of the park, and access is directly from the main A55(T). The Afon Rhaeadr Fawr, which flows from the Aber Falls, has cut a steep valley into the north slopes of Y Carneddau, now largely clothed in mixed oak woodland. The higher slopes are mainly of pure oak woodland, both pedunculate and sessile (and some inter-mediates), while the lower slopes are damper and slightly more fertile, support-ing a wider range of trees including ash, wych elm, alder, and hazel. As one walks up the valley towards the falls, the charac-ter of the woodland becomes more open, with grassy glades and marshy hollows in the valley, and screes on the slopes.

The flora is typical of ancient western oak woodland, with bluebells, prim-roses, wood-sorrel, wood anemone, and opposite-leaved golden-saxifrage all common, together with ferns such as hart's-tongue, scaly male-fern, hard-fern, and soft shield-fern. Tutsan is more local, and wood fescue is rare. In common with many such unpolluted western woods, the lower plant flora is exceptional. The trees and rocks are clad with a fine array of lichens, includ-ing many uncommon species. The area around the falls, where it is more humid, has a particularly rich bryophyte (moss and liverwort) flora, including many uncommon oceanic species. The falls themselves are both spectacular and interesting. They occur here because there is an outcrop of igneous granophyre rock, which is rather harder than the surrounding rocks and has therefore prevented the

Wales

The main stream in Coedydd Aber

stream from eroding back so far into the mountainside.

In late spring, the woods are alive with the sounds of birdsong. Besides the common woodland species, there are good numbers of pied flycatcher, redstart, and wood warbler in the wooded areas, and dipper and grey wagtail along the stream. On the high hill slopes where the woods thin out, there are ring ouzel, wheatear, peregrine, raven, and occasional hunting merlin.

The site is easily reached by taking the Abergwyngregyn turn off the A55, a few kilometres east of Bangor, then following signs towards Aber Falls. There is a good car park, and a walk of about 2 km to the falls. Informative nature trail leaflets are available from CCW.

SITE
44 Bardsey Island and the Lleyn Peninsula

An unspoilt mountainous peninsula projecting south-westwards from Snowdonia, with Bardsey Island at its tip.

Bardsey Island, or Ynys Enlli (SH 120220) is a remote island of 180 ha, lying about 5 km off the tip of the Lleyn Peninsula.

The island is steeped in history, with a long history of occupation and being a religious sanctuary. In recent years, it has

this part of north Wales. The upper drier fields are a mass of colour, particularly during June, with masses of common knapweed, yellow-rattle, eyebrights, lady's-mantle (*Alchemilla glabra*), together with large quantities of greater butterfly-orchids, common and heath spotted-orchids, and a fine array of grasses. The curious little adder's-tongue (usually a good sign of an old grassland) occurs in patches. On the lower parts of the reserve, there is extensive seepage. Here there are bog-mosses, half a dozen sedges, the pretty little cranberry, spikes of northern marsh-orchid, marsh violet, and the beautiful bogbean, amongst others. Earlier in the year, cuckooflowers are abundant (used by green-veined whites as food-plants for their caterpillars), and in early autumn there is a haze of bluish devil's-bit scabious. This is primarily a botanical reserve, though it is also interesting historically as a remnant of a way of farming that has all but disappeared.

been intensively studied ornithologically, and a very long list of birds – including many unusual vagrants – has been recorded. Resident or breeding birds include common choughs, ravens, peregrines, and a strong population of Manx shearwaters. There is a bird observatory, and limited self-catering accommodation. Information and bookings may be obtained from Bardsey Island Trust, Stabal Hen, Tyddyn du, Criccieth, Gwynedd LL52 0LY.

On the mainland opposite Bardsey, the NT coastal land at Mynydd Mawr has some superb displays of coastal flowers, including heather and western gorse in late summer. Further east, there is an important fen (similar to the Anglesey fens in character) at Cors Geirch NNR (SH 315363), noted for its rare plants and insects, including small red and scarce blue-tailed damselflies. Access is by permit only, from CCW.

At the eastern end of the peninsula, on the slopes of the hills as they begin to rise towards Snowdonia, there is an attractive little grassland reserve owned by Plantlife and managed by the WT – Caeau Tan-y-Bwlch (SH 431488). Although only small, this is a lovely site, representing one of the best remaining fragments of old flowery grassland in

Greater butterfly-orchid *Platanthera chlorantha*

SITE 45 Snowdonia (Eryri) National Park

Wales

A large and spectacular mountain NP covering 2142 square kilometres, and occupying about half of the county of Gwynedd.

The Snowdonia NP, the second largest in Britain, includes some of the most spectacular scenery in the country, and a vast range of habitats. Apart from containing the highest mountains in England or Wales, it also includes 37 km of coastline with sand dunes and estuaries, lakes of all sizes, upland and lowland deciduous woodlands, large areas of heath and moor, and many lesser habitats. Although most of the park is in private ownership, there are also a number of nature reserves and other protected areas; the core mountain ones are mentioned here, but more peripheral ones, such as sand dunes, and the isolated mountain mass of Cadair Idris, are treated separately.

The core of the park lies around the peaks of Snowdon itself (Yr Wyddfa), which reaches 1085 m. A large area of the high Snowdonia massif (16 677 ha) is protected as an NNR, covering the best examples of high cliffs, mountain grassland, and upland woodlands, with a good range of plants such as purple saxifrage, moss campion, and several club-mosses. It is also a noted area for lichens, with a number of upland and northern rarities. Most of the Welsh upland breeding birds occur, including ring ouzel, chough (often breeding in disused copper mines), raven, and peregrine. In general, the uplands of Snowdonia are not particularly rich in invertebrates, though there is an attractive leaf beetle known as the Snowdon rainbow beetle which occurs sparingly on wild thyme here, but nowhere else in Britain, and a range of other uncommon upland beetles and spiders.

A separate, smaller NNR to the north at Cwm Idwal (SH 640590) covers about 400 ha of a superb amphitheatre of cliffs around the glacial lake of Llyn Idwal. It is particularly noted as a site for mountain flowers, commencing with purple saxifrage which flowers as the snow melts in spring, and continuing with Snowdon lily (at one of its few British sites), moss campion, globeflower, starry saxifrage, and others.

Further east, the small NNR of Cwm Glas Crafnant lies at the head of the Crafnant Valley (SH 737603). This is a beautiful, quiet spot where red squirrels and pine martens can be seen, as well as a good range of upland insects, and flowers such as grass-of-Parnassus.

Further south in the Park lie the Rhinog Hills, with a rather different character to the main Snowdonia massif. These are more rounded, reaching 720 m at Rhinog Fawr, with scattered, ice-smoothed rock outcrops. They are covered with some of the finest heather moor in the country, scheduled as a Biogenetic Reserve in the European network, and managed as an NNR (SH 640300). Black and red grouse live in the heather, peregrine, merlin, and hen harrier hunt over it, and ravens and

Ring ouzel *Turdus torquatus* (Robert Dickson)

ring ouzels live in the rockier areas. There are several attractive natural lakes in the Rhinogs, of which Llyn Cwm Bychan is one of the most accessible, as well as being a good access point for the hills via some ancient Roman steps. The beautiful blue water lobelia and other upland water plants occur in these lakes.

Although Snowdonia is not particularly well wooded, there are some fine remnants of native oak woodlands, especially in the vale of Ffestiniog. Some are in superb gorges, which provide a humid atmosphere for mosses, liverworts, and ferns to flourish. Ceunant Cynfal (SH 703412), for example, is one of the finest in the country, clothed with luxuriant woodland and intersected by waterfalls. Ceunant Llennyrch (SH 662391) is similar, with spectacular high cliffs; the luxuriant lower plant flora includes Wilson's filmy-fern and hay-scented buckler-fern. Other protected woodlands include reserves at Coed Gorswen (SH 755707) and Coed Dolgarrog (SH 769665) in the vale of Conway, and Coed Ganllwyd (SH 715244) around the Rhaeadr Ddu waterfall, north of Dolgellau. The lovely reserve of Hafod Garregog NNR (SH 600445), south of Beddgelert, has a mixture of woodland, bog, heath, and a small lake, collectively rich in plants and invertebrates such as silver-studded blue butterflies.

SITE
46 Coedydd Maentwrog

Ancient woodland owned by the NT and managed as an NNR by CCW.
Grid ref: SH 665415.

The woods making up this attractive reserve lie in three blocks along the north slopes of the Vale of Ffestiniog, facing roughly southwards across the valley. They rise to about 200 m up the slopes of the Moelwyns, on acidic Cambrian rocks. The whole area has a high rainfall, of about 180 cm annually, which allows a rich bryophyte and fern flora to flourish. The woods are mainly composed of sessile oak and probable hybrids, with birch and rowan as less dominant components. The most westerly of the woods, Coed Llyn Mair, rises above a natural lake – Llyn Mair – which is not part of the reserve, but which certainly adds to its interest.

Typically, as with most acid western oak woods, the flowering plants are not a key feature. Primroses, bluebells, gold-enrod, lesser celandine, and others do

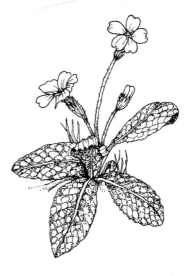

Primrose *Primula vulgaris*

occur, but the combination of acid soils and centuries of overgrazing have limited their numbers. Mosses and liverworts, on the other hand, thrive here and are probably best seen in winter; *Polytrichum* species *Dicranum scoparium*, *Plagiothecium undulatum*, and the attractive feather-moss *Thuidium tamariscinum* are all abundant, together with many others. The lichen flora is also rich.

The range of breeding birds is pretty much as one might expect: pied flycatchers, redstarts, wood warblers, nuthatch, buzzard, green and great spotted woodpeckers, as well as more common woodland species. Amongst the insects, there is a good range of fritillaries including high browns, numerous moths, and a particularly good selection of crane-flies and fungus gnats.

Apart from the natural history value, the woods are lovely places to walk, with superb views southwards. A woodland nature trail guide is available from CCW. The woods are easily found. They lie along the north side of the Vale of Ffestiniog (through which the Afon Dwyryd flows) either side of Maentwrog. The Oakley Arms Hotel on the A487 makes a good starting point. Llyn Mair lies about 2 km up the B4410.

SITE 47 Morfa Harlech and Morfa Dyffryn

Two major sand-dune systems near Harlech, both managed as NNRs.

Morfa Harlech NNR (SH 560350) is the larger and more northerly of the two reserves, covering almost 900 ha. The reserve includes a substantial expanse of saltmarsh and mudflat, as well as one of the most important areas of sand dunes in Wales. There is a rich flora here among both the older stabilized dunes and the more dynamic outer dunes: moonwort, sea spurge, sharp rush, cowslips, various orchids including marsh helleborine, and creeping willow. The most productive patches are usually in the dune slacks where water collects between the dunes.

The dune system as a whole is rich in invertebrates, mainly from less well-known groups, especially beetles, aculeate hymenoptera (solitary bees and wasps), and various flies. The attractive coastal tiger beetle *Cicindela maritima* is quite

Chrysomela populi

frequent, and the pretty red leaf beetle *Chrysomela populi* thrives on creeping willow in the dune slacks. Snail-killing flies abound around the dune-slack lakes, where thousands of aquatic snails become stranded as the lakes dry out each summer. The mudflats and saltmarshes are important for waders and wildfowl at passage periods and in winter. Common frogs, common toads, and grass snakes occur in the wet dune hollows.

Morfa Dyffryn (SH 560250) lies further south, between Harlech and Barmouth. There is an extensive section of old dunes, mainly contained within the NNR, and an area known as Shell Island which shelters an expanse of saltmarsh and mudflats at the mouth of the river. The flora is very rich, with an abundance of flowering plants and lichens in the extensive stabilized areas. It is broadly similar to that of Morffa Harlech, though the presence of green-flowered helleborine and seaside centaury is a bonus.

Access is easy via paths leading southwards from the end of a minor road just west of Llanbedr. There is open access to the shore area.

48 SITE Cadair (Cader) Idris

The southernmost high mountain of the Snowdonia NP, isolated by the Mawddach Estuary. It is partly NNR, partly NT.
Grid ref: SH 7213.

Cadair Idris reaches 893 m and forms a significant mountain mass, large enough to maintain its own climate and support an extensive range of montane habitats. Towards the top, there are high lakes, cliffs, screes, and mountain grassland, while lower down, there are bogs, unimproved grassland, streams, and woodlands of varying character. The higher parts are known for their mountain plants, often growing on cliffs and ledges where sheep cannot reach. These include purple and mossy saxifrages, moss campion, globeflower, Welsh poppy, and spring sandwort. The uncommon hairy greenweed occurs on the lower slopes, at its northernmost locality. There are uncommon ferns, too, including alpine woodsia, forked spleenwort, and green spleenwort, and a reasonable range of mountain mosses and lichens.

Ravens nest on the high crags, and ring ouzels occur in the rocky valleys, together with more widespread moorland birds such as meadow pipits. Overall, it is of considerable interest for its insects and other invertebrates, though most species occur in small numbers. There are colonies of marsh fritillaries on the lower

Moss campion *Silene acaulis*

Wales

slopes, and rare mountain specialists higher up, such as the spider *Micaria alpina*, and the ground beetle *Leistus montanus*.

Unlike Snowdon, there is no easy access to the top of Cadair, but there are several good paths, and the views from the top are spectacular.

In the Mawddach Valley just to the north, there is a Wildlife Information Centre at Penmaenpool (RSPB; SH 695185), open daily at Easter, and from Whitsun to September. The birds here include red-breasted merganser, redstart, and buzzard. Nearby, there are two reserves. Coed Garth Gell (RSPB; SH 687191) is a small oak wood with a river flowing through it, frequented by pied flycatchers, redstarts, wood warblers, and other woodland birds. Arthog Bog (RSPB; SH 619135) is a good example of a coastal bog, with interesting birds and flowers.

Peregrines often hunt here. On the slopes of Cadair Idris, the Cregennen Lakes, or Llynnau Cregennen (NT; SH 659143) are well worth a visit for their attractive setting and range of upland aquatic plants such as water lobelia and shoreweed.

A selection of other important sites in the county

Llyn Padarn Country Park (SH 586602): woodland, quarries; pied flycatcher, redstart, peregrine.

Llyn-y-Parc Woods (SH 791568): forest, river, lake; woodland birds, including goshawk, grey wagtail, dipper.

Powys

49 Lake Vyrnwy

A huge estate of about 10 000 ha, with the reservoir at its core. Owned by Severn Trent Water, but partly declared an NNR (covering 4300 ha) and partly managed by the RSPB. Nominal grid ref: SH 985215.

Lake Vyrnwy is an old reservoir, built in the 1880s to provide water for Liverpool,

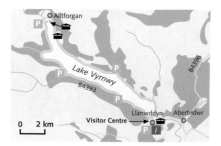

and many of the slopes surrounding it have been planted with conifers. From this unpromising start it has become a major site of interest, and even the dam is now a Grade 1 listed building. In recent years, much of the huge protective estate owned by Severn Trent has been the subject of conservation management and protection under the aegis of CCW and the RSPB. Vast sections are now of considerable importance to wildlife.

The lake itself, though old, is still relatively poor for wildlife thanks to its steep-sided profile, though the north-west end is much shallower and correspondingly better vegetated. The woods are mainly coniferous, managed commercially by Forest Enterprise, though they are by no means lacking in interest, with many breeding birds and mammals, and the tallest Douglas fir in Wales. The farmland is now mainly managed by the RSPB as a nature conservation site, and other parts are managed sympathetically. Hedges and flowery pastures are being restored, and sheep grazing has been much reduced in comparison with most of upland Wales, to provide better wildlife habitats. There is also a huge tract of lightly grazed heather moor – one of the best examples in Wales – on the higher hills.

Altogether, it is now a marvellous area for birds, with about 90 species breeding regularly on the estate, and over 140 occurring at some time or other. The high moors support red and black grouse, merlin, hen harrier, short-eared owl, ring ouzel, and curlew, amongst others, often in good numbers. In the woods, there are crossbills,

Globeflower *Trollius europaeus*

siskins, redpolls, buzzards, tawny owls, and sparrowhawks. Closer to the water, there are breeding goosander, common sandpiper, grey wagtail, dipper. and kingfisher amongst others. Mammals here include polecats; this site was one of this animal's strongholds and the starting point for its recovery and spread eastwards.

Botanically, the site is also surprisingly rich, thanks to the wide range of habitats. Over 200 species have been recorded, including grassland or fen species such as globeflower, yellow-rattle, petty whin,

Lake Vyrnwy , as a storm approaches

Ring ouzel *Turdus torquatus*

pignut, devil's-bit scabious, and heath spotted-orchid. There are bogs and associated marshy areas in many of the tributary valleys, and here you can find common butterwort, lousewort, sundew, bog asphodel, bog pimpernel, cottongrass and starry saxifrage. Lesser twayblade (an uncommon upland orchid) and cloudberry have been identified as two species that occur on the higher moorlands, and are in need of special protection here. Finally, there are also good numbers of butterflies, with 24 species recorded, including large heath and several fritillaries, and it looks set to prove of interest for other invertebrate groups, too.

Lake Vyrnwy is well sign-posted from the Dolgellau–Welshpool A458 road, or may be reached by minor roads from Bala to the north.

The Berwyn Mountains, and in particular the huge Y Berwyn NNR covering 3239 ha (SJ 300001) lie just north of Vyrnwy. They are one of the major sites for breeding upland birds in Wales, including red and black grouse, hen harrier, merlin, golden plover, and peregrine.

Roundton Hill reserve (WT; SO 293947, OS 137) is an attractive craggy hill with woodland and grassland, and noted for its plants. The grassland is largely ancient and becomes very dry in summer, so some of the plants that do well here are winter annuals. Specialities include shepherd's cress, upright chickweed, mountain pansy, and lesser chickweed. Sign-posted from the A489 from near Church Stoke.

Llanymynech Rocks reserve (WT; SJ 265220, OS 126) is an old limestone quarry, now rich in flowers and insects. Cowslips, early purple, bee, and pyramidal orchids, yellow-wort, and carline thistle make a fine display. Reached by a lane from the small village of Pant, on the A483 south of Oswestry.

SITE 50 Glaslyn

The flagship reserve of the WT, covering 216 ha of mixed upland habitats.
Grid ref: SN 828942.

This substantial reserve, not far from the town of Machynlleth, has a large expanse of heather moorland at its core, dominating the northern part of the reserve and dropping away northwards through rocky slopes into a deep ravine where the Afon Dulas flows (there is no access to the ravine). The moorland areas are home to red grouse, short-eared owls, meadow pipits, ring ouzels, golden plover, and wheatears, and birds of prey such as

merlin, peregrine, and red kite can often be seen hunting over them.

Southwards from the main moorland area, there is an attractive, though rather acid and species-poor lake. It supports an uncommon fern relative called quillwort, which is virtually confined to shallow upland lakes in Britain. Around the lake, and southwards to the reserve boundary, there is a mosaic of moorland, grassland, and bog, where sundew,

Merlin *Falco columbarius* (Mike Powles)

common butterwort, cross-leaved heath, and cottongrass grow.

There is open access to the reserve, except for the ravine, and a good viewpoint above the lake.

Eastwards across the county, near Montgomery, is Dolydd Hafren reserve (WT; SJ 208005), also open to the public. It is based around some of the loops of the river Severn, which has formed oxbow lakes at this point. The resulting lakes and marshy areas are excellent for birds, especially in winter and at passage periods, when good quantities of waders and wildfowl may visit. Otters turn up regularly, and may occasionally be seen from the more easterly of the two hides. Brown hares are frequent in the fields, and the damper areas are good for flowers and insects.

Wales

SITE 51 Nant Irfon

A mixed upland NNR, covering 142 ha, at the southern end of the vast Elenydd protected area.

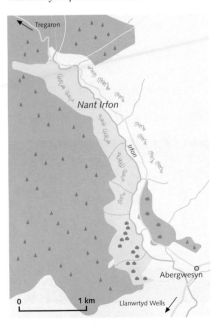

Although CCW classify this site as a woodland reserve, Nant Irfon (SN 840550) is actually a lovely mixture of upland habitats. It lies in a spectacular rocky valley that is partly clothed in some of the highest sessile oak woodland in Wales, growing close to its altitudinal limit. Within the reserve, there are also extensive areas of pasture, meadows, flushes, and upland streams.

The woodland is very humid (thanks to an annual rainfall of over 2000 mm), and has a luxuriant flora of mosses, liverworts, lichens, and the curious little Wilson's filmy-fern, which can only survive in high humidity. It has the usual range of breeding birds, including pied flycatcher, redstart, wheatear, wood warbler, and buzzard. The uplands have red kite, peregrine, merlin and short-eared owl and there is a red kite feeding station near Llanwrtyd Wells.

Wales

Wheatear *Oenanthe oenanthe* (Mike Lane)

The damp grassland sections have the most botanical interest, with globeflower, the pretty little ivy-leaved bellflower, sundews, common butterwort, bog asphodel, fragrant orchids, and the declining alpine and fir club-mosses, amongst others. The whole area is good for invertebrates, with dragonflies such as golden-ringed, butterflies such as pearl-bordered fritillary and purple hairstreak (amongst the oaks), and 26 species of caddis fly, to name but a few.

There are no public footpaths but general access is permitted, with entry points at either end of the reserve.

The reserve lies at the southern end of the vast Elenydd SSSI. This includes the 6670 ha of Abergwesyn Common, owned by the NT, which is probably the largest single open space in the country. It also includes Claerwen NNR (SN 830690), which protects one of the more varied parts of the area, including peat bog, moorland, and upland grassland, with breeding dunlin and golden plover.

SITE
52 Brecon Beacons National Park

Spectacular and varied mountain countryside covering 1351 square kilometres.

The Brecon Beacons are the most southerly range of significant mountains in Britain, reaching 886 m at Pen-y-Fan. The NP exists to conserve both the high parts of the Beacons themselves and much of the surrounding countryside, from Llandeilo in the west to the borders of England in the east. The uplands are composed mainly of hard, old red sandstone, and these are ringed by Carboniferous limestone outcrops, which provide a contrast in scenery and flora as well as harbouring numerous caves. The whole area is relatively unspoilt, with many small, hedged fields, hedgerow trees, and tracts of woodland.

The higher areas are mainly extensively grazed by sheep, and carpeted with uniform grassland of mat grass, bents, and cottongrass, like much of upland Wales. Where the ground is more broken, it is

Pied flycatcher *Ficedula hypoleuca*

The heavily-glaciated summit ridge of the Brecon Beacons (Peter Wilson)

possible to see what the flora must have once been like. For example, the northern side of the beacons has been strikingly sculpted by glacial action into high corrie cliffs (it is possible to be completely unaware of these when approaching from the south!), which are home to purple and mossy saxifrages, globeflowers, and other mountain species.

The whole park is notable both scenically and ecologically, but within it there are a number of specially protected areas which provide focal points. Craig Cerrig-Gleisiad a Fan Frynych NNR (SN 960230) covers about 500 ha of some of the best glaciated scenery in the park. Its high rocky cliffs and screes provide homes for over 500 species of plants, including arctic-alpines at the southern edge of their range in Britain, such as purple saxifrage. Peregrines, ravens, ring ouzels, buzzards, and other birds breed here, and 16 species of butterfly have been recorded. It is also an excellent place to study geomorphology and landform, with the recent history of the land clearly visible in its structure. Lower down to the west, the Ogof Fynnon Ddu NNR (SN 870165) protects one of the finest cave systems in the country, with a

surprising range of specialized and visiting wildlife. The cave extends to 45 km of passages, over a depth of about 300 m, but it can only be visited with a permit from CCW. However, the reserve also includes a fine example of limestone pavement and associated limestone habitats within its 420 ha, including the clints and grikes more typical of the limestone pavements of north-west England. There is access on foot to any of the above-ground parts of the reserve.

Craig-y-Cilau NNR (SO 187158) lies in the south-east corner of the park, and contains one of the best limestone cliffs in Wales in a quite spectacular setting. The reserve also contains an extensive cave system, which includes a winter roost for large numbers of lesser horseshoe bats. The cliffs are home to a range of unusual plants, including the extremely rare least whitebeam at its only site in the world, and alpine enchanter's-nightshade at its most southerly UK location. Within the reserve, there are also interesting patches of bog and grassland, and small areas of open woodland. Some 25 species of butterfly have been recorded, and birds such as peregrine,

Wales

ring ouzel, and redstart breed here. It is superb for walking as well as being a good place to see a range of wildlife. There is open access to the above-ground parts of the reserve on a network of footpaths.

In the north-east of the park is the lovely small woodland reserve called Pwll-y-wrach (WT; SO 165326), near Talgarth. It consists mainly of broadleaved woodland in a small, steep-sided valley, with an attractive waterfall. There is a rich flora here, including herb-Paris and carpets of bluebells, while pied flycatchers and wood

warblers call, and dippers fly along the stream. Talybont Reservoir (SO 098190), west of Llangynidr, is well known as a good winter wildfowl site, partly protected as a nature reserve.

One further location in the park that is worth a visit for its spectacular combination of scenery, waterfalls, and wildlife is the valley of the Afon Mellte southwards from Ystradfellte (SN 930135).

Other NNRs within the park are covered under Gwent. Llangorse Lake is treated as a separate site (below).

SITE 53 Llangorse Lake

A shallow lowland lake east of Brecon. Grid ref: SO 133262.

Although Llangorse Lake lies within the Brecon Beacons NP, it is very different from the mountain areas of the park, and significant enough to be looked at sepa-

rately. It is a quite large, natural shallow lake, with a circumference of about 8 km, naturally eutrophic, and considered to be of national importance. It has long been

Cattle at lake

Wales

known for its aquatic plant life and breeding birds; at one time it looked as though a combination of over-use for recreation and pollution from agricultural run-off was set to destroy much of its value; to some extent this problem has been conquered, but not before a few species had been lost. Interestingly, the whole lake surface, together with some adjacent land, is registered as common land, and has been known since medieval times as a place where fish and birds abounded.

Nowadays, it is fringed in places with reeds, and parts of the surface are covered with yellow and white water-lilies, and a variety of pondweeds. There are 23 plants here that are rare in Wales, plus a further 15 that are rare locally; these include greater spearwort, narrow-leaved water-plantain, golden dock, fringed water-lily, and a good range of duckweeds and pondweeds. There is a rich fish fauna, including perch, roach, pike, bream and tench, and it was once noted for its huge eels. Breeding birds include a large population of reed warblers, reed buntings, great-crested and little grebes, and various other waterside birds, and in winter there can be good numbers of waterfowl feeding and roosting here. It is also a good place for some of the more common lowland dragonflies such as southern hawker and common darters.

Access is limited, but there is a car park (SO 128271) just south-west of Llangorse village, and footpaths around parts of the perimeter.

A selection of other important sites in the county

Cors y Llyn NNR (SO 016553), north of Builth Wells, is a small area of bog, wet grassland, and herb-rich pasture. Footpaths pass close to the site. Permit to visit required from CCW.

Gilfach Farm (WT; SN 965717; 169 ha) is a substantial farm run as a nature reserve, about 5 km north of Rhayader. It has a fine mixture of habitats: woodland, grassland, river, rocky outcrops, and an old railway tunnel used by five species of bat. Dippers and common sandpipers nest along the river, with pied flycatchers and redstarts in the woods, and whinchat, wheatear, and stonechat on the hills above, to name just a few. The grasslands are bright with flowers, and the river gorge is good for bryophytes. There is a visitor centre, waymarked trail, and information boards.

Rhos Goch NNR (SO 190480), east of Builth Wells, close to the English border, is rather similar. Permit to visit required from CCW.

Dyfed

SITE
54 Dyfi Estuary

A marvellous mixture of estuary habitats protected in three main reserves at the mouth of the Dyfi river, west of Machynlleth.

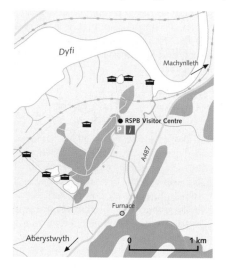

The Dyfi Estuary is not only beautiful and unspoilt, but it also contains a superb mixture of habitats, collectively recognized as being an internationally important Biosphere Reserve. The three key reserves, covering thousands of hectares between them are: Dyfi NNR, which includes Ynyslas sand dunes (SN 640955); Cors Fochno bog NNR, which lies immediately south of Dyfi and has very limited public access; and Ynys-hir reserve (RSPB; SN 683963), a little further up the estuary. Anywhere within this area is worth a visit.

The whole area is good for birds at all times, though the estuary does not attract the numbers that the Dee or some of the English estuaries do. Probably the best place to see birds easily is on the RSPB reserve, where there are a nature trail and

hides overlooking wetlands. The reserve's attractive mixture of habitats (saltmarsh, open water, wetland, woodland, and grassland) supports about 70 breeding species including pied flycatchers, redstart, water rail, red-breasted merganser, common sandpiper, and all three woodpeckers. Small quantities of waders and wildfowl can be seen in autumn and winter, including some Greenland white-fronted geese – it is the only regular wintering site for this race south of the Scottish border. It is also a good place for otters and polecats, though you would be lucky to see either. Over 30 species of butterfly have been recorded, including pearl-bordered, dark green, and marsh fritillaries.

The dunes at Ynyslas, within Dyfi reserve, are a superb example of a dune system, rich in plants and animals. There is an information centre at Ynyslas, manned in summer, and with a pro-

Pied flycatcher *Ficedula hypoleuca*

Ynys-hir

gramme of guided walks between Easter and September. There is a full range of dune habitats, from foreshore to stable dunes, including wet dune slacks, and a correspondingly wide range of flowers and insects, such as marsh helleborine, early marsh-orchid, bee orchid, cowslips, and, amongst butterflies, dark green fritillary and grayling.

Cors Fochno is a marvellous example of a bog, with a full complement of bog species. Permits to visit it, and further information, can be obtained at the Ynyslas centre or direct from CCW.

55 Coed Simdde Lwyd

SITE

A steep woodland reserve, managed by the WT, and declared as an NNR.
Grid ref: SN 713787.

This south-facing block of woodland, covering 36 ha, is part of a larger tract of surviving natural woodland within the Rheidol Valley east of Aberystwyth, much of it worth a visit.

It is primarily oak woodland, dominated by sessile oak (see box below), with some birch, rowan, alder, ash, wych elm, and even a little small-leaved lime – the latter an excellent indicator of

Wales

Rheidol Valley

ancient woodland where it grows naturally. The usual range of western
oak-wood breeding birds can be found
here, including pied flycatcher, redstart,
wood warbler, buzzard, and raven, and
red kites are not infrequently seen overhead. It is not a particularly rich area for
flowers, as the soil is rather acid, though
there is wood-sorrel, yellow pimpernel,
sheep's-bit, and common cow-wheat,
amongst others. It is a good area for
bryophytes and lichens, though being
south-facing it does not have the luxuri-
ance of some of the north-facing or
gorge woodlands. In the wider region,
including parts outside this reserve,
there is a good range of butterflies,
including purple hairstreak and pearl-
bordered fritillaries.

There are good footpaths through the
wood, and parking at the western end,
near where there is a waterfall.

Common oak *Quercus robur* and sessile oak *Q. petraea*

The two species of native oak in
Britain are rather similar and easily
confused. Sessile oak is commonest in
upland areas; it has leaves with stalks
1 to 2.5 cm long, but unstalked acorns.
Common (or pedunculate) oak has
virtually stalkless leaves, but the
acorns are clustered at the end of a
stalk up to 10 cm long. In general, sessile oak is a straighter tree, and the
leaves are slightly different; common
oak has distinct auricles (ears) at the
leaf base, while the base of a sessile
oak leaf tapers gradually into the stalk.
Intermediate trees of presumed
hybrid origin are common in areas
where both species occur.

56 Cors Caron (Tregaron Bog)

A superb bog, just north of the small town of Tregaron, in the valley of the Teifi. Nominal grid ref: SN 690640.

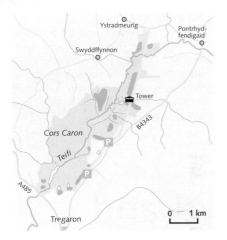

Cors Caron is a remarkable place, one of the finest examples of a bog in lowland Britain. By British standards it is huge (over 800 ha), stretching away into the distance, filling the wide valley of the Teifi River. Since 1993, it has been nominated as one of Britain's internationally important Ramsar Sites. It is primarily a true raised bog; that is, it has gradually raised itself, over thousands of years of development, well above the water table, and is now fed largely by rainwater. Most such bogs in accessible places have been drained or cut for peat, and are in poor condition; parts of Tregaron have been used in the past for peat cutting, though

One of the newly-restored areas at Cors Caron

Wales

not since 1960, and much of the bog was unaffected by it. Parts of the bog that were damaged by peat cutting are currently being restored by raising the water table locally and allowing bog-moss to become dominant again.

The bog has most of the plants you would expect in a prime site, including crowberry, the beautiful little cranberry, bog asphodel, all three British sundew species, white beak-sedge, and the cottongrasses, amongst others. At one time polecats were almost confined to this area of Wales, though they are now spreading again, and this valley remains an important centre. Water voles, otters, and water shrews are all resident, and there is a rich and varied fish population in the Teifi. This part of Wales is still the stronghold of the red kite, and they can often be seen soaring overhead. About 40 species of birds breed on the reserve.

Access is limited, because of the fragile and rather dangerous nature of the habitat. There is a good walk on the eastern edge of the bog on the old railway line, and it is also possible to get a permit to walk on the longer riverside walk, which gives closer encounters with the bog itself. Permits may be obtained from the warden on 01794 298480.

Not far to the north-west is the Llyn Eiddwen reserve (West Wales Naturalists Trust; SN 606674). This is a remarkably unspoilt lake, with many uncommon plants such as awlwort, least bur-reed, shoreweed, water lobelia, and lesser and floating water-plantains.

57 Gwenffrwd and Dinas

A pair of RSPB reserves a few kilometres apart, between them covering almost 500 ha of fine upland and woodland.
Grid ref: SN 787470.

These two lovely reserves cover a fine range of the best of the upland habitats of mid-Wales. Dinas, the smaller, more easterly site, is almost wholly upland oak wood on a wooded knoll, while Gwenffrwd includes a wider range of hill habitats such as upland grassland and scrub. The whole area is very beautiful, lying in the hilly country of the upper Tywi valley.

These are classic western upland bird sites, with redstarts, wood warblers, woodcock, tree pipits, all three woodpeckers, and pied flycatchers in the wooded areas; the population of the last-named has been greatly increased by the use of nest boxes. Along the river and tributaries, there are breeding common sandpipers, grey wagtail, dipper, and goosander, with sand martins nearby. Buzzards are frequent, of course (they are an ever-present feature in mid-Wales), together with ravens, and red kites are often seen.

On the moorland stretches above the woods at Gwenffrwd, there are boggy areas with bog asphodel, marsh St John's-wort, bog pimpernel, and other plants of acid wet places. Wheatear, red grouse, and stonechat call from the heather, and skylarks sing overhead. The woods are rich in ferns, bryophytes, and lichens, with relatively few flowers, like most acid upland woods. Ferns of particular interest

Wales

Ivy-leaved bellflower *Wahlenbergia hederacea*

include oak fern, lemon-scented fern, and Wilson's filmy-fern, a very delicate plant looking rather like a liverwort. There are bluebells in places, and the pretty little ivy-leaved bellflower occurs in more open grassy places.

There are resident polecats, and otters along the streams feeding on brown trout or migrating sea trout and salmon. The lovely little smoky-winged beautiful demoiselle (damselfly) occurs along the streams where there is dappled sunlight, and the larger and more powerful golden-ringed dragonflies can turn up anywhere, though their larval habitat is in the faster-flowing streams. There are purple hairstreaks

among the oaks, small heaths on the grassy areas, and several fritillaries occur here.

Access is easy via minor roads north from Llandovery to Rhandirmwyn, bearing right on the Llyn Brianne road for Dinas or left on the Lampeter road for Gwenffrwd. Both sites have nature trails and longer walks.

The whole area is very attractive, with numerous walks and drives.

A little to the west is the upland woodland reserve of Allt Rhyd y Groes NNR (SN 760480; 70 ha) which lies along a rocky valley side. 'Allt' means wooded hillside, which accurately describes this dramatic reserve, where ancient sessile oak woodland grows along a steep, north-facing slope, falling sharply towards a river. The woodland itself is humid and shady, providing ideal conditions for ferns, mosses, lichens, and other plants. The list of species here includes Wilson's filmy-fern, beech fern, oak fern, the increasingly rare stag's-horn club-moss, alpine club-moss, and many others. Pied flycatchers, redstarts, wood warblers, dippers, grey wagtails, and many more common birds breed here, and the woodland is alive with birdsong in the spring. May is an ideal time to visit, as there are carpets of bluebells then as well. Below the woods, there is a series of flowery meadows, with unusual plants such as wood bitter-vetch, greater butterfly-orchid, and dyer's greenweed, giving beautiful displays in June. There is free access to the reserve along various paths.

58 Welsh Wildlife Centre

SITE

A fascinating combination of an important reserve and an award-winning interactive visitor centre. Grid ref: SN 184455.

For the casual naturalist or family on an outing, this is the perfect easy introduction to Welsh wildlife. The visitor centre (which is open every day from April to

October, or by arrangement in winter for groups) has displays, exhibitions, and information about the reserve and Welsh wildlife in general; there are occupied

Wales

Lobaria pulmonaria

It is one of the best places in Wales to see otters in the wild, thanks to a strategically placed hide as well as the artificial holt. There is also a good range of flowers, butterflies, and dragonflies, together with badger setts, deer, and resident bats. Surprisingly, the centre is only about 2 km from Cardigan, from where it is well sign-posted.

Nearby, Coedmor NNR (SN 193436) contains a fine tract of ancient woodland, particularly rich in lichens (with almost 200 species, including the impressive lungwort *Lobaria pulmonaria*), and with a good range of butterflies and dragonflies such as the rare club-tailed dragonfly.

otter holts and owl boxes, discovery trails, and a series of hides. Many of the trails are suitable for wheelchair use. There is also a good café, and a cottage that can be booked for accommodation. The whole site is run by the Wildlife Trust, West Wales who can be contacted for bookings or information at their main office in Haverfordwest. Tel: 01437 765462; fax: 01437 767163.

For the more serious naturalist, there is a fine range of habitats within the 105-ha reserve, including old woodland, lagoons, riverside habitats, wildflower meadow, and a gorge. Birds include grey heron, Cetti's warbler, reed warbler, tawny owl, and a good range of wildfowl and waders. Red kites, peregrines, marsh harriers, and other birds of prey visit for the rich pickings here.

Another NNR, Rhos Llawr Cwrt (SN 411499) protects an outstanding stretch of upland grassland, with abundant flowers and insects, but a permit is required from CCW for a visit.

Otter *Lutra lutra*

59 Pembrokeshire Coast National Park

A spectacular coastline, islands, and inland areas of mountain, moorland, and woodland.

The Pembrokeshire NP covers 620 square kilometres of south-west Wales. It includes about 270 km of varied and beautiful coastline, all the nearby offshore islands such as Skomer, Skokholm, and Caldey, and substantial parts of the

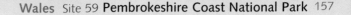

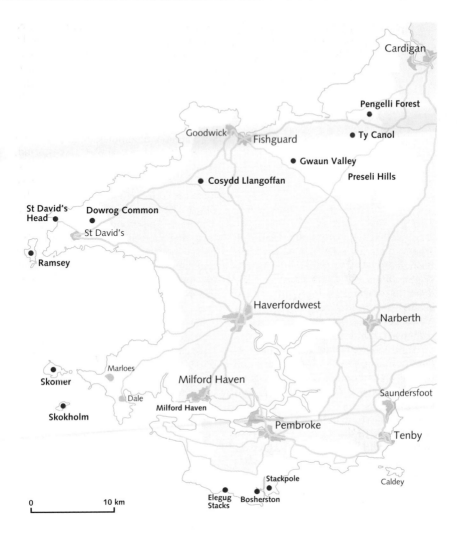

Cardigan

Pengelli Forest
•

Goodwick
Fishguard   • Ty Canol

• Gwaun Valley

• Cosydd Llangoffan   Preseli Hills

St David's   Dowrog Common
Head •   •
        St David's

•
Ramsey

Haverfordwest
                        Narberth

        Marloes
•   Milford Haven
Skomer
            Dale   Saundersfoot
•   Milford Haven
Skokholm   Pembroke
                                    Tenby

                    Stackpole
0   10 km   Caldey
                Elegug   Bosherston
                Stacks

Wales

Preseli Hills and Gwaun Valley. Overall, the park contains one of the highest densities of protected locations in Europe, with dozens of nature reserves, SSSIs, and other nationally or internationally recognized sites.

The coastline is the NP's greatest glory. The simple statistic of '270 km of varied and beautiful coastline' belies an enormous wealth of beauty and ecological value that cannot be described in detail here. It is best appreciated from the 299 km of official coast path that spans the whole park coastline, which is accessible at many points around the coast. Although the whole coast is of interest, we have selected a few special areas which are particularly rich in wildlife. In the early 1980s, native service-tree was discovered on the Pembrokeshire cliffs.

The area south of Pembroke has a considerable stretch of limestone outcrops which gives it a different character from the rest of the park. At Bosherston, the NT owns a large estate which includes Stackpole NNR (SR 983947), an area of great variety and beauty. Stackpole Warren is a fascinating sandy site, with

Wales

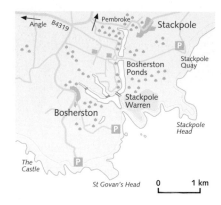

characteristics of the adjacent mainland including, often, spectacular displays of coastal flowers. But, in addition, they have marvellous colonies of seabirds, thanks to the absence of predators, and all are home to substantial populations of grey seals. Each is rather different in character.

Skokholm is one of the smaller islands, with an area of about 100 ha. It is made up of old red sandstone, and has less spectacular cliffs than Skomer, with fewer cliff-nesting birds, but this is counterbalanced by the large numbers of puffins, Manx shearwater, and storm petrels. There are superb displays of flowers including bluebells, and it is a great place to watch offshore mammals such as seals and common porpoises. There is a bird observatory, and accommodation which can be arranged through the Wildlife Trust, West Wales (see p. 361 for details).

Skomer is larger, with better seabird cliffs that support vast numbers of razorbills, guillemots, fulmars, and kittiwakes, plus large numbers of puffins, storm petrels, and Manx shearwaters. Other birds include peregrine, choughs, short-eared owls (which feed on the endemic Skomer vole – a subspecies of bank vole), and ravens. About 200 species of flowering plant have been recorded, and there are some excellent displays, especially in early summer. Skomer is open to day-trips by boat from Martinshaven (these may be booked in St David's, or on 01646 601636 – the Dale Sailing Company), but

many archaeological remains, and rare plants such as least restharrow. The Bosherston lakes, despite their artificial origin about 200 years ago from the damming of a small estuary, are of great ecological interest; parts have become typical marl lakes, with extensive beds of stoneworts. Their best-known feature is the impressive displays of white water-lilies in midsummer on the western and central lakes, though it is also a good place for otters, waterside birds, and many flowers and insects. Westwards from Bosherston, there are high cliffs with offshore rocks, largely on Ministry of Defence land, with fine displays of coastal flowers and good seabird colonies at places like Elegug Stacks (SR 926945).

Milford Haven, to the north and west of Stackpole, tends to be overlooked because of its partly industrial nature, but it is a fine winter bird site with a number of protected woodlands and other habitats around it, and some of it falls within a new Special Area of Conservation, indicating its value in a European context. Incidentally, it should be mentioned that virtually the whole of the Pembrokeshire coast has quite outstanding seashore and offshore marine life.

At the extreme western tip of the park lie the most important of the islands, all within the park: Skokholm, Skomer, Grassholm, and Ramsey, together with various smaller islands. They share many of the

Chough *Pyrrhocorax pyrrhocorax* (Mike Lane)

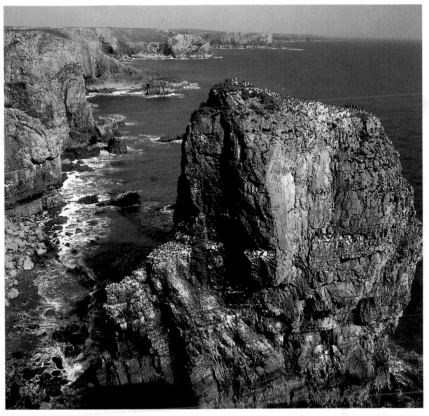

Elegug Stacks

there are many advantages to staying longer, not least the opportunity to hear the shearwaters and petrels which only come in at night; contact the Wildlife Trust, West Wales as above for details.

Grassholm is smaller and much further offshore, such that trips to it may often be cancelled in bad weather. It is the site of one of the finest gannet colonies in Britain, with about 30 000 pairs in 10 ha, together with a few other seabirds and some grey seals. The journey out and back provides good opportunities for seeing shearwaters at sea, and passing cetaceans or even basking sharks. Landing trips are limited now to avoid disturbance, and may be arranged through the RSPB regional office (01686 626678) or the Dale Sailing Company, as above.

Ramsey is the largest of this group, at 242 ha. It is a flat-topped island, covered with heath and grassland and ringed with cliffs. It is now run by the RSPB as a reserve, particularly noted for breeding common chough, and the large numbers

Grey seals *Halichoerus grypus*

Wales

Hermit crab *Pagurus bernhardus*

of grey seals that haul ashore in the autumn to breed. Many other birds breed or visit, and there is always something to see here. More information may be obtained from the RSPB as above, or from Thousand Islands on 01437 721686.

Although barely larger than a village, the cathedral city of St. David's is a fascinating place, well worth a visit in its own right and a good base for exploring the park. Just north-east of it lies Dowrog Common (NT; SM 775273), managed as a nature reserve. It is similar in character to the Dorset heaths (see p. 202) with many of the same species, including a range of damselflies and dragonflies such as small red damselfly, scarce blue-tailed damselfly, beautiful demoiselle, and keeled skimmer, good grasshoppers and crickets, and some rare flies. There is a fine heathland and bog flora, including yellow centaury, and characteristic heathland birds such as stonechats.

Other sites within the park that should be mentioned include the Preseli Hills, south-west of Cardigan, with extensive moorland, grassland and bog; Ty Canol NNR (SN 090370) for its superb ancient woodland on rocky slopes, with an exceptional lichen flora of about 400 species; and St David's Head (SM 734272) for its marvellous coastal heathland, cliffs, and cliff-top flowers and birds. Cosydd Llangoffan NNR (SM 904318) is a wetland reserve just outside the park, but visits are by permit only from CCW. Pengelli Forest (SN 124395) is a fine tract of ancient woodland with good access, managed as a nature reserve, just outside the park's eastern boundary.

A selection of other important sites in the county

Castle Woods (SN 615217): mixed deciduous woods; woodland birds and flowers.

Llanelli (SS 533984): wetland, mudflats; waders, wildfowl.

Glamorgan

<small>SITE</small>
60 Gower Peninsula

*A beautiful and varied peninsula extending south-westwards
from Swansea.*

Gower Peninsula is a superbly varied and historic area, despite its proximity to Swansea, and its popularity with holiday-makers. Within a relatively small territory, it encompasses a wonderful range of high quality habitats, protected by 3 NNRs, 3 LNRs, and 22 SSSIs, with everything else being protected by Heritage Coast or AONB designation, or NT ownership. Habitats within the peninsula include saltmarshes, dunes, limestone and other cliffs, common land, ancient woodland, open water, fore-shore, and moorland. The highest point is The Beacon on Rhossili Down, 193 m high and with marvellous views. The whole southern coast, in particular, has an excep-tional intertidal flora and fauna, and for this reason is popular with naturalists, chil-dren, bait diggers, and seaweed collectors.

Oxwich Bay NNR (SS 506870) provides a fine introduction to the peninsula. Its 300 or so hectares includes some superb dunes, with well-developed dune slacks, open water, limestone woodland, grass-land, and excellent adjacent intertidal

Yellow whitlowgrass *Draba aizoides* (Peter Wilson)

areas, all sheltered from the prevailing winds by Oxwich head. The flora is superb, with marvellous displays in the dune slacks in June. Species of interest here include round-leaved wintergreen, dune gentian, and a variety of orchids, while in the woods there are stinking hellebore, rock whitebeam, and small-leaved lime. In all, about 600 species of plants have been recorded. Cetti's war-blers are now resident, together with many other wetland and woodland birds. It is an exceptional site for invertebrates, of national importance, with an abun-dance of dragonflies including hairy dragonfly, a rare strand-line beetle *Nebria complanata*, the local Cepero's ground-hopper, and fine assemblages of solitary hymenoptera (such as mining bees) in the western cliffs. Butterflies include dark green and silver-washed fritillaries, and white-letter hairstreaks. The intertidal life includes an abundance of different sea-weeds, porcelain crabs, blue-rayed limpets, and hundreds of other species.

Westwards from Oxwich as far as Worm's Head there is a marvellous line of

Dark green fritillary *Argynnis aglaja*
(Alec S. Harmer)

Wales

Limpets *Patella vulgata* and barnacles
Semibalanus balanoides

limestone cliffs, with a particularly rich flora, and several reserves within it such as the 'South Gower cliffs' reserve (WT; SS 470844) west of Port Eynon, and the Gower coast NNR (SS 405873). Plants to be found here, sometimes in abundance, include spring squill, the rare yellow whitlowgrass, hoary rock-rose, green-winged orchids, rock sea-lavender, golden-samphire, small restharrow, wild cabbage, goldilocks aster, and spring cinquefoil – just to whet the appetite! It is also a good place for watching birds at sea, and occasional mammals, and the whole intertidal area is very rich. Choughs are tentatively returning to breed, and peregrines are regular.

From Worm's head, the great sweep of Rhossili Bay curves north, with dunes at its northern tip, followed by Broughton Bay which grades northwards into Whiteford Burrows. Whiteford NNR (SS 450955) marks a major transition point on Gower,

with harsher Atlantic conditions to the west and south, and the shelter of the Burry inlet to the north and east. Whiteford NNR contains a huge area of sand dunes, with many rare plants such as dune gentian and fen orchid amongst 250 or so other species. Eastwards lie the salt-marshes and mudflats, which can only develop thanks to the shelter provided by Whiteford Burrows. The number of birds visiting the Burry inlet can be huge, especially in winter when very large flocks of waders are often recorded. The transition between the dunes and the saltmarsh is occupied by an extensive seepage marsh – one of the best in Britain – which is home to a number of rare flies and other insects.

Just across the inlet, and readily visible from Whiteford, lies Pembrey Burrows and Forest (SN 3902). Although not on the Gower (and actually in Dyfed), the habitat is rather similar, with some excellent dunes. The forest consists mainly of Corsican pines on former dunes, but the combination of broad rides, sheltered glades, and some open water has made this into an excellent site for butterflies and some other insects. Plants of interest include fen orchid, bee orchid, marsh helleborine, moonwort, and lesser water-plantain, amongst many others. It is managed as a forest nature reserve.

SITE 61 Crymlyn Bog

A large urban fringe NNR, mainly fen, covering 1150 ha.
Grid ref: SS 695945.

Crymlyn Bog is a remarkable place. It lies in a valley just north of Swansea docks, hemmed in by industry, tips, and ware-housing. For years it was constantly threatened with damage and drainage, though now at last it is well-protected as an NNR. It is the largest area of lowland fen in

Wales, and the third largest in Britain, more akin to the best East Anglian fens than anywhere else. The vegetation here includes rich fen, reedbed, open water, and unimproved old pasture with anthills.

The bog is best known for its plant life, with typical fen species such as great fen-

General view looking east across the bog

sedge, slender cottongrass, sundews, lesser bladderwort, several marsh-orchids, bog pimpernel, marsh lousewort, and royal fern. Breeding birds include large populations of reed and sedge warblers (see box below), reed buntings, water rail, and other wetland species, while marsh harrier, peregrine, buzzard, and merlin can be seen hunting over the site at times. There is a large autumn pre-migration roost of swallows in the reeds – a marvellous sight as they fly in during the evening. It is a good place to see the rare hornet robberfly, Britain's largest fly, which occurs in the old pastures. It often perches on pony dung, where the females lay their eggs. Green woodpeckers also feed in these old pastures; they hunt for ants in the old anthills and leave their curious droppings, which look like cigar ash and are full of ant remains!

Access is via minor roads leading off the A4217 and A483 around Kilvey Hill. There is a visitor centre on the west side of the reserve. Eastwards, the bog extends into Pant-y-Sais LNR (SS 716942). Just north-east of Swansea is the Cwm Clydach reserve (RSPB; SS 685026) with oak woodland, heather moorland, and a stream. Park by the New Inn just north of Clydach.

Sedge and reed warblers

Sedge warblers and reed warblers are both summer visitors to Britain, breeding in rather similar places, especially reedbeds. They can be hard to see, and their songs are rather similar. They are easy enough to separate with a good view: the sedge warbler has a distinct light eyebrow topped with a dark crown (both absent from the reed warbler), and is generally more boldly marked. The songs can only be distinguished with difficulty; that of the sedge warbler tends to be more varied and insistent, a mixture of harsh and melodic notes, with more mimicry, often continuing for long periods.

Wales

SITE
62 Kenfig Pool and dunes

518 ha of dunes, with a large lake, recently declared an NNR.
Grid ref: SS 780820.

The dunes at Kenfig, despite being so close to Porthcawl and Port Talbot, have long been recognized as a major conservation site, managed since 1978 as an LNR and recently given national status. There is a very large area of calcareous dunes in all stages, with dune slacks and a 28-ha lake known as Kenfig Pool.

The site has an extremely rich flora and fauna. Over 500 species of flowers have been recorded, including early and southern marsh-orchids, marsh helleborine, fen orchid, and round-leaved wintergreen in the dune slacks, adder's-tongue, green-winged orchid, restharrow,

and burnet rose in the stable dune pastures, and typical dune plants such as sea-holly and sea spurge in the more open patches. Around the lakes, there is purple-loosestrife, yellow iris, marsh-marigold, creeping willow, and others, whilst in the water there are four species of pondweed, stoneworts, and amphibious bistort. Dunes can be surprisingly good for fungi, and there is a good range here, including the spring-fruiting morel. There is an enormous range of insects, with at least 20 species of dragonflies, most of the butterflies you would expect, including dark green fritillary, grayling,

Kenfig Pool

and brimstone. There is a particularly rare weevil, *Tychius quinquepunctatus*, that occurs only in a few other places.

It is not a great site for birds or mammals, though a range of more common species breeds, and the pool and saltmarsh attract quite a number of waders and wildfowl in winter and at passage periods.

Access is open, apart from a few areas that may be fenced off, and there is a good information centre, with guided walks available.

Not far away, the WT has its HQ and a large reserve at Parc Slip (SS 880840). Here 100 ha of mined land have been restored to a fine complex of flowery grassland, marsh, and open water, with developing woodland. There are nature trails, three hides, and a good new visitor centre.

A selection of other important sites in the county

Aberthaw Saltmarsh (ST 045657): cliffs, saltmarsh; seabirds, waders.

Cwm Col-Huw (SS 957674): grassland, woodland, cliff; peregrine, fulmar, migrants.

Lavernock Point (ST 182680): cliff, grassland, scrub; seabirds, migrants.

Llyn Fach (SN 905038): lake, bog, cliff; buzzard, raven, ring ouzel.

Peterstone Wentlooge (ST 269800): mudflats; waders, wildfowl.

Gwent

SITE
63 # Cwm Clydach

An attractive, valley-side beech wood. Grid ref: SO 218125.

The main reason for the existence of this site as an NNR is the presence of what is almost certainly the most westerly natural beech wood in Britain. The woods tumble steeply down the north-facing slope of the river Clydach gorge, partly on Carboniferous limestone and partly on more acid shales, and once extended much further down the valley as far as Gilwern. The best reason for visiting the reserve is simply to see a very fine example of a genuine western beech wood, but it is also of some interest for its

species. Both the bird's-nest orchid and the slightly similar yellow bird's-nest occur here under the beeches (see box below), together with soft-leaved sedge, wood-sorrel, ramsons, early dog-violet, and many other herbaceous species. The rare whitebeam *Sorbus porrigentiformis*, endemic to southwest Britain, occurs in small quantity. On the more acid soils, ferns such as scaly and common male-fern, hard-fern, and other species occur, and there is a reasonable, if unspectacular, range of bryophytes and

Wales

The old beech woods at Cwm Clydach

lichens. Breeding birds include dipper and grey wagtail along the river, green and great spotted woodpeckers, nuthatch, redstart, sparrowhawk, and tawny owl.

Ramsons *Allium ursinum*

Yellow bird's-nest *Monotropa hypopitys* and bird's-nest orchid *Neottia nidus-avis*

These two flowers are often confused, particularly because they often grow in the same places – in deep shade under beeches. The similarity really comes from their colouring – both are saprophytes (that is, they depend on rotting material for their nutrition, rather than producing their own food as green plants do), and both are therefore pale yellowish-brown. However, they are quite unrelated, and have totally different structures; yellow bird's-nest has narrowly tubular flowers in drooping spikes, while bird's-nest orchid has erect spikes of more open flowers, each dominated by a divided lower lip, with the upper shorter petals forming a hood.

Access is easy via minor roads running southwards from the A465 Abergavenny to Ebbw Vale road between Gilwern and Brynmawr.

Not far to the north-east, there is another woodland NNR at Coed-y-Cerrig (SO 294212), with a varied mixture of coppice woodland types on limestone.

SITE 64 Magor Marsh

A remnant of the Gwent Levels, run as a 26-ha reserve by the WT.
Grid ref: ST 427867.

The Gwent Levels were once an extensive, rich wildlife habitat, paralleling the Somerset Levels across the Severn Estuary. Sadly, however, little now remains, and this relatively small reserve is almost certainly the finest surviving example. All these coastal levels were once tidal, but have been gradually drained and reclaimed since Roman times. The present grid pattern of ditches (known locally as reens, equivalent to the Somerset rhynes), was established in the fourteenth century, so they are quite ancient features in themselves.

The reserve is maintained as an area of mixed habitat, with grazed fields, ungrazed tall fen, open water, hay meadows, and ditches. The hay meadows are cut late, then grazed afterwards. There are fine displays of flowers such as cuckooflower and marsh-

Grazing marsh with pollard willows at Magor

marigold in the spring followed by meadowsweet, greater and lesser spearwort, yellow iris, purple-loosestrife, wild angelica, and many others – a riot of colour and scent, and a magnet for insects. The ditches are beautiful in summer, fringed with iris, bulrush and reeds, with flowering frogbit, arrowhead, and the lovely pink flowering-rush in the water.

It is a good bird site at almost all times of year. There is a large colony of reed warblers, together with sedge, grasshopper, and occasional marsh warblers. Male reed buntings call from the tops of reeds, yellow wagtails frequent the open fields, and water rail and coot call from the denser patches of reeds. Being so close to the Severn Estuary, and part of its ecological system, the marsh acts as host to a wide range of birds in passage periods and during the winter, though numbers are usually small. Less common species

such as night heron and spotted crake have been seen, together with kingfisher, various ducks, snipe, and jack snipe. The hawthorns and other bushes are good places to see fieldfares and other thrushes in winter. This all attracts birds of prey: kestrel, buzzard, peregrine, and sparrowhawk are frequent visitors, with merlin and marsh harrier turning up less often. It is also a good place for insects, with over 170 of the larger moths recorded, together with good dragonflies, water beetles, and much else. There is a small parking area and information board at the entrance on the roadside. Trails start from here, and include access to the hide overlooking a small lake.

Although the remaining areas of levels do not match Magor for concentrated quality habitat, it is worth driving around locally to see examples of relict fen habitat, including a number of good ditches.

65 Wye Valley woods

Various woodlands along the Wye Valley, close to the border with England.

The beautiful Wye Valley, which reaches the sea at Chepstow, and forms the border between England and Wales for part of its length, is extremely well wooded. Many of the woods are of

Wood white *Leptidea sinapis*

planted conifers, but in places there are older woods, some of which are protected as nature reserves. Overall, the woods of this area are considered to be nationally important. Lady Park Wood NNR (SO 560155) is one of the best known locally; although considerably modified by felling in the past, it has been left as a non-intervention area, to follow the course of succession. There is a particularly good tree flora, with both large and small-leaved limes (a combination that is very rare in the wild in Britain), wild cherry, wych elm, wild service-tree, whitebeam, and many others, flourishing in the limestone soil. Pied flycatcher, buzzard, redstart, wood warbler, and many other birds nest in the wood, with peregrine and raven on nearby crags. The caves and old mines are used by bats, including greater and lesser horseshoe bats. Butterflies here include pearl-bordered and silver-washed fritillaries, wood white, and white admiral.

Fiddler's Elbow NNR (SO 527140) is broadly similar, and includes some of the rare and endemic whitebeams *Sorbus* species for which this area is known.

In addition to these NNRs, the WT has reserves at Margaret's Wood (SO 526069) and Prisk Wood (SO 532091), while Coombe Valley Woods NNR (SO 460930) is not far out of the valley.

Within the lower Wye Valley, there are also numerous nature trails and viewpoints, such as the Wyndcliff Nature Trail (ST 525973) which takes in the spectacular viewpoint of Eagle's Nest and passes through part of a forest nature reserve. More information can be obtained from the tourist information office at Tinterne.

The river Wye itself is also considered to be one of the finest rivers in Britain, with good fish populations and a rich invertebrate fauna. The rare club-tailed dragonfly breeds here, as does white-legged damselfly, together with a particularly rare mayfly *Potamanthus luteus*, amongst many other species.

A selection of other important sites in the county

Magor Pill (ST 437847): mudflats; waders.

Strawberry Cottage Wood (SO 315214): woodland; buzzard, pied flycatcher, redstart, wood warbler.

Wales

South-west England

Introduction

This is a very distinctive region, characterized by mild winters, higher-than-average rainfall, luxuriant vegetation, and a hilly landscape. It is the Atlantic fringe of England, equivalent – and in many ways remarkably similar – to south-west Wales and the north-west tip of France, Brittany. For our purposes, it is made up of Cornwall and the Scilly Isles, Devon, Somerset, Avon, and Dorset, plus the Channel Islands. Although it is a cohesive and distinctive region, there are gradual differences across the region, with a declining Atlantic influence and a softening geology eastwards, so that the differences between the extremes are considerable, though they also have much in common.

The climate of the south-west is distinctly milder and damper than that of central and eastern England. Atlantic depressions reach here first, bringing rain and strong winds. The winters are particularly mild, thanks to the presence of the ocean, the extreme southerly latitude, and the fact that it is furthest from the continent of Europe with its cold high-pressure systems. Summers tend to be cooler, breezier, and usually damper than places further east. However, anywhere that is sheltered and in something of a rain shadow has the best weather in the country, with early springs, short winters, and long, warm summers. Flowers, such

White Nothe (see p. 195)

Opposite page: Hambledon Hill; cowslips *Primula veris* (see p. 201)

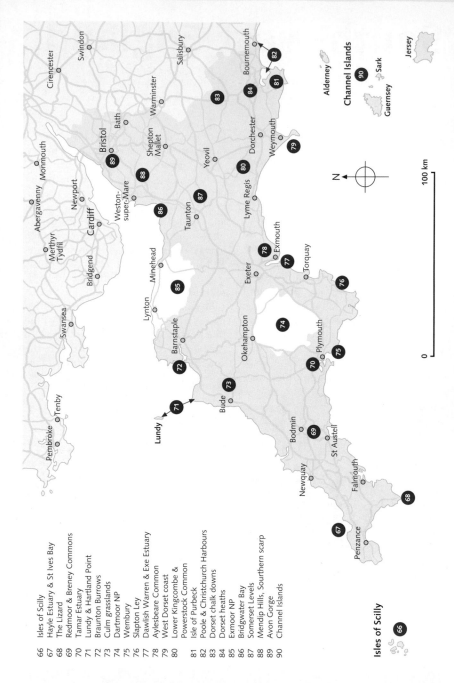

66 Isles of Scilly
67 Hayle Estuary & St Ives Bay
68 The Lizard
69 Redmoor & Breney Commons
70 Tamar Estuary
71 Lundy & Hartland Point
72 Braunton Burrows
73 Culm grasslands
74 Dartmoor NP
75 Wembury
76 Slapton Ley
77 Dawlish Warren & Exe Estuary
78 Aylesbeare Common
79 West Dorset coast
80 Lower Kingcombe &
   Powerstock Common
81 Isle of Purbeck
82 Poole & Christchurch Harbours
83 Dorset chalk downs
84 Dorset heaths
85 Exmoor NP
86 Bridgwater Bay
87 Somerset Levels
88 Mendip Hills, Southern scarp
89 Avon Gorge
90 Channel Islands

as primroses and lesser celandines, appear very early here, and common frogs are usually spawning by January in the warmer locations.

The western part of the peninsula is dominated by older, harder rocks, including granite, old red sandstone, and slates, which produce a hilly land-

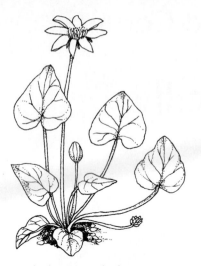

Lesser celandine *Ranunculus ficaria*

scape with some well-known high moorlands such as Bodmin Moor, Dartmoor, and Exmoor. Naturally enough such places, which reach to well over 600 m on Dartmoor, are wetter and cooler than the lowlands, and winters can be relatively harsh. Surrounding these high areas are softer sedimentary rocks such as new red sandstones, greensand, limestones, and chalk, giving rise to a softer landscape of vales and lower hills. A major feature, quite different from most of the landscape, is the Somerset Levels, which stretch inland from Bridgwater and Weston-super-Mare as a huge flat plain, barely above sea level. They are the remains of an inlet of the sea that has steadily been drained or dried out to become a distinctive and beautiful landscape of damp fields intersected by ditches overlying peat and alluvium.

The crowning glory of this region full of interest is the coast. Because it sur-rounds a long, thin, indented peninsula, it is particularly long relative to the area of land. In the west, the dominant features are cliffs and rocky foreshores, thanks to the hard underlying rock, and the exposure to the strong westerly winds and Atlantic breakers. Where there is shelter, such as in the Falmouth or Hayle Estuaries, saltmarshes and mud-flats more typical of the east develop, and these can be very rich bird sites. Further east along the south coast, there is more variety of rock, and the coast is less exposed as the relative shelter of the English Channel is reached. The coast of Dorset is extraordinarily beautiful and varied, as it cuts across the strata of many different rocks, and much of it is now a World Heritage Site. Going east-wards along the north coast, leaving behind the high rocky cliffs of Exmoor, there are extensive saltmarshes, mud-flats, and dunes in the shelter of the Severn Estuary.

It is a very beautiful region that, thanks to the climate and geology, and perhaps its relative remoteness, has escaped many of the changes that have affected eastern and central England. Many parts have a landscape of small fields with old hedges and banks, rich in the more common countryside species that have disappeared elsewhere. There are still large, wild, unploughed areas, such as Exmoor, Dartmoor, the southern slopes of the Mendips, the Quantock Hills, and the Dorset and Devon heaths, making it an exceptionally good place for the naturalist, with something of interest almost everywhere. Thanks to the mild climate, it is worth a visit at virtually any time of year.

Isles of Scilly and Cornwall

66 Isles of Scilly

An isolated archipelago off the extreme south-west of Cornwall.

The tourist literature calls the Isles of Scilly 'a world apart', which describes them perfectly. They are a low archipelago, lying about 40 km off Land's End, subject to the full force of the Atlantic gales but with an extremely mild climate. There are five inhabited islands with a total resident population of about 2000, and about 40 other islands of varying sizes. There is a rich flora of native plants, including a number of rarities, supplemented by many introduced plants that have found the climate to their liking. There is a strong population of seabirds, including some good breeding colonies, and the islands are famous for the range of unusual migrant birds, especially in October when large numbers of birdwatchers descend on the islands.

St Mary's is the largest and most populous island, where most people stay. The whole coast is of interest, both for its intertidal and marine life, and for its birds at all times. The flora is not exceptional, though there is a good range of more widespread more common species; the clear, unpolluted air allows an enormous variety of lichens to flourish here, especially on the rocks and trees. There are nature trails at Low Pool and Holy Vale.

Tresco is famous for its subtropical gardens, which are worth a visit for both the flowers and the tame garden birds that occur there. There are pools which attract a fine range of birds. Peninnis Head is a good vantage-point for seawatching. St Agnes, with its satellite island of Gugh, is beautifully unspoilt, with a good variety of breeding birds. Parts of the downland are managed as reserves by the Isles of Scilly Environmental Trust, and the flora includes all three species of native adder's-tongue, two of which are rare.

Bryher has particularly good sand dunes, which support some of the Scillies' special plants, such as orange bird's-foot and dwarf pansy, found only here and in the Channel Islands. There is also a range of more common dune species such as sea bindweed, sea stork's-bill, yellow horned-poppy, and sea-holly. There are also good headlands with spring squill and other attractive plants. St Martin's has a good range of habitats, including

Shag *Phalacrocorax aristotelis*

St Martin's (Liz Gibbons)

an exceptionally fine sandy bay. One unusual plant is the South African ice-plant relative, Hottentot-fig, which is abundantly naturalized on sea-cliffs in the Scillies, and elsewhere in this region.

About 15 species of seabirds breed on the islands, mainly on the uninhabited rocks. This total includes not just more common species such as shag, cormorant, kittiwake, and fulmars, but also rather rarer species such as storm petrels, Manx shearwater, and roseate terns. Most of the breeding areas are closed during the nesting season, though boat trips may be taken to view them. The land-bird populations on the Scillies are quite limited, with, for example, no woodpeckers, owls, or buntings, but those birds that do occur are found in unusually high densities. At passage periods, and in particular autumn, a vast range of birds can turn up,

including many rarities particularly from North America. The numbers are not usually large, as the islands are not on a main migration route, but the variety and interest is enormous. For example, Lapland and snow buntings are regular, and Richard's pipits and short-toed larks turn up almost every year. There is plenty of information on what birds are present on bird lines, and information boards at several venues on St Mary's.

There are relatively few mammals. The Scilly shrew (or lesser white-toothed shrew) is widespread here, although the Channel Islands is its only other British locality. The individuals on the Scillies are sometimes classed as a separate race. Grey seals are common around the islands, and common porpoises can often be seen during boat trips, or even from headlands in calm weather.

SITE 67 Hayle Estuary and St Ives Bay

Estuary and bay on the north Cornish coast, partly within an RSPB reserve.

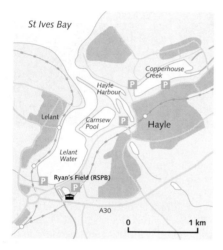

The river Hayle flows into picturesque St Ives Bay, in the far west of Cornwall. Though it lacks the peaceful beauty of some of the southern Cornish estuaries, it is, nonetheless, a very attractive area, which is easily accessible and particularly rich in bird life.

The estuarine part of the site has two arms; the larger southernmost arm runs from the junction of the A30 and A3074 past Hayle village, down to the sea, while the eastern arm runs inland to the north of Hayle town. The southern arm, which consists mainly of mudflats and salt-marsh, is readily visible from the old A30 which runs alongside it, and the eastern arm can be viewed from tracks around it. There is also a large freshwater pool, Carnsew Pool, which serves as a feeding area and high-tide roost for birds. On the western side of the river mouth, there is a fine patch of sand dunes at Porth Kidney

Sands, with a good slightly calcareous dune flora.

The rest of St Ives Bay extends from St Ives town at the western end to beyond the Hayle Estuary in the east, but the most interesting part lies around St Ives itself. The area is famous for the range of birds that can be seen at sea, and it is also a good place to see grey seals offshore. The seashore life is outstanding here, too, with impressive displays of mussels on the lower rocks, and a fine range of sea-weeds and seashore species that can withstand the force of the sea during westerly gales.

The outstanding feature of the whole site is its bird life, especially during passage periods and in winter, and it includes many rarities, particularly from North America. In autumn on the estuary, large numbers of waders and some gulls pass through, such as little stint, wood sand-

Peregrine *Falco peregrinus*

Hayle Estuary

piper, curlew sandpiper, spotted redshank, and occasionally little and Mediterranean gulls, to swell the numbers of resident oystercatchers, little egrets, turnstones, and others. In winter, there are reasonable numbers of waterfowl and waders, including wigeon, teal, Brent geese, gadwall, curlew, bar-tailed godwit, great northern diver, and many others. Peregrines are regular winter visitors.

In autumn, between late August and November, the number of birds that can be seen at sea from St Ives is remarkable. The best place is near the chapel on the island (not really an island, and accessible by car and on foot direct from the harbour). At times during this period, there can be good numbers of gannets, divers, storm petrels, occasional Sabine's gulls, and many others, both common and rare. Many birds such as common scoter, eider, and divers pass much of the winter here.

There is an RSPB hide at Ryan's Field near the Old Quay House Inn car park. Access is easy throughout, from St Ives, Hayle, and Lelant.

68 The Lizard

A large peninsula, the southernmost part of mainland Britain, noted for its rare flora. Nominal grid ref: SW 7012.

Unlike most of the Cornish coast, the Lizard Peninsula is not made up of granite, but of a more complicated mixture of rocks including serpentine and gabbro, giving rise to more base-rich soils. The

Cornish heath *Erica vagans*

South-west England

scenery is spectacularly beautiful, with moorlands on the plateau, ringed by cliffs and bays of great beauty. It is generally unspoilt, though there is an airfield, an RAF station at Culdrose, and small sections of unsightly tourist development. Large parts of the Lizard are now under protective management or ownership, by such bodies as the NT, EN, and the WT. The Lizard NNR (central grid ref: SW 720200) covers 1662 ha.

Botanically, the Lizard is quite outstanding, and undoubtedly one of the best places in Britain for flowers; it has 20 nationally rare species, and over 50 nationally scarce species, for some of which it is a key national stronghold. These numbers exclude lower plants such as liverworts, for which the Lizard is also important.

Heathlands are perhaps the most widespread habitat of the Lizard peninsula. These lie mainly on serpentine and gabbro rocks, and have escaped ploughing not only due to their inherent infertility, but also because of the presence of numerous gabbro boulders, known as

'crusairs'. Some of these heathlands have fine populations of Cornish heath, and smaller amounts of Dorset heath, in addition to the more common heathers. The tracks that cross the heath are often notable for their rare plants, such as three-lobed water-crowfoot, yellow centaury, pillwort, and pygmy rush, amongst others. Shallow pools on the heath have additional species such as shoreweed, lesser marshwort, and a particularly rich flora of stoneworts (charophytes) comprising 13 species, with a high proportion of rarities.

Towards the coast, especially on the west side, there are more grassy areas and broken ground where an exceptional range of plants grow. Rarities such as thyme broomrape, hairy greenweed, chives, fringed rupturewort, land quillwort, and a dozen or so clovers rub shoulders with more widespread species such as spring squill, green-winged orchids, kidney vetch, and bluebells. Aside from the high proportion of rarities, the displays of coastal flowers in May are quite outstanding, with thrift, kidney

Cornish heath

Hairy greenweed *Genista pilosa*

vetch, bird's-foot-trefoil, oxeye daisies, and bluebells particularly prominent. The best coastal area is between Mullion Cove and Lizard Point, on the west side, though it is by no means the only interesting location.

Although primarily a botanical site, there is much else to see. Peregrines and ravens breed around the cliffs, and the heaths are home to birds such as stonechats, and a wide range of dragonflies and damselflies in the wetter areas. The Lizard is noted for its particularly early dates for spawning common frogs, toads, and newts, sometimes as early as December.

Other sites nearby include Loe Pool (NT; SW 645240), where there is a sandy bar with a good flora holding back an extensive natural coastal lake, fringed with woods. The Helford River, which roughly marks the north-east limit of the Lizard, is a very beautiful secluded valley, lined with old sessile oak woods in part, and visited by numerous waders and waterfowl. Not far away to the west is Marazion Marsh reserve (RSPB; SW 505316), opposite St Michael's Mount, good for birds in all seasons.

SITE 69 Redmoor and Breney Commons

Two neighbouring reserves protecting substantial heath and wetland habitats. Grid ref: SX 076623.

Redmoor and southern Redmoor form a complex of various habitats, including heath, bog, marshy grassland, wet woodland, and open water, in a valley on the north-eastern edge of the St Austell granite. Boggy areas are bright with the orange spikes of bog asphodel, marsh cinquefoil, cottongrass, heath spotted-orchids, and sundew, amongst others. Fine clumps of royal fern grow here and there, and on the wet heaths there are displays of cross-leaved heath, devil's-bit scabious, and many other plants. The devil's-bit scabious is the foodplant for a good population of marsh fritillaries here, and there are reasonable numbers of dragonflies and damselflies.

Breeding birds include nightjars, tree pipit, sedge warblers, grasshopper warblers, reed buntings, willow tits, sparrowhawks, and many other birds. Adders, grass snakes, common frogs, common toads, and newts all do well in the combination of habitats here. In the woods, there are luxuriant growths of lichens, thanks to the clean air of Cornwall, including beard lichens *Usnea* species.

Breney Common (SX 054610) lies a few kilometres to the south-west, protecting 54 ha of heath, wet heath, bog, and scrub.

Another reserve of botanical interest, well to the north near Week St Mary, is Creddacott meadows (SX 234963), owned by Plantlife and managed by the WT. It protects one of the largest remaining areas of species-rich damp Culm grassland. Flowers here include meadow thistle, devil's-bit scabious, saw-wort,

Marsh fritillary *Eurodryas aurinia*

lesser butterfly-orchid, bog pimpernel, lesser skullcap, heath spotted-orchid, and many others. Small quantities of the rare wavy St John's-wort are found here. It is also a good area for butterflies, including marsh and silver-washed fritillaries.

SITE
70 Tamar Estuary

A reserve along the foreshore in the upper reaches of the Tamar Estuary. Grid ref: SX 436627.

The river Tamar is the largest of several rivers feeding the large and convoluted Tamar Estuary, that is contiguous with Plymouth Sound. It includes the inlets of the St German's or Lynher River, St John's

Kingfisher *Alcedo atthis* **(Mike Lane)**

Lake south of Torpoint, and the river Tavy on the Devon side. Despite its proximity to Plymouth, the whole area is very beautiful, with many secluded places, rich in birds. There is an SSSI of 1441 ha covering the key areas of the estuary, and it is considered to be of international importance.

The WT has a reserve covering 404 ha of foreshore and adjacent habitats running from Cargreen to Moditonham Quay along the shore of the Kingsmill Lake. The mudflats support an enormous density of invertebrates, especially molluscs, crustaceans, and worms, and these in turn support large populations of waders and wildfowl. Passage and wintering birds which use the reserve include black-tailed godwits, dunlin, curlew, redshank, whimbrel, lapwing, golden plover, and spotted redshank. Numbers of wintering avocets have built up in recent years (in common with several other south-western sites), usually staying from about October to March. Winter bird numbers go up considerably if estuaries further north are frozen. Shelduck nest in burrows on the upper saltmarsh or adjacent farmland, and can be seen out on the estuary. Kingfishers are common at most times of the year, and otters are not infrequent.

There is access to the reserve from Cargreen or Landulph villages, where there are information boards, or Moditonham Quay (SX 419613).

At Cotehele estate (SX 423681) a few kilometres to the north, there is an attractive nature trail that takes in woodlands and saltmarsh, with views onto the upper part of the estuary. Just across the border in Devon, there is a fine woodland reserve at Warleigh Point (SX 447610), with a rich flora and fauna.

A selection of other important sites in the county

Bude Marshes (SS 208057): pools, grassland, reedbeds; waterbirds.

Loveney Reserve (SX 183744): wetland; wildfowl.

Nansmellyn Marsh (SW 762541): reedbed, carr; warblers (including Cetti's), waterbirds.

Pendarves Wood (SW 640376): woodland, lake; woodland flowers and birds.

Stithians Reservoir (SS 715365): water, marsh; wildfowl, waders (often rarities).

Tamar Lakes (SS 295115): migrant waders (often rarities).

Devon

SITE
71 Lundy and Hartland Point

An island off the north Devon coast, surrounded by a marine nature reserve. Grid ref: SS 143437.

The island of Lundy lies about 16 km off the Devon coast, astride the entrance to the Bristol Channel. It is about 5 km long and less than 1 km wide, with a small resident population. Although it receives many day-trippers, and some resident

tourists, it is remote enough to retain an attractive air of isolation and solitude.

The area around Lundy is a Marine Nature Reserve, with an enormously rich marine and intertidal life. There is an underwater trail for divers, but much can

South-west England

The dramatic west coast of Lundy

be seen on the shore or from the headlands. In addition to the seaweeds and smaller invertebrates, it is a fine location for seeing basking sharks, cetaceans, the abundant resident grey seals, and interesting creatures such as sun-fishes and compass jellyfishes.

The island is no longer a great site for breeding seabirds – even the puffins after which the island was named have all but gone. There are a few auks, very small numbers of puffins, kittiwakes and various gulls, and a small colony of Manx shearwaters. At passage periods, a wide variety of migrants can turn up in the more sheltered parts, though numbers are never huge.

The plant life is generally what you might expect from exposed granitic cliffs, with relatively few higher plants, though the lichens are luxuriant, including rarities such as *Teloschistes flavicans*. One speciality is an endemic plant, the Lundy cabbage, which also supports two endemic leaf beetles. Other features of interest, apart from spectacular views, fascinating history, and a pub, include an abundance of minotaur beetles busily rolling dung about in spring.

Lundy can be reached by regular sailings from Bideford, or occasionally from Ilfracombe. Tel: 01237 470422 for details. Accommodation on the island can be arranged through the Landmark Trust.

Hartland Point is the nearest land to Lundy. It has some superb displays of coastal flowers and lichens, and bays such as Shipload Bay, just to the east, are marvellous for intertidal life. The coastal scenery, especially at Hartland Quay, is quite extraordinary.

SITE
72 Braunton Burrows

South-west England

One of the finest stretches of sand dunes in England. Grid ref: SS 464326.

Braunton Burrows is a vast expanse of sand dunes stretching northwards from the estuary of the Taw. Covering almost 1000 ha in all, it has the full range of dune habitats from sandy foreshore, through mobile dunes to ancient stable grassy dunes, with some sizeable wet dune slacks. It is also big enough to allow the natural processes of erosion – such as dune blow-outs – and accretion to occur without interference. Some of the dunes reach about 30 m in height, forming a miniature mountain landscape.

Its main interest, apart from being a prime habitat example, is as a botanical site. A vast range of coastal plants occurs here, over 400 in all, including many that are uncommon or rare, and many in great abundance. The sand is rich in shell fragments, giving a pH of over 8, so many lime-loving plants occur. Viper's-bugloss, bird's-foot-trefoil, wild thyme, yellow-rattle, common restharrow, evening-primrose, and several others give colour to the dunes as they flower in sheets. In dune slacks, there are masses of round-leaved wintergreen, creeping willow, marsh pennywort, marsh helleborine, and smaller amounts of water germander. More specialized plants on the dunes include sea-holly, sea bindweed, sea spurge, marram, sea rocket, dune pansy, and sand toadflax, which is well naturalized here.

Braunton Burrows harbours 14 species of dragonflies, and a good range of butterflies including grayling, abundant dark

Part of the vast dune system at Braunton

Sea bindweed *Calystegia soldanella*

green fritillaries, and small blues feeding on kidney vetch. One other insect that often gets noticed is the large, bright shiny red leaf beetle *Chrysomela populi* on creeping willow, frequently in considerable abundance.

Access is generally easy, with good parking and walks from the east side, but the southern part is used for military training and there may be restrictions at times.

The adjacent Braunton Marshes are like a small version of the Somerset Levels, with good ditches. Across the Taw-Torridge Estuary, there are some good dunes at Northam Country Park (SS 440310), just north of Westward Ho!

SITE 73 Culm grasslands

Five nature reserves, including one NNR, protecting some of the last remnants of 'Culm grassland' in Devon.

Culm grassland is the name given to a particular type of marshy grassland in north Devon and adjacent parts of Cornwall, rather similar to the 'rhos' pastures of Wales. It is called Culm grassland because it occurs here over the Culm Measures – strata of Carboniferous slates and sandstones. A survey in 1989 showed that 50% of the small remaining area of Culm grasslands had been lost in just 5 years, so considerable efforts were made to protect the remainder. The five reserves listed here protect a reasonable representative sample of the grassland.

Culm grasslands have a rather characteristic mixture of species, including meadow thistle, heath spotted-orchid, saw-wort, devil's-bit scabious, cross-leaved heath, marsh cinquefoil, sneezewort, and an abundance of sedges such as flea sedge, tawny sedge, and bottle sedge. Some sites have rarer plants such as lesser butterfly-orchid, whorled caraway, and the very local wavy St

John's-wort, a late-flowering species confined to this habitat in Britain.

Characteristic insects of Culm grasslands include marsh fritillaries, for which this is one of the main European strongholds, narrow-bordered bee hawkmoth, and marbled whites. The remaining sites tend to be attractive historic places, with small fields and thick hedges.

Mambury Moor reserve (WT; SS 385171) has five fields covering 22.5 ha, of which three are prime Culm grassland. Meshaw Moor reserve (WT; SS 761182) lies further east, near Gidley Cross. It has 13 fields in a total of only 14 ha! Vealand Farm reserve (WT; SS 288068) covers 41 ha, of which about 5 ha are Culm grassland, with a mixture of other habitats, while Volehouse Moor (SS 342172) covers 39 ha, of which about half is Culm grassland.

Dunsdon Farm NNR lies between Holsworthy and the Cornish border; at present it can only be visited with a permit from EN.

Dunsdon Farm

SITE
74 Dartmoor National Park

Dartmoor, an NP since 1951, covers 954 square kilometres of granite uplands, wholly within Devon. The NP includes many SSSIs, nature reserves, and other special sites.

Dartmoor is the largest and most significant area of uplands in southern England. It comprises the remains of a huge granitic intrusion, now greatly eroded, but still reaching 621 m at High Willhays (SX 580892), and over 50% of the park lies at over 300 m. It roughly resembles a shallow dome, with high central sections, and heavily dissected margins where the main rivers, such as the Dart and the Tavy, form deep valleys as they flow towards the sea.

It is large and high enough to make its own climate, and is well known for being distinctly wetter and cooler than the average for southern England, which in turn affects the vegetation.

On the high moors, there are two extensive areas of blanket bog, the largest being on the northern plateau, and these are surrounded by patches of heather moorland and acidic grassland. It is famous for its tors – dramatic hilltop granite outcrops.

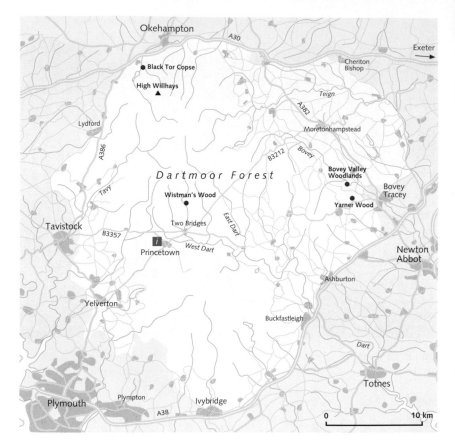

There are about 160 in all, and many, such as Hay Tor, Yes Tor, and Hound Tor, are well-known local landmarks. Towards the margins of the moor there is much more farmland, mostly under rather poor improved grassland, though there are areas of unimproved hay meadows and pastures here and there. In the valleys, especially the deeper, steep-sided ones such as the Dart Valley, there are extensive tracts of broadleaved and often ancient woodlands, and the rivers themselves are usually of great value for wildlife. Overall, Dartmoor is considered to be of international significance for its blanket bogs, upland heaths, upland oak woods, and cave systems, and of at least national importance for its valley mires, unimproved pastures, and grass moorland. Over 28 000 ha have been declared SSSIs, and there are many national and private nature reserves within its boundaries.

The bogs or mires in the high moorland areas are marvellous places for the naturalist. They have their own special plants, such as bog asphodel, bog-mosses, the insectivorous pale butterwort and round-leaved sundew, bog pimpernel, the pretty little ivy-leaved bellflower, and marsh St John's-wort, amongst others, though what often makes them stand out from a distance are the white fluffy heads of one or other of the cotton-grasses. In the wilder areas, golden plover, curlew, snipe, and even occasional dunlin breed. The rare southern damselfly breeds in a few sites on the southern part of the moor. The best areas of bog are in the high north-western parts of the moor, and the central southern upland areas.

Viviparous lizard *Lacerta vivipara*

Heather moorlands are scattered throughout the drier parts of the high moor, readily visible from most of the roads that cross the moor. They are quite spectacular in August when the heather, bell heather, and western gorse all flower together in a lovely carpet of purple and gold. At this time of year, the pink threads and flowers of the parasitic dodder can often be seen in masses on the heather and gorse. In places, bilberries are common, ripening in late summer. Birds on the heather moors are quite limited, and the most frequent are meadow pipits, skylarks, and stonechats, with red grouse in a few places. Adders and viviparous lizards are widespread, and the distinctive large bristly caterpillars of the emperor moth are a common sight. Interspersed with the heather moorlands are the upland grasslands, and in places the two grade into each other. The grasslands are relatively species-poor, though areas with bracken can be good for fritillaries such as high brown and pearl-bordered, feeding on the violets below. Some of the old grassy slopes are particularly good for waxcaps *Hygrocybe* species and other attractive fungi. Both the moorlands and the upland grasslands are grazed by Dartmoor ponies as part of the common rights exercised over most of the moor. The ponies are not wild – all are owned by someone – but they are free-ranging, and an integral part of the moor's ecology. At present, there are about 3000, many of them pure Dartmoor ponies.

The broadleaved woods of Dartmoor are outstanding places. There are two

Black Tor Copse

Western gorse *Ulex galli* and bell heather *Erica cinerea* on Ripon Tor

fascinating high-level woods that are quite unlike anywhere else; the better known of them is Wistman's Wood (SX 613770), in the upper reaches of the West Dart River above Two Bridges. It is a magical site of twisted common oak trees that have survived the effects of grazing thanks to the masses of granite boulders with which they share the slope. The harsh but humid climate has stunted and gnarled the trees, but allowed a luxuriant moss and lichen flora to develop. While not a place to see rare flowers, birds, or butterflies, it is a fascinating experience, well worth the walk. The less well-known wood, Black Tor (or Black-a-Tor) Copse (SX 562918) lies in the valley of the West Okement River, south of Okehampton. The dwarfing effects of climate are less marked here, but it is a fascinating wood in a beautiful place, and a regular site for ring ouzels. It is considered to be an exceptional site for lichens, and the list includes many rarities such as *Bryoria smithii* and *Parmelia discordans*. Both woods are NNRs.

The lower woods, such as those in the valleys of the Bovey, Dart, and Teign, are

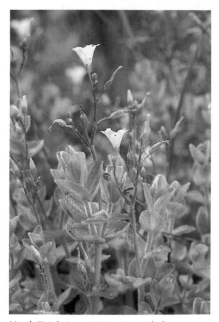

Marsh St John's-wort *Hypericum elodes*

Wood-sorrel *Oxalis acetosella*

St John's-wort, which occurs on a few dry acid rock outcrops along the valley sides. Yarner Wood NNR (SX 785788), just east of Haytor, is slightly different in that it does not clothe steep valley sides, though it is broadly similar in its plants and animals. The nearby Bovey Valley Woodlands NNR extends for several kilometres up the Bovey Valley from about SX 782796. English Nature have recently purchased land on Trendlebere Down to link the two woodland reserves into one extensive and varied site: the East Dartmoor Woods and Heaths NNR. Both high brown and pearl-bordered fritillaries occur on Trendlebere Down.

We should also mention that the archaeology of Dartmoor is quite outstanding. It has the largest collection of Bronze Age remains in the UK, and many of these can be readily seen on any walk or drive. They include field boundaries, ancient stone ranch boundaries stretching for kilometres, 18 stone circles, standing stones, burial places, and hundreds of dwelling places (marked as 'hut circles' on the maps). Their presence adds to the fascination of any visit.

Access to the moor is generally very easy, with the exception of the military training zone that covers a large part of the northern high moors; this is open at times, but areas flying red flags should never be entered. Some of the roads are narrow and winding, so take a good map. There are numerous information points in towns and villages within the park, and an all-year centre called the High Moorland Visitor Centre, at Princetown, Yelverton, Devon. Tel: 01822 890414. Outdoor Leisure 28, the excellent 1:25 000 OS map, covers the whole NP.

Outside the park, the boat trip from Totnes to Dartmouth gives excellent views of the beautiful Dart Estuary with its wooded banks and sloping hay meadows. Buzzards soar overhead, while grey herons and little egrets hunt in the creeks, and kingfishers perch on overhanging twigs.

fine examples of western acid oak woods, similar to those on Exmoor (p. 205). Pied flycatcher, redstart, and wood warbler breed, with dipper, grey wagtail, and occasional goosander along the streams, while the woodland mammals include dormice, wood mice, and badgers. High brown and pearl-bordered fritillaries can be seen in clearings and margins. A rare beetle, the blue ground beetle, has been recently found in several of the Dartmoor-edge woodlands. Like the high-level woods, the growth of lichens and bryophytes is rich and varied, with a fine range of species. Flowering plants include primroses, wood spurge, spurge-laurel, wood-sorrel, bluebells, and many other characteristic ancient woodland species. Both filmy-ferns – Wilson's and Tunbridge – occur in places, such as at the Blackadon reserve (WT) on a tributary of the Dart called the river Webburn, and in the woods along the main Dart Valley. Around Steps Bridge, in the Teign Valley, there is a spectacular display of true wild daffodils at the bridge and for several kilometres upstream, normally at its peak in late March or early April. This is also a site for the rare toadflax-leaved

SITE
75 Wembury

Over 6 km of foreshore and cliffs, with marvellous intertidal life
and a good visitor centre, run by the WT. Grid ref: SX 520485.

Although most of south-west England's coastline has interesting and varied marine life, that at Wembury is quite exceptional. The combination of numerous rocky reefs, sandy beaches, an offshore island, and clean unpolluted water provides ideal conditions for a wealth of species of all types. A 6.5-km stretch, from Fort Bovisand on the edge of Plymouth Sound east to Gara Point, is protected by a series of agreements and accessible to all.

The rocky reefs are characterized by the dense growth of seaweeds, including kelp forests at the lower levels. As the tide drops, dozens of rock pools are exposed, each full of life. Typical species to be found here include the lovely blue-rayed limpets, starfishes, sea urchins, snake-locks anemones, a variety of crabs that includes porcelain crabs, velvet swimming crabs, and spider crabs, bryozoans, whelks, and many others. The reefs are also particularly good for corals, including ross, yellow trumpet, and Devonshire cup, though the best displays of these lie in deeper waters, accessible only to divers.

In the bay, the conspicuous rock known as the Mewstone is a breeding site for cormorants, great black-backed gulls, and a few other seabirds. The mainland coastline, especially at Wembury Point, is generally good for birds such as turnstones, rock pipits, and other shore feeders, though numbers are rarely large. Peregrines can often be seen overhead and ravens are not uncommon. To see the best of the intertidal life, it is worth trying to visit when the lowest tides occur, a few days after full moon.

Seaweeds

South-west England

The visitor centre, Wembury Marine Centre, is near the shore on the edge of Wembury village. It makes a good starting point for any visit to this stretch of coast, and there are displays of features that it is hard for the ordinary visitor to see, such as a walk through a kelp forest, or a Devon coral garden.

SITE 76 Slapton Ley

An attractive coastal NNR of 211 ha, with a large lagoon separated from the sea by a shingle bank. Grid ref: SX 828444.

The nature reserve, which is managed by the Field Studies Council is dominated by the large coastal lagoon of Slapton Ley. This shallow natural lake is fringed with reeds and other vegetation, and some inlets are entirely vegetated with reedbeds, fen, or carr woodland.

It is a very rich locale for birds at all times of year. A wide range of wetland

Common reed
Phragmites australis

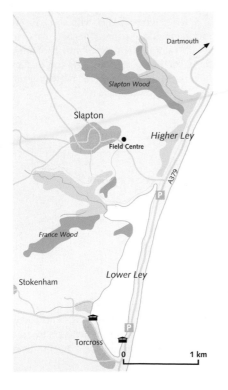

birds breed, including Cetti's warblers, sedge and reed warblers, great crested grebe, and cirl buntings not far away. Passage migrants of all sorts use the protected water, mud, and scrub, and in winter there are good numbers of waterfowl such as pochard and tufted duck. Almost 500 species of higher plants have been recorded, including the very rare strapwort on the fringes of the lagoon, and Ray's knotgrass on the shingle, together with more common plants such as yellow horned-poppy, viper's-bugloss, and purple-loosestrife. Some 1500 species of fungi have been recorded, including many rarities and about 30 not so far found anywhere else in Britain. It is also a good place for insects, with abundant dragonflies (such as migrant hawker and downy emerald), damselflies, caddis flies, mayflies, and others, with a good population of the rare and attractive Jersey tiger

Lagoon, Slapton Ley

moth, which flies in the day. Otters are not infrequently seen, and there are some appealingly tame badgers.

The Field Studies Council runs the nearby Slapton Ley Field Centre, which has a wide variety of courses on the natural world, including many that use the reserve. It manages the site, in conjunction with various other organizations. There are hides, paths, and viewpoints, though access to some areas is restricted to permit holders only.

Not far to the south lie Prawle Point and Start Point (SX 823374). This is an exceptional area for intertidal life, with some lovely rock pools. It is also one of the best places to see cirl buntings, and a good variety of other birds such as peregrines, and the bushes hold migrants on passage. Seawatching can also be very rewarding here.

77 Dawlish Warren and Exe Estuary

SITE

A complex of coastal habitats, south of Exeter, including two RSPB reserves, two WT reserves, and an LNR.

Where the river Exe reaches the sea, there is a broad bar of sand dunes stretching across from the west side, almost blocking the estuary. This is known as Dawlish Warren, partly nature reserves and partly golf course. The combination of estuarine habitats and sand dunes is particularly rich here.

South-west England

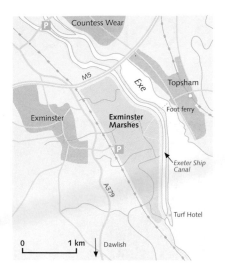

Dawlish Warren is famous both as a botanical site and as a birdwatching venue. The dunes have an impressive variety of flowers including sea-holly, yellow bartsia, evening-primrose, and viper's-bugloss, though it is best known as the only UK mainland site for the sand crocus, which flowers very early in the year and only opens in the sun. On the north side of the dunes, there are mud-flats and saltmarshes, with extensive beds of eelgrasses, cord-grass, and glassworts. These provide rich feeding areas for waterfowl and waders, especially in autumn and winter. There is a public hide here overlooking the estuary, best used around high tide as the birds are pushed towards the land.

The estuary as a whole is of international importance for its wintering bird populations, and is declared both as a Ramsar Site and a Special Protection Area under European legislation. Large numbers of waterfowl and waders congregate in winter, notably Brent geese, wigeon, red-breasted merganser, curlew, grey plover, purple sandpiper, redshank, greenshank, dunlin, and both black-tailed and bar-tailed godwits. The numbers of avocets have built up steadily, and the RSPB has been running winter

'avocet cruises' to see them and other birds. Short-eared owls and peregrines visit, amongst other birds of prey. At passage periods, there can be all sorts of interesting migrants.

It is also a good area for insects, with thriving populations of aculeate hymenoptera (solitary bees and wasps), bush-crickets, dragonflies, and the uncommon fen wainscot moth.

On the west side of the estuary, just north of Starcross, there is a large deer park at Powderham Castle (SY 970835) with a large herd of fallow deer. Exminster Marshes reserve (RSPB) lies some 6 km south of Exeter – there is a car park by the railway bridge beyond Swan's Nest Inn.

Nearby Haldon Woods (SX 884848, OS 192) includes woodland and heath, with butterflies such as wood white and high brown fritillary, and several rare birds of prey, including hobby and honey buzzard. There is a sign-posted bird of prey viewpoint.

Sand crocus *Romulea columnae*

SITE

78 Aylesbeare Common

Unspoilt east Devon heathland, managed as a reserve by the RSPB.
Grid ref: SY 057898.

Aylesbeare Common lies to the north of Budleigh Salterton. The 200 ha or so of reserve include dry heath, wet heath, bog, and open water. It is best known for its heathland birds, such as Dartford warbler, nightjar, stonechat, and linnet; Dartford warblers are rather at the western edge of their UK range here, and are prone to dying-out in hard winters, though at the moment they are doing well. The flora is rich, too, especially along the seepages and in the wet heaths, where you can find sundew, white beak-sedge, bog asphodel, pale butterwort, bog pimpernel, royal fern, and many others. On the drier heaths, there is western gorse and dodder, amongst the bell heather and heather. The ponds and seepages are particularly good for dragonflies, such as the keeled skimmer and southern and small red damselflies, and 32 species of butterflies have been recorded, with wood white and fritillaries being specialities. There are two nature trails and many paths.

Keeled skimmer *Orthetrum coerulescens*
(Peter Wilson)

The Otter Estuary lies not far away, at Budleigh Salterton. Although only small, it contains the largest piece of saltmarsh in Devon. The WT manages 23 ha of the estuary as a reserve (SY 076822), with footpaths along either side, two viewing platforms on the western side, and a hide on the east. There is a good range of saltmarsh plants such as sea aster, sea plantain, annual sea-blite, and common sea-lavender. A rare moss *Tortula solmsii* occurs at one of its only two British locations.

In winter and at passage periods, there are good numbers of birds, especially wildfowl and waders; redshank, greenshank, curlew, whimbrel, dunlin, grey plover, Brent geese, wigeon, teal, and many others occur, though rarely in large numbers. Reed and sedge warblers, reed bunting, and water rail are amongst the breeding birds.

A selection of other important sites in the county

Bowling Green Marsh (SX 972876): grassland, marsh; waders and wildfowl.

Chapel Wood (SS 483413): mixed woods; woodland and stream birds and flowers.

Old Sludge Beds (SX 952888): reedbeds, water, carr; Cetti's warbler, water rail.

Rackenford and Knowstone Moor (SS 858211): Culm grassland; flowers, willow tit, grasshopper warbler.

Dorset

SITE
79 West Dorset coast

One of the most impressive stretches of coast in England, rich in natural features.

The whole coast of Dorset, with the exception of a few built-up stretches, is of enormous interest to the naturalist, geologist, and anyone seeking spectacular scenery and wild country. The east Dorset coast is described elsewhere (pp. 198–201), and here we cover the coast from west of Lulworth to the county border at Lyme Regis.

Lulworth Cove and the Stair Hole are, of course, famous scenic and geological attractions, and just to the east there is a fine fossil forest. Westwards, there is steep chalk downland ending abruptly in superb cliffs, along Hambury Tout, Durdle Door, Swyre Head, and the appealingly named Scratchy Bottom. These have most of the typical chalk downland plants such as rock-rose, squinancy wort, and clustered bellflower, but also a more coastal element including henbane, sea stork's-bill, and wild clary. It is a fine area for butterflies, including the Lulworth skipper and dark green fritillaries, and there are grey bush-crickets

Sea campion *Silene uniflora* (Peter Wilson)

(amongst others) along the cliff edge. From White Nothe westwards, there are large areas of undercliff – an exceptional habitat caused by the cliffs slumping, so quite unsuitable for any exploitation and hard of access. Such places are usually alive with insects and birds, and flowers in selected places. White Nothe reserve (WT; SY 765812) covers about 50 ha.

Just north of Weymouth the RSPB has two fine coastal wetland reserves at Lodmoor and Radipole, both well signposted. These have open water, reedbeds, marshy grassland, and other habitats, and support a marvellous range of birds and other creatures. There are good hides and walkways, and a visitor centre and shop at Radipole. Birds here include bearded tit, Cetti's warbler, little egret, and Mediterranean gull.

The Isle of Portland must have been exceptional once, before quarrying and development, but there is enough of interest left to glimpse its riches. It is composed of limestone, which supports a rich plant and insect life, and its extreme southerly position, projecting into the English Channel, attracts many birds.

Sea pea *Lathyrus japonicus*

Dorset coast from Houns-tout

There is a bird observatory at Portland Bill. Church Ope Cove (SY 697710) is a good place to go for some of the more unusual plants such as rock stonecrop, ivy broomrape, hairy-fruited cornsalad, and hoary stock. Portland is also good for insects, including the special limestone form of silver-studded blue. Broadcroft Quarry reserve (BC) has silver-studded and small blues, and good orchids.

From Portland, Chesil Beach – one of the finest shingle beaches in Europe – stretches almost to Burton Bradstock, enclosing the major lagoon known as the Fleet. At the Portland end, around Ferrybridge, there is more stable habitat rich in uncommon plants such as four-leaved allseed, sea-lavenders, and yarrow broomrape. Westwards, it becomes more open shingle, with specialized plants such as sea-kale, sea pea, sea campion, and yellow horned-poppy. Little terns breed here in protected areas, and it is a famous invertebrate site. The Fleet varies between saline and fresh water according to position, weather, and tide, and it has a

varied flora and fauna. Fish are abundant, and in winter large numbers of wildfowl arrive to feed partly on the eelgrass beds, including Brent geese, wigeon, teal, and coot, often in thousands. At Abbotsbury, there is the famous Swannery, worth a visit at any time.

From Bridport westwards, there are huge areas of undercliff, particularly rich in fossils at Charmouth. The NT has a large estate around Golden Cap (SY 405922), and to the west of the hill there is a lovely unspoilt area of small pastures and high hedges.

Finally, west of Lyme Regis, and just into Devon though more appropriately described here, is the extensive Axmouth to Lyme Regis undercliff NNR. It covers about 325 ha of wild, jumbled undercliff, the result of numerous subsidences and collapses over the years. Over 50 species of bird breed here, including large populations of nightin-gales and lesser whitethroats, and it is a marvellous location for badgers, dormice, and other mammals. Access is on foot only, via the coast path.

SITE
80 Lower Kingcombe and Powerstock Common

Two WT reserves covering 270 ha of lovely, species-rich old grassland, woodland, and common land. Grid refs: SY 545985 and SY 540973, respectively.

The Lower Kingcombe Valley came to public notice when 'the farm that time forgot' came onto the market after the long-term owner died. Much of it was bought by the WT and other sympathetic organizations, and it is now run as a farm on traditional lines, to protect its outstanding conservation value.

Wandering around the meadows and pastures at Kingcombe gives you a glimpse of the countryside of a bygone age. There are dozens of small fields, with evocative names like 'Yonder cowleaze' and 'Lord's mead', mostly managed by grazing, with a few cut for hay, but all rich in flowers and butterflies. Most of the fields are damp or wet, with flowers such as lousewort, bugle, devil's-bit scabious, pepper-saxifrage, fleabane, marsh violet, and many others, though in drier areas, especially northwards onto the edge of the chalk, there are bee orchids, rock-

Rough pasture and old hedges at Kingcombe

rose, and wild thyme. The hedges are beautiful, all different, but almost all old and rich in shrubs and trees of many species. Although few real rarities occur, there are masses of insects, including marsh fritillaries, many different crane-flies, a long list of moths, and much more. There are 50 or more breeding birds recorded, including garden warblers, whitethroat and lesser whitethroat, blackcap, and yellowhammer. Dipper, grey wagtail, and kingfishers use the river Hooke that passes through the reserve, and otters are seen increasingly regularly.

Powerstock Common is separated from Kingcombe by just a few metres, and they collectively form a territory of great value. The old common land is similar to Kingcombe in many ways, except that it was never divided up into small fields. Unfortunately, much of the grassland was planted with conifers, though these are gradually being cleared to recreate species-rich habitat. An old railway line passes along the northern edge of the common, providing a lovely extra dimension in the form of sheltered calcareous downland, with abundant flowers including bee orchids, and butterflies such as marsh fritillary, Duke of Burgundy, and wood white. Up on the hill, there is some fine old coppice, with ancient oaks and coppiced hazel.

SITE
81 Isle of Purbeck

A peninsula in the south-east of Dorset with an extraordinary mixture of habitats and protected areas.

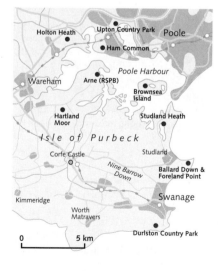

roughly from Wareham to Lulworth. Geologically, and therefore scenically, this area is complex and varied, which is the key to much of its present interest. The northern part, bordering Poole Harbour, is underlain by sands and gravels that give rise to heathy soils. Immediately to the south is a chalk ridge that runs from Lulworth in the west, through Corfe Castle, to outcrop at Foreland Point and Old Harry Rocks. South of this are the

Sand lizard *Lacerta agilis* **(Denny Cook)**

The Isle of Purbeck is not a true island, though it has some of the characteristics of one. It comprises that part of Dorset south of Poole Harbour, and along a line

clayey Wealden Beds, then a large area of limestone that forms much of the coastal hills and cliffs along the south of Purbeck.

For one reason and another, a huge expanse of natural habitat has survived on Purbeck, and because so many habitats lie adjacent they enhance each other, so that the whole is greater than the sum of the parts. Unlike many parts of the country, the habitat quality is probably getting better, as large areas are managed as reserves and lost habitats are being recreated. The NT owns many thousands of hectares, and there is a series of NNRs, RSPB reserves, WT reserves, and Country Parks.

The northern heathland and bogs are as good as anywhere, rich in characteristic species and grading northwards into the mudflats and saltmarshes of Poole Harbour (see p. 200). Boggy areas contain bog orchid, marsh gentian, lesser club-moss, bog asphodel, all three species of sundew, pale butterwort, bog myrtle, and dozens of other species, while in drier areas Dorset heath is abundant in one of its few British localities. Dragonflies and damselflies are common, including keeled skimmer, black darter, and southern and small red damselflies, often in abundance. Heath grasshopper, large marsh grasshopper, and wart-biter (in a single locality) are amongst the long list of orthoptera that occur. Drier heaths are particularly good for hymenoptera such as sand wasps, velvet ant, and the rare Purbeck mason wasp. Silver-studded blue and grayling butterflies both do well here.

Overall, this is a magnificent area for insects and other invertebrates.

It is also an excellent location for breeding birds, including large numbers of Dartford warblers (*the* heathland specialist), nightjars, stonechats, hobby, and others. It is one of the best places in the country for reptiles, and both sand lizards and smooth snakes have strong populations here.

The grazing marshes along the Frome are fascinating, not dissimilar to the Somerset Levels in a small way, though less accessible.

On the chalk ridge, there is a series of fine downland sites such as Ballard Down and Nine Barrow Down. These have a good range of downland plants including fragrant and early purple orchids, cowslips, squinancy wort, and clustered bellflower, and distinctive butterflies such as Adonis blue and chalk-hill blue in some abundance. There are many other insects of interest including glow-worms and stripe-winged grasshoppers.

Most of the soils over the Wealden Beds have been incorporated into more intensive agriculture, with the exception of Corfe Common, immediately south of Corfe Castle. This has a lovely combination of unimproved damp pasture with small bogs, rich in flowers and insects, as well as marvellous views of the ruined castle.

The coastal limestone areas are fascinating. Botanically they share much with the chalk, though the slightly different rock and the exposure to maritime influence has led to many differences. For example, the early spider-orchid is abundant between Durlestone Head and Worth Matravers, at one of its few UK areas. Chalk milkwort, the local early gentian, golden-samphire, wild cabbage, and ivy broomrape are other distinctive plants one can find. The butterflies are broadly similar, though the Lulworth skipper is a welcome addition. There are some small seabird colonies along the cliffs, with guillemots, razorbills, fulmars, kittiwakes, and a tiny number of puffins, as well as breeding peregrines and ravens.

Dartford warbler *Sylvia undata*

It is hard to go wrong on Purbeck – almost anywhere is good. Well-known protected sites include the heath, bog and harbour edge of the Arne reserve (RSPB; SY 984885); Studland Heath NNR (SY 0385) with heath, bog, sand dunes, and open water; Hartland Moor NNR (SY 961846); Ballard Down and Foreland Point (SY 050820) for fine chalk grassland and cliff edge habitats; Durlston Country Park (SY 032773) for limestone habitats, cliffs, and fine views of passing cetaceans at sea. The coast westwards from here is of great interest and beauty every metre of the way to Lulworth, and includes a Marine Nature Reserve and trail at Kimmeridge Bay.

SITE
82 Poole and Christchurch Harbours

Two large, bird-rich natural harbours on either side of the Bournemouth–Poole conurbation.

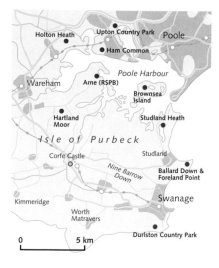

including dunlin, redshank, black-tailed and bar-tailed godwits, avocets, Brent geese, wigeon, shelduck, and curlew. One of the islands, Brownsea, is particularly noted for wintering avocets, and is the

Little egret *Egretta garzetta*

Poole Harbour is the larger of these two harbours, a major intertidal wetland of international importance. At high tide the waters cover about 3500 ha which, together with the islands and fringing habitats, makes a lovely combination. At low tide, vast areas of sheltered saltmarsh and mudflats are exposed.

It is a vital site for birds; in winter, thousands of waders and wildfowl visit, main breeding location for common and sandwich terns. It also has a heronry, Britain's first breeding little egrets (now numbering 50 pairs), a strong population of red squirrels, water voles, 17 species of dragonfly, and much more! It is owned by the NT, and partly run as a nature reserve by the WT. The RSPB reserve at Arne, and Studland NNR both protect parts of the shore, together with Upton Country Park just west of Poole, Ham Common Reserve (SY 983907), and Holton Heath NNR (SY 950912; at present closed to the public), though the whole area is a scheduled SSSI.

Christchurch Harbour lies on the border with Hampshire, at the extreme east of Dorset. It is a smaller harbour than Poole but has much to offer. The rivers Stour and Avon drain into it, and this often leads to local flooding as the river waters are backed up the valleys by the incoming tide. The intertidal areas of mud and saltmarsh serve as feeding grounds for abundant waders and wildfowl. Stanpit Marshes LNR protects much of the northern shore, while the southern arm of the harbour is formed by Hengistbury Head. Despite numerous visitors and a small amount of development, this has retained an abundance of flowers and insects, and high archaeological interest. There is a good car park and information centre, and easy access.

SITE 83 Dorset chalk downs

A number of surviving special downlands on outcroppings of Dorset chalk.

The main outcrop of chalk in Dorset (apart from the thin ridge across Purbeck – see p. 198) runs roughly south-westwards from the north-east of the county, reaching almost to the coast in the west. Vast sections of former downland have been ploughed and now lie under large arable fields, but wherever the slopes have been too steep to cultivate easily there are some fine areas of downland.

Botanically, the chalk of western England is slightly different from that of the east, though there are many similar species. There are fewer orchids here, though sawwort, devil's-bit scabious, and early gentian are more common. Cowslips are often abundant in spectacular displays, sometimes mingling beautifully with early purple orchids, such as on Hambledon Hill. Apart from the flowers, butterflies are probably the most popular feature of the chalk, and at good sites, in good years, there can be thousands on the wing at once. Species to be seen include the lovely Adonis blue,

Cowslip *Primula veris*

chalk-hill blue, silver-spotted skipper, marbled whites, and marsh fritillary, belying its name as it is the presence of devil's-bit scabious that is crucial, rather than the dampness of the habitat. Day-flying moths such as the burnet moths, cistus forester, and burnet companion can often be seen amongst them, and there are hundreds of other species of insects from all groups. There are few real chalk grassland bird or mammal specialists, though skylarks are frequent overhead, yellowhammers and whitethroats call from the scrub, and rabbits and brown hares graze the turf.

Sites of particular interest for chalk downland include Eggardon Hill (NT; SY 540946), with strikingly steep slopes; Fontmell and Melbury Downs (ST 884176) and other downs in the area such as Compton Down, managed by NT or WT; Hambledon Hill NNR (ST 845125) which includes a marvellous Iron Age hill fort, and the rather similar Hod Hill (ST 857107); Hog Cliff NNR (SY 620976), Maiden Castle (SY 668885), and Badbury Rings west of Wimborne (NT) for a superb combination of archaeology and nature.

SITE
84 Dorset heaths

Apart from the heaths on the Isle of Purbeck, there are extensive areas of heaths still remaining elsewhere in Dorset.

Dorset heaths are considered to be of very high nature-conservation value, protected by numerous national and international designations. The expanse of heath was once much greater and what survives is fragmented, although at least most remaining large fragments are protected in some way or other.

The drier heaths are dominated by heather and bell heather, with western or dwarf gorse, and cross-leaved heath in the damper parts. The wet heaths are botanically the richest, and it is here that marsh gentian, brown beak-sedge, bog pimpernel, and many other species occur. Track-ways across the heath often have a collection of tiny plants, some rare, including chaffweed, the tiny yellow centaury, and mossy stonecrop. Dartford warblers are often abundant, though they suffer badly from hard winters, and other breeding birds include nightjar, stonechat, hobby, and a few woodlarks. All the British reptiles occur on the Dorset heaths, including smooth snake and sand

lizard, which are both very restricted in their distribution.

For the entomologist and invertebrate specialist, the heaths are marvellous places, especially where they include bogs. Many grasshopper and cricket species occur, including heath grasshopper, mottled grasshopper, and bog bush-cricket. Dragonflies and damselflies are often abundant, and the list of species has many rarities such as southern dam-

Dartford warbler *Sylvia undata*

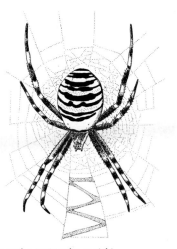

Wasp spider *Argiope bruennichi*

selfly, downy emerald, and scarce blue-tailed damselfly. There are more species of spider here than in any other British habitat, including some very rare ones, and distinctive species like the wasp spider *Argiope bruennichii* and the raft spider. Silver-studded blue butterflies and graylings are often abundant, and emperor moths and fox moths can also be seen in the daytime.

The remaining heaths lie in roughly two bands. The first runs from Christchurch northwards, west of the Avon, through the heathland of Hurn Forest (SU 104015) on to Avon Forest Park (SU 125035) west of Ringwood, as far as Cranborne Common reserve (SU 103112) near the county boundary. The second band goes across the county west from the Poole Basin to Dorchester. Heaths can often be found on the OS maps by the combination of 'heath' names and absence of field boundaries. Typical sites include Morden Bog NNR (SY 913916; 150 ha; limited access), with heath and valley bog; Holt Heath NNR (SU 047036), 500 ha of heath, bog, and ancient woodland, further inland; and Tadnoll/Winfrith reserve (WT; SY 795876) and Higher Hyde reserve (WT; SY 851902). There are also several heaths managed as reserves in and close to Poole, including Upton Heath, Canford Heath, Bourne Valley LNR, and Turbary Moor.

A selection of other important sites in the county

Garston Wood (SU 004194): mixed woods; woodland birds and flowers.

Sopley Common (SZ 132975): heath, woodland; hobby, nightjar, wood-lark, stonechat, Dartford warbler.

Somerset and Avon

---

85 Exmoor National Park

This is one of Britain's quietest and least-known NPs.

A place of great beauty and value, there are no nearby major conurbations, no motorway comes close, and its spectacular coastline has little in the way of safe bathing beaches, so it has escaped the mass tourism that affects many other

The dramatic Exmoor coast west of Lynton and the Valley of the Rocks

beautiful parts of Britain. The 693 square kilometres of the park straddles the Devon–Somerset boundary, lying mainly in Somerset. It is primarily a wild upland region, reaching 519 m at the highest point, Dunkery Beacon on the north-east edge of the moor, though sadly much of the high heather moorland has been ploughed and incorporated into farms – a process that carried on until very recently. The main sections of the park that are of interest to naturalists are: the high moorlands including their bogs, the valley woodlands, and the beautiful coastline. On the north-east edge of the moor, the NT owns the huge Holnicote Estate, where visitors are generally welcome; it is something of a microcosm of the moor, with all the major habitats represented by fine examples, and is worth describing here in a little more detail to give an idea of what the moor has to offer.

Holnicote runs from the coast at Bossington and Hurlestone Point inland to the top of Dunkery Beacon, with over 1600 ha of the higher reaches now being managed as an NNR, centred on Horner Combe

and Cloutsham. Above about 250–300 m, the slopes are open, heather-covered moorland, with bracken and gorse in places. In some of the highest valleys, there are good populations of the heath fritillary butterfly, only recently discovered but doing well, and high brown fritillaries have one of their strongholds in the area. Merlins still breed on the high moors, though their numbers have declined considerably. Exmoor is well known for its herds of red deer, which spend some of their time on the open moorland, and this can also be a good place to see Exmoor ponies, which are believed to be more like primitive native ponies than any other breed. The sides of the hills are cut into deep valleys (known locally as coombes) which are heavily wooded here with ancient oak-dominated woodland running down to the clear, fast-flowing rivers. Botanically, these valleys are very rich, particularly in lower plants. This is one of the finest national sites for lichens (as are several other Exmoor woodlands), with over 240 species recorded in the woodland alone, including many rarities and species of particular ecological interest. The clean air and high humidity allows a luxurious and impressive lichen growth. Among higher plants, Cornish moneywort, ivy-leaved bellflower, and hay-scented buckler-fern are species that occur because of the high humidity and mild climate.

There is a community of breeding birds that is characteristic of these western oak woods, which includes pied flycatcher, redstart, wood warbler, and buzzards, with dippers and grey wagtail along the streams. Although woodlands are notoriously difficult to survey accurately for bats, it is known that there are strong populations of several species here, and one ancient ash pollard was recently found to have a huge breeding colony of noctules. The rivers, such as Horner Water, are very clean and their oxygen-rich waters are home to many invertebrates such as caddis flies and stoneflies. The golden-ringed dragonfly breeds in the less shaded stretches, and can often be seen on nearby areas of moorland, or in woodland clearings.

Where the estate meets the sea, there is the fine coastal headland of Hurlestone Point, with superb views, good coastal flowers and lichens, and occasional peregrines and ravens. Dartford warblers have been breeding here in recent years, though it is probably not a permanent site for them. There is an impressive woodland of naturalized holm oak on the landward slopes of the headland. Below the point, in the great sweep of Porlock Bay, there are extensive areas of grassy stabilized shingle, and significant areas of marsh. Old records show the shingle to have once had a very rich flora, now much reduced, though the presence of autumn lady's-tresses, ivy broomrape, sea stork's-bill, and a number of clovers is of interest. The marshland, towards Porlock Weir, has steadily declined in size, though a recent initiative to allow the sea to breach the shingle defences and flood the land behind is recreating wetland habitats.

Away from this one estate, there are many other areas of interest to the naturalist. The whole coast from Minehead to Combe Martin is spectacular and unspoilt, and can be walked in its entirety on a section of the south-west coast path. Many of the coastal woods, such as those around Culbone (just west of Porlock Weir) and Lee Bay are home to some rare whitebeams, including endemic species such as *Sorbus devoniensis*. Seven species of

East Lyn River

South-west England

Gorse *Ulex europaeus*

whitebeam endemic to Britain occur along the Exmoor coast, three of which are found only in this area. The valley of the rocks, just west of Lynton, is spectacularly beautiful, and home to a fine herd of easily approached feral goats. Many of the coastal hills have outstanding displays of colour in August, when the bell heather, heather, gorse, and western gorse all flower at once in a glorious purple and gold carpet, often draped with the pinkish threads of parasitic dodder. Good sites to see this display include North Hill above Minehead, and the hills just west of Porlock, along the main A39. The coast itself is also of some interest as it changes from the sheltered semi-estuarine muddy coast at Minehead (where the remnants of some flowery dunes still hang on, just east of the town) to the clearer and more rocky exposed coasts at the western end of the park, where the rock pools are a delight.

Apart from the classic coombe oak woods at Horner and Cloutsham, there are fine woods in the valley of the East Lyn, especially around Watersmeet (where the presence of the rare Irish spurge is an additional bonus); in the valley of the river Barle near the ancient clapper bridge of Tarr Steps; in parts of the upper Exe; in

Hawkcombe west of Porlock; at Grabbist (or Grabhurst) Hill above Dunster (SS 983436); and around Woody Bay.

Good heather moorland areas are scattered throughout the park, often where there is a surviving piece of common land. The coastal main road passes through a number of such areas; Dunkery Beacon and the section to the west of it have extensive moorland, and there are other locations at such places as Molland Common (towards the south-east of the moor), Winsford Hill, and along the road from Minehead to Bossington Hill. Exmoor is rather marginal as an upland in Britain, and some of its more specialized upland plants, such as lesser twayblade, forked spleenwort, mountain pansy, and the club-mosses (and upland birds such as red grouse) tend to disappear and occasionally be refound, though there is a general tendency to decline. The high area around the Chains, inland from Lynmouth, is noted as being particularly wet and boggy. The WT has a reserve at Hurscombe (SS 974320) on the edge of Wimbleball Lake – a relatively new reservoir – which has a pleasant mixture of habitats in attractive surroundings.

Nowadays, the area is well protected by its NP status, with a good number of SSSIs in the key sites. Access to the unenclosed land is generally easy, though longer walks are required for some places. The best times to visit are between April and September, though October–November is quiet with good autumn colour and fungi. The NP office is in Dulverton, or tourist information offices in the main towns can help.

Golden-ringed dragonfly *Cordulegaster boltonii*

SITE
86 Bridgwater Bay

A huge area of estuarine habitat where the Parrett meets the
Severn Estuary, mainly included in an NNR. Grid ref: ST 278464.

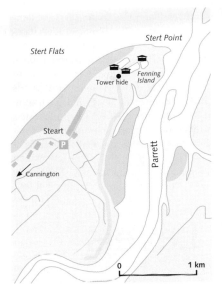

Bridgwater Bay NNR protects 2559 ha – a huge sweep of mudflats, saltmarsh, shingle, and coastal edge habitats. It is considered to be internationally important for its wintering and migrant waders and wildfowl, and is designated as both a Ramsar site and a Special Protection Area under European legislation. It interacts ecologically with the nearby Somerset Levels (see p. 208), and birds move between the two sites according to tidal and weather conditions.

The upper saltmarshes are dominated by common reed, sea aster, and other plants, with sea couch where there is sheep-grazing. There are large areas of cord-grass, which have grown from plantings in the early 1900s.

Huge numbers of birds visit the site. It is well known as the most important

Pool in dunes

moulting site for shelduck in the UK, with 2000 or more gathering in late summer in locations that are relatively safe from predators. Visiting waders include up to 15 000 dunlin, large numbers of whimbrel on passage, and smaller numbers of Icelandic black-tailed godwits, curlew, spotted redshank, little stint, and more common species such as redshank and oystercatchers. Raptors, including harriers, peregrine, and merlin are attracted to this abundance of prey, providing a spectacular sight if you are lucky enough to see them. Wildfowl here include wigeon, pintail, shoveler, and teal.

In spring, there are good numbers of yellow wagtails on the surrounding damp grasslands, together with reed and sedge warblers in the reedbeds. It is also quite an interesting site botanically, with uncommon species such as sea clover, knotted clover, honewort, and yellow horned-poppy in the drier grassy and shingle habitats along the south side of the bay.

Access is best from Steart (or Stert) village, and there are several hides (including a new tower hide) and information boards along the coastal trail. The Huntspill River NNR effectively extends the reserve eastwards up the Huntspill River, which is now being managed largely for wildlife conservation.

Across the estuary, and close to the northern edge of the NNR, there is a reserve at Berrow dunes (ST 294535), protecting a fine area of species-rich dunes and foreshore that is particularly good for orchids.

87 Somerset Levels

Vast expanse of low-lying wetland, protected under a series of national and international designations.

The Somerset Levels is the general name given to a huge territory covering over 500 square kilometres, defined roughly by the Mendip Hills (see p. 210) to the north, the Quantock Hills to the south-west, and wherever the land rises between Taunton, Glastonbury, and Yeovil to the south-east. It is land that was once under the sea, but has been steadily reclaimed over the millennia through a combination of falling sea levels and attempts at drainage by humans. The whole area is barely above sea level and still floods readily, especially when large amounts of flood water meet high tides in the Bristol Channel. Today, it is an appealingly historic landscape of damp pastures, intersected with ditches or 'wet fences', known locally as rhynes, and dotted with pollard willows, with settlements confined to the slightly higher-lying areas.

Of special interest to the naturalist are the ditches themselves, the unimproved wet pastures, areas that flood regularly, and a few fragments of older raised bog and fen vegetation that still exist here and there. There are also substantial areas of

Black-tailed godwit *Limosa limosa*

former peat workings that are being restored to sites of high wildlife value.

The ditches, which occur throughout the levels, vary enormously in their natural history value according to their management, neighbouring land use, and when they were last cleared. Overall, they are very rich in plants, including all the British duckweeds (not forgetting Britain's tiniest plant, rootless duckweed, just millimetres across!), frogbit, water-soldier, water-violet, bur-reeds, water dock, the insectivorous bladderworts, several species of water-crowfoot, flowering-rush, arrowhead, and many others. In the better meadows, there is marsh thistle, marsh-orchids, yellow iris, numerous sedges, cowslips, ragged-Robin, and so on, producing a wonderful tapestry of colour in midsummer. The areas of true bog have the typical bog plants such as bog asphodel, marsh cinquefoil, sundews, and bog pimpernel, with the much rarer marsh pea in a few peripheral patches.

The whole area is very rich in invertebrates. The ditches contain more common species such as whirligig beetles, pond skaters, water boatmen, and water measurers in abundance, but also include less common species such as water-crickets, water spider, raft spiders, water scorpion, about 60 species of diving beetles, and the uncommon great silver diving beetle. There are about 25 species of dragonflies associated with water bodies and the boggy areas, and uncommon species like the musk beetle are found in association with old pollard willows.

The levels are also known as a special place for birds. In winter, especially when the levels flood, large quantities can be found. These include whimbrel, Bewick's swans, teal, wigeon, ruff, godwits, and curlews. In the breeding season there are redshank, curlew, lapwings, snipe, a few black-tailed godwits, and marsh harriers, yellow wagtail, and whinchat, amongst others. Barn owls are common across the levels, thanks to the extensive areas of traditional farming and suitable feeding habitat. Otters seem to be increasing

A rhyne on the levels, with Glastonbury Tor beyond

here, brown hares occur throughout, and there are good populations of all the more common reptiles and amphibians.

Some sites to visit include the reserve at West Sedgemoor (RSPB; ST 360240), where there is a woodland heronry, and a large expanse of traditional grazing meadows, often flooded in winter, when the numbers of wildfowl and waders can be impressive; Shapwick Heath NNR and Westhay Moor NNR, in the varied area west of Glastonbury; and the sizeable 'Avalon Marshes' area where a number of conservation organizations are endeavouring to recreate high-quality wetland habitats from old peat workings. It lies mainly to the south of Meare and Westhay, west of Glastonbury, and there is a peatland information centre near Meare.

North of the Mendips, there is a smaller area of rather similar levels in the Gordano Valley, just north-east of Clevedon. The Gordano Valley NNR (ST 435727) protects 66 ha of this habitat, though access is restricted to footpaths at present.

SITE
88 Mendip Hills, southern scarp

Carboniferous limestone hills in north Somerset, with a series of reserves along their southern side.

The Mendip Hills form a solid block of high land across the north-east of the Somerset Levels. Between Brean Down, where a finger of limestone juts into the Bristol Channel, and Wells, almost all the southern scarp of this limestone ridge is of special interest to the naturalist. Most of it is now in sympathetic management, and efforts are being made to ensure the protection of the remainder.

It is probably best known as an area for special plants. There is fine limestone turf covering most of the steeper slopes, intersected by dramatic gorges at Cheddar and Ebbor. Plants include Cheddar pink (confined to this location within Britain), white rock-rose (abundant on Brean Down), and hybrids with common rock-rose, honewort, lesser meadow-rue, bloody crane's-bill, purple gromwell, rock stonecrop, pale St John's-wort, and most of the more common downland plants. Butterflies including dark green fritillary,

Cheddar pink *Dianthus gratianopolitanus*

Cheddar Gorge

brown argus and Duke of Burgundy abound in the more sheltered locations. Mammals such as badgers and dormice are common in the wooded areas.

Some special areas to visit include Brean Down (NT; ST 296589), with open access; the Crook Peak and Wavering Down area (NT; ST 390559) with superb stony limestone grassland; Cheddar Gorge (ST 468540), which has marvellous rare and uncommon plants in a spectacular setting, extending up to Black Rock and Long Wood; Rodney Stoke NNR (ST 486505), which is mainly woodland; and Ebbor Gorge NNR (ST 521485), a beautiful wooded gorge with many features of interest, just north-west of Wells. Black Down, to the west of Long Wood, has gorse and heather, with whinchats, stonechats, grasshopper warblers, and recently arrived Dartford warblers.

Not far away to the north, there are two long-established reservoirs which have developed into important bird sites. Chew Valley Lake (ST 570615) is the largest, with better access and visibility from the roads that skirt it. Large numbers of waterfowl pass the winter here, and good numbers of birds breed, including ruddy duck. The southernmost bay around Herriot's Bridge is a reserve, and there are several hides, some of which require a permit from the Bristol Water Company. Blagdon Lake, a few kilometres to the east, has plenty of interest, though it is harder to watch.

A few kilometres east of Chew Valley Lake, the WT runs a lovely old unspoilt farm – Folly Farm (ST 610603) – as a reserve. There are ancient flowery pastures, old woodland, and wet areas, rich in flowers and butterflies.

SITE
89 Avon Gorge

An impressive limestone gorge on the edge of Bristol, including the Avon Gorge NNR.

The Avon Gorge cuts through the limestone on the southern edge of Bristol. The best area for the naturalist lies downstream from the famous Clifton suspension bridge. It is a famous botanical locality. Although not as rich as it once was, because of development, pollution, and lack of management, it still retains many features of interest, especially on the bare limestone cliffs and rocks.

Peregrines and ravens are now regular breeders, and there is a special viewpoint (ST 564742) for the former. Kingfishers and dippers are both around, especially on the nearby river Trym.

The Avon Gorge NNR (ST 553731) consists mainly of woodland, centred around Leigh Woods on the west side of the river although there are open patches within it. Rare plants of special note here or nearby include Bristol rock-cress, virtually confined to this area within the UK, the western form of spiked speedwell, spring cinquefoil, fingered sedge, round-headed garlic, bloody crane's-bill, and several whitebeams including the endemic Bristol whitebeam *Sorbus bristoliensis* – at its only site in the world – and *S. wilmottiana*. The woodland reserve is also particularly rich in fungi, and the gorge is also a classic geological site. Butterflies, including white-letter hairstreaks, are abundant in summer.

At the mouth of the gorge, there is a reserve known as the Avonmouth Sewage Works (WT; ST 535794), covering 10 ha of open water and associated habitats. It lies on the Severn Estuary migration flyway and attracts large numbers of birds, espe-

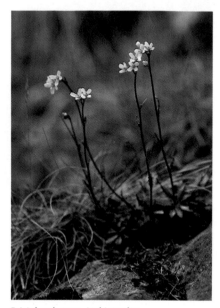

Bristol rock-cress *Arabis scabra*

cially at migration times. The Avon walkway, maintained by Bristol City Council, runs alongside the river and gives good views of feeding birds on the mud, and plants such as ivy broomrape and little-robin at the bottom of the gorge.

Not far to the west lies Weston Big Wood (WT; ST 456750), a reserve covering 38 ha of ancient woodland overlying limestone. Apart from fine displays of more common woodland plants such as bluebells and lesser celandines, it is also home to various less common plants such as herb-Paris, small-leaved lime, purple gromwell, and several uncommon whitebeams, as well as a good range of butterflies.

South-west England

A selection of other important sites in the counties

Catcott Lows (ST 400415): flooding meadows; waders, wildfowl.

Langford Heathfield (ST 106227): woodland, heath; good birds and flowers.

Sand Point/Middle Hope (ST 330660): grassland, scrub, saltmarsh; flowers, warblers.

Steep Holm (ST 229607): grassland, scrub; rich flora, great and lesser black-backed gulls breed, as do cormorants.

Walborough (ST 315579): grassland, scrub, saltmarsh; waders, wildfowl.

Willsbridge Mill (ST 665708): woodland, grassland, stream, pond; woodland birds and flowers, kingfisher, dipper.

^{SITE}
90 Channel Islands

Islands that lie closer to France than Britain, and are noted for their mild climate and abundance of southern species.

There is not space here to do full justice to the flora and fauna of the Channel Islands which, for their size, are as rich as any-where in Britain. Their southerly position and oceanic climate have allowed a particularly rich flora to flourish, including a

Spring flowers on the north coast of Guernsey

number of species that are very rare or absent in the UK. For example, lax-flowered orchid, which is common on the Continent southwards, is found in several sites here but not in mainland Britain; Jersey thrift, which within Britain only occurs in Jersey; and sand crocus, which is quite frequent in Guernsey and Jersey but only occurs elsewhere in Britain at one site (see p. 193). There are also special insects here such as the Glanville fritillary (only otherwise reliably on the Isle of Wight), and reptiles such as green lizard and common wall lizard that are not native elsewhere in the UK. Dartford warblers are common in heathy areas, and many other birds occur.

On Jersey, key sites include L'Ancresse Common and dunes; Les Landes (OS 547554), a substantial area of exposed heathland in the north-west; and the superb reserve of Les Quennevais (OS 573493), with a wonderfully rich flora and fauna, including many rarities.

On Guernsey the sites are less clearly defined. The coast path from St Peter's Port to Pleinmont passes through various habitats, and the flowers of Pleinmont Point itself include sand crocuses and spring squills. It is also good for watching birds at migration times. Fort Hommet and Port Soif also have fine coastal flowers.

Alderney has particularly good birds, including a gannet colony and other breeding seabirds. Sark and Herm are both small islands with good flowers, and particularly good birds.

Virtually the whole coastline of the Channel Islands is of interest for its rich intertidal and marine life, and the smaller islands are particularly exciting in this respect.

A selection of other important sites

Colin McCathie Reserve (Vale Pond): brackish pond, reeds; waterbirds, little egret.

La Claire Mare: reeds, pasture; waders, water rail, kingfisher.

Central England

Central England

Introduction

Central England is essentially a region of rather flat or gently undulating landscapes, though augmented by areas of higher ground such as the Shropshire Hills in the north, the Malverns, Herefordshire Hills, and Black Mountains in the west, and the Cotswold Plateau in the south.

The east is dominated by the wide valley of the Trent, draining north through Nottingham to the Humber Estuary. The other major rivers are the Severn, winding in an arc through Shropshire, Worcestershire, and Gloucestershire, and the Thames, with its water meadows, flowing along the southern edge of the region. In the west we find largely a pretty patchwork of wood-

land and pasture, while the lower land in the east is much more intensively cultivated, although even here patches of woodland remain as remnants of once more extensive ancient forests.

The typical central English countryside is one of farmed fields, both arable and grazed, delineated by hedgerows (many of which have sadly been grubbed out) or trees (usually elm or oak). Scattered here and there are (mainly) small woods, remnants of once more extensive forest. Today most of Central England is not very well wooded, although it certainly was at the time of the Domesday Book (1086). Staffordshire, for example, is estimated to have lost 80% of its woods since that

Knapp & Papermill (see p. 228)

Previous page: Buckholt Wood (see p. 233)

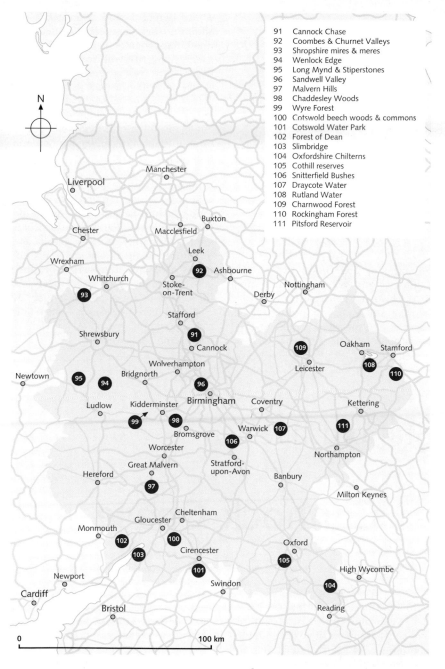

91 Cannock Chase
92 Coombes & Churnet Valleys
93 Shropshire mires & meres
94 Wenlock Edge
95 Long Mynd & Stiperstones
96 Sandwell Valley
97 Malvern Hills
98 Chaddesley Woods
99 Wyre Forest
100 Cotswold beech woods & commons
101 Cotswold Water Park
102 Forest of Dean
103 Slimbridge
104 Oxfordshire Chilterns
105 Cothill reserves
106 Snitterfield Bushes
107 Draycote Water
108 Rutland Water
109 Charnwood Forest
110 Rockingham Forest
111 Pitsford Reservoir

time. Leicestershire has very little woodland, with what remains being largely restricted to Charnwood Forest in the west and scattered woods in the east.

Northamptonshire has wooded enclaves, too – notably Rockingham Forest in the north-east and Salcey Forest in the south. The most wooded part of Oxfordshire is

Central England

Fen violet *Viola persicifolia* (recently rediscovered in Oxfordshire – see p. 242)

while Hereford and Worcester and Shropshire have a generous scattering of woods throughout.

The Malverns and Shropshire Hills towards the west of the region have a somewhat wilder aspect than much of the generally more agricultural lowlands. The underlying geology is complex, but many of the lowland soils derive from Jurassic marls or sandstones, and the higher plateaux, such as Cannock Chase, from Triassic sandstone. These conditions give rise generally to rather acid soils and a tendency towards a sandy, heath-like vegetation or ground cover in acid woodland. The Cotswolds are based mainly on clays, marls, and limestone and the vegetation is very different, with important areas of chalk grassland. In the south-east of the region, the Chilterns are underlain largely by chalk and there are also some splendidly rich grassland sites here, as well as beech-dominated woods.

around the Chilterns in the extreme south-east, with another cluster centred on Wychwood. Gloucestershire, however, is quite well endowed with woodland, especially in the west, in the Forest of Dean and along the Cotswold Plateau,

Staffordshire

91 Cannock Chase
SITE

Remnants of an original forest, now with a good mix of woodland, heath, and boggy sites.

Cannock Chase (SJ 980190, OS 127/8) lies just to the south-east of Stafford, and consists mainly of heath, with pine plantations and pockets of birch and oak woodland. There are also bogs, streams, and a gravel pit. This was once an extensive royal hunting forest and it still covers a large territory between Cannock and the valley of the Trent. It is

well worth a visit, especially in spring and summer, but can be crowded in places at weekends.

Some remnants of mixed woodland do persist, mainly dominated by sessile oak and birch, with stands of alder and willows on the damper soils in the valleys. Plants of the heath include heather, bell heather, bilberry, crowberry, and cow-

Central England

Roe deer *Capreolus capreolus* (Robert Dickson)

berry. An unusual plant found here is the rare hybrid between bilberry and cowberry, which is known from a handful of sites in Staffordshire, Derbyshire, and Yorkshire. It is known locally as the Cannock Chase berry. In the valley mires and more acid bogs can be found such species as bogbean, marsh cinquefoil, grass-of-Parnassus, cross-leaved heath, bog asphodel, cranberry, bog pimpernel, marsh pennywort, common butterwort, both round-leaved and great sundews, marsh valerian, and marsh violet.

The birds include woodpeckers, pied flycatcher, redstart, wood warbler, and hawfinch, with siskins and redpolls also regular (the latter two especially in the alders). The felled areas have recently attracted woodlarks and tree pipits, and this is one of the best northern sites for nightjars, and also grasshopper warblers. Watch also for ravens, buzzards, and goshawks. In winter the heathland brings in short-eared owls, and sometimes merlins and great grey shrikes. Amongst the birds of the plantations are crossbill (winter), coal tit, goldcrest, long-eared owl, and sparrowhawk.

Deer are prominent in Cannock Chase, with red, roe, sika, and muntjac, as well as the more common fallow, but they are generally rather shy and best spotted early or late in the day. With luck you may also spot red squirrels amongst the pines.

Butterflies are well represented, too, with green hairstreak, dingy skipper, and small pearl-bordered fritillary, in addition to more common species, and there are emperor and oak eggar moths.

Chartley Moss

Other sites nearby

Blithfield Reservoir (SK 058238) is one of the top reservoirs in the region, with huge numbers of ducks and gulls, especially in winter, and good movements of passage waders, particularly in drier years when the mud is exposed. Osprey and little gull drop in from time to time, and it is worth looking for ruddy duck and goosander.

Chartley Moss NNR (SK 0227; 42 ha) contains Britain's best floating bog (*Schwingmoor* – a German term for this mire formation). Access is by permit only, and the bog is rather dangerous. The pools have a floating carpet of bog-moss and peat as part of succession to a raised bog. The central pools are surrounded by birch and pine woodland. Bog plants abound, with cottongrasses, cranberry, bog-rosemary, round-leaved sundew, and cross-leaved heath. The dragonflies are rather special, too, with white-faced, black, and yellow-winged darters, four-spotted chaser, and keeled skimmer.

SITE 92 Coombes and Churnet Valleys

Wooded valleys with clear rivers, on the south-west edge of the Peak District.

Red campion
Silene dioica

These pretty valleys are excellent walking country, combining unpolluted streams and rivers with attractively wooded valley sides. The ancient nature of some of the woodland is attested to by the diversity of insects, especially the beetles, and there is much to divert both specialist and generalist.

Coombes Valley (RSPB; SK 005530), about 5 km south-east of Leek, is set in a steep valley, much of it clothed with woodland of varying age, some of it with old oaks dominant. Brown trout inhabit the clear waters of the Coombes Brook, which winds and tumbles through the reserve. The woodland has birch, ash, holly, rowan, and wych elm, with some small-leaved lime. Bluebells, wood anemones, foxgloves, and red campions grow well here,

with primrose, lousewort, moschatel, dog-violet, and adder's-tongue in the more open spots. There are also common spotted- and greater butterfly-orchid. The birds are those typical of such woodland – woodpeckers, woodcock, long-eared and tawny owl, redstarts, and a growing colony of pied flycatchers, aided by provision of nest boxes. Along the stream and at the pool you may see grey wagtail, dipper, and kingfisher. This is a good site for badgers. The insects include 1200 species of beetle and 24 butterflies, including high brown fritillary, the latter a declining species, with strongholds in the southern Lake District and Malverns. There are two hides, and an information centre.

Churnet Valley Woods (RSPB; SJ 990489) consists of three woods near the village of Consall. This is another good site for woodland birds, with redstart, pied flycatcher, and wood warbler, and siskins and redpolls in the winter. The butterflies include white-letter hairstreak.

Dimmings Dale also lies in the Churnet Valley, some 15 km south-west of Ashbourne, not far from the famous theme park at Alton Towers and arguably more worthwhile to visit. A car park between Alton and Oakamoor has a tea room nearby, and from here a track takes you past a pool, with woodland close by. Birds here include wood warbler, pied flycatcher, redstart, and nuthatch.

Also in the Churnet Valley is Hawksmoor (NT; SK 035445) with its mixture of woodland, pasture, and river. Here there are healthy populations of fox, badger, stoat, weasel, and brown hare, while the woods (mainly mixed oak) have woodpeckers, warblers, and redstarts. In the wetter areas and along the river expect kingfisher, dipper, yellow and grey wagtail, and common sandpiper. There is a fine spring display of bluebells, ramsons, and wood anemone. These mainly acid habitats also have cow-wheat and wood-sorrel and there are large areas of birch and bracken.

Other sites nearby

Manifold Valley (SK 100543). This beautiful valley in the Peak District NP lies just north of the NT property of Ilam Hall, north-west of Ashbourne (Derbyshire). Limestone cliffs, meadows, wooded dales, and clear river.

Castern Wood SSSI (WT; SK 119537, OS 119; 21 ha) is a steep woodland dominated by ash, alongside the Manifold. Good woodland birds. Flowers include cowslip, primrose, and hybrids (false oxlip). Old (grilled) mineshafts are used by hibernating bats.

A selection of other important sites in the county

Aqualate Mere NNR (SJ 774204, OS 127; 192 ha; access restricted) is a large mere, with diverse flora and heronry.

Croxall Pools (National Forest) (SK 181152), near Burton upon Trent, is a series of pools and pits, with wet meadows nearby. It attracts large numbers of wildfowl, including all three swans, and geese including bean and Brent. Garganey, and wintering scoters and smew. Little gulls are regular in spring, and there is a growing list of waders.

Doxey Marshes (WT; SJ 915239, OS 127; 145 ha) is one of Staffordshire's largest reserves, much of which has SSSI status. The main habitats here are marsh and grassland in the floodplain of the river Sow, which contain a good wetland flora and attract many wildfowl and waders.

Hem Heath Wood (WT; SJ 885412, OS 118; 9 ha) has wood warblers. Plants include wild cherry and marsh cinquefoil.

Loynton Moss (WT; SJ 7825) is a wetland with alder carr, reedbeds, and raised bog; greater spearwort and bog myrtle.

Mottey Meadows NNR (SJ 840130, OS 127; 37 ha). Fine old meadows with fritillaries and marsh-orchids.

Rod Wood (WT; SJ 997529, OS 118) has woodland, grassland, and marsh, with adder's-tongue, dyer's greenweed, twayblade, and early purple orchid.

Shropshire

93 Shropshire mires and meres

Some of the finest raised bogs and other mires, with a special flora and insect fauna characteristic of these rare habitats.

North Shropshire, towards the border with Wales, has some fascinating wetland sites, amongst which some of the most interesting are the mires (wet peatlands) and meres (bodies of open water). Good lowland mires, although highly character-istic of Britain, are a great rarity as so many have been ruined through peat extraction and drainage.

Fenn's, Whixall, and Bettisfield Mosses NNR/SSSI (SJ 4936; OS 126) comprises three adjacent mires on the Welsh border, just to the south-west of Whitchurch. With a total of about 510 ha, this site preserves the central core of one of the best lowland raised bogs in the country. Like many mires, this site was badly damaged in the past by commercial extraction of the peat, and a restoration programme is underway. This involves tree and scrub clearance, combined with a raising of the water levels by damming. This management has already yielded results, with a substantial

Purple moor-grass
Molinia caerulea

recolonization by bog species, which bodes well for the future. Plants include bog-rose-mary, cranberry, and white beak-sedge. There are over 1800 species of insect recorded here, with large heath, northern footman moth, bog bush-cricket, and a rare caddis fly (*Hagenella clathrata*). The 27 species of dragonfly include white-faced darter, and the raft spider is also found here. The mammals include water vole and brown hare, and the birds skylark, nightjar, linnet, reed bunting, and tree sparrow. The site can be visited throughout the year, although a permit is needed away from footpaths. Roadside parking is available.

Nearby Wem Moss NNR (WT; SJ 472342; OS 126) is a smaller reserve of about 30 ha, and part of the same general mire complex. It lies near Northwood, some 6 km east of Ellesmere. This mire has a fringe of carr and woodland, with fen communities developed over mineral-rich groundwater, dominated by willow, alder, and alder buckthorn. Other areas have purple moor-grass in profusion, and there are also well-developed expanses of bog-

Reed bunting *Emberiza schoeniclus*

Central England

A peaty pool in Whixall Moss

moss, with scattered pools. Here grow all three British sundews, cranberry, cotton-grass, bog-rosemary, white beak-sedge, cross-leaved heath, and the spicily scented shrub bog myrtle, as well as early marsh- and lesser butterfly-orchids. Wem Moss is one of the most southerly sites for the local large heath butterfly. Visitors are warned that the reserve also has a large population of adders. Although there is no car park, a nearby lay-by can be used, and there is a footpath around the site. For access, apply to the Shropshire WT.

Brown Moss (SJ 564394) near Whitchurch is a similar site, with bog surrounded by woodland (in this case the latter is rather acid and heathy). The pools here have broad-bodied chaser and other dragonflies.

Ellesmere lies just east of the town of the same name. This large lake is the biggest of Shropshire's meres and an attractive site, with fringing vegetation and mixed woodland clothing the banks, especially on the northern shore. The site has a visitor centre and café, and lakeside walks giving good views over the water. In spring and summer there are sand martins and great crested grebes, with buzzards and hobbies possible, and spotted and pied flycatchers in the woodland. In winter the mere brings in plenty of wildfowl – including goosander, golden-eye, and sometimes smew.

Prees Heath (SJ 558368; OS 126) nearby is an area of heath and scrub with silver-studded blue and small skipper.

SITE
94 Wenlock Edge

One of Shropshire's (and England's) most famous landmarks – a
wooded ridge rising over the adjacent valleys.

Wenlock Edge (SO 595988) is a magnificent limestone escarpment, running about 20 km from Much Wenlock to Craven Arms, with crags, scrub, woodland, grassland, and marshy spots. This romantic spot, made famous partly through A. E. Housman's *A Shropshire lad* (set to music by Ralph Vaughan Williams), also justifies a visit for its natural history, although much of the original woodland has been either cleared or planted with conifers. It is one of the most famous landmarks in the region. On its western flank, the hillside shows signs of quarrying for stone and lime; some of the rocks here are rich in fossils. The eastern side is gentler, descending gradually into Corve Dale.

The views from the ridge are outstanding. This is a very wooded range, although much of it carries relatively recent plantations.

There are also pockets of limestone grassland, in places quite rich, with quaking-grass, sainfoin, autumn gentian, yellow-wort, carline thistle, and many orchids.

There are a number of woods here, mainly owned by the NT, with excellent woodland birds and flowers. These include Blakeway Coppice (SO 595988; 86 ha), Easthope Wood (SO 570965), and Harley Bank (SJ 605002; 29 ha). These are primarily mixed woods, with oak, beech, ash, hazel, wild cherry, and birch, and in some cases with an understorey of holly, rowan, spindle, and guelder-rose. Poorly drained sites have sessile oak and ash communities, with wych elm, often with ramsons, sanicle, and woodruff in the herb layer.

The fine Elizabethan house of Wilderhope Manor (NT) is about 11 km south-west of Much Wenlock.

Cowslips *Primula veris* in an old pasture on Wenlock Edge

SITE 95 Long Mynd and Stiperstones

Two magnificent ridges, lying roughly parallel, some 20 km south-west of Shrewsbury.

Just west of Church Stretton lies the ridge of Long Mynd (NT; SO 430940), rising to over 500 m and offering wonderful views in clear weather. Climbing these hills takes one rather suddenly into an upland habitat, with moorland animals and plants more usually associated with more northerly and westerly ranges.

Common spotted-orchid
Dactylorhiza fuchsii

The reserve covers part of a plateau rising up from the plain. The curved mass of the Long Mynd ('Mynd' from the Welsh for 'Mountain') is cut by several deep valleys (known locally as hollows or batches) which serve to break up the landscape and add to the general diversity of habitats. The highest point lies at 516 m, and there are excellent views in clear weather, across to Wenlock Edge and Stiperstones, and further as far as the Brecon Beacons and Cadair Idris in Wales.

Extensive sheep pastures on the Long Mynd

The ridge, once forested like so much of England, now carries mainly heather moor managed to encourage red grouse, like much of the moorland further north in Britain. It is reminiscent in general appearance of parts of Dartmoor and Exmoor, with its gently rolling foothills and numerous valleys.

Other upland birds to be seen here are ravens and curlews, along with ring ouzel, wheatear, and stonechat, with dipper and grey wagtail on the streams. Buzzards are fairly common, and wood warbler, redstart, and pied flycatcher breed in the pockets of woodland on the lower slopes. Long Mynd is a fine spot to see moorland shrubs such as heather, bilberry, and bracken, and flowers like tormentil, heath bedstraw, shepherd's cress, and navelwort. The boggy sites are found mainly in places where springs rise at the plateau's edge. Here, flush communities carry such flowers as common butterwort, sundew, bog pimpernel, marsh lousewort, and marsh pennywort. Other plants to see here are heath bedstraw and common spotted-orchid.

Stiperstones NNR (EN; SO 3798) is mainly upland heather moor and bog. It lies closer to the Welsh border than Long Mynd, covers about 480 ha, and rises up as a majestic, largely heather-clad ridge, topping out at nearly 540 m. A series of valleys cuts into its flanks and areas of mainly birch woodland and the occasional boggy patch add to the overall interest. The crest of the ridge has rather strange tors of quartzite, one famously known as the 'Devil's Chair'. Large parts of the hillsides carry an upland moor, with heather, bilberry, cowberry, crowberry, and bell heather and western gorse tending to dominate on the warmer, south-facing slopes. Notable plants here are moonwort and stag's-horn club-moss, and the acid grassland is brightened by the flowers of mountain pansy. On boggy patches there are cranberry, bog-mosses, cottongrass, bog asphodel, and marsh violet.

At the northern end there are some groves of ancient pollarded holly trees – a highly unusual feature which dates back to the time when the local farmers managed this as a wood-pasture, using holly as winter animal fodder. It is estimated that some of these trees may be as much as 400 years old; many are certainly well into their third century. There are also remnants of oak woodland, some rich in birch and rowan. One pollarded rowan measures 225 cm in girth – a British record.

Red grouse and curlew inhabit the moorland, along with stonechat, and this habitat is maintained by a programme of regular cutting and burning. The insects include hairy wood ant, grayling, green hairstreak, pearl-bordered fritillary, and emperor and fox moths.

The Stiperstones NNR lies near Minsterley, and there is a convenient car park at the southern end of the site.

A selection of other important sites in the county

Atcham (SJ 538084; OS 126), on the banks of the river Severn just south-east of Shrewsbury. White-legged damselfly, banded demoiselle, club-tailed dragonfly.

Berrington Pool (SJ 526073; OS 126): downy emerald, variable damselfly, red-eyed damselfly.

Clunton Coppice SSSI (WT; SO 343806, OS 137; 23 ha), of sessile oak coppice woodland, with birch, holly, and yew. Buzzard, wood warbler, and pied flycatcher.

Llanymynech Quarry (SJ 266218; OS 126) is a disused quarry with both pearl-bordered fritillaries and dingy and grizzled skippers.

West Midlands

SITE 96 Sandwell Valley

A fine reserve within the Birmingham conurbation, with easy access and a good information centre.

This RSPB reserve (SP 036931) in the valley of the river Tame is an example of how conservation can succeed, even in an urban environment. In this case the site is completely encircled by greater Birmingham, but nevertheless well worth visiting.

At the heart of the reserve is a lake with an island, surrounded by marshy areas with scrub. The wet areas have been designed to provide plenty of mud for migrant waders. The bird list is surprisingly long, with kingfisher, water rail, and jack snipe in winter. Breeding birds include great crested and little grebe, tufted duck, little ringed plover, snipe, lapwing, and many warblers.

A visitor centre offers fine views and facilities, including for the disabled, and footpaths take a circular route around Forgemill Lake and the slightly more distant Swan Pool. The pools are surrounded by reeds, wet scrub, and areas of grassland.

Winter and spring are the best times to come to Sandwell, when the wildfowl in particular are at their most impressive. There are large numbers of pochard and shoveler, alongside wigeon, teal, and goldeneye, but perhaps most notable are the regular winter flocks of goosander – numbering up to about 50. Other birds include water rail, kingfisher, and little ringed plover, and this is also a good site for willow tits, a species normally quite hard to spot.

Nearby Sutton Park NNR (SP 113962), close to Sutton Coldfield, is another oasis in a built-up area. This park covers some 970 ha and holds a wide range of habitats – from oak, birch, and conifer woodland, to heath and bog, to open ponds. The wet heaths and mires have species such as cranberry, bog pimpernel, butterwort, round-leaved sundew, and grass-of-Parnassus. Raptors such as hen harriers and merlins sometimes hunt over the heathland in winter.

A selection of other important sites in the county

Kinver Edge (NT; SO 835830) is just to the west of Stourbridge in Staffordshire. This wooded hill has good heathland and scrub and is the haunt of lizards, adders, and slow-worms.

Wren's Nest NNR (SO 937917, OS 139; 35 ha) is an educational reserve in Dudley, centred on fossil-rich limestone cliffs and quarries, famous for its trilobites.

Wigeon *Anas penelope* (Mike Lane)

Central England

Hereford and Worcester

97 Malvern Hills

Walking country par excellence, with footpaths following the ridge through a mixed patchwork of woods, grassland, and scrub.

The Malvern Hills lie just to the west and south-west of Great Malvern and stretch for some 13 km, running south to north. The geology is varied, the main rock being ancient granite, but there are also some areas with limestone and others with sandstone. The tops of the hills are mostly rather bare or clothed with a short, rough grassland. The lower slopes tend to be quite well wooded, and these very mixed communities have ash, oak, birch, field maple, cherry, holly, hazel, rowan, and yew. Between the woods and the more open habitats are areas of scrub, also very mixed, with gorse, elder, hawthorn, roses, and willows.

The South Malvern Hills to the east of Ledbury are well worth visiting, and this stretch, between Little Malvern and Hollybush, offers excellent walking. British Camp is an Iron Age fort on the side of Herefordshire Beacon and makes a good starting point. From here a trail follows the ridge, through woodland and open country, skirting News Wood, to Swinyard Hill, past Gullet Quarry, and south to Midsummer Hill (NT; SO 759375), noted for its ancient holly trees. Just to the east lies Castlemorton Common, an area of wet heath that has very good butterflies, including dark green, small pearl-bordered, and high brown fritillaries. The Malverns are one of the strongholds of the high brown, a species which has suffered a marked decline over most of its range. The woods hold pied flycatchers, and the grassy slopes have some colonies of glow-worms. Other butterflies to expect are dark green and pearl-bordered fritillaries, marbled white, green hairstreak, and grayling.

Woodland flowers include purple and broad-leaved helleborine, wild daffodil, columbine, and greater butterfly-orchid.

The North Malvern Hills, immediately west of Great Malvern are, somewhat surprisingly, a prime site for migrant birds, especially from September through November. North Hill and Worcestershire Beacon and their associated valleys are well worth exploring at this time of year. Ring ouzel and redstart are regular, and snow bunting, dotterel, and shore lark possible. Worcestershire Beacon is the best midland site for snow bunting, from late September.

Knapp & Papermill (WT; SO 748522) is a fine reserve a few kilometres north of Great Malvern, near the village of Alfrick in the valley of the Leigh Brook. It encompasses ancient meadows, orchards, and woods and has something to interest all

Sparrowhawk *Accipiter nisus*

Central England

Bluebells *Hyacinthoides non-scripta*, Malvern Hills

naturalists. The brook itself has trout and otters, kingfishers, grey wagtails, and dippers, and a hide is sited with a view of a regular kingfisher nesting site. Buzzards and sparrowhawks are usually about over the woods. The old meadows and pastures have many good flowers, such as yellow-rattle, green-winged and spotted-orchids, greater broomrape, and cowslips, and bluebells carpet the woods in spring. The site has records for 30 species of butterfly.

Nearby Ravenshill Wood (WT; SO 740539) is a mixed wood on limestone,

with spindle, broad-leaved helleborine, and herb-Paris, woodcock, and also wood white butterfly.

Brockhampton (NT; SO 682546) is an attractive park just east of Bromyard, with mixed woodland, streams, and ponds. The flowers include yellow archangel, enchanter's-nightshade, and dog's mercury; and the woodland birds buzzard, sparrowhawk, raven, woodcock, pied flycatcher, and redstart. The manor house is a splendid fourteenth-century half-timbered building, well worth a visit.

SITE 98 Chaddesley Woods

Typical central English oak wood, with a good flora and high invertebrate interest.

Chaddesley Woods NNR lies about 2 km east of Chaddesley Corbett, between Kidderminster and Bromsgrove. It con-

sists of about 50 ha of oak woodland, probably the remains of the medieval Royal Forest of Feckenham, with a similar area of plantation and some scrub and grassland. The site is on sandy loam, with clay-rich loam on the lower ground.

The reserve presents a classic lowland oak wood, with hazel, ash, rowan, and holly, and its diversity is improved by a series of streams, lanes, and small meadows. Notable flowers here are bluebells, herb-Paris, and early purple orchid. Butterflies include white-letter hairstreak and white admiral and the unusual terrestrial caddis fly is also found here. The usual woodland birds occur, and crossbills sometimes breed in the conifers. The

grassland, which is mainly managed by cattle-grazing, is floristically rich, with saw-wort, betony, knapweed, and common spotted-orchids.

Car parking is possible on the road running through the reserve, and there is a nature trail.

Pepper Wood (WdT; SO 940750, OS 139; 54 ha), which lies very close to Chaddesley, is a 'community wood' where visitors are encouraged to help with the traditional management, and rekindle lost links between local people and the living woodland.

Other sites nearby

Clent Hills (NT; SO 9480) is a country park with heath, grassland, streams, and mixed woodland. The latter has bird cherry, wood warbler, and redstart. Good butterfly site.

Monkwood (WT; SO 804607, OS 150). Mixed woodland about 8 km northwest of Worcester. Excellent woodland reserve for butterflies. Also for moths, with over 500 species recorded. Wood

white, dingy skipper (late May to June), silver-washed fritillary, white admiral (July), purple hairstreak (August).

Trench Wood (WT; SO 925587, OS 150) is a replanted ancient wood good for butterflies, with white admiral and white-letter hairstreak, brown argus, and grizzled skipper. Also common twayblade and adder's-tongue.

99 Wyre Forest

One of the largest remaining tracts of ancient forest, with delightfully varied and attractive habitats.

Wyre Forest is a large (over 2600 ha) remnant of ancient woodland, with grassland, old orchards, and streams. The Wyre Forest NNR (SO 730760) protects about 550 ha of this varied habitat with its rich flora and fauna. It developed under intensive management for charcoal and for bark used in the tanning industry.

Lily-of-the-valley
Convallaria majalis

The reserve has a great variety of habitat, from acid oak wood, through neutral woods

on clay to wet ash–elm woodland, to meadows, woodland glades, and rich riverside communities. It lies close to the river Severn and a clear stream, the Dowles Brook, runs through it. Much of Wyre is dominated by sessile oak woodland, with a mixture of other trees such as birch, ash, alder, small-leaved lime, and the occasional wild service-tree. The ground flora is varied, with bilberry, heather, bracken, wavy hair-grass, wood-sorrel, woodruff, wood crane's-bill, lily-of-the-valley, and narrow-leaved helleborine. There are also patches of afforestation. Pedunculate oak also grows here, but tends to be on the more clay-rich soils. Other interesting woodland flowers one might see are intermediate wintergreen, bloody crane's-bill, and columbine. In places, the closed woodland gives way to grassland or abandoned orchards, and the plants here include cowslip, betony, harebell, yellow-rattle, wild thyme, adder's-tongue, saw-wort, meadow saffron, green-winged orchid, and lousewort.

The insect fauna of the forest is very diverse, with 34 species of butterfly recorded, 500 species of moth, and the now rather famous terrestrial caddis fly, *Enoicyla pusilla*, found here at one of its few British sites. The butterflies include wood white, white admiral, purple and white-letter hairstreaks, dingy and grizzled skippers, silver-washed fritillary, and one of the largest English populations of pearl-bordered fritillary. The moths are noteworthy, too, with alder kitten, great oak beauty, and five species of clearwing. The beautiful demoiselle and white-legged damselfly both occur here, as do club-tailed dragonfly and southern hawker.

The forest is a good site for woodland birds, with all three woodpeckers, nuthatch, wood warbler, pied flycatcher, redstart, and hawfinch, and dippers, kingfishers, and grey wagtails on the streams. Buzzards and ravens also breed. Fallow deer are numerous, and both otters and polecats are found. Rodents include common dormouse, yellow-necked mouse, and water shrew, and there are good numbers of common pipistrelle and brown long-eared bats. The forest is also home to viviparous lizards, slow-worms, grass snakes, and adders.

The Dowles Brook which flows through the reserve has salmon, brook lampreys, and white-clawed crayfish.

There is a good car park and visitor centre about 3 km west of Bewdley.

An old farm at the heart of the Wyre Forest

A selection of other important sites in the county

Bradnor Hill (NT; SO 282584) lies right against the Welsh border, close to Hergest Ridge and part of Offa's Dyke. The hill has wonderful views and good grassland, heath, and scrub.

Bredon's Hardwick (SO 908347) near Tewkesbury has a series of water meadows and pools in the Avon Valley. These attract numbers of migrant waders and wildfowl, including geese and swans.

Bredon Hill NNR (SO 9639) is a famous landmark, with fine views, some old trees, and good unimproved grassland (with glow-worms).

Croft Castle (NT; SO 455655). Parkland with woods, grassland, and ponds. Famous for its large, ancient oaks and associated insect life. Old hornbeams attract hawfinches, and there are buzzards and pied flycatchers. Silver-washed fritillary.

Devil's Spittleful (WT; SO 8176), is one of the largest and richest heaths in the county.

Leeping Stocks (WT; SO 549161, OS 162; 8 ha): mixed wood with good flowers and fungi.

Lugg Meadows (WT; SO 527411, OS 149; 16 ha): meadows with fritillaries and flowering-rush.

Moccas Park NNR (SO 340424, OS 148/9; 39 ha) is an ancient deer park, with some old trees.

Piper's Hill & Dodderhill Common SSSI (WT; SO 960649, OS 150; 16 ha). Wood and wood-pasture with some ancient trees. Rich in fungi.

Tiddesley Wood (WT; SO 929462, OS 150; 80 ha): large wood, with small-leaved lime, wild service-tree, wild pear, crabapple, and plum.

Upton Warren (WT; SO 932674) has inland salt habitats as a result of past salt extraction. The resultant lagoons attract waders and gulls, including unusual species such as Temminck's stint and little gull. There is a breeding colony of ruddy ducks.

Gloucestershire

SITE
100 Cotswold beech woods and commons

Well-developed beech woods with patches of rich limestone grassland.

The Cotswold Beechwoods NNR (EN), between Gloucester and Stroud, includes a number of individual sites of international importance with some of Britain's finest beech woods. Nearby are several expanses of limestone grassland known as the commons, which have a rich flora and butterfly fauna. The whole area forms a patchwork of habitats, with woodland, clearings, grassland, and streams.

Not surprisingly, beech is the dominant tree in most of the woods, and some of these trees are very old. Often mixed in with beech are pedunculate oak, ash, and sycamore, as well as field maple, holly, yew, whitebeam, and wych elm. The ground flora of these woods has ivy, bramble, dog's mercury, sanicle, wood anemone, and bluebell, with in some places green hellebore, common wintergreen, bird's-nest orchid, and broad-leaved helleborine, as well as rarer species such as fingered sedge, stinking hellebore, and yellow star-of-Bethlehem. Woodland birds include buzzard, tawny owl, and wood warbler, and the butterflies white admiral, white-letter hairstreak, and silver-washed fritillary.

Buckholt Wood (EN; SO 8913, OS 162/3), on the Cotswold limestone just north of Cranham, is one of the best mature beech woods in Britain. The tree-layer is dominated by tall, well-grown beech trees, beneath which grow sapling beech, along with whitebeam, wych elm, ash, oak, and, in damper places, alder and willows. The shrub-layer may contain hawthorn, hazel, wayfaring-tree, holly, cherry, yew, sycamore, bramble, and dog rose. There is a rich flora typical of ancient woods, with many interesting species such as enchanter's-nightshade, primrose, woodruff, and wood spurge, with occasional clumps of green hellebore. The very rare red helleborine also occurs here, and at nearby Witcombe Wood. Frith Wood (WT; SO 8809) is another fine beech wood. Other notable plants found in these woods are white, narrow-lipped and green-flowered helleborines, columbine, lily-of-the-valley, bird's-nest orchid, greater butterfly-orchid, yellow bird's-nest, mezereon, and angular Solomon's-seal.

Between Stroud and Cheltenham lies a string of splendid sites with rich limestone grassland, connected by the northern section of the Cotswold Way. Painswick Hill (SO 8713) has rich chalk

Cranham Common

Central England

Wood warbler *Phylloscopus sibilatrix* (Mike Lane)

grassland with dwarf thistle, squinancy-wort, bee, fly, musk, frog, and greater butterfly-orchids, and autumn lady's-tresses. The butterflies include chalk-hill and small blues. Cranham Common is another good orchid-rich grassland site, with some juniper and whitebeam. Crickley Hill (NT; SO 930165) is an area of woodland and limestone grassland just south of Cheltenham on the northern Cotswold slopes, with wild thyme, clustered bellflower, and autumn gentian.

The Cotswold edge south of Stroud levels out into a plateau, with important areas of limestone grassland rich in flowers. Amongst the best of these are Minchinhampton Common (NT; SO 850010) and Rodborough Common (NT;

SO 850038). Regular grazing, mostly by cattle, keeps this habitat ideal for flowers and butterflies. This is particularly good for orchids, with 11 species, and the butterflies include small and chalk-hill blue, marbled white, and dark green and marsh fritillaries. These two commons are amongst the best places to appreciate the riches of limestone grassland. The soil on the plateau is generally fairly deep, but much shallower on the slopes at the edges, giving interesting variety to the flora. On the thinner soils can be found such flowers as carline thistle, herb-Robert, yellow-wort, and common restharrow, while in the coarser grassland there are species such as yellow-rattle, greater knapweed, kidney vetch, and common spotted-orchid. Where the sward is shorter, the flowers include harebell, bird's-foot-trefoil, eyebright, cowslip, common milkwort, wild thyme, autumn gentian, and rock-rose. A terraced effect caused by soil creep is evident on some of the slopes, and this favours marjoram, horseshoe vetch, and clustered bellflower. Bee, early purple, green-winged, fragrant, and pyramidal orchids also grow on the reserve, as well as pasqueflower and wild liquorice, the latter both rather local species.

101 Cotswold Water Park
SITE

Large concentration of old gravel workings in the Thames Valley. A top site for birds, especially wildfowl and migrant waders.

This splendid wildlife site has been developed around a series of flooded gravel pits on the border with Wiltshire, just south of Cirencester. There are more than 100 lakes in all, many of which have well-grown fring-ing vegetation, making them even more attractive to wildlife. Although recreation is one of the functions of the park, the area is so large and the bodies of water so diverse that the naturalist is also well catered for.

Nightingale *Luscinia megarhynchos*

Many migrant birds follow river systems, including the Thames Valley, and this undoubtedly draws in a great many travelling birds in spring and autumn. Black terns are regular such migrants, as are garganey, green, wood, and curlew sandpiper, greenshank, spotted redshank, ruff, and osprey. Breeders of note include redshank, lapwing, common tern, both ringed and little ringed plover, sand martin, yellow wagtail, nightingale, and hobby. In winter, these pits are thronged with bird life, with notable species including ruddy duck, goosander, jack snipe, and the occasional smew and Bewick's swan.

Nearby Whelford Pools (WT; SU 174005), near Fairford, has similar habitats, and is less disturbed by leisure activities such as boating and water skiing. Kingfishers are frequently spotted here, and the waterfowl include tufted duck, pochard, and coot, with occasional ruddy duck and red-crested pochard. Winter brings in wigeon, Canada geese, grebes, and shoveler. The smaller pools are good spots for dragonfly-watching, with 11 species, such as emperor and red-eyed damselfly.

102 Forest of Dean
SITE

One of the largest areas of woodland in the region, with an attractive range of habitats.

A wander through the Forest of Dean offers a glimpse of the original wildwood which once clothed much of lowland Britain. In all there are some 1000 ha of ancient woodland, although today it is a mosaic of mixed oak woodland, conifer plantation, and felled clearings. The woods are broken by the occasional rocky outcrop and stream. The semi-natural landscape that results is well endowed with wildlife and worth a visit at any season. Fallow and roe deer are frequently seen, and there are many badgers, although you are more likely to come across their regularly used tracks rather than spot the animals themselves. Polecats are also found here, and there are otters in the streams. Dormice still inhabit the area, attracted by the combination of woodland

Kestrel *Falco tinnunculus* (Peter Wilson)

Wood anemone *Anemone nemorosa*

and kingfishers on the streams. The butterflies include white admiral, silver-washed, dark green, high brown, pearl-bordered, and small pearl-bordered fritillary, holly blue, brown argus, and grayling.

Nagshead SSSI (RSPB; SO 606085, OS 162) is an excellent reserve at the heart of the Forest of Dean, and one of the best places to see woodland birds such as pied flycatcher, wood warbler, hawfinch, marsh and willow tits, nuthatch, siskin, and crossbill. Buzzards and sparrowhawks breed in the area, as does the rarer goshawk, the latter mainly in the mature plantations. Other birds to expect are raven, woodcock, and nightjar (the latter most likely to be found at nearby Oakenhill Wood). One of the specialities here is firecrest, a tiny, active bird best located by its song.

Nagshead is also known for its invertebrate fauna, with 35 species of butterfly and 21 dragonflies. These include small pearl-bordered and silver-washed fritillary, grizzled skipper, and beautiful demoiselle. The extremely local club-tailed dragonfly is also found feeding in clearings in parts of the forest (it breeds along stretches of the Wye). Common woodland flowers such as foxglove and

cover and a shrub-layer rich in hazel and honeysuckle. Watch for bats on summer evenings – the forest holds good numbers of both greater and lesser horseshoe bats.

Large sections of the forest still support semi-natural woodland, mainly of sessile oak and beech, although some parts have been planted with conifers such as larch and spruce. Ash, wych elm, lime, sweet chestnut, rowan, and holly are also common trees here. One reason why the Forest of Dean has so much to offer the botanist is that its soils encompass a range of different types, from acid to limestone, with corresponding changes in the flora. In addition, there are streams, pools, and small areas of bog which repay a visit. The flowers include meadow saffron, herb-Paris, bird's-nest orchid, stinking hellebore, white helleborine, and the spectacular martagon lily with its large, pink-purple nodding flowers.

Woodland birds abound, with all three woodpeckers, nuthatch, treecreeper, sparrowhawk, woodcock, pied flycatcher, redstart, wood warbler, goldcrest, siskin, hawfinch, and crossbill. Buzzards and ravens are frequent, and there are dippers

Meadow saffron *Colchicum autumnale*

Central England

bluebell are abundant here, and more local species include autumn crocus and ivy-leaved bellflower. Cannop Ponds (SO 608110) has breeding mandarin duck, little grebe, kingfisher, grey wagtail, and dipper. Speech House (SO 620120), at the centre of the forest, is known for its impressive collection of ancient oaks.

On the western fringes of the Forest of Dean lie two sites of note: Symonds Yat and Lady Park Wood. Symonds Yat (RSPB; SO 563196) is a limestone viewpoint perched above the river Wye, offering stunning views over the countryside with its wooded valleys. The peregrine viewing point is now famous and open from early April through August from 10.00 am (weather permitting), providing one of the easiest ways of getting good views of this magnificent bird of prey. There are other raptors here, too: buzzards and sparrowhawks are common, and kestrels, hobbies, and goshawks regular, and there

is always the chance of a passing red kite, osprey, or honey buzzard. Ravens also nest nearby. Lady Park Wood NNR (SO 547145; 45 ha) clothes a steep slope on the banks of the Wye. Its importance lies in the fact that it is close to the original wildwood in structure and has, at least in part, been relatively little affected by humans. It is a very mixed wood, with oak, beech, ash, lime, elm, and birch.

Nearby Betty Daw's Wood (WT; SO 696284, OS 162; 9 ha) is an ancient sessile oak wood, with small-leaved lime and wild service-tree. It has an impressive display of wild daffodils, wood anemones, bluebells, and primroses. Pied flycatchers and marsh tits breed here, and the butterflies include white admiral, wood white, and silver-washed fritillary. Collin Park Wood is another wood near Newent and in many ways even more interesting, with sessile oak, small-leaved lime, and many wild service-trees.

103 Slimbridge
SITE

A superb site for getting to know wildfowl, with excellent facilities that include hides and an observation tower.

Slimbridge (WWT), the creation of Sir Peter Scott, is best known for the large numbers of wintering wildfowl, especially for the hundreds of Bewick's and whooper swans which congregate here each winter.

Here is wildlife-watching at its most comfortable, and the site has all possible conveniences, including shops, restaurant, visitor centre, and even a lecture theatre and art gallery. The birds may be watched in luxury from hides which they are accustomed to approach closely, and individual swans may be recognized by their unique bill patterns. A fine collection of captive wildfowl allows beginners to get to grips with their field characters

at very close range, before venturing out to look at the real thing!

White-fronted goose *Anser albifrons* (Mike Lane)

A good system of footpaths allows the more energetic visitor to wander into somewhat wilder country and there are a total of 15 hides. Some of these offer views over pools and wet marshland to (usually rather distant) flocks of wild geese – greylag, pinkfooted, white-fronted, and the occasional lesser white-fronted, or even more rarely, red-breasted. A telescope is essential to get good views of these. The white-fronts usually peak after Christmas, but have all gone by March.

Hunting peregrines are frequently seen here, perched on a post or tree, or soaring over the marshes on the lookout for waders or ducks. Other birds of prey to look for are merlin, sparrowhawk, and short-eared owl. Little owls breed in the willows towards the marsh, and a hunting barn owl is a fairly regular sight, particularly towards dusk. There are large flocks of wigeon, along with pintail, shoveler, gadwall, and teal. There are also muddy pools which attract waders such as greenshank, ruff, spotted redshank, and black-tailed godwit. In spring, the wetland flowers such as purple-loosestrife, marsh-marigold, and ragged-Robin add a dash of colour. Slimbridge is also one of the strongholds of the water vole, now nationally threatened.

Slimbridge is between Bristol and Gloucester, on the banks of the Severn Estuary. It is open daily (except Christmas Day), 9.30 am to 5.00 pm (4.00 in winter). It has good access for the disabled, with wheelchairs available.

A selection of other important sites in the county

Ashleworth Ham and Meerend Thicket SSSI (WT; SO 830265, OS 162) has old meadows on the Severn floodplain, with adjacent wooded bank. Wetland birds include wintering wildfowl.

Dover's Hill (NT; SP 137397). Cotswold edge overlooking Vale of Evesham. Grassland and woodland. Flowers include meadow saxifrage.

Highbury Wood NNR (EN; SO 540085, OS 162; 47 ha): ancient wood on Offa's Dyke, with both limes.

Highnam Woods (RSPB; SO 778190) is a broadleaved wood with good woodland birds.

Lancaut SSSI (WT; ST 539966, OS 171/2; 24 ha): fern-rich wood with rare whitebeams; saltmarsh on tidal Wye gorge.

Littleworth Wood (NT; SP 086338) is a mixed wood with orchids and adder's-tongue.

May Hill (NT; SO 695215) is a 275-m hill with heath and acid grassland. Marshes and ponds with newts; also bog plants.

Prestbury Hill (SO 992242, OS 163) is an area of heath and grassland, just east of Cheltenham. It has good butterflies – Duke of Burgundy, brown argus, small and chalk-hill blue, dark green fritillary, grayling, and marbled white.

Oxfordshire

SITE
104 Oxfordshire Chilterns

Chalk hills rising up as a gently undulating feature and character-ized by woodland and chalk grassland.

The Chiltern Hills stretch roughly from Goring in Oxfordshire to Dunstable in Bedfordshire, and there are fine sites in both these counties (see also pp. 292, 296). Much of the finest Chiltern woodland is dominated by beech, which produces impressive displays of autumn colours. The pure beech stands are mostly old plantations, but beech also occurs here quite commonly in mixed oak woodland of a more natural provenance. The open chalk grassland has several local plants (notably woodland orchids) and butter-flies, and the woods are the haunt of deer, dormice, and that Chiltern speciality, the edible dormouse, the latter restricted to this part of the country. The recently rein-troduced red kites are thriving and buz-zards are increasingly common, adding to the overall wildlife interest of the area.

Common milkwort
Polygala vulgaris

The Warburg Reserve (WT; SU 720879, OS 175; 109 ha) is an excellent large reserve, in the Chilterns AONB just north-west of Henley, and is one of the best places to experience the diversity of Chilterns wildlife. It occupies a dry valley, and the habitats include mixed broadleaved wood-land, beech woods, and some coniferous plantation, as well as scrub, and acid as well as chalk grassland. Over 450 species of higher plants grow here, including (in the woodland) broad-leaved, violet, and narrow-lipped helleborines, bird's-nest and fly orchid and common twayblade, and (in grassland) pyramidal orchid, squinancywort, and Chiltern gentian. The butterflies feature purple emperor, white admiral, and silver-washed and dark green fritillaries. Viviparous lizards, grass snakes, adders and slow-worms add to the inter-est, and common frog and smooth newt breed in the ponds. In addition to the expected mammals such as rabbits, brown hares, foxes, badgers, voles, shrews, and mice, there are plenty of fallow, roe, and muntjac deer, and dormice thrive in the hazel coppice.

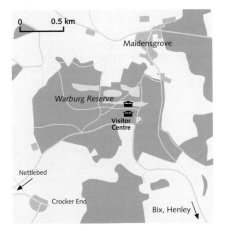

0   0.5 km

Maidensgrove

Warburg Reserve

Visitor Centre P

Nettlebed

Crocker End

Bix, Henley

Red kite *Milvus milvus* **(Mike Lane)**

Aston Rowant NNR/SSSI (SU 731967, OS 165; 129 ha) and Aston Rowant Woods SSSI (SU 750982; 211 ha) lie some 8 km south of Thame. Here there is the typical mix of chalk grassland, scrub, and beech woods. The unimproved grassland has patches of juniper grading through scrub to mature woodland. Though sadly bisected by the M40, the site is well worth a visit and access is easy, with car park and nature trail. There is also a convenient FC car park at Cowleaze Wood.

The reserve is centred upon a large area of rich chalk downland on a fairly steep chalk slope at the edge of the Chiltern Hills. The

scrub has species such as blackthorn, bramble, hawthorn, and dogwood. In some places there is also quite a lot of juniper, and yew is also present in some quantity. Deadly nightshade, with its black, glistening, highly toxic berries, is frequent in the scrub close to the beech woods. In the woods there are flowers such as sanicle, wood-rush, and yellow archangel, as well as orchids such as white and violet helleborine. On the open grassland grow rock-rose, wild thyme, eyebright, common milkwort, horseshoe vetch, bird's-foot-trefoil, common centaury, oxeye daisy, marjoram, and common spotted-orchid, as well as two Chiltern specialities – Chiltern gentian and candytuft.

The butterflies of this reserve include silver-spotted skipper, chalk-hill blue and small blue, brown argus, dark green fritillary, green hairstreak, dingy and grizzled skippers, and Duke of Burgundy. There is a good chance of spotting the red kites which have successfully been reintroduced into the area, and the woods have sparrowhawks, woodpeckers, and hawfinches.

Other sites nearby

Watlington Hill (NT; SU 708937, OS 175), near Christmas Common, has fine chalk grassland with 30 species of butterfly including chalk-hill blue and silver-spotted skipper. Also scrub and woodland, with some yew. Plants: horseshoe vetch, rock-rose, squinancywort, frog, bee, and pyramidal orchids, autumn and Chiltern gentian. This is also one of the best places to watch for red kites which are thriving in the area. A reintroduction programme began in this area in 1989 using kites from Spain, and the numbers have now built up to some 120 pairs. Meanwhile, buzzards have continued their gradual eastward expansion and are now also to be seen here. The best season for the kites is early spring on a dry, sunny day when they can be seen displaying and soaring over the hills and beech woods. Hobbies may also be seen in the vicinity, as can woodcocks.

Chinnor Hill (WT; SP 766002, OS 165; 28 ha) lies right on the border with Buckinghamshire some 6 km south-east of Thame and displays good Chiltern habitats, with scrub, woodland, and chalk grassland. Access is easy and there are good footpaths, including a section of the Icknield Way, and there are good views across the Vale of Aylesbury. There is oak and ash woodland, with beech at the ridge and patches of juniper on the slopes; also yew, whitebeam, and wayfaring-tree. Look for carline thistle, rock-rose, and wild thyme. Corn buntings, yellowhammers, and linnets breed and the site is also good for warblers, turtle dove, and the occasional quail.

Oakley Hill (WT; SU 753994, OS 165; 12 ha): chalk downland and beech woods.

SITE 105 Cothill reserves

A cluster of complementary and rather varied reserves in the heart of the county.

The Cothill reserves (OS 164) lie near the village of Cothill, just north-west of Abingdon. Three are easy to visit, with open access, while Parsonage Moor, which contains the small Cothill NNR, has access restricted to a footpath.

Dry Sandford Pit (WT; SU 467997; 8 ha), based around an old quarry, is next to the Sandford Brook. Note that the fossiliferous cliffs of the quarry are very friable and dangerous! The sandy banks are one of the best sites in Britain for burrow-nesting species of wasps and bees, for which this reserve is well known. The main habitats here are woodland, scrub, fen, open water, and small patches of heath – remarkably varied for such a small site. The fen communities contain species such as common spotted- and early marsh-orchids, and marsh helleborine, with a carr of willows,

Creeping-Jenny *Lysimachia nummularia*

alder, and birch, while the ponds and other wet areas have grass snakes, common frogs, common toads, and newts, as well as dragonflies. Other insects include marbled white, glow-worms, and great green bush-cricket.

Hitchcopse Pit (WT; SU 452996; 0.8 ha) is a small disused sandpit with interesting insects, including many burrowing bees and wasps and some rare species of beetle.

Lashford Lane Fen (WT; SU 468011; 7 ha) is a compact wetland site with a rich valley fen community around the Sandford Brook. This is an extremely rare habitat and the reserve is something of a little jewel. The reeds are dotted with the flowers of hemp-agrimony, meadowsweet, and great willowherb, with creeping-Jenny brightening the ground flora.

Parsonage Moor (WT; SU 462998; 17 ha) completes the quartet of Cothill reserves. Footpaths lead through the reserve and it is dangerous to stray from these onto the treacherous surface. Woodland, fen carr,

Marsh helleborine *Epipactis palustris* (Martin Walters)

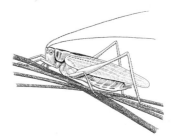

Great green bush-cricket *Tettigonia viridissima*

Cothill Fen

and lowland fen are the main habitats, and the mire communities are complex, with areas of alkaline and acid reaction. The wetland species here include common butterwort, southern marsh-orchid, grass-of-Parnassus, and both round-leaved and oblong-leaved sundews, amongst beds of bog-mosses. There is a healthy population of the attractive scarlet tiger moth, whose food-plant common comfrey is abundant.

A selection of other important sites in the county

Farmoor Reservoir (SP 450064): winter wildfowl and passage waders.

Foxholes (WT; SP 254206, OS 163) is a remnant of Wychwood Forest with a rich flora. Butterflies include white admiral.

Iffley Meadows (WT; SP 525036, OS 164): fritillary.

Otmoor (RSPB; SP 569126) is mainly grassland, with a small reedbed. The rare fen violet has recently been rediscovered here.

Stanton Harcourt Pits (SP 402056): disused gravel pits with carr and reeds.

Sydlings Copse & College Pond (WT; SP 559096, OS 164; 16.8 ha). Mixed habitats in steep valley. Marbled white and dark green fritillary.

White Horse Hill (NT; SU 301866). Famous landmark in Vale of White Horse and close to the Ridgeway track. Some good chalk grassland.

Wychwood NNR (SP 338165, OS 164; 260 ha; access restricted). Largest wood in west Oxfordshire, with grassland and ponds. Site for Roman snail.

Warwickshire

SITE
106 Snitterfield Bushes

Remnant of ancient woodland, near Stratford-upon-Avon, with good butterflies and birds.

Snitterfield Bushes (WT; SP 200604, OS 151; 50 ha) is one of the best woodland reserves in the county, even though it has been much altered, especially by being partly felled and converted into an airstrip in the Second World War. Nevertheless, a ground flora typical of ancient woodland has been largely preserved and the woodland shrubs and herbs have quickly clothed and disguised the concrete paths and runways.

The trees are now mostly ash and birch with some oaks, underneath which grows a shrub-layer with field maple, dogwood, wayfaring-tree, and guelder-rose. This is a good bluebell wood and with primroses, and these flowers carpet it in spring. Other species here include herb-Paris, early purple, greater butterfly, and common spotted-orchids, twayblade, and broad-leaved helleborine.

All three woodpeckers breed here, as have (occasionally) nightingales at the northern edge of their British range. Snitterfield is a good spot for butterflies, too, with common and holly blues, brown

Reserve in spring

argus, grizzled skipper, purple hairstreak, marbled white, and white admiral. An open area in the centre has a few ponds with breeding smooth newts.

Ryton Wood SSSI (WT; SP 387728, OS 140; 85 ha), just to the south-east of Coventry, is another fine Warwickshire wood and provides a nice contrast to Snitterfield. Ryton is very ancient and contains some coppiced small-leaved lime trees which are some 600 years old. In spring there are masses of bluebells, wood anemones, wood-sorrel, and lesser celandine, with red campion. The dominant trees are mainly oak with hazel or lime. A tower hide allows the patient naturalist to scan the forest and glades for butterflies and perhaps to glimpse a grazing muntjac or roding woodcock. The butterflies include white admiral, purple and white-letter hairstreaks, marbled white, small pearl-bordered and silver-washed fritillaries, and brown argus. This is another, rather northern, locality for nightingales.

SITE
107 Draycote Water

Large reservoir which attracts wildfowl, especially during the winter.

Draycote Water is about 5 km south-east of Rugby, close to the M45. This is primarily a site for birders, especially in the winter months when the reservoir brings in a good range of wildfowl. A Country Park has been developed on the south shore and a road surrounds the reservoir, allowing good views over the water. There is also a car park and hide near the end of Toft Bay, which lies at the northern end and offers the best birdwatching.

Alongside the usual mallard, there are teal, tufted duck, and pochard, with goldeneye and large numbers of wigeon joining in winter. Sea ducks such as long-tailed duck and scaup, and divers turn up pretty regularly in the winter, as do smew, goosander, and red-breasted merganser. Winter storms sometimes drive in skuas or a Leach's petrel.

A large gull roost adds to the winter bird interest and there are many thousands – mainly black-headed, with common, herring, and lesser black-backed, plus occasional kittiwakes or rarer species such as Iceland, glaucous, and Mediterranean. Terns are fairly frequent on passage, with black terns and little gulls a possibility.

In the autumn, waders pass through, especially if the water level is low enough to reveal marginal feeding areas.

Kingsbury Water Park (CC; SP 204958, OS 139), south of Tamworth, is another good wetland site for birds. Reed, sedge, grasshopper, and garden warblers all breed here, as do little grebe, little ringed plover, and common terns (the latter in a large colony on Canal Pool). In winter, there may be Bewick's and whooper swans, and goldeneye. This flooded gravel pit is also a good site for dragonflies, with red-eyed damselfly, emperor dragonfly, black-tailed skimmer, and migrant hawker.

Migrant hawker *Aeshna mixta*

A selection of other important sites in the county

Alvecote Pools SSSI (WT; SK 254047) is a beneficiary of an abandoned colliery and subsidence, leaving pools, reedbeds, and scrub. Redshank, shelduck, and yellow wagtails breed and there is a large gathering of moulting mute swans in the autumn.

Brandon Marsh SSSI (WT; SP 386761, OS 139; 92 ha). Wetland reserve with pools, near river Avon.

Charlecote Park (NT; SP 263564) is an old deer park on the banks of the Avon, with some fine old trees, includ-ing the rather local black poplar. Flooded fields attract winter wildfowl.

Clowes Wood (WT; SP 101743, OS 139; 44 ha). Oak–birch woodland, heath, damp meadows. Lily-of-the-valley, cow-wheat, wood horsetail.

Ufton Fields SSSI (WT/CC; SP 378615, OS 151). Old limestone workings with scrub, grassland, and ponds. This is a good site for orchids and also for but-terflies (26 species), including purple and white-letter hairstreaks, grizzled and dingy skippers, brown argus, small blue, marbled white, and wall.

Leicestershire (and Rutland)

108 Rutland Water

Large reservoir, with landscaped surroundings – a magnet for visiting wildfowl.

Rutland Water (WT; SK 897059), between Oakham and Stamford, was created in the 1970s and is one of the largest artificial lakes in Europe; in Britain, only Kielder Water (see p. 80) is bigger. Although very much an amenity lake, with angling and sailing, it is also important for its wildlife. At the western end, the shoreline is broken up by finger-like promontories and sheltered bays, and there are mead-ows and woods close to the water. There are two main reserves here: the Lyndon Reserve between Manton and Edith Weston, and the Egleton Reserve near the village of Egleton. Both have hides and visitor centres and a handy car park. It is also possible to view the lake from the

Osprey *Pandion haliaetus*

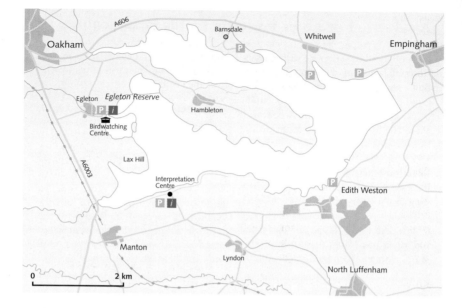

north shore – there are convenient picnic spots off the A606, near Whitwell.

Rutland Water is one of the best places in the country for wildfowl. Breeding birds include ruddy duck, shoveler, oyster-catcher, and common tern. Migrants often stop-by to feed at or near the lake, and spring visitors include little gull, garganey, and black-necked grebe, with osprey and hobby regular visitors. In winter there are many species of duck, with pochard, tufted, gadwall, goldeneye, goosander, and

Rutland Water (Peter Wilson)

occasional red-breasted merganser and smew, and sometimes long-tailed duck, divers, scoters, or whooper and Bewick's swans. The reserve also has a thriving population of tree sparrows – a species in marked decline in most other areas.

The birdwatching and information facilities at Rutland Water are being expanded, partly to enable visitors to view the ospreys which have begun to breed here (2001) after a reintroduction programme using chicks from the healthy Scottish population.

Other sites nearby

The Vale of Belvoir (pronounced like the large aquatic rodent) is an attractive part of the county with great historical interest, centred on the impressive Belvoir Castle. However, it is also a good natural history area, with a mix of woodland, lakes, and farmland, and is well worth visiting.

Knipton Reservoir (SK 818302), with its adjacent woodland, lies just to the north of Branston. This area has birds of traditional farmland, such as corn bunting, grey partridge, turtle dove, and quail, while the water attracts goosander and sometimes pink-footed geese in winter. Raptors are good here, with kestrel, sparrowhawk, buzzard, and barn owl all breeding, and the chance of passage merlin, hen harrier, red kite, osprey, honey buz-

zard, and goshawk. In the woods there are marsh tits, siskins, and sometimes crossbills.

Eyebrook Reservoir (Corby Water; SP 850960, OS 141) lies some 12 km south of Rutland Water, and about 3 km south of Uppingham. This large reservoir is easily visited by car (there are two car parks and a number of useful lay-bys). It has migrant waders in August: little stint, curlew and wood sandpiper, and black-tailed godwit are regular. Spring may bring little gull, black tern, and garganey. The site often attracts passing osprey, buzzard, hobby, and red kite. In winter you may see goldeneye and goosander, and the gull roost often has Mediterranean and glaucous gulls. A plantation clothes the eastern shore.

109 Charnwood Forest

Remnants of an ancient forest close to Leicester.

The great ancient forest of Charnwood once covered a wide area to the north-west of Leicester, and this region is still one of the most wooded parts of what is now a relatively treeless county. Now only a few remnants of the original forest remain, but some of these still hold interesting wildlife.

One of the best of such remnant woods is Swithland Wood (SK 537117, OS 129/140; 58 ha), about 9 km north of Leicester. This wood is now largely mixed deciduous, with sessile oaks and birch on the acid soils, and hazel coppice where the soil is richer. Other trees here are small-leaved lime, with alder and ash in

Tormentil *Potentilla erecta*

the wetter sites. The flowers of this reserve include woodland species such as enchanter's-nightshade, wood sage, and bluebell, and the colourful foxglove and rosebay willowherb. The overall diversity is increased by the presence of disused and flooded slate quarries, and by pasture, which has flowers such as common spotted-orchid, betony, adder's-tongue, and saw-wort. Woodpeckers and nightingales breed here.

Ulverscroft (NT/WT; SK 490126, OS 129; 60 ha) is a mixed site with remnants of Charnwood Forest, though most of it is planted woodland. The ridge here rises to 240 m and there are the remains of heath and botanically interesting old meadows, the latter with fragrant orchid. The woodland, mainly oak with some beech, has redstart, nuthatch, and all three woodpeckers.

Lea Meadows (WT; SK 506115, OS 129; 12 ha) preserves unimproved meadows, alongside an unpolluted stream. The latter has white-clawed crayfish, bullheads, minnows, and brook lampreys, in addition to three-spined sticklebacks, and is also the haunt of kingfishers. The meadows boast harebell, betony, great burnet, and common and heath spotted-orchids.

Other important sites nearby

Buddon Wood is a little to the north-east. Although but a shadow of its former self, being now largely quarried, it still holds interesting wildlife, with some ancient lime stools, along with alder carr and birch. It is also famously a site for the rare spreading bellflower.

Martinshaw Wood (WdT; SK 510073, OS 140; 103 ha) is a large mixed wood with easy access.

Burroughs Wood (WdT; SK 492062, OS 102; 37 ha) has woodland and adjacent grassland.

Pear Tree Wood (WdT; SK 498065, OS 140; 18 ha) is a mixed wood, with some marsh.

Cloud Wood (WT; SK 417214, OS 129; 81 ha) is slightly further west, north of Coalville. Part of an SSSI, it is a traditionally coppiced ancient wood. This is rich in flowers, such as wood anemone, bluebell, primrose, and also Solomon's-seal, bee, bird's-nest, and greater butterfly-orchids, and violet helleborine. Keep away from the quarry, as it is dangerous.

Cropston Reservoir lies just south of Swithland Wood. It is good for waders and ducks, including ruddy duck.

Bradgate Park, which is adjacent, has grassland and heath, with tormentil and harebell, as well as whinchat, viviparous lizard, and a herd of fallow deer.

Central England

A selection of other important sites in the county

Cribbs Meadow SSSI (WT; SK 899188, OS 130; 5 ha) is old grassland with green-winged orchid, common spotted-orchid, and adder's-tongue.

Muston Meadows NNR (SK 824367, OS 130; 9 ha) is neutral grassland with a large colony of green-winged orchids.

Prior's Coppice (WT; SK 834052, OS 141; 71 ha) is mainly ash woodland with good flowers.

Watermead Country Park (SK 606106), near Leicester, is one of the best Midlands wetland reserves. Well supplied with hides and tracks, this complex of habitats alongside the Grand Union Canal is a haven for wildlife, with winter wildfowl a speciality. Summer: grey heron, garganey, terns, warblers, sand martin, hobby. Winter: smew, goosander, bittern, grey heron, short-eared owl, peregrine.

Northamptonshire

SITE 110 Rockingham Forest

Flower-rich woodland sites, survivors of a once-extensive royal forest.

The great Royal Forest of Rockingham once occupied a large tract of land in the north of Northamptonshire, roughly between Corby and Peterborough. Several remnants remain, amongst which the best and easiest to visit is probably Bedford Purlieus SSSI (FC/WT; TL 040994; 215 ha). The flora of this wood is remarkably diverse, with many species typical of ancient woodland, and botanists consider it to be one of the richest of all British woods. This is partly due to the range of soil types, which support both lime-loving species and those requiring more acid soils. In addition to more common woodland species such as bluebell, ramsons, and dog's mercury, there are rarer flowers, including fly and greater butterfly-orchids, stinking hellebore, deadly nightshade, wild liquorice, nettle-leaved bellflower, wood spurge, caper spurge, toothwort, lily-of-the-valley, and columbine. Not surprisingly, this wood also supports a good selection of butterflies, with white admiral, high brown, dark green, pearl-bordered and silver-washed fritillaries, and white-letter and brown hairstreaks.

White admiral *Limenitis camilla*

Central England

Short Wood, coppice (Peter Wilson)

Short Wood (WT; TL 015913, OS 141; 25 ha), near Oundle, lies mainly on boulder clay, with some patches of more freely draining acid soils. It is one of the finest bluebell woods in Northamptonshire. The main community is oak–ash woodland with ash, field maple, and hazel coppice, dogwood, spindle, and the occasional wild service-tree. The ground flora has dog's mercury, bluebell, enchanter's-nightshade, yellow archangel, and wood-sorrel. Some areas of the wood are particularly good for orchids, with early purple, common spotted-, common twayblade, greater butterfly-, and bird's-nest, plus broad-leaved and violet helleborines. There is also a rich insect fauna, including purple and white-letter hairstreaks. In addition to the usual woodland birds there are all three woodpeckers, hawfinch, and both marsh and willow tits.

Nearby Glapthorn Cow Pasture (TL 003902, OS 141; 28 ha) is one of the best sites for black hairstreak, which has only about 30 colonies, all in the East Midlands. This species requires mature blackthorn and sunny clearings, and the adults fly between June and August. Nightingales breed here, as do woodcock, nuthatch, and tawny owls. The flowers include bugle, early-purple and common spotted-orchids, meadowsweet, bluebell, and primrose.

Collyweston Great Wood & Easton Hornstocks NNR (TL 014004, OS 141; 156 ha) is on the border between Northamptonshire and Cambridgeshire, and consists of three woods, with Wittering

Woodcock *Scolopax rusticola*

Coppice in addition to the two named. These are in the main rich remnants of Rockingham, with coppiced small-leaved lime and a diverse flora, plus ground flora species such as wood anemone, lily-of-the-valley, yellow archangel, wood spurge, woodruff, ramsons, and dog's mercury.

Access is restricted, however, and by permission only.

Geddington Chase is a mixed wood, much affected by afforestation but with patches of surviving ash, maple, and lime coppice, and a rich flora, with wild daffodils growing in some of the more open sites.

SITE 111 Pitsford Reservoir

Large reservoir near Northampton, well known by birdwatchers especially for its winter wildfowl and waders.

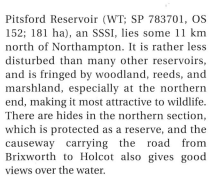

Pitsford Reservoir (WT; SP 783701, OS 152; 181 ha), an SSSI, lies some 11 km north of Northampton. It is rather less disturbed than many other reservoirs, and is fringed by woodland, reeds, and marshland, especially at the northern end, making it most attractive to wildlife. There are hides in the northern section, which is protected as a reserve, and the causeway carrying the road from Brixworth to Holcot also gives good views over the water.

Although pleasant to visit at any time of the year, Pitsford is at its most exciting in winter, or during the spring and autumn migrations, as the bird list, which stands at over 256 species, attests. Some

55 species breed here, including grey heron, sparrowhawk, and shoveler.

Goldeneye and goosander add to the wildfowl interest in the winter, and there are occasional Slavonian, black-necked, and red-necked grebes, eiders, long-tailed duck and, more rarely, little auk. There is a large gull roost, and unusual species such as glaucous, Mediterranean, and little gulls all turn up from time to time. The winter wildfowl usually number about 4000, peaking at 10 000, and include grebes, coot, swans (sometimes including Bewick's and whooper) and (more rarely) geese, in addition to the 14 species of duck recorded here. Tree sparrows may be spotted amongst the small birds attracted to the feeding station.

Raptors are also regular at Pitsford, with all three harriers having been recorded, in addition to kestrel, sparrowhawk, buzzard, rough-legged buzzard, osprey, hobby, merlin, and peregrine.

There is more than the bird life to interest the naturalist here. Pitsford is one of the best locations in the county for dragonflies, with 16 species, of which common blue and emerald damselflies and ruddy darter are the most prominent. This reserve is also a good site for the rather elusive harvest mouse.

Recently, the woodland near to the reservoir has begun to be slowly converted from alien stands of conifers to native oaks and ash, with natural regeneration encouraged. This has increased the wildlife value enormously, with many more butterflies and birds moving in. The fringing vegetation is also well developed, with damp willow scrub grading into reedbeds, and mixed wetland habitats with reed canary-grass, rushes, common fleabane, and water mint. Another habitat represented here is neutral grassland, with pepper-saxifrage, bird's-foot-trefoil, and yellow-rattle, as well as the rather rare swamp meadow-grass.

There is a large car park on the western side of the causeway, and further car parks at the southern end, near the village of Pitsford.

Summer Leys LNR (SP 885634, OS 152) is about 8 km east of Northampton, between Great Doddington and Wollaston.

This wetland reserve lies close to the river Nene and consists of a series of gravel pits and lagoons, with islands and a scrape. It is a haven for wildlife, and perhaps the best site in the county for waterbirds. Free access from a car park (adjacent to picnic area) and four hides, all with wheelchair ramps. Ringed and little ringed plovers, redshank, oystercatcher, gadwall, and common tern breed, and hobbies may be spotted feeding on the abundant dragonflies. In autumn the passage waders include curlew, green and common sandpiper, little stint, greenshank, dunlin, ruff, spotted redshank, and black-tailed godwit. Marsh harriers, black terns, and little gulls are also seen quite often. Winter brings in good numbers of pochard, shoveler, wigeon, and goldeneye, and there is often a golden plover roost. Watch for tree sparrows and bramblings at the feeding station. The ducks include garganey in spring or summer, and smew in winter.

A selection of other important sites in the county

Ashton Mill, National Dragonfly Museum (TL 053883, OS 142). Open weekends June–September. Emperor dragonfly, ruddy darter, migrant hawker, red-eyed damselfly. Ashton Water Dragonfly Sanctuary (TL 077875) is nearby.

Ditchford Lakes (SP 931678, OS 153; 31 ha). Gravel pits, grassland, and scrub. Crosswort, great burnet, and spiked sedge. Occasional Cetti's warbler.

High Wood & Meadow (WT; SP 588548, OS 152; 17 ha) is an ancient wood with adjacent acidic meadow. The wood has wild cherry, moschatel, opposite-leaved golden-saxifrage, and over 80 species of bird including wood warbler and redstart. The meadow also has a rich flora.

Irthlingborough Newt Ponds (SP 941716, OS 141; 0.4 ha): small reserve with colonies of the rare great crested newt.

Salcey Forest (WT; SP 8191): rich ancient woodland, with nightingales and grasshopper warblers.

Stanford Reservoir (WT; SP 604807, OS 140; 71 ha) is good for wetland plants, wildfowl, and also for bats, some of which roost in the outflow pipe. Daubenton's, Natterer's, noctule, common pipistrelle, and whiskered have all been seen here.

Stanwick Gravel Pits (SP 973716, OS 141) lie alongside the Nene and attract regular waders, with frequent rarities.

Thrapston Gravel Pits and **Titchmarsh LNR** (WT; TL 007813, OS 141). This site has a large heronry with about 50 pairs, and is good generally for wildfowl, especially in winter. There are 17 species of dragonfly.

Eastern England

Eastern England

Eastern England

Introduction

This region stretches roughly from the Humber south to Greater London and the Thames Estuary, taking in the bulge of East Anglia. The main ecological areas are the Lincolnshire Wolds, the Fens, Breckland, North Norfolk and the Broads, the Suffolk coast and heaths, the Chilterns, and the Thames Estuary. Whilst there is little high ground, the habitats are nevertheless quite varied, with the coasts in particular offering some of the finest reserves and protected areas in the country.

The Wash is a large square mass of shallow sea between Lincolnshire and Norfolk. This is a wild, often windy area with wide vistas over mudflats and sandbanks. At low tide, large expanses of mud provide rich feeding grounds for many thousands of migrating waders and wildfowl, either wintering or on passage.

In the European context, it is perhaps the fenland which is of most interest, as this rare habitat is not well represented elsewhere, except perhaps in the polderlands and adjacent wetlands of The Netherlands. There are ambitious plans to extend the fenland into areas currently occupied by agricultural land, from the nucleus of Wicken Fen, going some way towards recreating the Great Fen which once stretched almost from Cambridge to Lincoln.

The Norfolk Broads, like the Breckland and the Fens, is a habitat essentially created by humans. It comprises a network of important wetlands, with rare and local species such as marsh harrier, swallowtail butterfly, Norfolk hawker, and rare water plants such as water-soldier.

Brickpits, Wicken Fen (Martin Walters) (see p. 286)

Previous page: **Redgrave & Lopham Fens** (Peter Wilson) (see p. 279)

Eastern England

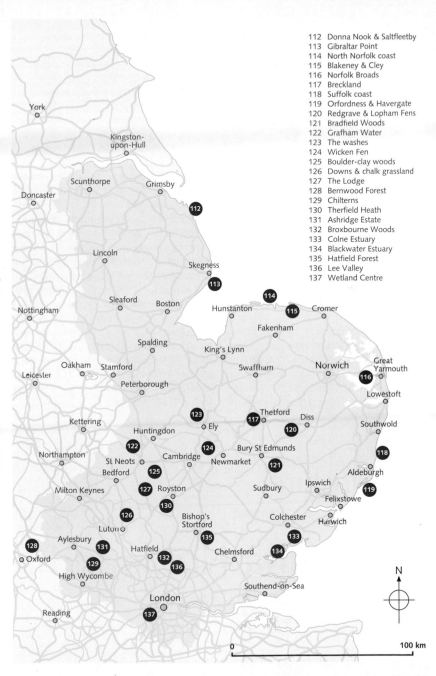

112 Donna Nook & Saltfleetby
113 Gibraltar Point
114 North Norfolk coast
115 Blakeney & Cley
116 Norfolk Broads
117 Breckland
118 Suffolk coast
119 Orfordness & Havergate
120 Redgrave & Lopham Fens
121 Bradfield Woods
122 Grafham Water
123 The washes
124 Wicken Fen
125 Boulder-clay woods
126 Downs & chalk grassland
127 The Lodge
128 Bernwood Forest
129 Chilterns
130 Therfield Heath
131 Ashridge Estate
132 Broxbourne Woods
133 Colne Estuary
134 Blackwater Estuary
135 Hatfield Forest
136 Lee Valley
137 Wetland Centre

The coasts of both Norfolk and Suffolk are well protected and superb areas for the naturalist, with a string of top-quality reserves including the famous sites of Blakeney and Cley (Norfolk) and Minsmere and Walberswick (Suffolk). These include coastal reedbeds where it is still possible to hear the eerie boom-

Pasqueflower *Pulsatilla vulgaris*

continental climates in western Europe. The churring of nightjars is an evocative sound and can be heard in many Breckland spots, especially where forest and heath merge, as can the wonderful song of the nightingale and the odd clicks and croaks of roding woodcocks. Stone curlew can still be found in several places, and you may be lucky enough to hear their ghostly wails floating across the heaths late in the evening. A new project aims to recreate and extend the area of traditional Breckland, with its associated special wildlife.

In much of the region the landscape is dominated by agriculture, making nature reserves especially important for wildlife conservation. Notable amongst the inland habitats are the boulder-clay woods, several with impressive displays of bluebells and that regional speciality the oxlip. Many of these woods have an ancient history, exhaustively and eloquently documented by Oliver Rackham. Mention should also be made of the surviving patches of chalk grassland, with its rich flora, including the beautiful pasqueflower, and butterflies such as chalk-hill blue.

ing call of the bittern – one of Britain's rarest birds.

Breckland has a unique character – on a fine summer's day the open heaths can be baking hot, the well-drained sandy soil heating up quickly. This area has an almost steppe-like flora in places, associated with one of the driest and most

Lincolnshire

112 Donna Nook and Saltfleetby

A fascinating coastal site famous for its sand-dune systems, which cover some 440 ha, and also for its saltmarshes and mudflats.

Donna Nook (WT) is a fine reserve that borders the Saltfleetby–Theddlethorpe Dunes NNR (EN) at its southern end. The broad sand- and mud-flats of these two reserves, which form a long sweep along the coast from Saltfleet to Mablethorpe,

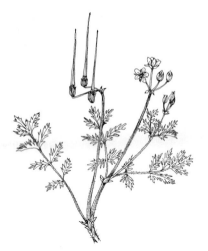

Common stork's-bill *Erodium cicutarium*

are an excellent offshore feeding ground for waders and wildfowl, whilst the salt-marsh and dune systems are extremely rich in plant and insect species – especially butterflies.

The extensive saltmarshes have thrift, annual sea-blite, sea-lavenders, and sea-purslane. Other notable plants of the reserve are autumn gentian, bog pimpernel, marsh pea, carline thistle, and fairy flax. The dunes also have a number of orchids; these include bee, pyramidal, and early and southern marsh-orchids, which can make an impressive show in early summer.

Occasional pools in the dune slacks offer ideal breeding conditions for the rare and rather local natterjack, along with common frog, common toad, and smooth newt.

This site is also well known for its rich insect fauna. Butterflies to watch for include green hairstreak, dark green fritillary, and brown argus, and this is also a good place for dragonflies and damselflies, with at least 10 species.

Breeding birds include oystercatcher, redshank, snipe, and shelduck. In late summer there are large gatherings of terns, especially Sandwich. In autumn, especially following easterly winds, the reserves can be active with newly arrived migrant birds, particularly in the scrub at the upper shore. In winter

the saltmarsh is also worth checking for birds, and often has flocks of Lapland buntings and occasionally shore larks. Skuas are regular here, too, and may sometimes be seen harrying the gulls and terns over the sea. Brent geese arrive to winter along the shore, and there are large numbers of wigeon, and many waders.

Apart from the mudflats and saltmarsh, another important habitat here is provided by the thick scrub which has developed on the older dunes, with hawthorn, elder, and sea buckthorn. The more open dunes have a specialized flora, with mouse-ear hawkweed and stork's-bill. Birds nesting in the scrub include whitethroat, dunnock, linnet, and redpoll, while the berries and shelter bring in winter visitors such as redwings and fieldfares. Other notable winter birds are woodcock, sparrowhawk, hen harrier, and merlin.

English Nature has created a number of freshwater pools in the marsh and these have several interesting plants, including water-parsnip, water-plantain, and yellow iris. Water voles, water shrews, and horse leeches also live here.

At low tide it is sometimes possible to spot grey and common seals on the sand, especially in the autumn.

There is easy access and adequate car parking available at these two reserves, which are within easy reach of both Grimsby and Mablethorpe, off the A1031. There is a good nature trail, partly with level surface for wheelchair use. The best times to visit are May–June for the dune flowers, spring and autumn for migrant birds, and winter for the wildfowl.

Nearby

Tetney Marshes (RSPB; TA 345025) is a good birdwatching site. This area of saltmarsh, dunes, and sandflats at the mouth of the Humber contains a large colony of little terns, with wintering bar-tailed godwit and Brent geese.

Eastern England

SITE
113 Gibraltar Point

One of the best coastal reserves on the east coast, with a rich flora and extensive dunes, saltmarsh, and mudflats; a magnet for countless migrant birds.

Gibraltar Point NNR/SSSI/Bird Observatory (WT/TNC) is a superb coastal reserve, and no visitor can fail to be impressed by the huge area of saltmarsh which stretches away between the extensive dune systems. The landscape is very flat, and can be bitterly cold and windswept during bad weather, especially in autumn and winter, but for many it has a certain magnetic attraction in any season. Recent acquisition of adjacent arable land is steadily improving the reserve, which covers about 430 ha.

Botanists and birders alike will find much to their liking here, with species colonizing dunes at all stages of their development, from shifting sand near the shoreline, to old dunes on the landward side where a more stable, greyer soil is clothed in mixed scrub of elder, hawthorn,

Armeria maritima

sea buckthorn, wild privet, and roses. The most venerable of the dunes are probably at least 175 years old, while another ridge seawards began to stabilize about 100 years ago, and the wind-blown sand is constantly creating new dunes. Early plant colonizers are sea-holly and sea rocket. Pyramidal orchid may be seen in the more open grassy spots, along with spring-beauty. Natterjacks have been successfully reintroduced to the reserve.

In high summer, swathes of the saltmarsh are purple with the massed flowers of common sea-lavender, amongst which can be found sea-purslane, annual sea-blite, sea-milkwort, thrift, and sea aster. The shrubby sea-blite also grows here, at

Sea lavender *Limonium*, Gibraltar Point

Nearby

Frampton Marsh (RSPB; TF 354384), on the north side of The Wash just south-east of Boston, includes a large area of mudflats and saltmarsh, and brings in good numbers of wintering wildfowl (especially Brent geese) and waders. It also has the largest black-headed gull colony in Britain, and regular marsh harriers. Seals (mainly common) are frequent here.

one of its most northerly sites, as does marsh-mallow, the latter in the fields near the freshwater marsh.

Birdwatchers tend to visit during spring or autumn migration, or in winter for the waders and wildfowl. At this time hen harriers and short-eared owls can often be seen hunting, and the latter also breed on the reserve. Regular migrants include snow bunting, twite and, in irruption years,

waxwings. The mere has public hides and is a good place to see a variety of wildfowl, gulls, and waders, with little ringed plover, stints, curlew and wood sandpipers, and spotted redshank all possible.

Gibraltar Point lies some 4 km south of Skegness, at the north-westernmost corner of The Wash. There is parking available, a good visitor centre, nature trails with hides, and a picnic area.

A selection of other important sites in the county

Baston-Langtoft Pits (TF 140139; OS 142) near Market Deeping. Speciality birds: red-crested pochard (breeds in small numbers); black-necked grebe (autumn); smew, goosander, and goldeneye (winter); hobby, marsh harrier, and yellow wagtail (summer).

Far Ings SSSI (WT/TNC; TA 011229, OS 112): flooded pits close to the Humber.

Little Scrubs Meadow (WT/TNC; TF 145744, OS 121). Good for butterflies (26 species, including grizzled and dingy skipper, purple hairstreak, and white admiral).

Snipe Dales (WT/TNC; TF 319683, OS 122): woodland, grassland, and streamside habitats.

Southrey Wood (TF 127682, OS 121). This is a good site for butterflies, with purple and brown hairstreaks and white admiral. Woodcock and nightingale.

Whisby Nature Park (WT/TNC; SK 914661, OS 121). Nesting common terns, goldeneye in winter. Good invertebrates, with Essex skipper, migrant hawker, black-tailed skimmer.

Norfolk

SITE 114 North Norfolk coast

Unspoilt coastline with numerous top-flight sites for flora and fauna.

North Norfolk has a justifiable reputation as one of the top natural history sites in the whole of Britain, and much of this coastline is protected from development and boasts a string of superb nature reserves.

Almost the whole of the Norfolk coast is of great natural history interest, and some 7890 ha are protected in the North Norfolk Coast BR/SSSI. Here the visiting naturalist is almost spoilt for choice. Two of the most famous and popular of

Eastern England

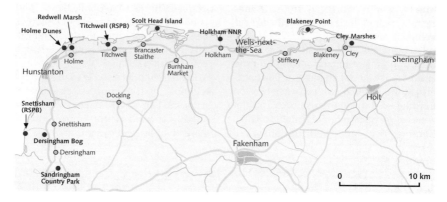

the sites, Blakeney and Cley, are treated in a separate entry. From Holme near Hunstanton in the west, to Sheringham some 45 km to the east, this marvellous coastline boasts a string of sites of un-rivalled natural history value and beauty. The attractive harbour town of Wells-next-the-Sea makes a good centre for exploring the nearby reserves, many of which may be reached from here by foot or bike.

Holme Dunes WT (TF 697438) and Bird Observatory lies between Holme and Hunstanton. Here there are fine sand dunes, with pines, scrub, and grazed marshland. The slacks have many unusual plants, including marsh helleborine, and there are colonies of natterjack. The observatory is a Norfolk Ornithologists' Association reserve (members only – non-members need a permit). It has several hides, and is known as a hot spot for migrants.

Redwell Marsh (TF 702436) may be viewed from the footpath from Holme to Broadwater Road. It is a grazed marsh, with a scrape which attracts many waders.

A little further east lies Titchwell (TF 749436), a typically well-managed RSPB reserve, with two hides and an embankment footpath offering views over reedbed and marshland. Marsh harriers are easy to spot here, as are avocets, and there are usually bearded tits about, with the chance of water rail and bittern. At the seaward end of the reserve there are colonies of little and common tern, and ringed plover and oystercatcher. Winter brings hen harriers and short-eared owls. Much of the reserve is wheelchair-accessible.

Moving eastwards again, the gentle curve of Brancaster Bay is backed by dunes and saltmarsh, and at low tide the flat beach reveals areas of mudflat, with good feeding for waders. Winter brings large flocks of Brent geese. The sea-lavenders and sea aster here are very colourful in summer. Scolt Head Island NNR (NT; TF 8146) may be reached by boat from Brancaster Staithe (TF 800450). This impressive island covers some 660 ha of saltmarsh, sand dune, and shingle, and is home to large colonies of mainly Sandwich, common, and little terns. The scrub harbours migrant songbirds in spring and autumn, with rare warblers possible. Natterjacks also breed on the reserve.

Holkham NNR (TF 892447) is a real jewel, with habitats ranging from sandy beaches and flats, through dunes and

Sandwich tern *Sterna sandvicensis* (Mike Lane)

Eastern England

fringing Corsican pine woods, to scrub, carr, birch groves, lagoons, grazed wet marshland, and pasture. Nearby is the splendid stately home of Holkham Hall, with its walled, landscaped grounds, grazed meadows, woodland, and large ornamental lake. Several pairs of Egyptian geese breed around the lake, which also has a cormorant roost on the island. A public road and footpaths run through the estate. Hawfinches and bramblings can occasionally be seen under the beech trees. Holkham Hall is well worth a visit in its own right. Few of the north Norfolk sites are as atmospheric as Holkham, and, using its network of footpaths, it is usually possible to escape the crowds. During the high season and holidays the beach close to the head of Lady Ann's Road can be busy, but most visitors are day-trippers who choose not to wander far.

The pines and scrub shelter migrants, especially in autumn, and almost anything can turn up here – icterine, barred, yellow-browed, and Pallas' warbler, red backed shrike, wryneck, and firecrest. More regular migrants such as wheatear and the occa-

Springbeauty *Montia perfoliata* (Martin Walters)

sional ring ouzel often feed on the meadows, or on the golf links near Beach Road at Wells. The marshes and reed-fringed pools are a favoured hunting ground for marsh

Holme

Reed-beds and grazing marsh at Holkham, Holme (Peter Wilson)

harriers (which also breed), and the wet fields attract large numbers of geese each winter – mainly pink-footed, Brent, and white-fronted, and there are often big flocks of golden plover. Other rare or local birds breeding in the vicinity are bittern, avocet, bearded tit, and garganey. Rare plants of Holkham include Jersey cudweed.

There is a population of natterjacks in the dunes. The unusual springbeauty, with its flowers nestling in a collar of fused leaves, is common here.

Car access to the reserve is either from the large park on Beach Road, Wells-next-the-sea, or from Lady Ann's Road, opposite Holkham Hall, off the A149 coast road.

Other sites nearby

Snettisham (RSPB; TF 648335), being alongside The Wash with its huge expanses of mudflats and sandbanks, is a great site for waders and wildfowl. These are best seen at high tide when they are concentrated closer to the shore. The numbers of knot and dunlin in particular can run into tens of thousands. Pink-footed geese are best seen between November and January; over 40 000 have been recorded.

Dersingham Bog SSSI/NNR (TF 672286; 159 ha). Bog with sundews.

Sandringham Country Park (TF 689287), close to the Royal Estate, is open all year. Mainly woodland and heath, with a dense cover of rhododendrons, an invasive exotic which produces a fine show of flowers in late spring. Good for woodland birds, including crossbill in the conifers.

SITE 115 Blakeney and Cley

Two of Britain's most famous reserves, which together epitomize East Anglia's coast, with a fascinating range of habitats.

Blakeney Point NT/NNR (TG 015464) and the adjacent reserves of Blakeney Marshes RSPB and Cley Marshes WT (Walsey Hills NOA) are famous mainly as birdwatching sites, and are probably visited by more 'twitchers' than anywhere else in Britain. Incidentally, Cley is usually spoken to rhyme with 'eye'. In these days of mobile phones and dedicated birdlines news travels fast, and birders soon gather if a rarity is reported. Rare birds are easily found here by watching for huddled groups of birders, especially at Cley along the East Bank and near the famous Arnold's Marsh, particularly in spring and autumn.

Blakeney Point itself is one of the most important sites for breeding terns; little, Sandwich, and common terns having large colonies here, and the relative inaccessibility gives them a degree of protection from predators. Other breeding birds are ringed plover, oystercatcher, and redshank, and over 260 species of birds have been recorded here. Regular on migration are bluethroat, dotterel, red-breasted flycatcher, and barred, icterine, and greenish warblers.

This is one of the finest examples of a shingle spit and it extends for some 11 km

Sea sandwort *Honkenya peploides* (Martin Walters)

from Cley, arching over the mudflats and channels of Blakeney and Morston. Its precise outline changes with the erosive effects of wind and sea. The habitats include sandy beach, huge areas of pebbles, and shingle, topped by dune systems, with fertile saltmarsh and mudflats on the sheltered landward side.

One highlight of a visit to Blakeney is a boat trip out to the point, to admire the seals which are usually hauled out at the tip, or lolling in the sea nearby. Most of these are common seals, but there are usually a few grey seals to be seen as well. The boat trip also gives good views of the tern colonies, which contain common, Sandwich, Arctic, and little terns. Boats normally leave from either Blakeney or Morston quays and are reasonably priced. Oystercatchers and

Ringed plover *Charadrius hiaticula* (Robert Dickson)

Cley Marshes (Peter Wilson)

ringed plovers also breed on the shingle. Blakeney Point may also be reached by a long trudge up the shingle spit from the south. This is an exhausting option, however, as the shingle is pretty heavy going.

Plants of the saltmarsh include glasswort, sea aster, sea-lavenders, and sea-purslane, with common stork's-bill, tree lupin, sea campion, sea sandwort, and yellow horned-poppy on the dunes and shingle.

Inland, the fine saltmarshes of Morston and Stiffkey (Stiffkey Saltmarshes NT; TG 956439) are a welcome feeding ground for hundreds of wintering geese, and in summer are dotted with the flowers of common sea-lavender and sea aster.

Cley Marshes (TG 054441), justly famed internationally as a birdwatching site, is blessed with both saltwater and freshwater marshes. These are set in a landscape of grazed marsh, with fringing reedbeds. These pools attract migrant waders in spring and autumn, and sedge, reed, and grasshopper warblers breed in the reeds and scrub. Other breeding birds are avocet, bittern, bearded tit, and reed bunting. This,

Britain's first bird reserve, was founded in 1926, since when it has become well known as one of the country's top birding sites. Birds include marsh harrier, bittern, water rail, little grebe, long-eared owl, bearded tit, and avocet. In spring and autumn there are always rare migrants here, often flagged by a cluster of twitchers lined up on one of the banks. Expect the unexpected is a good maxim here, and sightings of unusual species such as crane and spoonbill are a regular feature.

Cley is worth a visit at any time; the boardwalk gives good access even in wet

Water rail *Rallus aquaticus*

conditions, and there are viewing facilities for visitors in wheelchairs from some of the hides. In winter there are large numbers of wildfowl, notably wigeon, teal, pintail, and shoveler, while the shingle bank may hold flocks of snow bunting or shore lark. The visitor centre, set on a hill, is a good spot from which to scan the reserve.

Other sites nearby

Blickling Hall (NT; TG 178286) has an estate with woodland and riverside meadows, and the wildlife is surprisingly rich. The woods have twayblade and lily-of-the-valley, and breeding woodpeckers, redstarts, wood warbler, and hawfinches. Look out for Egyptian geese near the lake, and kingfishers and water voles on the river Bure.

Sheringham Park is an attractive mixture of woodland, with an impressive understorey of varied rhododendrons, and open grazing land sloping down towards the coast, where the cliffs support a colony of fulmars.

Swanton Novers Wood NNR/SSSI (TG 014313; 85 ha). This woodland complex lies some 16 km inland from Blakeney, just south of the Holt–Fakenham road.

Its main claim to fame is for the honey buzzards that breed in the area and which (with luck) can be spotted from the 'raptor watch point' just to the south of the wood. Entry to the wood itself is by permit only. Look out for hobbies, too. It is worth checking out any buzzards seen in this part of Norfolk as they may well be honey buzzards, and there is plenty of suitable country for these rather strange and secretive birds of prey, which seem to be increasing.

Walsey Hills (NOA; TG 062441) has good views over Cley and Salthouse marshes. The scrub often holds rare migrants. The woods and heaths to the south of Salthouse are good places to hear nightjars and nightingales in the summer, and if you are very lucky, to spot a great grey shrike in the winter.

SITE
116 Norfolk Broads

England's largest wetland area, with a mixture of habitats and featuring several shallow lakes occupying low-lying land, mainly between Norwich and the North Sea coast.

Broadland has a unique atmosphere, with its interconnected meres and broads, and associated fringing marshland and reedbeds. The whole area, covering 303 square kilometres, has been protected since 1989 and now has NP status. The lakes are nearly all artificial, constructed originally by peat diggers in medieval times, and some of

Meadowsweet
Filipendula ulmaria

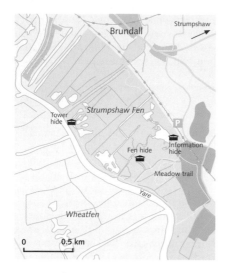

these shallow habitats have recently been recreated by planned excavation.

Though many of the waterways suffer from excessive boat traffic and consequent pollution, this region remains something of a wildlife haven. Its specialities include key marshland species such as marsh harrier, the rare swallowtail butterfly, Norfolk hawker dragonfly, and fen orchid. In addition to the more common sedge and reed warblers, Cetti's warbler breeds in broadland – usually in scrub or carr – but is more often heard than seen. The aquatic plants of broadland include the rather delicate stoneworts, water-soldier, and frogbit.

The Broads are also the main stronghold in Britain of the rare ramshorn snail (sites where it is found include, for example, Carlton Marshes, Suffolk, and Halvergate Marshes, Norfolk).

Hickling Broad NNR (TG 410220, OS 134), lies to the east of the A149 Yarmouth–Cromer road, and is signposted from Hickling village. This is the largest of the broads and covers nearly 500 ha of wet woodland, marsh, reedbed, and sedgefield, as well as the open water of the broad itself. Although, like many broads, it suffers from overuse, especially summer boat traffic, the walks, nature trails, and hides are well worth exploring. The breed-

ing birds include marsh harrier, bearded tit, bittern, grey heron, and common tern. This is a good site for the rare Savi's warbler, which has a similar song to a grasshopper warbler, but which prefers reedbeds. Grasshopper warblers are also found here, in the bushy areas. In spring, the broad attracts passing migrants, including osprey and black tern, and in winter the ducks include goldeneye, and the occasional smew. The reserve has a wide range of wetland and fen plants, including milk-parsley (the food-plant of the swallowtail), water-violet, purple-loosestrife, marsh pea, marsh fern, and early and southern marsh-orchids. The dragonfly pools are well worth inspecting, and this is also one of the best sites for that symbol of broadland, the swallowtail butterfly, now sadly restricted to broadland as a regular breeder (watch for the adults between May and August).

Bure Broads & Marshes NNR/SSSI (TG 350155), which includes Ranworth Broad (WT), cover some 740 ha of fen, reedbed, alder carr and open water in the valleys of the rivers Bure and Ant. At Hoveton Great Broad (TG 315164) there is a nature trail

Water-soldier *Stratiotes aloides*

Bure Marshes (Peter Wilson)

and hide. Ranworth Broad lies just south of the river Bure, off the B1140 Norwich–Acle road. This broad benefits from being free of boat pressure and is an excellent reserve in which to absorb the flavours of broadland. A boardwalk leads to an information centre, which is open April–October. The habitats here range from oak woodland, through alder and goat willow carr – look out for clumps of tussock-sedge and the beautiful royal fern. Other plants include meadowsweet and the much more local milk-parsley. Common terns nest here, and there is a large cormorant roost.

At the southern edge of the Broads NP lie the reserves of Berney Marshes (RSPB) and Breydon Water LNR/SSSI (TG 488070; 515 ha). These grazing marshes and estuarine mudflats are open throughout the year and lie just to the west of Great Yarmouth. The grasslands of Berney Marshes attract wildfowl and waders, such as wigeon, pintail, shoveler, teal, gadwall, redshank, avocet, and lapwings, and also Bewick's swans and geese in the winter. The mudflats of Breydon Water are perfect feeding grounds for waders, and the open brackish water attracts goldeneye and mergansers. Flowers include common sea-lavender, sea aster, and scurvygrass, and this is also one of only a handful of sites for the rare Norfolk hawker dragonfly.

Marsh pea *Lathyrus palustris*

Swallowtail *Papilio machaon*

Strumpshaw Fen (TG 341067, OS 134), which can be reached from the A47, east of Norwich, is another fine RSPB reserve, with typical broadland habitats of reedbeds, wet woodland, and meadows. It is well equipped with hides and nature trails and open daily from dawn until dusk. This is another of the places where it is still possible to spot the beautiful swallowtail butterfly. Also found here are Norfolk and migrant hawkers and black-tailed skimmer. Occasional views of the introduced Chinese water deer are possible. The breeding birds include bearded tit, marsh harrier, and Cetti's warbler. Over 400 plant species are recorded, with water-soldier, marsh pea, greater spearwort, and marsh sow-thistle.

Nearby Buckenham Marshes is famous as one of the few sites where bean geese can be reliably spotted. The geese, numbering a few hundred, turn up here each winter and are best seen in December and January, before they start the return flight to their breeding grounds in Sweden.

Some other important reserves within or near the Norfolk Broads

Ant Broads & Marshes NNR/SSSI (TG 364212; 743 ha): broadland habitats, otters.

Barton Broad (WT): reedbeds, carr, bearded tit, swallowtail.

Horsey Mere (TG 456224): warblers, wildfowl.

Ludham Marshes NNR/SSSI (EN; TG 404177; 103 ha): broadland habitats.

Martham Broad NNR (WT; TG 4621) has swallowtails and a rich fen flora. The reedbeds have marsh harrier and bearded tits, and red kites sometimes pass through.

Surlingham Broad (WT): fenland, open water.

Surlingham Church Marsh (RSPB; TG 306064): reedbeds, sedge fen, open water, nature trail.

Upton Broad SSSI (TG 391137; 195 ha): fenland vegetation.

Upper Thurne Broads and Marshes SSSI (TG 438209; 1184 ha): water plants, wildfowl.

Waveney Forest (TG 467008), near Fritton, is a mainly coniferous wood next to the river Waveney. Good site for woodcock and crossbills, and for waders, wildfowl, and raptors over the adjacent marshes in winter.

Wheatfen (the Ted Ellis NR, named after this famous local naturalist) is a reserve of about 40 ha, with a good network of footpaths, leading through alder and willow woodland, tidal grazing marsh, and fen, to the southern bank of the river Yare.

Winterton Dunes NNR (TG 4921) has shallow dune ponds with breeding natterjacks. Stonechat also breed here. In winter the higher dunes give good views inland over the marshes (hen harrier and short-eared owl) and over the sea (divers and long-tailed ducks possible).

SITE 117 Breckland

This fascinating area of semi-natural habitats on well-drained soil in the heart of East Anglia is a patchwork of heath and woodland, with many unusual and rare species.

The East Anglian Breckland straddles the border between inland Norfolk and Suffolk, with a small extension into Cambridgeshire. This is essentially a landscape moulded by humans, but none the less interesting for that. Its characteristics are a mosaic of conifer plantations, old Scots pine hedges (now grown out into gnarled trees), and groves, extensive heaths, stony fields, and pasture. Large tracts are controlled by the Ministry of Defence with limited public access, but there are also many visitable reserves, and a network of footpaths through the extensive FC holdings.

The area has one of the driest climates in western Europe and the most Continental climate in Britain, with relatively hot summers and cold winters. A visit to the open Breckland heaths can therefore be bracing on a windy day in winter, but surprisingly hot on a still day in good weather in the summer. Although it shares many species with the heaths of southern England, the Breckland has quite a different feel to it, being more arid, with any rainfall tending to drain away quickly through the porous sandy soils. One of the key features of Breckland, for flowers, is the underlying chalk, which makes it different from other heath areas, and the soils here vary from acid to quite alkaline. In a few places there are unusual ponds – known as the Breckland meres – which fluctuate with the ground water, and these have their own special plants and animals. The winter annual, mossy stonecrop, is one such plant.

Breckland's special birds include woodlark, nightjar, wheatear, and stone curlew. Look for woodlarks in areas that have been replanted with conifers, especially adjacent to open heath and taller forest. This edge habitat is also preferred by nightjars and tree pipits.

Rabbits are abundant in Breckland, and indeed have played (and still play) a key role in keeping the grassy sward low, to the benefit of many of the birds and flowers. The rabbits, introduced as a food 'crop' by the Normans, were formerly kept in managed warrens, which have given their name to several sites. Roe, fallow, red deer, and muntjac are all found in the forests and woods.

Breckland has several special plants that are rare elsewhere in Britain but which find the conditions of this unusual habitat to their liking. These include spiked, breckland, and spring speedwells, breckland thyme, sand and Spanish catchfly, field wormwood, and rue-leaved saxifrage. Spanish catchfly even has its own special moth, the confusingly-named viper's-bugloss, whose larva feeds on this species.

Biting stonecrop *Sedum acre*

Eastern England

Stone curlew *Burhinus oedicnemus* **(Peter Wilson)**

East Wretham Heath SSSI (WT; TL 910882) is slightly unusual in that it has large areas of grassland, and also two of the Breckland meres – Langmere and Ringmere. There are also tracts of Scots pine, with goldcrests, crossbills, and long-eared owls, and hornbeam woodland where hawfinches can sometimes be seen. The grassland has viper's-bugloss and harebell, with biting stonecrop in patches. The meres attract passage waders such as snipe, curlew, ringed plover, and green sandpipers. The flora and fauna of the meres have to be adapted to occasional drought, as is the rare leech *Dina lineata*, which occurs here. Amphibious bistort grows in the meres, with shining and fennel pondweeds, and a fringing growth of reed canary-grass. Grass snakes, adders, and viviparous lizards are fairly frequent, and common toads and smooth and great crested newts breed in both meres.

Thompson Common (WT; TL 934967, OS 144) contains the large shallow lake of Thompson Water, as well as a number of pingos (shallow ponds formed by ice action at the end of the last ice age). The wetland and aquatic plants are good here, with marsh-marigold, marsh-orchid, greater spearwort, bogbean, stoneworts and water-violets. In winter, the ponds attract wildfowl. Thompson Common and Frost's Common, Great Hockham (TL 945935, OS 144) both have the rare scarce emerald damselfly, along with several other dragonflies.

Wayland Wood (WT; TL 924995, OS 144) is a truly ancient wood with aspects of original wildwood. It is mainly oak with hazel and ash coppice and has splendid bluebells, as well as yellow archangel, early purple orchid, and yellow star-of-Bethlehem (at its only Norfolk site). The birds include woodcock and golden pheasant.

Lynford Arboretum (OS 144) is a fine, varied Breckland site with mixed woodland, gravel pits, and fields. This is a good site for hawfinches (associated with the hornbeams) and crossbill, and Egyptian geese breed near the pits.

Thetford Forest is a large area of plantation in various stages of growth, and this complex of woodland and heath dominates the central part of Breckland. A good nature trail leads from Santon Downham (TL 8287) through a variety of typical habitats. The special birds to expect here are woodlark, nightjar, and tree pipit. This site has a particular poignancy for true birders as the last (official) breeding site (1988) of red-backed shrike in Britain. The habitat still seems ideal for the species, and it is possible that this striking bird may return to Breckland. Just to the north of Santon Downham is the famous old flint mine of Grimes Graves (TL 8290).

Weeting Heath NNR/SSSI (TL 757882; 142 ha) is one of the classic sites for stone curlew. This reserve, just north of Brandon, has hides from which these birds (at their most active late in the day) can be watched in relative comfort for both watcher and bird. Several pairs of woodlarks also nest on the reserve, and little owls, green woodpeckers, and crossbills may be seen. This is a good spot to see Essex and dingy skippers, grayling, and brown argus. Weeting's Breckland plants include spiked speedwell, Spanish catchfly, purple-stemmed cat's-tail, maiden pink, wall bedstraw, quaking-grass, bearded fescue, spring sedge, wild thyme, and mouse-ear hawkweed.

Mayday Farm (TL 7887, OS 143/4) has become well known for its woodlarks, which are usually fairly easy to see here, and for nightjar, but perhaps most of all for goshawks which breed in the area. They are easiest to see when they indulge in their display flights in the spring, from February to April. There are also hobbies from May, and crossbills, woodcock, and occasional golden pheasant in these woods. There is a car park, and tracks leading to a hide, from which woodlarks and tree pipits may be seen. The best way to locate the elusive goshawks is to choose a fine morning, then scan the skies for birds soaring and displaying above the trees.

Lakenheath Washes (RSPB; TL 7286, OS 143) lie just north of the Little Ouse River. Here we are very much on the western edge of Breckland proper, with some of the atmosphere of the nearby fenland. The washes attract large numbers of wildfowl in winter. This can be quite a magical

Cavenham Heath (Peter Wilson)

area, with the chance of the sight (or more likely sound) of one of East Anglia's rarest breeding birds – golden oriole – or a passing marsh harrier or hobby. The low-growing marsh vegetation is ideal for barn owls, which may be spotted hunting here. Black tern and garganey are regular in spring. One of the RSPB's newest reserves is now being created on the south side of the Little Ouse River, between Lakenheath Station and Botany Bay, and the area is becoming increasingly attractive to wetland birds and plants. The ground bug *Sphagristicus nebulosus* – a species new to Britain – was recently found in this area.

Cavenham and Icklingham Heaths NNR/SSSI (TL 751731; 399 ha) is one of Breckland's best examples of acid heath. Access is by public road and track running through the area, although some parts require permission from EN. The river Lark runs through it and is bordered by wetland vegetation and damp meadows, providing an interesting contrast to the dry heath. Much of the reserve sup-

ports heather and gorse, broken up by pockets of damp birch and alder woodland, patches of bracken, and small areas of fen. Willow carr is well developed towards the river, where there are also sedge and reedbeds, with flowers such as yellow iris and purple-loosestrife. Some of the damp woodland has marsh fern in the undergrowth, and in open areas sand sedge spreads rapidly to colonize the soil. The keen-eyed might spot the tiny mossy stonecrop, Britain's smallest land flowering plant and a Breckland speciality.

Summer birds include nightjar, woodlark, grasshopper warbler, whinchat, nightingale, and woodcock. Curlew and stone curlew also breed on or near the reserve. In winter, the heath may attract hen harriers and occasionally a great grey shrike. Green woodpeckers feed on anthills on the heath and grassland, and the air is often loud with the songs of tree pipits performing their parachute displays. Buzzing flocks of redpolls are a feature, especially in the birch woods, and snipe and redshank breed in the damp, grazed fields. The well-

Thetford Heath (Peter Wilson)

Eastern England

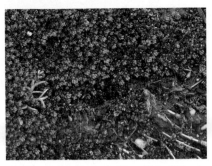

Mossy stonecrop *Crassula tillaea* (Peter Wilson)

drained, sandy soils dry out and warm up quickly, making this habitat ideal for reptiles. Adders, grass snakes, and viviparous lizards are all found on the reserve. Adders can be a danger, especially early or late in the season when they are sluggish, so boots are recommended. The butterflies and moths include grayling, small heath, small copper, and emperor moth.

Not far from Cavenham Heath lies West Stow Country Park (West Stow Heath SSSI

(TL 792713; 44 ha)), which has a good mixture of Breckland habitats, including lush riverside vegetation alongside the river Lark. The pretty maiden pink is common here – search for it in places where rabbit grazing pressure is relatively low.

Nearby Lackford Wildfowl Reserve (WT; TL 800708, OS 155; 42 ha), is a fairly recent reserve and a prime Breckland site for wetland birds. The series of flooded gravel pits alongside the river Lark attract winter wildfowl, with occasional visits from goosander, goldeneye, and divers, and breeders include kingfisher, great crested grebe, and little ringed plover. Hobby and osprey are regular visitors.

Foxhole Heath, near Eriswell SSSI (TL 736781; 86 ha), has a rabbit-grazed sloping hillside and is a regular breeding site for stone curlew. Please note that there is no access, so the birds should be viewed, or listened to, from the roadside. In the evening, their wailing calls can often be heard here.

Some other Breckland sites

Norfolk

Brettenham Heath NNR (TL 925869; 236 ha; permit required): dry heath with rich flora; also red, roe and muntjac deer.

Stanford Training Area SSSI (TL 866945; 4655 ha): Ministry of Defence land with rich wildlife, including stone curlew.

Suffolk

Barnham Heath SSSI (TL 882798; 77 ha).

Berner's Heath, Icklingham SSSI (TL 798764; 234 ha; no access): breckland with rare flora.

Deadman's Grave, Icklingham SSSI (TL 779742; 127 ha).

Knettishall Heath SSSI (TL 952803; 92 ha): grassy heathland.

RAF Lakenheath SSSI (TL 746826; 112 ha): defence land with some protected habitat.

Lakenheath (RSPB) (Lakenheath Warren SSSI (TL 763803; 588 ha)): heath with Spanish catchfly, woodlark and stone curlew.

Little Heath, Barnham SSSI (TL 850781; 46 ha).

Thetford Heath NNR/SSSI (TL 852802; 98 ha; permit required): heather and lichen heath with many rare plants.

Wangford Warren SSSI (WT; TL 755841; 68 ha; no access): inland dunes and sandy heath; good insects.

Weather and Horn Heaths, Eriswell SSSI (TL 784774; 133 ha; no access).

Eastern England

Suffolk

SITE
118 Suffolk coast

Superb nature site with coastal shingle, marsh, pools, heathland, woodland, and the largest continuous reedbeds in Britain.

For the naturalist there is perhaps no finer area in this region than that stretching between the charming coastal towns of Southwold and Aldeburgh. A gently shelving bank of shingle protects the fragile marshes,

Bittern *Botaurus stellaris* **(David Element)**

lagoons, and reedbeds from the occasional ravages of the North Sea, whilst the slopes on the landward side contain precious remnants of heath and woodland.

The complex of wetland, coastal marsh, and adjacent woodland and heath that stretches from the village of Walberswick south through Dunwich, and on towards Minsmere, includes a wonderful swathe of continuous reedbed. It is probably the sheer extent of this rare habitat which explains why it holds such good numbers of local birds such as marsh harrier, bearded tit, and the very rare bittern. In early May, the surrounding copses resound with the trills and fluting notes of recently arrived nightingales, and the occasional abrupt song of Cetti's warbler, while common, little, and Sandwich terns ply along the shore, fishing in the adjacent shallows.

Stacked reeds, Benacre

Westwood Marsh is the single largest expanse of reedbed in the country, but this marvellous habitat is only about 50 years old, having been flooded during the Second World War as part of Britain's coastal defence measures. Concrete pillboxes also provide an echo of this period. Reedbed such as this remains very much a managed habitat, and regular cutting, combined with controlled flooding and drainage, is employed to keep the conditions ideal for animals and plants alike. An attractive feature of the reserve is also the close juxtaposition of wetland with woodland, the wooded hills lending protection and privacy to the reedbeds. Some of this woodland derives from natural cover, but others, such as Hoist Covert, were planted in the early nineteenth century as game cover. Plants to look out for in the reedbeds or pools are the marsh sow-thistle, a majestic species overtopping the reeds when fully grown, wild celery, bog pimpernel, louse-wort, sneezewort, bogbean, frogbit, and greater bladderwort.

The patches of heath are remnants of the once much more widespread Suffolk sandlings, which came into being largely through intensive grazing by sheep on the thin, sandy soils. Special plants of these heaths include suffocated and subterranean clovers, mossy stonecrop, and fenugreek. The local butterfly, silver-studded blue, is also found on the sandlings, laying on heather, gorse, or bird's-foot-trefoil. In winter, the heaths and marshland attract birds of prey and owls, including hen harriers, merlins, short-eared owls, and sometimes rough-legged buzzards.

Resident mammals include otters and five species of deer, and more than 120 species of bird have bred here. The invertebrate fauna is also very rich, with solitary bees and wasps, and 500 species of lepidoptera, including white admiral and silver-studded blue. This is also one of a handful of sites in the area (Minsmere is another) where the recently discovered antlion *Euroleon nostras* breeds. Natterjacks have been reintroduced.

Part of the reserve follows the attractive estuary of the river Blyth, where waders and wildfowl can be watched from footpaths skirting the woodland, or from the hides.

Dingle Marshes (WT/RSPB) lies between Dunwich and Walberswick and is a similar mix of coastal habitats and reedbeds, with breeding avocets, marsh harriers, and bitterns. Recently, the rare bug *Orthotylus rubidus* was discovered here.

The nearby reserve of Benacre NNR/ SSSI (TM 530830; 393 ha) is a fascinating patchwork of reedbeds, dunes, shingle, woodland, and brackish pools and lagoons. A public hide can be reached from the coastal footpath. Marsh harriers breed here, and little egret are regular in winter, as are snow buntings and shore larks along the shingle.

Minsmere (RSPB; TM 465665) is one of Britain's most famous nature reserves, and this flagship site is justly famous for its diversity of birds in particular. It is an example of a reserve managed and maintained with the express aim of fostering a wide range of coastal habitats for the birds – so much so that to the purist naturalist it almost has the feel of an open-air zoo, though the birds are truly wild and come and go as they please. It is easy of

access, with good facilities. Paths lead through reedbeds, marsh, heath, and woodland and to the coastal shingle, and to the well-sited hides which give easy viewing over the varied habitats. The scrape, with its shallow lagoons, is particularly famous for its waders, especially in spring and autumn. Good views of avocets are pretty much guaranteed, and you may also see rarer waders and the occasional spoonbill. Savi's warbler breeds sometimes, as well as the very common reed and sedge warblers. At the edge of the marsh, where bush meets reedbed, listen for the distinctive song of Cetti's warbler, or for the monotonous reeling of a grasshopper warbler. The woods have all three woodpeckers, tawny owl (sometimes long-eared owl), nightingale, and redstart. The reserve's richness is underlined by the fact that Minsmere also has 243 species of spider. Although taking second place to the birds, Minsmere's flowers are not without interest. The grassy ditches have common spotted-orchid and southern marsh-orchid, and the marsh edges have water dock, hemp-agrimony, and yellow iris, as well as the

Gorse and reedbeds, Walberswick (Martin Walters)

Avocet *Recurvirostra avosetta*

tall and rare marsh sow-thistle. The heathland has heather, bell heather, and gorse, and the adjacent mixed oak woods are also worth investigating.

Close to Minsmere is Dunwich Heath (NT; TM 475683, OS L 156), a patch of coastal heathland lying just inland from a line of crumbling cliffs. The heath has gorse and heather, with bell heather and occasional clumps of birch and pine. This threatened habitat has breeding nightjar, and silver-studded blues. Dartford warblers have recently colonized, which is an encouraging sign. They were first recorded as breeding in the mid-1990s at Westleton, since when there has been a steady

increase and spread, with a cluster of sites in the area, centred on Dunwich Heath. The southern edge of the heath gives commanding views over the adjacent reedbeds towards Minsmere, and from here marsh harriers can often be spotted, and (much more rarely) bitterns. The sandy cliffs house a colony of sand martins, and at the foot of the cliffs there are lesser marsh grasshoppers and glow-worms, the former an insect with its stronghold in coastal East Anglia. The cliff-top paths around the nearby village of Dunwich are a good place from which to scan the waves for scoters, divers, and skuas in particular, and to ponder the fate of those parts of the village now submerged by the sea.

Nearby North Warren (RSPB; TM 467575), just north of Aldeburgh, protects a tract of rare coastal heath, as well as woodland, reedbed, grazing marsh, and shingle. Breeding birds here include marsh harrier, nightingale, and woodlark, the latter with over 80 territories in 2000 – one of the densest populations in Britain. The marshes attract wildfowl in the winter, and bitterns have started to breed here.

Eastern England

SITE 119 Orfordness and Havergate

A fine coastal site; one of only three major shingle landforms in Britain, and amongst the most important shingle features in Europe.

Although access is impossible except by boat, this is such an extraordinary feature that it is worth inclusion. It also has important wildlife, notably its gull colonies. The spit may be viewed from the landward side of the river Ore, and similar habitat exists further south, for example at Shingle Street.

Orfordness is almost unique in Britain in combining a shingle spit with a foreland, and it is this 'nose' or ness which gives rise to the name for the whole area. The area has protected status as Orfordness-Havergate NNR. The spit is a complex sequence of shingle ridges and swales (valleys), deposited over centuries,

Eastern England

Sea campion *Silene uniflora*

and the whole structure extends for an astonishing 15 km, deflecting the flow of the Alde River from just south of Aldeburgh, past Orford and Havergate Island, to its eventual entry into the sea as the river Ore at Hollesley Bay.

Orfordness contains one of the largest stretches of unimproved brackish marsh and lagoons in Suffolk. These lagoons were dug as 'borrow-pits' and the clay which was extracted was used mainly to make river walls. They now support a group of unusual plants and animals, adapted to the fluctuating salinity of the water. Only very few species can tolerate these changing conditions, and some of those here are very rare. One of the most noteworthy is the starlet sea anemone.

There are patches of shingle heath – one of the rarest of all habitats in Britain. Plants include sea campion, and there are many kinds of lichens growing here (116 species have been found), some very rare. Another local rarity is the sea pea which grows along the drift-line behind the beach, in a band stretching for kilometres. Gratifyingly, this is now on the increase and benefits from the isolated nature of the location. Sea-kale is another special plant of this site, especially towards the southern end. The shingle is home to about 50 pairs of little terns, and large numbers of ringed plover and oystercatchers. Rare beetles and spiders are also to be found here.

Reedbed communities are relatively scarce on Orfordness. Recently this valuable habitat has been extended, and

islands created on deeper water. The results are already showing, with marsh harrier and bearded tit moving in.

Another habitat here is grazed marshland, probably reclaimed under royal patronage in the thirteenth century. These fields were farmed for arable crops until 1989, then abandoned. Management has allowed natural regeneration of grassland, which now attracts breeding waders (notably lapwing and redshank) and wintering wildfowl. Kings Marsh is a brackish saltmarsh, enclosed by river walls. This grazed pasture, which often floods, is ideal as a feeding ground for waders and wildfowl, while the remaining ungrazed sections attract birds such as short-eared owl. Flooding at Lantern Marsh creates tidal lagoons, mudflats, and new saltmarsh. Species which have benefited from this are spoonbill (now nesting!), little egret, avocet, redshank, whimbrel, curlew, bar-tailed and black-tailed godwits, little tern, and shore lark. The reserve is also used by hunting raptors such as marsh and hen harrier, peregrine, merlin, and barn owl.

Orford is justly famous for its gulls, and the mixed colonies now consist of up to 22 500 pairs of lesser black-backed gulls (about 10% of the European population) and over 5500 pairs of herring – one of the largest in Europe. This is also an extremely important breeding area for little tern with some 70% of the total Suffolk population breeding here.

Havergate Island (RSPB; TM 425496), a nature reserve since the late 1930s, is perhaps best known for its large breeding population of avocets – over 100 pairs.

Oystercatcher *Haematopus ostralegus*

The reserve is carefully managed, mainly for the birds, with lagoons of varying depth and islands. The numerous Sandwich and common terns are joined by a few Arctic terns at what is for this species a very southerly breeding site. Autumn and winter waders include both godwits, little stint, spotted redshank, and whimbrel. The rare lagoon sandshrimp has recently been found here and at Snettisham. Access is by permit only. Boats ferry to the island from Orford Quay between April and August, on the first and third weekends.

Other sites nearby

Landguard and Bird Observatory (WT; TM 279320, OS 169) forms the eastern flank of Harwich Harbour, just south of Felixstowe. The geography is a perfect welcome for tired migrant birds – a shingle spit backed by grassland and scrub. From August through to November almost anything can turn up here. Regulars are firecrest, snow bunting, ring ouzel, black redstart (also breeds), long-eared owl, purple sandpiper, and Mediterranean gull, with divers, grebes, and sea ducks offshore.

Trimley Marshes (WT; TM 360268) lies just up river from here and is a good site for waders and wildfowl. There are five hides.

SITE 120 Redgrave and Lopham Fens

One of the largest fens in lowland England. It holds threatened habitats and has a diverse and special invertebrate fauna.

Redgrave & Lopham Fens NNR/SSSI (WT; TM 048797; 125 ha) is a fine reserve lying in the valley of the river Waveney, on the border between Suffolk and Norfolk. These fen communities have developed on ground kept wet by springs draining into the valley. Such spring-fed fen is so unusual that it has Special Area of Conservation candidate status, and is already an SSSI and Ramsar Site.

The reserve holds a mixture of fenland habitats, ranging from open water, through extensive beds dominated by great fen-sedge and purple moor-grass, to reed fen with peaty pools, to areas of

Grasshopper warbler *Locustella naevia* (Mike Lane)

Eastern England

Pools at Redgrave and Lopham, fringed with hemp agrimony *Eupatorium cannabinum* (Peter Wilson)

dry and wet heath, to carr and alder and birch woodland. Here, there are acid as well as calcareous conditions, which adds considerably to the diversity of the site.

The fenland vegetation has plants such as water dock, meadowsweet, common and marsh valerians, hemp-agrimony, fen bedstraw, wild angelica, meadow-rue, water mint, and purple-loosestrife. The more acid patches of wet heath harbour heather and cross-leaved heath, with tormentil, common cottongrass, grass-of-Parnassus, and sundew. Recent improvements to the water regime have seen an enrichment of the flora with butterwort and marsh fragrant orchid appearing.

Invertebrates are a special feature, with more than 120 rare species, including one of only two British sites for the fen raft spider. This magnificent spider is a specialist fen huntsman, lying in wait, often on floating leaves, for passing insects, and can even tackle small fish. As you might expect this is also a good site for dragonflies.

Breeding birds of the fen include nightingale, reed, sedge and grasshopper warblers, water rail, snipe, marsh harrier, short-eared owl, sparrowhawk, and hobby, with bearded tit and siskin in winter.

Water voles and water shrews are found on the reserve, although they are difficult to spot.

The reserve can be found between Redgrave and South Lopham, and there are car parks and a visitor centre. The whole site can be very wet, so adequate footwear is recommended. There are three nature trails, and disabled access.

121 Bradfield Woods

SITE

Largest area of traditionally managed ancient woodland in Suffolk, with a diverse flora.

Bradfield Woods NNR/SSSI (WT; TL 932575; 65 ha) is an ancient woodland, much of it under a coppice-with-standards regime that promotes a rich ground flora which varies with the stage of coppicing. Some parts of the woods – particularly Felshamhall Wood and Monk's Park Wood – have been managed in a similar fashion since 1252.

Bradfield is one of the richest woodland sites, not just in East Anglia, but in

A ride with coppiced margins in Bradfield Woods

the whole country. This richness is partly due to the management, but also a result of the varied soils; some parts are calcareous, while others are on a more acid soil. Ponds, ditches, and woodland glades add to the interest.

The main woodland types here are dominated by pedunculate oak, often with brambles and bracken below, and ash and field maple, frequently carpeted by dog's mercury. In some of the more acid patches, the coppice has a mixture of alder, hazel, small-leaved lime, holly, and birch. Ash, elm, field maple, guelder-rose, spindle, and dogwood are more characteristic of the more calcareous soils. More than 370 species of higher plants are known at Bradfield. Notable species are green-flowered helleborine, wood spurge, water avens, and fragrant agrimony, and the local pale sedge. Other plants of the woodland floor include bluebell, primrose, wood anemone, ramsons, herb-Paris, dog's mercury, early purple orchid, and the beautiful and rather local oxlip. Some of the ash stools are over 5.5 m across and possibly 1000 years old! Active coppicing here yields useful, sustainably produced items such as spars for thatching, poles, tool handles, firewood, and ash for glazing pottery.

Given the range of habitats it is no surprise that these woods are also rich in bird life. All the expected woodland species can be seen, such as woodcock, all three woodpeckers, tawny owl, willow tit, sparrowhawk, blackcap, garden warbler, whitethroat, chiffchaff, and willow warbler. Many a visit will be rewarded by a nightingale serenade, and the sharper-eared may pick out the feebler trills of the rather elusive wood warbler.

Fallow and roe deer both frequent the woods and glades, and there are badgers, stoats, weasels, and foxes, along with small mammals such as wood mice and bank voles, and dormice, the latter towards its northern British limit. Adders and grass snakes are both found here, as well as common toads and common frogs, and viviparous lizard.

There are more than 20 butterfly species, including white admiral, purple hairstreak, Essex skipper, orange tip, wall, brimstone, and comma.

Three nature trails wind through the reserve, and there is also a birdwatching hide. The best seasons to visit are probably spring and summer, when the woods are loud with birdsong and the woodland flowers are at their finest.

A selection of other important sites in the county (for Suffolk Breckland sites see Norfolk)

Carlton Marshes (WT; TM 505918): grazed marsh, dykes, wet woodland; rich fen flora.

Castle Marshes SSSI (WT; TM 473917, OS 134): Norfolk hawker, scarce chaser, hairy dragonfly.

Deben Estuary SSSI (TM 293438; 979 ha): saltmarsh and intertidal mudflats, with the most complete range of saltmarsh community types in Suffolk; wintering waterbirds, especially avocet.

Hen Reedbed (WT; TM 470770): reedbeds and pools with marsh harrier, bearded tit, bittern and garganey.

Orwell Estuary SSSI (TM 321377; 1309 ha): seabirds, waders.

Wolves Wood SSSI (RSPB; TM 054440, OS 155). This ancient mixed woodland has warblers, nightingales, woodpeckers, and occasional hawfinches. It is also a good site for butterflies, notably purple and white-letter hairstreaks.

Cambridgeshire

SITE 122 Grafham Water

Huge inland reservoir with varied bird life, especially good in winter and during the migration.

Grafham Water SSSI (Anglian Water and WT; TL 140681; 807 ha) is a large reservoir lying between Huntingdon and St Neots. Although worth visiting at any time of the year, it is perhaps best known for the large numbers of wintering waterbirds, including teal, gadwall, wigeon, goldeneye, goosander, tufted duck, coot, and great crested grebes. Rarer winter wildfowl are divers, the rarer grebes, scaup, scoters, long-tailed duck, and smew. The roosts are worth checking for rare gulls.

In summer the woods have nightingale and garden warbler, and the scrub grasshopper warbler. Regular on passage are wood sandpiper, greenshank, little gull, black tern, and osprey. If the Rutland Water ospreys expand their range, then Grafham is another likely breeding site.

There are several hides, two of which have wheelchair access, nature trails, and an information centre and wildlife garden. The reserve, which is on the western end of the reservoir and covers some 150 ha, can be entered from the car park near the village of West Perry, and is open all year round.

Nearby

Brampton Wood SSSI (WT; TL 185698, OS 153; 132 ha), not far from Grafham Water, is the second largest ancient wood in Cambridgeshire (after Monks Wood), and composed mainly of ash and field maple, with hazel. More than 300 species of plants recorded, with yellow archangel, wood spurge, and wild pear. It has good butterflies, amongst which feature purple, white-letter, and black hairstreak, and white admiral. Nightingale, grasshopper warbler, woodcock, and all the woodpeckers also breed here.

SITE 123 The Washes

Superb wetland site, flooded in winter and providing ideal conditions for a range of wildfowl, notably ducks and swans.

The parallel channels of the Old and New Bedford Rivers are part of a system which drained some of the fenland in the seventeenth century to win the rich soil for agriculture. The land between them is flat, and stretches away from south-west to north-east, broken here and there only by ditches and lines of willows.

Winter, pollard willows

In summer the area is dominated by rich grazing pasture, with occasional pools. This rare habitat attracts waders such as redshank, snipe, and lapwing, which all breed here, as does garganey. However, there are also uncommon species such as spotted crake, black-tailed godwit, and ruff, which breed sporadically. Marsh harriers are regularly spotted hunting over the washes.

In winter, the washes are quite different, being transformed into a huge expanse of shallow water – perfect feeding grounds for wildfowl. There are tens of thousands of wigeon, and large numbers of Bewick's and whooper swans. Hen harriers, short-eared owls and, more rarely, merlins and peregrines, hunt over the washes. Although much of the washland is protected, there is occasional shooting by wildfowlers in the winter, on adjacent private land.

There are two main bands of washland, both draining ultimately into The Wash: the Ouse Washes stretch roughly from Earith in the south to Downham Market;

the Nene Washes lie just north of Whittlesey, eastwards to Guyhirn. The RSPB and WT both have reserves and hides on the Ouse Washes (near Manea), as does the WWT, the latter at Welney. The Nene Washes are best seen from the RSPB reserve just north of Whittlesey.

Ouse Washes SSSI (RSPB/WT; TL 474856; 2479 ha) and Welches Dam (WT) lie about 4 km from Manea (TL 471861), and are free to members. There are 10 hides in all, 2 of which are wheelchair-accessible. These adjacent reserves are managed together, thus conserving a fine stretch of wetland.

The commonest ducks in winter are wigeon, pintail, shoveler, pochard, mallard, and teal, joined by occasional goldeneye and smew. The stars are undoubtedly the huge flocks of Bewick's swans which gather on the reserve – often as many as 2000 – with perhaps a couple of hundred whooper swans as well.

In summer, pools and ditches are revealed amongst the lush grassland pasture and reed-fringed ditches. Now is the

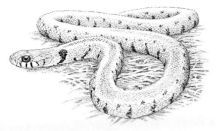

Grass snake *Natrix natrix*

time to watch for displaying ruff and black-tailed godwit, both of which breed here. The fields are also the ideal habitat for yellow wagtail. Black terns and little gulls are regular visitors, and have bred.

The washes are not without botanical interest, too. The deeper water of the rivers and ditches may hold fringed and yellow water-lilies and frogbit, with comfrey, meadowsweet, yellow iris, and purple-loosestrife at the margins. One rather special plant here is mousetail, a rare annual which grows here in wet, trodden ground.

Welney (WWT; TL 546946, OS 143) is an internationally important wetland, most impressive in winter when good views may be had of hundreds of visiting Bewick's and whooper swans, and many duck, such as large numbers of pochard, wigeon, pintail, gadwall, shoveler, and teal. Feeding of corn brings the wild swans to the hides for an evening display, which gives great close-up views of wild birds, but which may be a little too zoo-like for some tastes. In summer, meandering along the boardwalks can give good views (and sounds) of reed and sedge warblers, with breeding waders such as snipe and the rare black-tailed godwit, and the occasional garganey. These rich meadows and reedbeds have fine displays of great willowherb, purple-loosestrife, and marsh woundwort. The insects are good, too, with 19 species of dragonfly regular, including scarce chaser, hairy dragonfly, and red-eyed and variable damselflies.

Welney lies about 12 km north of Ely, and is open from 10.00 am to 5.00 pm, except Christmas Day. Free entry for children under four and WWT members. Gift shop and tearoom.

The Nene Washes SSSI (RSPB; TL 302995; 1517 ha), some 8 km east of Peterborough, are similar, with a mixture of marshland, wet meadows, and drainage ditches. Star breeding birds here are garganey and black-tailed godwit, with passage ruff, and wintering Bewick's swans, merlins, and hen harriers. The RSPB reserve (TL 277992) is reached via the Thorney road, just north of Whittlesey. The damp meadows here hold good numbers of breeding lapwing, snipe, gadwall, and shoveler, and rarities such as garganey, spotted crake and, most impressively, black-tailed godwit. Marsh harrier and hobby are regular in summer, while the winter visitors include large numbers of wigeon, pintail, teal, and Bewick's swans. Short-eared owls are regularly seen hunting at this time of year.

At Eldernell (TF 319988) there is a fine watchpoint on the south side of the Nene Washes, and a footpath running alongside. This spot is a favoured roosting site for birds of prey. From mid-August to mid-September there is usually a communal roost of marsh harriers in the reeds, and the winter gatherings of various raptors can be even more impressive – with hen harriers and short-eared owls in the reeds, and the chance of merlin, peregrine, and barn owl. Ruff and black-tailed godwits also gather nearby in the winter.

Stanground Wash (WT; TL 208975, OS 142; 25 ha), at the western end of the Nene Washes, is a mosaic of wet pasture and rough grassland in summer, and flooded most of the winter.

Yellow iris
Iris pseudacorus

Eastern England

SITE
124 Wicken Fen

One of Britain's finest wetland reserves; a remnant of once
extensive fenland.

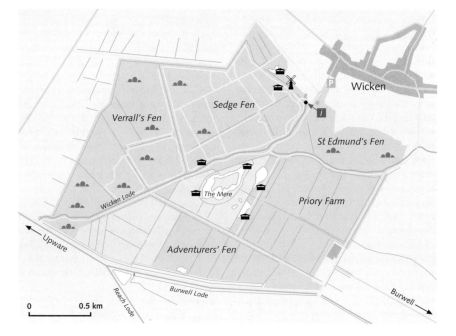

Wicken Fen NNR/SSSI (NT; TL 554702) lies 14 km north-east of Cambridge and 5 km south-west of Soham. The first reserve to be acquired by the NT, it is one of Britain's oldest nature reserves. It has been gradually enlarged over the years (a continuing process) and now covers about 325 ha.

The open, some would say bleak, landscape of fenland is not to every taste, but this area has its own characteristic set of animals and plants and a unique aura. Today, only patches remain, in a sea of fertile fields on the rich, peaty soils.

The survival of this world-famous fenland reserve is in large measure due to the activities of a group of Victorian naturalists who valued it for its wetland plants and birds, but perhaps above all for its insects, especially the butterflies – and most

notably the swallowtail. Partly because it has been so closely studied, Wicken boasts one of the longest species lists of any British reserve: about 300 species of higher plants, more than 2000 species of flies, 1000 species of beetle, 1000 species of moth, and 212 species of spider. Amongst

Fen violet *Viola persicifolia* (Martin Walters)

Eastern England

the larger insects, the dragonflies are prominent, with emperor dragonfly, hairy dragonfly, black-tailed skimmer, and red-eyed and variable damselflies.

This NNR is the third largest in Cambridgeshire, after the Ouse and Nene Washes. As with so many reserves, the character of the fen is due partly to traditional management for crops of great fen-sedge, which has been harvested for hundreds of years, and also peat extraction, which has been dug here since the seventeenth century.

Wicken is surrounded by cultivated fields which have isolated the reserve from other fenland pockets, and this may be one reason why some fenland specialities have declined or disappeared. Thus, the swallowtail was once common, but now only clings on through repeated introduction (now discontinued pending expansion of suitable habitat). The fen ragwort has been successfully reintroduced. In recent years, with the relative decline in intensive agriculture, packets of adjacent land have been acquired, thus enlarging the reserve, and there are now ambitious plans to extend it still further. On Adventurers' Fen there is an area of open water known as the Mere, and good views over this, and of the reedbeds and flooded meadows, are possible from the tower hide, or from the public footpath running alongside the southern edge of Wicken Lode. A pleasant walk of some 4 km brings one out eventually to the village of Upware. The

Old peat diggings

sedge fen itself lies to the north of Wicken Lode, and consists of a mixture of habitats: carr, sedge fields, reedy ditches, wet pasture, and thickets of more mature woodland. A system of boardwalks leads through part of this, from the picturesque restored windpump, the latter still occasionally used to bring water onto the reserve, symbolically reversing its original function.

Breeding birds include marsh harrier, teal, wigeon, shoveler, pochard, tufted duck, gadwall, garganey (spring), bearded

Other sites nearby

Holme Fen NNR/SSSI (TL 208889; 266 ha): fenland vegetation, warblers, nightingale.

Kingfisher's Bridge (TL 544728; 65 ha) is a privately owned restoration project just north of Wicken Fen. It links to Upware North Pit, one of only a few locations in East Anglia for the rare water germander, and is developing into a fine wetland site. A footpath

runs along part of the boundary, and public access is planned for the future.

Woodwalton Fen NNR/SSSI (WT/EN; TL 231848, OS 142; 208 ha). By permit only from EN. A fine old reserve with woodland, fen, and open water, and a very rich flora including fen violet. Chinese water deer. Hairy dragonfly, scarce chaser, red-eyed damselfly.

tit, Cetti's warbler, cuckoo, nightingale, long-eared owl, woodcock, sparrowhawk, and hobby. There is usually a hen harrier roost in winter.

Botanical highlights are the pretty fen violet, marsh pea, Cambridge milk-parsley, marsh fern, bladderwort, and a narrow-leaved, stingless variant of common nettle. Other interesting Wicken flowers are great fen-sedge, yellow-rattle, meadowsweet, hemp-agrimony, wild angelica, and southern marsh-orchid.

SITE
125 Boulder-clay woods

Pockets of ancient managed woodland on heavy, poorly draining soils, with a special flora highlighted by oxlips, a regional speciality.

The boulder-clay woods of Cambridgeshire are special for a number of reasons. Centuries of careful woodland management have resulted in a patchwork of

Great spotted woodpecker *Dendrocopos major* (Peter Wilson)

ancient habitats, all the more welcome in the intensively cultivated landscape of this county. In spring, many of these woods are bright with swathes of bluebells, flowers we tend to take for granted in Britain but which are rarely seen in such abundance elsewhere in Europe. The bluebell is endemic to Europe and almost restricted to the north-west fringe of the continent. Oxlips, however, are a real rarity, being restricted in Britain to some of these clay woods.

Monks Wood NNR (157 ha), about 1 km west of Woodwalton, is one of the finest ancient ash–oak woodlands in the region. The trees and shrubs here are varied, with blackthorn, both hawthorns, hazel, field maple, aspen, spindle, wild privet, dogwood, wayfaring-tree, guelder-rose, and wild service-tree. The flowers include star-of-Bethlehem, yellow archangel, small teasel, and crested cow-wheat, and many orchids such as twayblade, early purple, bird's-nest, spotted-orchid, and greater butterfly. Surprisingly, oxlip does not grow here, but cowslips and primroses do, along with their hybrid, known as false oxlip. Glades and rides add variety to the woodland scene, and this benefits the wildlife, especially the butterflies, which include both black and white-letter hair-streaks. Over 1000 species of beetle alone have been recorded here, including the rare *Osphya bipunctata*. There are also streams and ponds within the reserve. Woodland birds abound, including woodcock and nightingale.

Hayley Wood (TL 294534; 50 ha) is a fine boulder-clay wood, lying off the B1046 between Cambridge and Sandy, alongside the old Cambridge–Oxford railway. Hayley Wood is truly ancient, and first recorded by name in 1251. Coppicing continues on a rotational basis, creating herb- and shrub-layers at different stages and of varied composition. The woodland birds are good, with nightingale, woodland warblers, marsh tit, nuthatch, treecreeper, woodcock, and woodpeckers. But it is the woodland flora which is perhaps Hayley's greatest asset. There are magnificent displays of flowers in the spring, and it is perhaps best known for its rare oxlips (one of the largest populations in Britain) and the sheets of bluebells which appear every April and May. A herd

Oxlip *Primula elatior*

of fallow deer regularly moves through the wood, though they are hard to spot, being

Bluebells, Hayley Wood

Eastern England

Common dog-violet *Viola riviniana*

rather shy and nimble. The deer are also not entirely welcome as they are partial to oxlips, although careful creation of fenced deer exclosures has improved the ground flora. Oliver Rackham has estimated the population of oxlips here at well over one million plants! The main trees are pedunculate oak and ash, but there are other species such as field maple, aspen, elm, hazel, and hawthorn, in a mixed community. Some of the oaks are 200 years old, and many of the coppiced 'stools' (mainly ash) are even older. Other woodland flowers here are herb-Paris, dog's mercury, wood anemone, archangel, enchanter's-

nightshade, lesser celandine, early purple and common spotted-orchid, and both common and early dog-violets. The careful observer may even spot the strange bird's-nest orchid, inconspicuous amongst the leaf litter of the woodland floor. The wood is very damp, and boots are recommended, even in dry weather.

Waresley & Gransden Woods SSSI (WT; TL 260550, OS 153; 54 ha) lies some 22 km west of Cambridge. A circular track and rides allow easy access, but the northern part of Gransden Wood is private. No dogs. As with all these woods, it can be very wet and sticky underfoot, so waterproof footwear is pretty essential. There are fewer old trees than at Hayley, but a similar coppice regime has operated here. The main trees are ash, oak, aspen. and birch, with hazel coppice. Invasive sycamore is being discouraged. In the wetter parts oxlips dominate, grading into primrose areas where the drainage is better; there are occasional hybrids where the two meet. Bluebells, herb-Paris, and dog's mercury all grow here as well. Wood is harvested in Waresley Wood for use by traditional 'bodgers' to produce hurdles and other artefacts.

Another important boulder-clay wood is Brampton Wood (see p. 283).

Other important woods nearby

Buff Wood (TL 283509) also has fine oxlips, as well as many primroses, and hybrids between the two. It also has good orchids and green hellebore, as well as commoner woodland flowers such as wood anemone, bluebell, and lesser celandine.

Eversden Wood SSSI (TL 344530; 38 ha): private; mixed boulder-clay wood with oxlips.

Gamlingay Wood SSSI (TL 241533; 48 ha) provides a fascinating contrast to

Hayley and Buff, being partly on acid greensand. It also has oxlips and bluebells, as well as the rare wild service-tree.

Hardwick Wood SSSI (TL 352575; 16 ha): ancient woodland with bluebells and oxlips.

Kingston Wood SSSI (TL 326541; 47 ha): private, but footpath alongside.

A selection of other important sites in the county

Barnack Hills and Holes NNR/SSSI (TF 075045; 23 ha). Just south of Barnack, near Peterborough, 5 km from Stamford, Lincolnshire, along the B1443. Lowland grassland in the area once occupied by Rockingham Forest. A rare habitat in eastern England, where most has been converted to agriculture. Good insect fauna. Mixture of limestone grassland and woodland, developed over former Roman stone quarries on Jurassic limestone. The grassland is mainly dominated by tor-grass, with upright brome. Flora is rich and varied, including nationally scarce species, notably pasqueflower, man orchid, fragrant orchid, purple milk-vetch, dwarf thistle, and quaking-grass. Over 300 species of vascular plant have been recorded on the reserve. Part of the reserve carries mixed scrub: mainly hawthorn, with a small amount of woodland, dominated by the introduced turkey oak. The butterflies include brown argus, marbled white, Essex skipper, and chalk-hill blue, and a particular speciality are the glow-worms, which live on the reserve in quite large numbers. The best time to visit is between late April and early July.

Castor Hanglands NNR/SSSI (EN; TF 119019, OS 142; 90 ha). Varied reserve with ponds as well as limestone grassland, scrub, and woodland, some of it ancient, with oak and ash dominant. Good butterfly fauna includes black hairstreak. Good for birds, also great crested newt. Fallow and muntjac deer. Birds: woodcock, long-eared owl, turtle dove, cuckoo, hobby, nightingale, grasshopper warbler. Passing buzzards, red kites, and honey buzzards are increasingly being spotted here.

Chippenham Fen NNR/SSSI (TL 648694; 156 ha): fenland habitats (footpath only).

Devil's Dyke/Ditch SSSI (WT; TL 616616; 38 ha): one of the county's most important stretches of chalk grassland, with lizard orchid.

Fleam Dyke SSSI (TL 554536; 11 ha): similar to Devil's Dyke, with juniper.

Fowlmere SSSI (RSPB; TL 406453; 42 ha). Disused watercress beds, fed from spring. Reedbeds, open water, woodland, and scrub. Good variety of breeding warblers including reed, sedge, and grasshopper, water rail, and kingfisher. In winter, corn bunting roost.

Fulbourn SSSI (WT; TL 528560; 27 ha). Damp grassland with alder woods. Early marsh-, southern marsh-, common spotted-, and bee orchids.

Milton Country Park (TL 480620, OS 154). Disused gravel pits near Cambridge. Good dragonflies and birds. Black-tailed skimmer, emperor dragonfly, migrant hawker, hairy dragonfly. Hobby, kingfisher, great crested and little grebe. Muntjac.

Paxton Pits LNR/SSSI (TL 194633; 128 ha). Gravel pits close to the A1, northwest of St Neots. Noted for the highest population of nightingales in Cambridgeshire (25 singing males in 2000). More than 60 breeding birds, including grey heron, little grebe, kingfisher, and a large cormorant colony (c.100 nests). Lapwing, redshank, ringed plover, common tern, and oystercatcher breed. Spring and autumn migrants often include avocet and black-tailed godwit. Smew, goosander, and black-necked grebe are regular in winter, and bittern occasional. Favoured by hobbies.

Bedfordshire

126 Downs and chalk grassland

A series of sites on calcareous soils, with a rich flora and associated characteristic insects.

Clustered mainly around Luton and Dunstable in the south of the county are several sites with well-preserved chalk grassland. Barton Hills NNR and nearby Knocking Hoe NNR are being managed under grazing regimes designed to maintain a rich flora and to benefit adjacent abandoned farmland. Barton Hills SSSI (TL 093295, OS 166; 48 ha) lies in a steep-sided valley and features chalk grassland, scrub, and ancient woodland habitats. The flowers here include pasqueflower, clustered bellflower, and several orchids, and the butterflies dingy skipper, brown argus, chalk-hill blue, marbled white, and white-letter hairstreak. Knocking Hoe SSSI (TL 131306, OS 166; 8 ha; permit required) is a small site protecting similar chalk grassland with pasqueflower, moon carrot, and spotted cat's-ear.

Pegsdon Hills SSSI (WT; TL 120295, OS 166; 75 ha) is in the same area. This reserve, which contains part of the Deacon's Hill SSSI, has fine chalk grassland and scrub with good butterflies: chalk-hill blue, brown argus, and dingy skipper. The flowers include horseshoe vetch, common rock-rose, wild thyme, and clustered bellflower, with annuals such as Venus's-looking-glass, poppies, and cornsalad in the former arable land. Glow-worms may be seen here on summer evenings. The birds are typical of such sites: skylark, meadow and tree pipits, grey partridge, corn bunting, grasshopper warbler, turtle dove,

Autumn gentian
Gentianella amarella

as well as hobby, buzzard, woodcock, little, tawny, and long-eared owls, and the occasional quail. Hoo Bit (WT; TL 117290, OS 166; 4 ha) is adjacent to Pegsdon Hills and has a similar range of species.

Sharpenhoe (NT; TL 067300; 55 ha) is a Chiltern grassland site just to the west of Barton-le-Clay. Careful management has increased the proportion of grassland here, and there is also an area of beech wood. The grassland flowers include horseshoe vetch, wild thyme, clustered bellflower, autumn gentian, and orchids.

A little south of Dunstable is Dunstable & Whipsnade Downs SSSI (TL 001189; 73 ha). Lying close to the other Chiltern sites of the Ashridge Estate (see Hertfordshire), these downs are famous as the site of Whipsnade Zoo. The west-facing slopes give fine views, and the chalk grassland has (in places) a rich flora with dwarf thistle, autumn gentian, and frog orchid. The butterflies include chalk-hill and small blue, grizzled skipper, and Duke of Burgundy.

Totternhoe Knolls SSSI (WT; SP 978220, OS 165; 14 ha) has areas with good chalk grassland, as well as a quarry and beech wood. The site of a Norman castle, it now consists partly of open grassland with patches of scrub, and much of the site shows the signs of old quarrying for stone, which has left an uneven surface now largely clothed by rich chalk grassland. Along with more common flowers such as lady's bedstraw, bird's-foot-trefoil, and wild thyme, are species such as horseshoe vetch, adder's-tongue, clustered bellflower, and autumn gentian. Orchids include common spotted-, fragrant, and common twayblade. Duke of Burgundy and green hairstreak may be seen here, especially at the scrub margins.

Blows Down (TL 033216, OS 166; 46 ha) is another excellent chalk downland reserve within the Chiltern AONB, and also of great interest despite its close proximity to urban areas. It has developed a reputation as a good spot for migrant birds, with wheatears, ring ouzels, and redstarts all pretty regular on passage here. The woods have fine displays of bluebells. Blows Down is a site for small and chalk-hill blues, marbled white, and brown argus, as is Sewell Cutting (TL 004227, OS 165/6).

SITE 127 The Lodge

Headquarters of the RSPB, and a reserve well worth visiting in its own right.

This reserve, which covers some 40 ha, lies on a ridge of sandstone (greensand) and has a correspondingly acid soil, with areas of oak–birch–pine woodland and heath, a habitat rather rare in the area. Well known as the headquarters of the RSPB, The Lodge building itself houses offices and research quarters. It is nevertheless a welcoming place, with information for visitors and grounds that are surprisingly rich in wildlife. This is an ideal place to learn about garden and woodland birds; there is a shop and picnic area, a series of paths lead round the reserve, and there are also hides. The Lodge is also the only British locality for the rare fungus *Hygrophorus speciosus*.

All the expected woodland birds may be seen here, including all the woodpeckers, nuthatches, and treecreepers, and hobbies are regular. Siskins, redpolls, and bramblings often visit in winter. The lake has grey herons and kingfishers. Muntjac are present in some numbers, and other mammals include yellow-necked mouse, fox, stoat, and weasel. There is a small colony of natterjacks, which were introduced in the 1980s. Not surprisingly the site has been well recorded and the insect fauna includes some 300 species of moth, including rosy footman, cream-spot tiger, emperor moth, and pine hawkmoth.

Other sites nearby

Sutton Fen (RSPB; TL 205475) lies on the same ridge of greensand as The Lodge. It has large areas of birch scrub, growing on peaty soil adjacent to the ridge. The birds here include woodcock, turtle dove, cuckoo, many warblers, and marsh and willow tits. Siskins, redpolls, and sometimes crossbills and bramblings can be seen in the winter.

Willington Gravel Pits is an excellent wetland site alongside the Great Ouse about 8 km west of The Lodge. It has a large sand martin colony, kingfishers, and barn owls, and is a favoured haunt of hobbies as well as waders and wildfowl.

A selection of other important sites in the county

Cooper's Hill (TL 028376, OS 153; 12.5 ha): largest greensand lowland heath in the county.

Felmersham Gravel Pits SSSI (WT; SP 990583, OS 153; 22 ha). A good site for waterbirds, swamp plants such as yellow and purple-loosestrifes, and yellow iris, and also for its dragonflies, among which are emperor dragonfly, white-legged and emerald damselflies, ruddy darter, four-spotted chaser, and banded demoiselle.

Flitwick Moor SSSI (WT; TL 048352; 32 ha). Valley mire with wet woodland and meadow, with diverse flora including the rare narrow buckler-fern. Birds include water rail and grasshopper warbler. The county's largest wetland.

King's Wood, Heath & Reach NNR (SP 932298, OS 165; 104 ha). Part of the largest semi-natural woodland in Bedfordshire, once a royal estate, hence the name. Partly on greensand,

partly with heavy clay soils. Notable for small-leaved lime and largest lily-of-the-valley population in the county, rare mosses, fungi, and purple emperor. Nearby Rammamere Heath (Bucks) is also of interest.

Marston Vale Country Park (OS 153) is a fine mixed reserve created as part of the millennium community forest enterprise. It has a good information centre, and a network of tracks. It includes Stewartby Lake and a newly created wetland, The Pillinge. In addition to the regular wetland birds, this reserve attracts rarer species such as divers, grebes, ruddy duck, and glaucous, Iceland, and Mediterranean gulls.

Woburn Park (SP 950332), between Ampthill and Leighton Buzzard, has fine landscaped grounds with deer herds (including the rare Père David's deer), a safari park, and a grand house. There are breeding mandarin ducks and Lady Amherst's pheasant.

Buckinghamshire

128 Bernwood Forest

Mixed woodland with a rich flora. Also a prime site for butterflies, with a number of local species.

The ancient Royal Forest of Bernwood once covered a large area on the border with Oxfordshire, and a number of reserves now protect remnants of its woodland. Several of these woods are prized for their butterflies, and above all for the black hairstreak, a national rarity.

This sedentary butterfly is a speciality of the Midlands, being generally restricted to blackthorn thickets in the region between Oxford and Peterborough. It likes a tangle of blackthorn lying in a sheltered, sunny site, such as along the edge of woodland or in a hedgerow. A curious feature of this species is its camouflaged pupal case, which closely resembles a bird dropping. Look for the adults on sunny days in June and July. Brown hairstreaks and white admirals also occur in these woods.

Whitecross Green Wood (WT; SP 600150, OS 164; 62 ha) has a rich ground flora indicative of its ancient origin, although much of the tree cover has been felled and replanted. Some parts of the wood still carry an oak–ash tree cover, with hazel beneath. Woodland flowers such as bluebells, ramsons, enchanter's-nightshade, and yellow archangel are well represented. It has wood and marbled whites, purple emperor, white admiral, and the occasional black hairstreak. Nightingales and grasshopper warblers breed on the reserve, and the mammals include roe, fallow, and muntjac deer.

Finemere Wood SSSI (WT; SP 721215, OS 165; 40 ha), although cleared and replanted in the 1950s and 1960s, is surprisingly rich in flowers, with 200 species recorded, including bluebell, woodruff, and yellow archangel. Some patches of more ancient coppice woodland remain.

The birds include all the woodpeckers and woodcock, and there are grass snakes, viviparous lizards, and muntjac and foxes. But it is the butterflies which are special here – over 20 species, including wood white, white admiral, purple emperor, and purple and black hairstreaks.

Burrows Reserve (WT; SP 624114, OS 164/5) lies in the same general Bernwood Forest area and is another locality for the rare black hairstreak, for which this site was purchased.

Nearby Bernwood Meadows (WT; SP 606111, OS 164/5) is an expanse of hay meadows adjacent to Bernwood Forest. The meadows boast a rich flora, with over 100 species recorded. The speciality is the green-winged orchid, and also adder's-tongue. The ancient 'ridge and furrow' pattern is clearly visible here, and this is accentuated by differences in flora between the drier ridges and damper furrows.

Rushbeds Wood & Lapland Farm SSSI (WT; SP 672154, OS 164/5; 59 ha) preserves an ancient woodland and meadow, a remnant of Bernwood Forest. Butterflies here include black hairstreak.

Blackthorn (*Prunus spinosa*) hedge

^{SITE} 129 Chilterns

A series of mainly woodland and grassland sites astride the chalk
ridge of the Chiltern hills, mostly dominated by beech woods.

The Chilterns stretch roughly from the Thames between Reading and Goring north-westwards to Dunstable Downs in Bedfordshire. These are gentle hills, reaching no higher than about 265 m, but nevertheless very picturesque, being capped in many places by stands of beech wood with its associated flora and fauna. Common whitebeam is conspicuous in these woods.

Plants of the beech woods include several orchids, such as the rather strange ghost orchid and red helleborine, as well as wood vetch, coralroot, cow-wheat and mezereon. Patches of grazed grassland nestle on the slopes and these are rich in flowers such as yellow-wort and orchids. Special mention should be made of the gentians, since some of these Chilterns sites have early gentian and Chiltern gentian as well as the more common field gentian. Even rarer is the fringed gentian. Another notable Chiltern flower is the lovely pasqueflower for which this region is one of the main areas.

The patchwork of woodland is ideally suited to the red kite, whose numbers are now increasing rapidly after successful recent introductions. The lucky visitor may be treated to the sight of several of these agile raptors soaring together as they hunt over the hills.

Several of the clear streams have healthy populations of trout and grayling and some also have white-clawed crayfish. Watercress (once harvested) abounds in some streams, as does river water-drop-wort, and the flowers of water-crowfoot brighten the surface in spring.

Although seldom seen, the star mammal of the Chilterns is undoubtedly the edible dormouse. This shy and mainly nocturnal rodent was introduced in the Tring area in the early 1900s and has maintained a presence here, though without spreading far. Its total population now stands at around 10 000. Muntjac, roe deer, foxes, and badgers abound in this varied landscape.

Dancersend (SP 900095; 33 ha) & The Crong Meadow (SP 904088; 1 ha) (WT; OS 165) are two adjoining reserves that form part of a larger SSSI. Located near Wendover, together they give a fine flavour of Chilterns habitats, covering woodland, scrub and rich grassland, on one of the highest points of these hills (255m). Although the underlying rock is chalk, as in many Chiltern sites, the conditions range from quite acid in the higher woods to alkaline on the lower, more chalky slopes. Notable woodland flowers here are stinking hellebore, Solomon's-seal, and wood vetch, with autumn fungi, including earth-star. The unusual yellow bird's-nest, which lacks chlorophyll, can grow even in the darkest shade. The expected woodland birds are much in evidence, especially woodpeckers, nuthatches, and tawny owls. Areas of chalk grassland are managed with a grazing regime beneficial to the flowers,

Duke of Burgundy *Hamearis lucina*

Eastern England

Coralroot *Cardamine bulbifera*

pedunculate oak, holly, hornbeam, white-beam, rowan, birch, and cherry. Much of the wood is on well-drained, rather dry soil, but there are wetter patches which tend to have a richer ground flora. Species to look out for here include marsh St John's-wort, lesser skullcap, juniper, orpine, bladderseed, sundew, bog aspho-del, hoary cinquefoil, and wood horsetail. The birds are also of note, with all three woodpeckers, nuthatch, woodcock, hawfinch, redstart, tree pipit, wood war-bler, and sparrowhawk all breeding here.

Church Wood reserve (RSPB; SU 968873) lies close by. This mixed broadleaved wood has woodpeckers, nuthatch, turtle and stock doves, warblers, and woodcock, and also muntjac deer, white admiral, and purple and white-letter hairstreaks. The flora runs to some 200 species, with bugle, butcher's-broom, and green hellebore.

especially to the orchids, which include common spotted-, bee, fragrant, and pyramidal. Chiltern gentian, adder's-tongue, cuckooflower, and coralroot also grow here. Butterflies are something of a feature, too, with grizzled skipper, green hairstreak, dark green fritillary, marbled white, ringlet, and the rare Duke of Burgundy, whose caterpillar feeds on primrose and cowslip.

Burnham Beeches NNR/SSSI (SU 948855, OS 175/6; 383 ha) lies some 4 km north-west of Slough, south of the main Chiltern range, and is a famous and much-visited site. Established mainly on acid soil, it occupies a low plateau, with a number of small valleys. There is a mix-ture of ancient, mature woodland interspersed with coppice, scrub, and clearings with grassy vegetation. The main dominant tree is beech, but there are a good many other species, too, including

Some other important Chiltern sites

Bradenham Woods (beech woods), **Park Wood** (former Tudor deer park, returning to woods), & **The Coppice SSSI** (SU 826981; 134 ha; mixed woodland, mainly beech).

Coombe Hill SSSI (NT; SP 849065; 52 ha). Woodland, scrub, and chalk grassland, reaching 260 m, with great views. The slopes have a rich flora, with horseshoe vetch and good butterflies. Occasional patches of juniper, and some oak and beech woodland.

Ellesborough and Kimble Warrens SSSI (SP 830058; 70 ha): woodland, calcareous grassland.

Grangelands and Pulpit Hill SSSI (WT; SP 827050; 26 ha): woodland and downland.

A selection of other important sites in the county

Ivinghoe Beacon (NT; SP 960169): fine chalk grassland habitat, with pasqueflower and Duke of Burgundy.

Willen Lake, Milton Keynes (OS 152) was formed by flooding in 1973 and is now a top-notch wetland for waders and wildfowl. Access is easy from junction 14 of the M1. The North Basin is particularly good, with its island and scrape. Birds here include greenshank, ruff, and godwits, with garganey, black tern, and hobby possible. The winter gull roost should be checked out for rarities.

Hertfordshire

SITE
130 Therfield Heath

Hillside with areas of chalk grassland – a good habitat for flowers and butterflies.

Therfield Heath SSSI (WT; TL 335400; 168 ha) lies near Royston. The name is something of a misnomer, as the site is dominated by chalk grassland rather than heath. Chalk grassland is a rather rare habitat in the east of England, although some remnants survive – nowhere better than at Therfield, which is one of the finest remaining examples. The reserve here also has mature beech woods, developed on the well-drained soil at the crest of the hill. Although there is a large golf course, the adjacent grassland is home to a range of

Pasqueflower *Pulsatilla vulgaris*

downland flowers, insects, and birds. The landscape is sloping and undulating, providing differences of aspect; with cooler, north-facing slopes, and much warmer and drier south and west-facing slopes.

Therfield is a great place to learn the flora of chalk downland and to meet species such as cowslip, common milkwort, common rock-rose, salad burnet, wild thyme, clustered bellflower, wild mignonette, purple milk-vetch, dropwort, and horseshoe vetch. Other flowers here include wild candytuft, bastard toadflax, spotted cat's-ear, field fleawort, and bee and fragrant orchids.

However, there is one special species for which this reserve is famed, and that is the pasqueflower. Therfield is one of only a few sites where this beautiful plant still thrives in reasonable numbers. April and May are the months to visit to catch the pasqueflower at its best.

As for the butterflies, blues are particularly well represented, with common, holly, and chalk-hill blues all breeding here, and it is worth watching for small blue as well, since the conditions are certainly suitable for this local species. Other species include brown argus, and dingy, large, Essex, and small skippers.

The 'heath' provides nesting and hunting sites for open country birds such as skylark, meadow pipit, corn bunting, and kestrel, and in or near the woods there are both wood and grasshopper warblers.

> ## Other important sites nearby
>
> **Fox Covert** and **Fordhams Wood** (TL 3440) lie just to the south. These are fine woods containing many flowers, including white helleborine.

Eastern England

131 Ashridge Estate

Large tract of chalk downland, with a range of typical habitats and some fine vantage points with good views.

This large site lies on the county border, just north of Berkhamsted. It has a good network of footpaths and nature trails and is an excellent place in which to soak up the atmosphere of downland. The NT owns this large estate, which extends from Ivinghoe Beacon in the north (Bedfordshire), south to Berkhamsted Common in the south, comprising over 1100 ha of mixed habitats. The area is designated as the Ashridge Commons and Woods SSSI (SP 9812).

The mixed woodland (mainly oak, ash, beech, sycamore, and birch) has fallow, muntjac, and Chinese water deer, and this is also a site for the edible dormouse.

Ancient beech pollards at Ashridge

The chalk flora has rock-rose, squinancy-wort, gentian, restharrow, and hairy violet, and several species of orchid, and the woodland plants include narrow-lipped and green-flowered helleborines, yellow bird's-nest, and stinking hellebore.

Notable amongst the usual woodland and downland birds are redpoll, woodcock, wood warbler, nightingale, redstart, hawfinch, nuthatch, and the occasional firecrest.

Nearby Tring Reservoirs SSSI (BW; SP 904130, OS 165; 100 ha) is a series of artificial lakes. This is a haven for waterbirds and a good dragonfly site. Passage birds include regular black terns and ospreys. Car parks and footpaths allow easy access to the reserve and hide. Wilstone Reservoir (WT; SP 905134) in particular is favoured by newly arrived hobbies in spring, when it is not unusual to see several together. The waders are also varied, with greenshank and ruff, and always the chance of rarer species. The winter wildfowl include ruddy duck, wigeon, and goldeneye. There are two heronries. The site is not far from one of the red kite reintroduction centres and these raptors can occasionally be spotted here. The waters are rich in vegetation and insect life – hornwort, water-milfoil, and Canadian waterweed thrive – and a third of the British fauna of water beetles are found here. Fringing plants include, along with reed, bulrush, reed sweet-grass, meadowsweet, gypsywort, yellow iris, skullcap, and water mint. On summer evenings bats, including noctule, may be seen feeding here.

Nearby

College Lake Wildlife Centre (WT; SP 933139, OS 165), just north of Tring, is an old chalk quarry which has been restored as a wildlife centre. The reserve (actually in Buckinghamshire) now has a lake, several large islands, shingle beaches, floating nesting-rafts, bird hides, and a visitor/information centre. A variety of waders, terns, and other species are regularly seen on passage, and breeding birds include lapwing, redshank, and little ringed plover. In addition to the lake there are large stretches of grassland and hay meadow. The Susan Cowdy Information Centre houses a splendid collection of fossils found on the reserve. The reserve is open 7 days a week from 10.00 am to 5.00 pm. Visitors to the site must collect a permit, available from the warden's office on site. Entry is free to WT members. The site is accessible to elderly and disabled visitors, and wheelchairs can be borrowed free of charge on site.

SITE
132 Broxbourne Woods

Some of the best Hertfordshire woodlands, with oak–hornbeam communities – a relatively rare habitat in Britain.

Broxbourne Woods NNR lies south of Hertford and is owned and managed by the WT and Hertfordshire CC. It is a composite site, consisting of Bencroft Wood, Broxbourne Wood, and Wormley–Hoddesdonpark Wood SSSI (the latter at TL 342078; 339 ha), which together form part of the largest area of woodland in the county.

The woods are mainly developed on acidic soils formed from gravels overlying London clay. The dominant trees are oak,

Eastern England

with a good representation of hornbeams, the latter being a distinctly southern element in Britain. A series of small streams flows through these fern- and moss-rich woods, and there are small grass-rich heathy areas in amongst planted conifers. Also growing here are cow-wheat, pendulous sedge, wood anemone, bluebell, yellow archangel, woodruff, honeysuckle, wild service-tree, and alder in the wetter places.

Although the woods are much visited, being close to urban areas, the wildlife is quite rich, with grey squirrel, muntjac deer, badger, weasel, and grass snake. Some 27 species of butterfly have been recorded, including grizzled skipper, white admiral, and purple hairstreak. The birds include woodpeckers, treecreeper, hawfinch, sparrowhawk, woodcock, and the occasional buzzard – the latter slowly increasing in this part of England.

There are car parks at Broxbourne and Bencroft woods.

Nearby lies Northaw Great Wood SSSI (TL 278037). This wood is just to the north of Potter's Bar. In the drier parts, bracken and brambles dominate in the undergrowth, and there are good displays of spring bluebells and wood anemones, with wood-sorrel. Other flowers are dog's mercury, lesser celandine (on damper ground), sanicle, lords-and-ladies, wood sage, foxglove, enchanter's-nightshade, bugle, early purple orchid, and broad-leaved helleborine. In damper sites look for ragged-Robin, herb-Robert, wild strawberry, corn mint, brook-lime, and cuckooflower. The wood has muntjac, fallow deer, badger, fox, brown hare, rabbit, weasel, grey squirrel, bank vole, field vole, wood mouse, and common and pygmy shrews. Hawfinches can occasionally be seen here, and have a liking for hornbeam and wild cherry seeds. Redstart and wood warbler are two other rather local birds which occur here in small numbers.

Some other Hertfordshire woods

Knebworth Woods SSSI (TL 223224; 129 ha): ancient woodland on poorly drained acid soils; rare flowers include water violet and the fine-leafed water dropwort.

Redwell Wood SSSI (TL 212025; 53 ha): mixed woodland, mainly oak and hazel.

Sherrardspark Wood SSSI (TL 228138; 75 ha): oak–hornbeam wood near Welwyn Garden City, with some very old standard trees; plants include moschatel and broad-leaved helleborine.

A selection of other important sites in the county

Hertford Heath SSSI (WT; TL 351109; 29 ha): open heath and woodland with ponds and bogs.

Rye Meads SSSI (RSPB/WT; TL 387101; 60 ha): nine breeding warblers; bittern, water rail in winter.

Stocker's Lake (WT; TQ 044931, OS 176; 38 ha): heronry; good wildfowl – smew, goosander, ruddy duck, red-crested pochard, and rare grebes.

Lords-and-ladies *Arum maculatum*

Essex

133 Colne Estuary

Important coastal site, with habitats ranging from shingle to saltmarsh and mudflats. A vital stopover for migrant birds, especially waders and wildfowl.

This estuary stretches for some 10 km, from Wivenhoe, just south of Colchester, to the open sea at Colne Point. The main channel is joined by a number of smaller tributaries and creeks, and on the western side lies the large island of Mersea. The area is interesting in any season, although perhaps most exciting in autumn and winter when the food-rich mudflats and coastal grasslands are alive with waders and wildfowl.

The Colne Estuary covers about 2700 ha, including the Upper Colne Marshes SSSI (TM 030222; 114 ha), and the WT reserves of Colne Point (TM 108125) and Fingringhoe Wick (TM 041195).

Fingringhoe Wick (Peter Wilson)

Brent geese *Branta bernicla*

In the late summer the saltmarshes are perhaps at their most colourful, with the pink and purple shades of sea aster, common sea-lavender, and thrift. Other saltmarsh plants found here are golden-samphire, annual sea-blite, sea-purslane, glasswort, and sea arrowgrass, while on the shingle and sand the species include yellow horned-poppy, sea-holly, sea bindweed, sea beet, sea wormwood, and shrubby sea-blite.

Prominent bird visitors to the mudflats and saltmarsh are Brent geese, which gather in large numbers on the mudflats in winter, flighting in noisy arrow-shaped skeins. Along with mallard, shelduck, pintail, teal, and wigeon, there are also regular goldeneye.

There are nearly always good numbers of waders on the tidal mudflats – dunlin, curlew, bar-tailed godwit, knot, golden, grey, and ringed plovers, redshank, and turnstone. During the migration, expect others as well, notably whimbrel and greenshank.

Colne Estuary NNR/SSSI (TM 096121; 580 ha) consists of three distinct areas: Brightlingsea Marsh, East Mersea, and Colne Point. Brightlingsea Marsh consists of grazing marsh lying directly behind the sea wall, near the small town of Brightlingsea. Mainly of unimproved grassland, cut by ditches, it is managed by cattle grazing as well as by sluice control of the water levels. These marshes are west of Brightlingsea on the Colne Estuary, off the B1029. The nearest car park is in Brightlingsea, and the marshes may be viewed from the sea wall. At East Mersea the processes of coastal erosion and deposition have exposed fossils of national importance. Colne Point is an extensive shingle spit, in the lee of which is a further area of saltmarsh. At low tide, shingle banks and shell beds are exposed. The nearest car park to the reserve is at St Osyth. There is no disabled access to the site, and public access is limited to holders of day permits, issued by the Essex WT. Colne Point is on a major migration route and so good for passage birds. Breeding little tern, ringed plover, redshank, and oystercatcher.

Fingringhoe Wick has good facilities, with an information centre, trails, hides, and an observation tower. From here there are fine views over the saltmarshes and mudflats. This site also has areas of woodland and scrub, favoured by migrant songbirds. Waders and wildfowl are winter specialities here, too, and the woodland and scrub has woodpeckers, and warblers and nightingales in spring and summer.

Nearby

Abberton Reservoir SSSI (WT; TL 977182; 726 ha) is one of the best reservoirs for birds. It attracts large numbers of wintering goldeneye as well as the usual ducks, and goosander and smew may also be spotted. Spring often brings in black terns and little gull. Cormorants nest in nearby trees – an unusual sight. Visitor centre, nature trail, and five hides.

SITE
134 Blackwater Estuary

Large estuary with a series of top birding sites: creeks, mudflats, islands, and adjacent meadows and marshes.

The mudflats of the wide estuary of the Blackwater River are of supreme importance as feeding grounds for a wide range of waders and wildfowl. A footpath follows the sea wall, and the conditions can be bleak, so wear warm clothes in winter. Waders and wildfowl congregate here in huge numbers. At high or rising tides, the birds will be closer inshore, but a telescope is often essential for good views. Flocks of twite and snow bunting are often about in the winter, and the estuary may have grebes, divers, and long-tailed ducks.

Blackwater Estuary NNR/SSSI (EN/RSPB; TL 978100; 4397 ha) consists of two distinct areas: Old Hall Marshes and Tollesbury Flats. A regime of cattle-grazing maintains a suitable sward, both for grazing by wintering wildfowl and for nesting waders in summer. The water levels are also controlled to enhance the grasslands as a bird habitat.

Old Hall Marshes (RSPB; TL 950117; permit required) protects the largest tract of traditional Essex marshland, much of it grazed, with reedbeds filling-in the wetter sites. Breeding birds include yellow wagtail, bearded tit, avocet, shoveler, gadwall, and common tern. Merlin, hen harrier, and barn and short-eared owls are regular in winter. This reserve is west of West Mersea, north-east of Tollesbury, on the B1023. There is no public access to the site, although the marshes can be viewed from the sea wall. The marshes include unimproved and improved neutral grassland, one of the largest areas of freshwater creeks, and the largest reedbed in Essex. There is a big expanse of intertidal mud which attracts large numbers of waders and wildfowl, especially Brent geese.

Tollesbury Flats is an extensive area of intertidal mud, sand, and shingle on the north shore of the Blackwater Estuary, forming another important feeding ground for waders and wildfowl. Tollesbury Wick Marshes lie south of Tollesbury on the B1023. There is a nature trail around the perimeter of the reserve, and a leaflet available from the site.

The south side of the Blackwater Estuary also has good wildlife sites. Dengie NNR/SSSI (TM 044031; 2366 ha) is a large expanse of intertidal mudflats off the Dengie Peninsula, on the Essex coast, near Bradwell-on-Sea, on the B1021, and Burnham on Crouch, on the B1010. The nearest car park is in Bradwell-on-Sea. A long strip of salt-marsh follows the coast, varying in width from about 100 m to well over 1 km.

Golden-samphire *Inula crithmoides*

Eastern England

Offshore, the flats vary from soft silt to hard sand. Cockles are common here around high water, and bass, mullet, and sole are regularly fished. Dengie has tens of thousands of wildfowl in the winter, giving it international significance. There are also local and rare plants here, including sea-kale, sea barley, golden-samphire, lax-flowered sea-lavender, and three species of eel grass. Bradwell Bird Observatory lies nearby, at the mouth of the Blackwater Estuary.

Northey Island (NT/WT; TL 872058) is reached by causeway at low tide and access is by permit only. Some 2000 Brent geese gather here or nearby in the winter. Saltmarsh plants here include sea-lavenders, sea-purslane, common scurvygrass, and sea plantain. One of the best spots near here is Goldhanger Creek, near Osea Island, which often attracts seaducks, divers, and Slavonian grebes.

Common sea-lavender *Limonium vulgare*

Other sites nearby

Blake's Wood and Lingwood Common SSSI (TL 772066; 86 ha): woodland with nightingale.

Crouch and Roach Estuaries SSSI (TQ 847966; 1736 ha): tidal mud; wintering waterbirds, especially Brent geese.

Danbury Common SSSI (NT; TL 783043; 69 ha) is an area of mixed heath, scrub, and woodland, with a good insect and bird fauna. Close by lies Thrift Wood, Bicknacre, one of the best sites for heath fritillary.

Hanningfield Reservoir SSSI (WT; TQ 733983; 401 ha): mixed woodland, reservoir; woodland birds and flowers, waterfowl, gull roost, hobby, osprey.

Hockley Woods SSSI (TQ 832917; 92 ha): woodland birds and flowers.

Mucking Flats and Marshes SSSI (TQ 706811; 312 ha): brackish grazing marsh, flooded clay and chalk pits, saltmarsh, and broad intertidal mud-flats; wintering waterbirds including grebes, geese, ducks, and waders.

Norsey Wood SSSI (TQ 706867; 65 ha): woodland birds.

Pitsea Marsh SSSI (TQ 742869; 91 ha): saltmarsh, scrub.

Thorndon Park SSSI (TQ 603921; 148 ha): woodland birds.

Two Tree Island (WT; TQ 825855; 73 ha): waders and wildfowl, migrants.

Vange and Fobbing Marshes SSSI (TQ 733838; 166 ha): saltmarsh.

Woodham Walter Common SSSI (TL 791065; 80 ha): woodland birds, notably hawfinch and redstart.

^{SITE}135 Hatfield Forest

One of the finest remnants of ancient woodland in Britain, with a rich flora and bird life.

Hatfield Forest NNR/SSSI (NT; TL 538201) is one of the last medieval royal forests to retain largely its original character and composition. It is all that is left of the once huge Forest of Essex, a royal hunting preserve since before the Conquest, but at 425 ha this is still a substantial chunk. This fine remnant of ancient woodland lies just east of Bishop's Stortford. There is a good mixture of habitats here – from closed woodland with magnificent oaks and hornbeams, to woodland pasture and glades, open water, and marshy ground. It is a mosaic of open grassland, with numerous old pollarded trees and areas of coppice. The forest has a very long history, and at various times has been managed for timber, partly under a coppice-with-standards regime, where the main trees are oak, ash, hornbeam, maple, and hazel. There are over 850 veteran trees, ranging from 400 to 700 years old.

Much of the woodland consists of ash–maple and oak–hornbeam communities on wet soil. The old pollards – principally hornbeam, beech, field maple, and oak – support important lichens and invertebrates, and many also carry clumps of mistletoe. In the understorey are field maple, hawthorn, hazel, and spindle. The forest has herb-Paris, violet helleborine, and several nationally scarce plants, including oxlip and stinking hellebore.

The woodland pasture, an uncommon habitat, includes species-rich grassland, ranging from acidic, with harebell, upright chickweed, and small-flowered buttercup, to mildly calcareous, with bee and pyramidal orchids and adders-tongue fern. The marshy areas have yellow iris, lesser spearwort, and marsh cinquefoil and are the only Essex localities for broad blysmus and bog pimpernel.

The birds of Hatfield include nightingales and woodpeckers, and there are

Old pollards

Eastern England

fallow deer in the forest. With luck, hawfinches and tree sparrows may be spotted, and the open areas have tree pipits and woodcock, with great crested and little grebe on the lake.

The abundance of old timber has resulted in a rich invertebrate fauna, Hatfield being regarded as one of Britain's top sites for insects, including the rare beetles *Procraerus tibialis* and *Malthodes crassicornis*.

Hatfield Forest is managed by the NT, with the aim of further improving the habitats. This is done by coppicing the ancient woodland compartments; maintaining the deer population at sustainable levels; grazing with cattle and sheep in selected areas; limited pollarding of veteran trees; creation of new pollards as the next generation of veterans; removal of areas of secondary scrub to enhance the wood pasture habitat; and by improvement of marshland habitats through restoration of river meanders.

Hatfield Forest is sign-posted off the A120 at Takely, near the M11 junction. The main car park is free to NT members. There are toilet and refreshment facilities on site, and limited disabled access. Information leaflets and panels are available for visitors. The site can be visited at any time, although access is easiest in summer, when the conditions are usually drier.

Epping Forest SSSI (TQ 402959; 1760 ha) is another large tract of woodland, close to London. This is a very good site for woodland birds, and also for autumn fungi. Beech, oak, hornbeam, and birch are the major trees of the forest here and the site is a patchwork of woodland, open rides, ponds, and heathy grassland. In some places holly forms a dark lower storey in the forest, and wild service-tree can also be found. Some of the open areas have been invaded by scrub of hawthorn and blackthorn, or groves of birch. Epping has a very rich insect fauna, boasting almost 1400 species of beetle alone. The butterflies include purple hairstreak, holly and common blues, and large, small, Essex, and dingy skippers, the latter a declining species. Woodland birds include all three woodpeckers, nuthatch, treecreeper, and redpoll, as well as less widespread species such as redstart and hawfinch.

A selection of other important sites in the county

Benfleet and Southend Marshes SSSI (TQ 860846; 2370 ha): the impressive emperor moth breeds on the heath, as does the bog bush-cricket.

Southend Pier (TQ 889830) is a great spot for birds, especially seabirds, notably gulls, with Mediterranean gulls regular around the pier end.

Chalkney Wood SSSI (TL 875277; 74 ha) is a fine small-leaved lime wood.

Foulness SSSI (TQ 998877; 10 969 ha; no access): grazing marsh, saltmarsh, mudflats, shell banks, and sandflats; waders and wildfowl, notably Brent goose.

Hamford Water NNR/SSSI (TM 228254; 2187 ha): in winter, thousands of Brent geese gather here; goldeneye, eider, and red-breasted merganser offshore or in Walton Channel.

Stour Estuary (RSPB; TM 189309; 240 ha), foreshore and woodland, and nearby **Stour Wood** (WdT; TM 190315; 54 ha). The latter is mainly oak, with much sweet chestnut, and has woodpeckers, woodland warblers, and nightingales. The butterflies are good, too, with white admirals, and there are dormice. The estuary, which may be viewed from three hides, attracts many wintering waders, including black-tailed godwit in good numbers, as well as Brent geese, shelduck, and pintail.

Greater London

SITE
136 Lee Valley

A string of fine reserves with riverside habitats and adjacent lakes and gravel pits.

The river Lee (or Lea) flows south towards London, eventually entering the Thames. The Lee Valley has over 100 reservoirs and lakes, and stretches from Ware in Hertfordshire right down into London between Enfield and Epping Forest, to Hackney.

This is one of the best sites in the region for breeding waterfowl, with tufted duck and great crested grebe in some numbers. Hobbies are regularly seen feeding on dragonflies over these wetlands, and the valley is also noted as one of the best places to see wintering bitterns (from certain hides).

Below are a number of selected Lee Valley sites.

Amwell Quarry NR and Gravel Pits (Herts) (TL 375134), in the upper Lee Valley, have a patchwork of woodland and reed-fringed lakes and are excellent for wildlife – especially birds and insects. Hobbies hunt here regularly, and common terns nest on rafts. Notable breeding species: ruddy duck, Egyptian goose, little ringed and ringed plover. Osprey and garganey are regular.

Rye House Marsh (RSPB; TL 385100) has a mixture of scrapes, pools, lakes, willow carr, and reedbeds. Notable amongst the birds is a thriving colony of common terns, and the reeds are alive with sedge and reed warblers in summer, with cuckoos and reed buntings common. Artificial sandbanks provide ideal breeding sites for kingfishers, and hides give good views over the wetlands. Green sandpiper and jack snipe are reg-

ular in winter. Harvest mouse has been recorded in the reserve.

Turnford & Cheshunt Pits (TL 368024) has patches of damp scrub and woodland. Good site for willow tits.

Lee Valley Park includes a special dragonfly sanctuary at Cornmill Meadows (TL 380013, OS 166). This is easily visited from the countryside centre near Waltham Abbey and is one of the finest dragonfly sites in eastern England, with 18 species regular, including white-legged and red-eyed damselflies, banded demoiselle, migrant hawker, and hairy and emperor dragonflies. A fine place to get to grips with this beautiful group of insects. Butterflies here include Essex skipper, and the plants flowering-rush and shiny pondweed.

Fisher's Green (TL 376032) is good for goosander, smew, and goldeneye in the winter. It has achieved recent fame amongst birders as one of the most reliable spots to see bittern in winter – there is a special bittern hide with views of a small reedbed where these strange

Ruddy duck *Oxyura jamaicensis* (Mike Lane)

herons regularly lurk. Other special winter birds here are long-eared owl, smew, water rail, goldeneye, siskins, and redpolls. Common terns nest here on special rafts.

Hall Marsh (TL 374005) has breeding redshank, little ringed plover, and lapwing, and passage waders.

There are a number of large reservoirs in the Lee Valley, the main ones being King George V and William Girling Reservoirs, Banbury Reservoir, Lockwood Reservoir, and Walthamstow Reservoirs. These all attract wintering wildfowl and may have rare grebes. There is another good reserve at nearby Walthamstow Marshes.

Nearby

The Chase (TQ 515860; 50 ha), in Dagenham, is London WT's largest reserve, with shallow wetlands, pasture, reedbeds, woodland, and scrub. This is a great site for birds with about 150 species recorded, and is particularly good in winter. The scrub is dominated by hawthorn and willow, and the rare black poplar also grows here. The grassland has birds-foot trefoil, early hair-grass, crested dog's-tail, and spiny restharrow, with rushes, lesser spearwort, and gypsywort in the wetter sites. Over 140 species of bird have been seen here, including reed warbler, kingfisher, great spotted woodpecker, short-eared owl, and lapwing. Teal, shoveler, and gadwall winter here, and spring and autumn waders include green sandpiper, redshank, and little ringed plover.

137 Wetland Centre

SITE

Fine, purpose-built wetland reserve, developed from a set of old Victorian reservoirs close to the Thames.

This is a very new WWT reserve, beautifully designed to attract a wide range of birds, a rich flora, and diverse insects. It lies off the A3003, in Barnes (TQ 522176). The artificial lagoons and scrapes are well served by paths, boardwalks, and hides, and the reserve offers a great introduction to wetland habitats. Non-WWT members pay an entrance fee. The facilities include educational material, a restaurant, and shops. There is a visitor centre, and no fewer than seven hides, one of which has three storeys. There are also pens with wildfowl from around the world.

Natural regeneration has been aided by planting with 250 000 aquatics and other plants, and 30 000 trees and shrubs, a process which began in 1997. The vegetation is now well established and it is difficult to imagine that this is not a natural habitat. Certainly the wildlife has no problem with the artificial origin! Wetland birds have been quick to adopt the reserve, and large numbers now breed, including ruddy duck. Proximity to the Thames helps to bring in passage birds such as hobbies and waders, and rarities turn up, especially on migration.

Spring–summer birds: reed and sedge warblers, hobby, ringed, and little ringed plovers. Autumn–winter: bittern, marsh harrier, water rail, peregrine, Slavonian and black-necked grebes, wildfowl, and waders,

Water vole *Arvicola terrestris*

with possible little egret, spoonbill, and black tern on passage. Breeding wildfowl include teal, shoveler, pochard, tufted duck, and shelduck.

Water voles, one of Britain's most threatened mammals, are set to become a special feature of the Wetland Centre, with an active programme of introduction. Once a familiar sight, they have disappeared from 90% of their range in recent years, partly through predation by escaped American mink. The habitat here is ideal for them, and (so far) remains a mink-free zone.

Nearby

Staines Reservoirs (TQ 050730), which are just in Surrey, lie to the south-west of Heathrow Airport, close to the confluence of the rivers Colne and Thames. Despite their location in a heavily populated area they have considerable wildlife interest, and are easy to scan from a public causeway. This is a good spot for grebes, with visits from red-necked, black-necked, and Slavonian. Little gulls and black terns may drop in, and it attracts its fair share of rarities. In winter the waterbirds congregate here to feed and also to roost in relative safety. Occasionally, large areas of mud are exposed if the water levels are low and there may be many waders at such times. Pochard and tufted duck are common, with rarer species such as goldeneye, goosander, and smew.

A selection of other important sites in the county

Bedfont Lakes Country Park (TQ 079729). Reedbeds, grassland, and lakes, with warblers and wildfowl. Hobbies and ring-necked parakeets regular. Smew, water rail, and bittern in winter.

Morden Hall Park (NT; TQ 259687), on Wandle River, has good wetland flora, dragonflies; grey wagtail, kingfisher.

Rainham Marshes SSSI (RSPB; TQ 5480): new reserve on north side of Thames Estuary.

Richmond Park (TQ 942190; 955 ha) is a huge royal park, and although well visited its ancient trees and rough grassland attract many birds, including woodcock, tree pipits, and a few redstarts. The herds of red and fallow deer exhibit their autumn rutting behaviour seemingly oblivious of the many human visitors.

Selsdon Wood (NT; TQ 357615): woodland, grassland, and pond; bluebells; white-letter and purple hairstreaks.

Sydenham Hill Wood (WT; TQ 346726): woodland birds, including hawfinch.

Southern England

Southern England

Southern England

Introduction

This region is favoured by a relatively mild and sunny climate, and characterized by rolling downland, woodland, and heath. The main areas of downland are the North and South Downs, the Berkshire and Marlborough Downs, the Hampshire Downs, and the South Wessex Downs (the latter also stretching into the south-west England region). In addition, there are the extensive heaths and woodland of the New Forest, The Weald with its patchwork of rich woodland sites, the coastal marshes of Kent, which include the southern Thames Estuary and Romney Marsh in the south, and the cliffs and estuaries of the south coast, stretching to the Solent and the Isle of Wight.

The dry, chalky soils of the North and South Downs can produce quite a warm, sometimes even hot microclimate, especially on south-facing slopes in summer. Such conditions favour certain southern plants, such as horseshoe vetch, round-headed rampion, and ground-pine. Orchids are also a major feature of the downs, with one species, lady orchid, virtually confined to open woodland on the chalk downs of Kent and Surrey, where it grows at its northern European limit. One famous southern plant is box, which gives its name to Box Hill. Several butterflies also flourish on these warm slopes – notably the rare and rather local Adonis blue.

Southern England is mostly well wooded, the county of Kent in particular having more ancient woodland (about 30 000 ha) than any other in Britain. Many of the woods lie on The Weald, which extends through Sussex and Surrey. In Norman times there was even more woodland, although even then the forests

would have been mostly managed and would not have been in a primeval, wildwood state. The Wealden woods of Surrey offer a fascinating contrast with the open downland. These are some of Britain's most diverse woods, with a fine array of flowers, as well as being amongst the best for insects, particularly butterflies.

The New Forest is neither new nor is it a forest – rather it is a mixture of pockets of ancient woods interspersed with tracts of lowland heath, grassland, and valley bogs. It is certainly a naturalist's paradise, with a very diverse flora and fauna. The lowland heath protected here is one of Europe's most threatened and valued habitats, giving the New Forest NP international importance.

The region also boasts some of Britain's finest coastal wetlands, such as those of the Solent and Chichester, whose mudrich estuaries are superb feeding sites for millions of waders, wildfowl, and other birds. These contrast with the stark, rather desolate expanse of shingle that is Dungeness, at England's south-eastern tip. This is an almost desert-like environment, home to large numbers of coastal birds, and to plants adapted to the harsh conditions of shifting pebbles.

Lapwing *Vanellus vanellus* (Mike Lane)

Previous page: **Beech woodland at Holm Hill in the New Forest**

Southern England

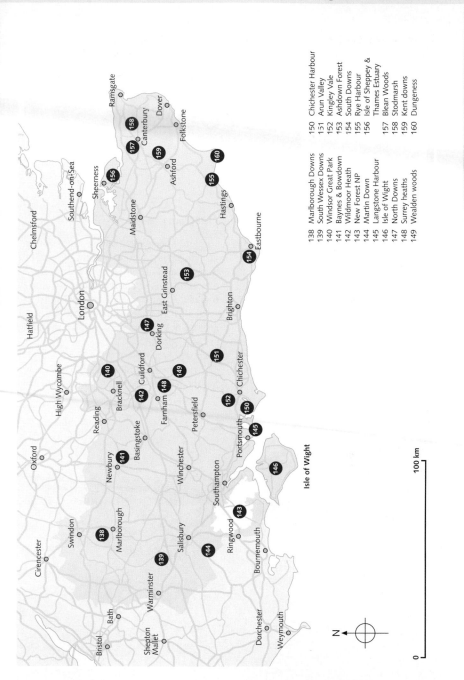

138 Marlborough Downs
139 South Wessex Downs
140 Windsor Great Park
141 Baynes & Bowdown
142 Wildmoor Heath
143 New Forest NP
144 Martin Down
145 Langstone Harbour
146 Isle of Wight
147 North Downs
148 Surrey heaths
149 Wealden woods

150 Chichester Harbour
151 Arun Valley
152 Kingley Vale
153 Ashdown Forest
154 South Downs
155 Rye Harbour
156 Isle of Sheppey &
     Thames Estuary
157 Blean Woods
158 Stodmarsh
159 Kent downs
160 Dungeness

100 km

0

N

Wiltshire

^{SITE}138 Marlborough Downs

An area with some of the finest chalk grassland sites in the region.

The smoothly undulating Wiltshire Downs are covered in many places by chalk grassland – a special habitat harbouring many species adapted to its conditions, including beautiful orchids and butterflies.

Decades of grazing by sheep have shaped this habitat, which is therefore one of many which must be managed to perpetuate its unique character. The thin soil is surprisingly rich, with as many as 40 plant species in a single square metre. The downland here has many ancient barrows and other earthworks, a number of white horses carved from the chalky turf, and stone circles, all adding to the appeal of the area. Spring and summer are the best seasons to visit, for the flowers and butterflies.

Fyfield Down NNR (SU 135710, OS 173) lies north-west of Marlborough and covers nearly 250 ha, on a high plateau of chalk

Pewsey Downs

grassland cut by a series of dry valleys. It forms part of a World Heritage Site, partly because of its archaeological interest – it has the finest collection of sarsen stones in Britain, some of which support unusual lichens. Although we think of these as chalk downs, in fact the soils here vary in reaction from calcareous to acidic, with most being neutral. This gives a range of grassland types, maintained by a mixture of grazing regimes, using sheep and cattle.

Pewsey Downs NNR (SU 1264, OS 173; 165 ha) protects one of the best stretches of chalk downland in England. It lies in the Vale of Pewsey, between Devizes and Pewsey, about 10 km south-west of Marlborough on the southern edge of the Marlborough Downs. The reserve is on the ancient Ridgeway track, popular with distance walkers, and close to the Wansdyke. There is also a famous landmark, a white horse, carved into the chalky flank of Milk Hill (294 m). There are two main types of grassland here, each with a different grazing regime. Milk Hill is mainly grazed year round by cattle and sheep, whereas Walkers and Knap Hills receive light cattle-grazing in the summer, and winter grazing by sheep, with a break in April. The latter regime allows a taller sward to grow. The main grassland type is a mixture of red and sheep's fescues, with upright brome. Other plants found here include glaucous sedge, salad burnet, dwarf thistle, bastard toadflax, field fleawort, chalk milkwort, horseshoe vetch, clustered bellflower, and wild thyme. Like many other downland sites, Pewsey is rich in orchids. Look out for burnt, common spotted-, bee, frog, fragrant, green-winged, and pyramidal orchids. Other flowers of particular interest are round-headed rampion, betony, devil's-bit scabious, and tuberous thistle. Butterflies abound, especially the blues, with common, chalk-hill, small, and brown argus. The presence of its food-plant, devil's-bit scabious, allows the marsh fritillary to survive here as well.

On the western end of the Marlborough Downs lie the Morgan's Hill (WT; SU 028672; 30 ha) and Kingsplay Hill (WT; SU 006658; 30 ha) reserves. These have good chalk downland with orchids and some areas of woodland and scrub. Both afford fine views over the surrounding countryside; Morgan's Hill reaches 258 m. Cherhill Down & Oldbury Castle (NT; SU 046694) has good chalk grassland, especially on the warmer southern slopes, where lesser butterfly-orchid may be seen. The butterflies include chalk-hill blue, marbled white, brown argus, and dingy skipper. Nearby is the famous stone circle of Avebury, and the remarkable Silbury Hill, the largest prehistoric mound in Europe.

Stoke Common Meadows (SU 065904), just south of Cricklade, has traditional meadows, with pepper saxifrage, sweet vernal grass, heath spotted-orchid, adder's tongue fern, and brown hair-streaks. In an ambitious restoration project, seed from here is currently being used to recreate similar habitats on a 240-ha disused airfield at Blakehill.

SITE
139 South Wessex Downs

Excellent downland lying on the southern edge of Salisbury Plain, towards the borders with Hampshire and Dorset.

Parsonage Down NNR (EN; 275 ha) lies near Shrewton, about 15 km north-west of Salisbury. Managed grazing by cattle and sheep maintain the grass swards in a state which is most beneficial to the wildlife. About 150 ha consists of rich chalk grassland with many rare and characteristic species.

Prescombe Down NNR, about 12 km east of Shaftesbury, is another good site, preserving about 75 ha of downland SSSI. Although not the easiest to visit (a permit is required, and a 3 km walk) the keener visitor will be well rewarded as this is one of the richest of the south Wiltshire downland sites. Large sections are dominated by the very local dwarf sedge, and in addition to the commoner downland flowers Prescombe boasts a large population of early gentian, in some years numbering hundreds of thousands.

Harebell
Campanula rotundifolia

Not surprisingly, the butterflies are good, too, with a strong population of Adonis blue. As with the other protected downland sites, a carefully managed programme of grazing is essential to maintain this traditional semi-natural habitat.

Wylye Down NNR is near Wylye village, between Salisbury and Warminster. About

Fritillary *Fritillaria meleagris* at North Meadow NNR (see p. 318)

35 ha of mainly east- and west-facing chalk grassland lie across a dry valley. The flora is rich, with dwarf sedge and fragrant orchids especially noteworthy. Access is by arrangement with the local farmer.

Coombe Bisset Down (SU 111256, OS 184; 35 ha), about 5 km south-west of Salisbury, preserves a patch of rich chalk grassland and is a very convenient site to find many of the most typical species. There is also some scrub and a beech wood. This is another site for dwarf sedge, but the real star amongst the flora here is burnt orchid, a very local species. Butterflies here include brown argus, and chalk-hill, small, and Adonis blues.

Some other good downland sites nearby

Chickengrove Bottom (WT; SU 040216; 8 ha) is a flower-rich chalk downland site with woodland and scrub. The orchids here include spotted-, early purple-, and greater butterfly-orchid.

Great Cheverell Hill (WT; ST 978523; 9 ha), on the northern edge of Salisbury Plain, has good orchids and Adonis blue.

Middleton Down (WT; SU 049233; 26 ha) has fine orchids in spring and summer, with dwarf sedge.

Grovely Down (WT; SU 086327; 10 ha): another good orchid site near Middletown.

White Sheet Down (NT; ST 800348), near Mere, is another downland site with old-established chalk grassland and a correspondingly rich flora and butterfly fauna. Rock-rose flowers here in quantity, along with cowslip, primrose, harebell, bird's-foot-trefoil, yellow-rattle, salad burnet, wild thyme, and lady's bedstraw, and several orchid species. Chalk-hill and small blues, grizzled and dingy skipper, marbled white, and marsh fritillary. Stourhead (NT), with its famous garden, is nearby.

A selection of other important sites in the county

Bentley Wood (Charitable Trust NR; SU 259292, OS 184), on the border with Hampshire, is a splendid site for butterflies, including white admiral, marbled white, high brown, dark green, silver-washed, and both pearl-bordered fritillaries, and purple and white-letter hairstreaks. This is probably the best place in Britain to observe perhaps our finest native butterfly, the purple emperor, which can sometimes be spotted in the car park, gliding down to rotting fruit. There are public rides and footpaths. Listen for nightingales.

Blackmoor Copse (WT; SU 333616; 31 ha): oak and birch woodland with a fine butterfly fauna (fritillaries).

Clouts Wood (WT; SU 137794; 13 ha) is a mixed wood on a slope, and a site for spiked star-of-Bethlehem.

Jones's Mill (WT; SU 168613; 12 ha): wet woodland and fen meadows with a good range of birds, bogbean, and marsh-orchids.

Morgan's Hill (WT; SU 019671, OS 173): chalk downland with Roman road; lesser butterfly-orchid.

North Meadow, Cricklade NNR (EN; SU 0994) is a Thames floodplain reserve famed for the largest British population of fritillary (peak flowering in late April to early May).

Ravensroost Wood (WT; SU 023882; 39 ha) is an ancient coppiced wood with midland hawthorn, small-leaved lime, and wild service-tree.

Smallbrook Meadows (WT; ST 878443, OS 183): wet meadows and willow woodland; water avens, marsh-marigold, yellow iris, meadowsweet, ragged-Robin; dragonflies.

Berkshire

SITE
140 Windsor Great Park

Fine old forest fragments with magnificent ancient trees, set in parkland rich in insect and bird life.

This ancient royal forest lies just to the south of Windsor (SU 9674, OS 176). It has many ancient oak trees, some of which are more than 500 years old, a few probably even older, and its open, parkland structure makes it attractive to a range of wildlife. Many of the trees were planted centuries ago to ensure a supply of timber for the Navy. About half the park is wooded, some under a coppice regime, and there are areas with near-natural oak–beech communities, a somewhat unusual combination in the region. The range of timber, in various stages of decomposition, makes Windsor Great Park particularly rich in inverte-brates. The park occupies what used to be an ancient hunting forest, rather like the New Forest in Hampshire, although most of the habitats here are very different. Like the New Forest, it is in part open and park-like, with old trees set in grassy meadows, but it also has areas of closed woodland and scrub. Lakes add to the overall diversity of habitat, providing food and cover for a wide range of wildlife. In the south there is a section of lowland heath with a rather different set of animals and plants.

The bird life here is typical of lowland woodland and parkland, with species such as sparrowhawk, tawny and little owl, all three woodpeckers, nuthatch, treecreeper, warblers, tits, spotted flycatcher, redpoll, and redstart. The relative abundance of well-grown hornbeams makes this a good place to spot hawfinches, a rather local and elusive species. On the heath patches towards the south there are nightjar, woodlark, stonechat, and hobby. Deer are common here, with red, fallow, roe, and muntjac all present.

Windsor is famous for the diversity of its insect life, and over 2000 different species of beetle alone have been logged. The butterflies include white admiral, painted lady, five species of skipper, holly blue, and that heathland speciality, the silver-studded

Southern England

Ancient oak (Peter Wilson)

blue, a species which has declined recently and which is now found mainly in parts of Dorset and the New Forest. The damselflies include southern and small red.

At the southern end of the park lies the attractive lake of Virginia Water (SU 9769).

This is worth visiting for its wildfowl, and is one of the surest place to see wild mandarin ducks, which breed here and are present throughout the year. Look for them particularly at the east end of the lake, and just north of the car park.

SITE
141 Baynes and Bowdown

Mixed heathy woodlands, close to a large reedbed.

Baynes and Bowdown reserves (WT; SU 511651 and SU 501655, OS 174; 38 ha), near Newbury, form the WT's largest woodland reserve in Berkshire. They are close to Greenham Common air base, which came to public prominence through its peace

camp. The site is quite varied, with woodland, heath, and acid grassland, and close by lies the contrasting habitat of Thatcham Reedbeds, part of one of the largest reedbeds in southern England and an excellent spot to see wetland plants and

Great spotted woodpecker *Dendrocopos major*

animals. Both reserves are components of a large piece of land designated as an SSSI.

Roe deer and muntjac are very active in these woods, and special nest boxes are used to try and increase the numbers of common dormice. These rather local rodents are well suited by the sheltered habitat with its hazel and honeysuckle, which provide food and bedding material. Woodland birds are well represented, with all the woodpeckers and woodcock, as are reptiles, with grass snakes, adders, viviparous lizards, and slow-worms. No fewer than 32 species of butterfly are known here, including dark green and silver-washed fritillaries and white admiral, as well as purple hairstreak, ringlet, and small skipper, and there are 15 species of dragonfly.

Greenham and Crookham Commons lie on a plateau, and the reserve is on a slope cut by several streams leading down to the valley of the river Kennet. Clay soils predominate near the bottom of the slope and carry a rich flora, with moschatel, herb-Paris, early purple orchid, and Solomon's-seal. On the wetter sites there are alder and willow groves, and a nice plant to look for here is opposite-leaved golden-saxifrage. A mixed woodland grows at the top of the slope, where the ground is drier, and more acid. Oak is the predominant tree here, but there are also rowan, hazel, birch, and wild cherry, and the heathy ground flora with bluebells, foxgloves, and ferns grades into areas of open heath with bell heather. The former airbase is gradually returning to heathland, and has nightingale, nightjar, woodlark, tree pipit, Dartford warbler and hobby.

Thatcham Reedbeds (SU 5067, OS 174), about 3 km east of Newbury, lies alongside the Kennet and Avon Canal and can be viewed from the towpath. There is a varied wetland flora with water-plantain and yellow iris. The birds are good, too, and water rails are much in evidence, especially in winter. The dragonflies include common blue damselfly and broad-bodied chaser.

SITE
142 Wildmoor Heath

An accessible heathland oasis in the heart of the home counties,
with a diverse mixture of threatened habitats.

Heathland is a rare habitat in Berkshire, a county which once boasted large expanses, mainly in the south and east. A staggering 98% of the heathland which existed in the county 250 years ago has been lost, mainly to urban development or agriculture, with the result that the landscape has changed enormously, largely to the detriment of the wildlife. All the more important, then, to find Wildmoor Heath (WT;

Oblong-leaved sundew *Drosera intermedia*

SU 842627, OS 175; 99 ha), a jewel of a nature reserve with woodland, dry and wet heath, mires, and grassland.

Heathland specialist birds are well represented here, with woodlarks, stonechats, and nightjars. The song of the woodlark is one of the most attractive of all birds – a rather mournful series of trills and fluted notes, usually delivered in a fluttering songflight, and surprisingly early in the year,

February being a good month to hear them. The birches attract redpolls, and siskins may also be spotted. Reptiles are also well represented, with grass snakes and adders, viviparous lizards, and slow-worms.

It is the wetter parts of the reserve which are the most unusual, and these have great botanical and entomological interest. Wet heath and the associated mires are even rarer than dry heath and have special treasures. In addition to nine species of bog-moss, there are white beak-sedge, cottongrass, bog asphodel, bog pimpernel, and both round- and oblong-leaved sundews. The insect stars here are the dragonflies – 14 species, including keeled skimmer and the pretty golden-ringed dragonfly. Emperor and fox moth are also found on the reserve, as are grayling and silver-studded blue butterflies.

Public footpaths give good access to the reserve from nearby car parks, and there are also boardwalks.

A selection of other important sites in the county

Basildon Park (NT; SU 611782; 164 ha) has woodland (with yew and box) and open grassland. Plants include dwarf thistle, bee orchid and four species of helleborine. White admiral is also found here.

Decoy Heath (WT; SU 615635, OS 175; 7 ha) is the richest site in the county for dragonflies, with 23 species, including downy and brilliant emeralds. Also grayling, silver-studded blue, and Essex skipper.

Dinton Pastures Country Park (SU 787718, OS 175), just east of Reading, is centred on a group of old gravel pits alongside the river Lodden. There are hides and wader scrapes, and an information centre. The winter wildfowl are very good: goldeneye, smew, black-necked grebe, red-crested pochard and ruddy duck.

Hartslock (WT; SU 616796, OS 175; 4.4 ha): rich chalk grassland overlooking Goring Gap.

Hosehill Lake LNR (OS 175) between Reading and Newbury, and nearby gravel pits, is a great place to see birds (over 150 species recorded) and insects (notably butterflies and dragonflies). The best times for birds are during the migrations. Breeding birds include sand martin, water rail, kingfisher, and marsh and willow tits, and this is a good site for passing raptors, such as hobby, osprey, buzzard, honey buzzard, and peregrine.

Inkpen Common (WT; SU 382643, OS 174; 10 ha): heath and bog.

Inkpen Crocus Field (WT; SU 370640, OS 174; 3 ha): flower-rich meadows with spring crocus, a naturalized species with its biggest population here.

Lardon Chase (NT; SU 588809) and **Lough Down** (NT; SU 588813) lie just north of Streatley and together form one of the largest remnants of chalk grassland in the county. Clustered bellflower, chalk milkwort, and autumn gentian. Good for blue butterflies.

Loddon Reserve (WT; SU 785758, OS 175; 14 ha): large gravel pit.

Moor Copse (WT; SU 633738, OS 175; 27 ha): mixed woodland with white admiral.

Sole Common Pond (WT; SU 413707, OS 174): mainly bog and heath; woodcock and wood warbler.

Theale Gravel Pits (SY 676703) lie west of Reading, and close to the Kennet and Avon Canal. Good birdwatching, especially for waders, wildfowl, terns, and gulls.

Walbury Hill (SU 3663), rising to some 330 m, is the highest chalk down in England, and offers fine views. This is a good area for raptors, with red kite possible alongside buzzard, kestrel, and sparrowhawk, and peregrine, merlin, and hen harrier in autumn and winter.

Hampshire and Isle Of Wight

SITE 143 New Forest National Park

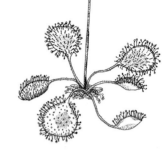

An extraordinary survivor of a medieval landscape, with a rich and special flora and fauna.

The New Forest is a remarkable and unexpected remnant, thanks to a number of chance occurrences and a gradually increasing awareness over the last hundred years or so of its exceptional importance.

It is essentially an almost complete, large (580 square kilometres), medieval hunting forest, declared originally a little over 900 years ago. Hunting forests were rarely composed entirely of woodland – they were much more likely to be a combination of woodland and open habitats such as heathland, making for better hunting, and the New Forest was exactly that. Although originally wholly wooded

Round-leaved sundew *Drosera rotundifolia*

after the ice age, by medieval times it was a matrix of heath, bog, grassland, and forest

Hobby *Falco subbuteo*

Most of the many English hunting forests have gradually fallen into private ownership and been turned into agricultural or residential land; the New Forest, however, has remained in Crown ownership (through the office of Forest Enterprise nowadays), and retains most of its traditional habitats and customs, albeit in a modified form. Today it covers almost 40 000 ha and is made up of a wonderful patchwork of lowland heath, bog, scrub, open woodland, enclosed woodland, and grasslands, together with streams and small rivers, and a number of artificial lakes and ponds. With the exception of certain enclosures set aside specifically for forestry, it is grazed by ponies and cattle (and a few donkeys) as a huge common. This has the effect of encouraging a landscape free of boundaries – the habitats all grade into each other, without clear-cut edges, and these transition zones move according to the intensity of grazing, which varies over the years.

From the natural history point of view, this has both good and bad effects. The strong points of the forest's regime are its vast size, the way in which many different habitats all adjoin each other (a rarity in modern lowland Britain), and the long continuity of these habitats. Its drawbacks include the lack of certain rich habitats such as coppiced woodland, and the heavy grazing of all habitats, which reduces the flowers, insects, and species that depend on them. For example, there are remarkably few small mammals (in species and numbers) in the New Forest, because there are so few areas of long grass, and very few strong populations of woodland or grassland butterflies.

The New Forest is considered to be nationally and internationally important for its habitats and species. It is an SSSI (with a few small reserves within it), a Special Protection Area, an internationally important Ramsar wetland, and a candidate Special Area for Conservation.

The woodlands are perhaps its best-known feature. The ancient woods that have a long history of being open to grazing are distinctive by virtue of their many old trees, and the lack of an understorey of shrubs, as well as an almost complete absence of spring flowers, except in a few locations. These ancient unenclosed woodlands are known as the 'Ancient and Ornamental' woods (or A & O for short). They are dominated by beech or pedunculate oak, and are particularly good for invertebrates of old wood (such as stag beetles), many bats, birds such as redstarts, honey buzzards and wood warblers, and lichens. They are well used by deer (there are five species in the forest) and will provide cover or food for most species at some time. There are also

Raft spider *Dolomedes fimbriatus*

Pillwort around a New Forest pond

many younger woods that have invaded areas of open habitat naturally, which are dominated by birches, holly, or younger oaks. Along the river valleys there are often alder and willow woods, which may have a richer flora, and birds such as siskins. There are also vast tracts of managed plantations, often fenced against grazing, known as the Enclosures. Although they consist normally of alien species in a heavily managed environment, they do provide a useful alternative and often ungrazed habitat, and may act as strongholds for certain birds such as sparrowhawks, deer, and some flowers and butterflies which cannot tolerate heavy grazing. The woods as a whole are exceptionally important for fungi, with huge numbers of species recorded.

There are vast stretches of heathland within the New Forest, dominated by heather and bell heather. They cover many of the drier hills, and grade into wet heath and bog in the valleys or where there are wet flushed patches. The dry heaths are the stronghold of some of the forest's rari-

ties, especially Dartford warbler, hobby, stonechat, nightjar, smooth snake, the beautiful wild gladiolus, grayling butterflies, and many other species. They are also good areas for lichens, especially *Cladonia* species. The heaths are by no means uniform, and the most interesting are often those with a few trees, or bushes of gorse, allowing feeding and cover for a wider range of species. The wet or damp heaths, intermediate between bog and heath, are often dominated by cross-leaved heath, and have uncommon plants such as marsh gentian, marsh clubmoss, and sundews, and were the only UK site for summer lady's-tresses before it became extinct.

There are very large areas of bogs in the New Forest, particularly valley bogs, and hillside bogs where sand and gravel overlie clay, giving rise to an acidic springline. These are wonderful places for the naturalist, particularly rich in flowers and insects. Some of the special flowers include all three species of sundew, the rare bog orchid, pale butterwort, all the cottongrasses including

Southern England

slender cottongrass, early marsh-orchid, lesser bladderwort, bog asphodel, and many species of bog-moss.

The New Forest as a whole is exceptionally good for dragonflies, and the bogs are the strongholds of many of the less common species such as southern, small red, and scarce blue-tailed damselflies, keeled skimmer, black darter, and many others. The raft spider, a striking species, is common in the boggy areas, in addition to many other invertebrates. They are also prime feeding sites for hobbies in search of dragonflies as prey.

There are also extensive areas of natural grassland in the New Forest, often known as 'lawns', kept open by heavy grazing from ponies, cattle, and deer. They are frequently quite species-rich, though it may be hard to see the plants as they rarely flower. Some particular specialities of the grasslands, which usually do succeed in flowering, are the pennyroyal (a mint, now virtually extinct elsewhere in Britain), small fleabane (virtually confined to the New Forest), and

wild chamomile, which is generally rare. The grasslands are also key feeding sites for green woodpeckers (which eat the yellow meadow ants) and other birds.

Within this general matrix of heath, forest, and grassland, there are also other minor habitats. The rivers and streams of the forest are largely unspoilt and consequently rich in invertebrates, aquatic plants, and a few semi-aquatic mammals such as water shrews. In the southern part of the forest, there are many old marl pits dug into the calcareous Headon Beds clay, and these have subsequently developed into attractive wildlife sites, often surrounded by damp calcareous grassland. They are good places for flowers such as coral-necklace, yellow centaury, Hampshire-purslane, and other rarities, many dragonflies, two or three species of groundhopper, water spiders, and much else. Some of the more acid ponds in the north part are good for plants such as pillwort (a rare semi-aquatic fern-ally), dragonflies, and damselflies, and are often key breeding sites for common

Ponies grazing a streamside lawn on the Ober Water

frogs and toads. There are also one or two ponds, which dry up in summer, where the rare tadpole shrimp occurs, or the beautiful and uncommon fairy shrimp.

The New Forest is not easy to know, nor somewhere to find species quickly – it is large, and the features of interest are often widely spread, so it is not a place to be hurried. Some good locations to start include Cranes Moor and the adjacent Kingston Great Common NNR, on the west side of the forest near Burley, for bog and wet heath species. There are fine ancient woods around Mark Ash Wood in the centre of the Forest, Shave Wood in the north-east, and Denny Wood, Tantany Wood, and Stubbs Wood towards the south-east. Some of the most interesting lawns are north of Cadnam and around Minstead, and the best marl pits are in the south, near East End, Boldre, and Norley Wood. Heathland areas are wide-spread, in places such as Beaulieu Heath, and to the north of Burley. Dartford warblers are easily found, at the time of writing, in any heath with old gorse, because the population levels are currently very high; this will change if the area experiences a hard winter.

The New Forest perambulation (boundary) also includes a small stretch of the shore of the Solent, between Lymington and Beaulieu. There is a major NNR – the North Solent NNR – around Beaulieu, which includes examples of many of the best habitats, covering 820 ha. Access is via public footpaths (e.g. from Beaulieu south to Buckler's Hard) or by permit from EN.

The New Forest is currently being turned into a NP, though its boundaries are not yet fixed. It will almost certainly cover a wider area, stretching to Christchurch Harbour and the Avon Valley. The whole area is of enormous interest to the naturalist.

144 Martin Down

SITE

An NNR of 320 ha in the far west of Hampshire, mainly chalk grassland.

Martin Down is an outstanding reserve, hidden away in the quiet countryside on the borders of Hampshire, Wiltshire, and Dorset, just west of Martin village. It is large enough to support its own ecosystem, and provide space for some of the more demanding species of chalk. Most remaining fragments of our once vast chalk grasslands are on scarps too steep to plough; Martin is unusual in that it includes large patches of relatively level chalk grassland, in addition to some steep slopes and a few ancient earthworks. Besides the big areas of chalk grassland, some short and some rough, there are also tracts of scrub and woodland, with many zones of interface between the two.

It is an outstanding area botanically, with most of the plants that you might expect on western chalk grassland. Orchids are frequent, including burnt, man, fragrant, pyramidal, greater butterfly-, frog, southern marsh-, and common spotted-orchid. Kidney vetch, horseshoe vetch, and bird's-foot-trefoil (all key butterfly larval food-plants) abound, together with bastard toadflax, greater knapweed, field fleawort, chalk milkwort, dwarf sedge, cowslip, clustered bellflower, and many others. Pasqueflowers have been recorded, but are almost certainly introduced. The linear Romano-British earthwork, the Bokerley Dyke, crosses the site, forming its boundary in places (and the Hampshire–Dorset boundary), and this is an excellent place to start looking for the special chalk flowers.

It is a particularly good place for butterflies, and many other insects; 43 species of butterflies have been recorded in recent years, making it one of the best such sites in the country. Dark green fritillaries can be abundant in some years in rough grassland, together with commoner species such as marbled white and meadow brown. Shorter, hotter grassland supports Adonis and chalk-hill blues, silver-spotted skipper, and brown argus, amongst others. The little Duke of Burgundy is easily missed, but not uncommon, in more sheltered areas where cowslips grow, and marsh fritillaries occur in patchy colonies around its food-plant, the devil's-bit scabious. In the more wooded parts, especially in the Kit's Grave section north of the Blandford–Salisbury road, woodland butterflies such as white admiral and silver-washed fritillaries are common in

Burnt orchid *Orchis ustulata*

some years, feeding mainly on brambles. Other insects are abundant, too. There are large numbers of glow-worms, and numerous robberflies, including the striking hornet robberfly, one of our biggest flies. Bumble bees are abundant, including some scarce ones, and the vast resources of summer nectar are also used by hoverflies, longhorn beetles, and sawflies. Moths include small elephant hawkmoth, privet hawkmoth, and the cistus forester moth. On a warm evening, the place is alive with moths, often accompanied by bats or nightjars.

It is also a surprisingly good place for birdwatching. Apart from nightjars, there are abundant skylarks, common and lesser whitethroats, turtle doves, and nightingales breeding on the site, and hobbies, stone curlews, and barn owls often feed over the area. In winter, there are often masses of thrushes – redwings, fieldfares, and others – feeding on the berries. Apart from widespread mammal species, such as rabbits and foxes, there are also brown hares (now rare in the surrounding farmland), harvest mice, and dormice in the more wooded areas.

Access is open, with entry points at the end of Sillen Lane from Martin village, or on the main A354 where the reserve extends across the road. It is an interesting place at any time, though late April to early August is outstanding, as is September–October for late butterflies, passage birds, and some autumn colour.

The village of Breamore, a little to the east in the Avon Valley, has a fascinating goose-grazed common marsh, dotted formerly with ancient willow pollards and ringed with old cottages – the atmosphere is extraordinarily medieval – and there are also a few rare plants around the ponds, such as brown galingale.

There are a number of other good chalk grasslands surviving in Hampshire, including Old Winchester Hill NNR (actually well east of Winchester, just south of the village of West Meon); Butser Hill near Petersfield, and St Catherine's Hill, just on the south-eastern edge of Winchester.

SITE
145 Langstone Harbour

A major site for birds and other wildlife, especially in winter.

Langstone Harbour is the central one of three major harbours along the north shore of the Solent, between Southampton and Chichester. These are large sheltered inlets, and at low tide they almost empty, to reveal huge areas of glistening, food-rich mud. Their particular importance is for birds, especially as a feeding area and refuge in winter and at passage periods. Two of the three harbours (Portsmouth and Langstone) lie in Hampshire, and the third (Chichester) in West Sussex (see p. 337). Of the Hampshire two, Langstone is less developed, and generally richer.

Some recent counts give an idea of the wealth of birds to be found here. In winter, one year, there were maximum numbers of almost 50 000 dunlin, 4000 grey plover, 2000 each of redshank, curlew, and bar-tailed godwits, about 1000 black-tailed godwit, and almost 17 000 Brent geese, with smaller numbers of pintail, goldeneye, wigeon, and many others. Passage periods bring similar species, though in lower numbers, plus the characteristic passage-only birds such as spotted redshank and whimbrel, and there are usually a few rarities. The numbers of waders and waterfowl peak at over 95 000 in winter and over 40 000 on passage, making it an internationally important site. Amongst the wintering birds, the Brent geese are the most obvious, as they are noisy and quite tame, frequently flying between the harbour and nearby grasslands. In early summer, there are breeding common and little terns here,

Dunlin *Calidris alpina* (Mike Lane)

together with shelduck, yellow wagtail, and reed and sedge warblers.

The Hampshire WT has a reserve of about 120 ha on the north side of the harbour, called Farlington Marshes. It consists mainly of damp coastal grassland and marsh on a peninsula almost surrounded by sea, providing a valuable feeding area and high-tide roost. It is also an important site botanically, with grassland and coastal species such as grass vetchling, strawberry clover, yellow-rattle, and many uncommon sedges and grasses. There is access from the A27 or from Broadmarsh coastal park, just to the north-east.

Hayling Island lies to the east of the harbour. Although built-up, it still retains some patches of good habitat, especially at the southern end and around the coastal fringes.

SITE
146 The Isle of Wight

A surprisingly unspoilt and varied island, with a wealth of special plants and animals.

The Isle of Wight is a large island lying astride the entrance to the Solent and Southampton Water. Although only about 3 km from the Hampshire mainland at its closest point, it is a world apart in many ways (thanks partly to the high ferry costs!). It is geologically varied, rather like the Isle of Purbeck, and some of its features, such as The Needles, the undercliffs around Ventnor, and the multi-coloured sands of Alum Bay, are particularly famous.

The north coast is part of the Solent system, and shares many characteristics and species with places such as Langstone Harbour. Probably the best location is around Newtown Harbour on the north-west coast. This is a small drowned valley similar to Langstone Harbour, but smaller and surrounded by lovely, unspoilt countryside. Almost 300 ha of NT land are managed as an NNR, comprising the estuary itself (considered to be the most unspoilt

Bee orchid
Ophrys apifera

estuary on the south coast of England), saltpans and lagoons, ancient woodland, and some lovely old meadows set in a framework of ancient hedges. Birds in the harbour include Brent geese, black-tailed godwit, redshank, wigeon, teal, shelduck, and a host of other waders and waterfowl. In the ancient coppice woodland there are red squirrels (a feature of the island,

Compton Down

Walter's Copse

along the cliff edges, including the beautiful sea stock and white horehound.

Just inland of the south-west coast, there is a line of fine chalk downland which meets the coast at Tennyson and Compton Downs, where there is a wonderful combination of downland and coastal species. These downs are one of the best sites in the country for the endemic early gentian, which can occur in millions in good years, together with a wealth of other downland flowers such as cowslips, bee and pyramidal orchids, bastard toadflax, yellow-wort, and horseshoe vetch. Butterflies do well in the more sheltered parts, with species such as Adonis and chalk-hill blues, Duke of Burgundy, and dark green fritillary. There is a rich assemblage of insects and spiders here, including strongly coastal species such as the grey bush-cricket. Access is largely open, and there are many NT properties here.

Further east, Luccombe Chine (northeast of Ventnor) has good insects and flowers, and there is a good botanic garden at Ventnor. Ventnor also boasts one of only a handful of British sites for the common wall lizard – on walls in the town and near the beach. It is well established here, and may even be native. The cliffs east of Sandown, particularly Red Cliff and Culver Cliff, are a noted botanical site for a number of species, including the rare yarrow broomrape. Around Bembridge and St Helen's, at the easternmost point of the island, there are some superb intertidal limestone ledges with particularly rich seashore life of all types. Other places of interest on the island include Ventnor Down, Firestone Copse (south-west of Ryde), and Brading Marshes, just east of Brading village. The latter is regarded by the RSPB as one of the region's best wetlands, with the largest expanses of reedbed and grazing marsh on the island. It has marsh harriers, bearded tits, and wintering bitterns, as well as thriving water voles, dormice, and red squirrels, and the rare starlet sea anemone in the lagoons. The RSPB bought this 168-ha marsh in late 2001.

Access to the island is by ferry from Lymington, Southampton, and Portsmouth, or by air.

untouched by grey squirrels) and dormice, and a rich woodland flora including 28 species recognized to be particularly associated with ancient woodland. The meadows have green-winged orchids, restharrow, lady's bedstraw, adder's-tongue, an abundance of dyer's greenweed, and many other flowers of heavy clay. Butterflies are abundant and diverse, though without special rarities. The easiest access is from the hamlet of Newtown itself and along the road to the east. The Yar Estuary, south of Yarmouth, further west, is similar, though not as rich.

The south coast is quite different in character, dominated by cliffs exposed to the waves, without any sheltered harbours. There are extensive areas of undercliff – slumped land below the higher cliffs – which are often completely unspoilt habitats, as in Dorset. On the south-west coast, particularly around Compton and Brook, is the only native British site for the Glanville fritillary, which feeds on ribwort plantain but clearly needs the warmth of this area to help it survive. Some rare plants grow

A selection of other important sites in the county

Hook-with-Warsash (SU 490050): shingle, marsh, reedbed; geese, Cetti's warbler.

Lower Test (SU 364150): saltmarsh, grassland, reedbed; waders, Cetti's warbler, bearded tit.

Lymington–Keyhaven NNR (SZ 315920): marsh, lagoons; passage waders and wildfowl.

Lymington Reedbed (SZ 325963): extensive reedbed, carr; Cetti's warbler, water rail, otter.

Titchfield Haven NNR (SU 535025): wet meadows, reedbeds; bearded tit, Cetti's warbler, water rail, waders, and wildfowl.

Surrey

^{SITE}
147 North Downs

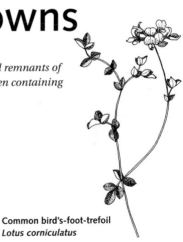

Common bird's-foot-trefoil
Lotus corniculatus

Undulating countryside with chalk grassland and remnants of woodland, many on quite steep gradients and often containing yew – a rare woodland type.

The chalk hills of the North Downs stretch in a long arc, roughly from Guildford in the west towards Dover in the east. They are divided from the South Downs by the sandy ridges and clay vales of The Weald which lies between. These hills would once have carried fairly dense woodland of ash, beech, hornbeam, and yew, except on the steeper slopes, but only scattered remnants remain. Most of the woodland was cleared to make way for agriculture, and especially for sheep as it was soon discovered that chalk grassland makes excellent grazing, and what we now often regard as typical downland habitats are indeed such grazing grounds. These traditional semi-natural habitats are very rich in flowers and insects and have themselves in turn come under pressure from urbanization and arable farming, and now require active conservation in their own right.

Box Hill (TQ 1751) is a famous beauty spot near Dorking. It lies on the North Downs Way footpath and is a well-known vantage point with a fine view. Although this site takes its name from the box which grows so well here, it is the taller yew which really gives it its unique atmosphere, box generally forming the understorey. Yew and box produce a dark woodland on the crest of the hill, and the ground flora includes deadly nightshade

Rufous grasshopper *Gomphocerripus rufus*

and common twayblade. The grassy slopes are rich in flowers, with horseshoe and kidney vetch, marjoram, and orchids: bee, fragrant, pyramidal, musk, and autumn lady's-tresses, and there are chalk-hill blues and silver-spotted skippers. The large and edible Roman snail thrives here on the warm, chalky slopes. Box Hill is something of a honeypot with many visitors, but a brisk walk will take you away from the crowds and it is well worth a visit.

A little further west is Ranmore Common (NT; TQ 1451). This wooded common has beech, oak and ash, and a sprinkling of yew, with bluebell, foxglove, wood anemone, and white helleborine. All three woodpeckers,

wood warbler, and woodcock may be seen, and there are foxes and roe deer. The butterflies include purple hairstreak, white admiral, dark green and silver-washed fritillaries, with Adonis and chalk-hill blues and silver-spotted skipper on the grassland.

To the south of this lies Leith Hill (NT; TQ 139432), which reaches 294 m, making it the highest point in the whole of southeast England and giving fine views over the rolling hills and woods of this attractive countryside. The reserve itself has sloping woodland with a mixture of trees – oak and birch, with Scots pine. Woodland birds are a feature, and this is a good butterfly site, with white admiral. Bluebells are a particular feature in spring.

Hackhurst and White Downs (TQ 096486) have some of the finest stretches of chalk downland, with all the typical habitats well represented. This site also straddles the North Downs Way and is well supplied with footpaths that allow easy exploration. A visit here in spring or summer should reveal a wealth of flowers, with specialities such as round-headed rampion, and several species of orchid. This is a good site for chalk-hill blues, and the grasshoppers include the local rufous grasshopper.

Box Hill

Headley Heath (NT; TQ 204538) is an unusual downland site, since it combines heathland with chalk downland. Heather and bracken clothe the sandy soils, with patches of birch woodland, but lower down the chalk is at the surface and the flora changes to a typical downland community with rock-rose, wild thyme, bird's-foot-trefoil, milkwort, marjoram, and musk mallow notable. The butterflies include chalk-hill blue, skippers, and Duke of Burgundy.

SITE
148 Surrey heaths

Fine heaths within easy reach of London. Dry and wet habitats with a range of characteristic heathland species.

The countryside of west and south-west Surrey is characterized by mostly rather acid, sandy soils. These soils would naturally carry an oak–birch woodland, often degraded into the related habitats of heathland and scrub. A series of reserves protects this valuable landscape in an area roughly from Woking south to Haslemere.

One of the finest of these reserves is Thursley Common NNR (EN; SU 900417, OS 186; 325 ha), 8 km south-west of Godalming. It is composed of heath, woodland, and bog and is a prime site not only for heathland plants and birds, but also for insects, especially dragonflies. Thursley Common is a superb remnant of a threatened habitat – lowland acid heathland. As well as pure dry heath, the reserve has many gradations to wetter communities, including wet heath and bog. There is

Cross-leaved heath
Erica tetralix

also a considerable amount of woodland, mostly birch and pine.

The dry heath is dominated by heather, gorse, dwarf gorse, and bell heather, and the wet heath has purple moor-grass and cross-leaved heath. The boggy sites have many interesting plants, including two species of sundew, common cottongrass, bog asphodel, and bladderwort. The mires and wet heaths are some of the best in southern England. There are also patches of royal fern, well to the east of its usual haunts.

The reserve has 27 species of dragonfly, with 16 breeding, including downy and brilliant emerald, keeled skimmer, and small red damselfly, in addition to emperor dragonfly and broad-bodied chaser, and white-faced darter at a southern outpost. There are silver-studded blue, grayling, and purple emperor, and the nationally rare large marsh grasshop-

White-faced darter *Leucorrhinia dubia*

Thursley Common

per is also to be found in the locality. Other interesting invertebrates here are sand wasps (*Ammophila* species) and the raft spider. Thursley holds good populations of Dartford warbler and woodlark, and hobbies are regularly spotted. It is probably at its best in late spring or early summer, although woodlarks breed very early and would be in full song much earlier (even in February). Other birds to look for here are curlew, woodcock, nightingale, and grasshopper warbler; and with luck tree pipits and redstarts may be spotted along the edge of the woodland. The common gets occasional visits from wintering hen harriers and great grey shrikes. Reptiles are a feature, too, with natterjack, sand and viviparous lizards, and smooth and grass snakes. Adders are common here, so reasonably stout footwear is recommended, especially early or late in the season, when the snakes may be sluggish.

The site is open to the public, and there is a network of bridleways and paths, with boardwalks to the wetter areas.

Selected further Surrey heathland sites

Esher Common (TQ 125625, OS 187), and adjacent West End and Fairmile Commons, have open access, and are particularly good for dragonflies: brilliant and downy emeralds, white-legged and red-eyed damselflies, black-tailed skimmer, banded demoiselle.

Frensham Common (NT; SU 8540) has a mixture of heath (dry and wet) and woodland. The dry heath has heather, bell heather, gorse, with birch and Scots pine, and there are also boggy areas with sundew. There are also two ponds fringed by reeds, with yellow iris, bulrush, and sweet-flag. The birds include snipe, redshank, whinchat, stonechat, nightjar, wood and reed warblers, and nightingales.

Hindhead Common (NT; SU 8936). Fine heathland, including the famous Gibbet Hill and Devil's Punchbowl. Also mixed woodland.

Lightwater Country Park (SU 921622): gravel quarries with adjacent woodland, heath and bog. Hobby, nightjar, woodlark, tree pipit, Dartford warbler and stonechat.

Witley & Milford Commons (NT; SU 9240) consists of woodland, heath, and downland. Although much disturbed by army camps, this site is still of interest, with a good mixture of acid heath and more calcareous soils, with species such as dwarf thistle and marjoram. Both roe and red deer may be seen. Viviparous lizards and adders are quite frequent.

SITE
149 Wealden woods

Some of the richest woodland sites in Britain, especially for insect fauna, with many being excellent for butterflies.

The Weald is a dome-like terrain of mainly clays and sands, sandwiched between the North and South Downs, and lying like a wedge across Surrey, Sussex, and Kent. The natural history of The Weald differs markedly from the mainly chalk habitats to the north and south, and the soils here vary according to which underlying rocks are exposed.

This area has been clothed in woodland for centuries; indeed the name 'weald' means 'forest' in Anglo-Saxon and is cognate with the German 'Wald'. Today it remains the part of England with the most native woodland, which probably explains the richness of its woodland flora and (especially invertebrate) fauna. No longer unbroken forest, what we see today are patches of woods in a landscape which also includes scattered heaths and grassland.

Chiddingfold Woods (FC; SU 9835) lies some 8 km south of Godalming. This region consists of a group of woods, plantations, pastures, and small farms close to the border with West Sussex. These woods are actually some of the best in Britain for butterflies, with good populations of common species and the added spice of a number of rather rare or local species, notably purple emperor and fritillaries. With fine weather, a visit timed for the target species, patience, and good luck, it is possible to see dozens of species here, such as the wood white, a local species on the wing in late May and June. Silver-

Ashtead Common

Southern England

White admiral *Limenitis camilla*

washed fritillaries are attracted to flowers such as bramble along the woodland rides and these woods are also home to the white admiral. Woodland and hedgerow species such as brimstone, peacock, orange tip, and comma abound, and these woods also have small, large, grizzled, and dingy skipper, both pearl-bordered and small pearl-bordered fritillaries, and four out of the five species of hairstreak: green, purple, white-letter, and brown.

The general natural history interest is high, with flowers such as primrose, violets, woodruff, marsh thistle, and spotted- and greater butterfly-orchids. Many of the woods have rather dense undergrowth, which is ideal for woodland warblers such as blackcap, garden warbler, whitethroat and lesser whitethroat,

willow warbler, and chiffchaff, and for nightingale. Sparrowhawks and, increasingly, buzzards breed here, and the plantations have firecrest as well as the commoner goldcrest.

Oaken Wood (BC; SU 994338, OS 186) is a mixed woodland site, with areas of scrub and grassland; it is particularly noted for its butterflies. Wild service-tree grows here, as does greater butterfly-orchid. There are silver-washed and both pearl-bordered fritillaries, purple emperor, wood white, brown hairstreak, and grizzled skipper. The moths are also impressive, with clear-wings and broad-bordered bee hawkmoth.

Nearby Barfold Copse (RSPB; SU 914324) is mainly oak with hazel coppice. It is excellent for woodland birds, but also has wild daffodil, and good insects, including white admiral.

Further east, between Cranleigh and Horsham, lies Wallis Wood (WT; TQ 121388, OS 187; 13 ha), a fine oak–hazel coppice wood with wild apple, cherry, Midland hawthorn, and wild service-tree. Bluebells, primroses, wood anemones, and wild daffodils grow here, as do broad-leaved and violet helleborines. This wood is another great place for butterflies, with purple emperor, silver-washed fritillary, purple hairstreak, and speckled wood.

A selection of other important sites in the county

Ashtead Common NNR (TQ 1759; 200 ha) has marvellous ancient oak pollards and an associated invertebrate fauna, with over 1000 beetles alone. A remarkable site so close to London (just within the M25). There are some 2000 oak pollards (mainly pedunculate oak), and most are 300–400 years old. Over 100 of the beetles are of special interest and there are more than 20 'Red Data Book' rarities. The beetles include stag beetle and jewel beetles (e.g. genus *Agrilus*). Purple emperor and white admiral may be seen here, and the orthopterans include long-winged cone-head and Roesel's bush-cricket.

Bookham Commons (NT; TQ 1256) offers a mixture of habitats of grass-land, woodland, scrub, and ponds and streams. Oak with holly in places. Woodpeckers, woodcock, kingfisher, grey heron, nightingales. All three newts are found in the ponds.

Nower Wood (TQ 193546): woodland, ponds; woodland birds, mandarin duck.

Riverside Park, Guildford (TQ 005515): meadow, lake, woodland; hobby, warblers, water rail.

West Sussex

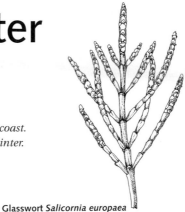

150 Chichester Harbour

One of the largest mudflat areas on the south coast. Best visited for its wildfowl, in autumn and winter.

The south coast has a large number of fine coastal sites, and there are none better than the rather intricate bays and inlets of Chichester Harbour and nearby Langstone Harbour (for the latter see p. 328). For centuries these natural harbours have sheltered boats of all shapes and sizes, but they simultaneously provide safe havens for birds, especially passage waders and wildfowl, and today attract sailors and naturalists alike, for the most

Glasswort *Salicornia europaea*

part co-existing amicably, though the hobbies can be difficult to combine.

Towards the eastern end of Chichester Harbour lies the ancient and picturesque village of Bosham, with its Saxon church and harbour slipway, where the highest

Saltmarsh, Pagham Harbour

Bar-tailed godwit *Limosa lapponica*

of little egrets on Thorney Island. This beautiful heron is now becoming a regular feature of certain south coast sites (see also Brownsea Island, p. 200).

East Head (NT; SU 766990), at the entrance to Chichester Harbour, is dominated by shifting shingle and sand, with dunes and saltmarsh. Apart from the wildfowl and waders, this site has a rich and rather special flora, with unusual species such as sea bindweed and sea-heath, as well as fine stands of sea-lavenders and thrift.

A little further east is Pagham Harbour LNR (CC; SZ 856966, OS 197), just west of Bognor Regis. This is a superb place for wintering wildfowl and waders, notably Brent geese, shelduck, pintail, goldeneye, black-tailed godwit, and grey plover, with the chance of divers, Slavonian grebe, eider, common scoter, and smew. Other waders often seen here during the migrations are green and wood sandpipers and little stint. The shingle has a thriving colony of little terns, with oystercatchers and ringed plovers, and shelduck also breed nearby. Little and barn owls both breed in this area, and with luck you might spot a ring-necked parakeet, which breed around Church Norton. The saltmarsh has plants such as cord-grass, glasswort, and sea-purslane, with sea-kale, yellow horned-poppy, and sea campion on the nearby shingle. Selsey Bill, to the south, is a favoured seawatching site with pomarine skuas a speciality in early May.

tides fill part of the main road with seawater and ducks swim happily across the street. There are some splendid walks around the bays here and fine views over the water and mudflats, even from the comfort of the local pubs.

The bays attract huge winter flocks of dunlin and knot, with redshank, curlew, black- and bar-tailed godwits, sanderling, greenshank, and grey plover. The wildfowl include wigeon, shelduck, pintail, teal, goldeneye, and red-breasted merganser, and both Slavonian and black-necked grebes regularly show up here. It is hard to miss spotting the very large numbers of Brent geese – often over 5000 – swinging in over the saltmarshes and flats in loose skeins.

At the centre of Chichester Harbour lies Thorney Island (actually a peninsula). The RSPB has a reserve here (Pilsey Island), which is famous for its impressive wader roost. There is also a regular roost

SITE 151 Arun Valley

Excellent wetland sites with a fine array of wildlife, notably waterbirds.

The Arun rises just south of Billingshurst and meanders southwards to reach the sea at Littlehampton. There are several locations in the Arun Valley with interesting riverside meadows which are regularly

flooded, and these are well worth a visit. Such meadows are a magnet for winter waders and wildfowl. About 100 Bewick's swans regularly winter in the Arun Valley, mainly at Pulborough, Waltham, and

Amberley Wildbrooks

Amberley, although they are sometimes seen at Arundel. Other winter visitors are hen harrier and short-eared owl.

The Arun Valley ditches (notably at Amberley Wildbrooks and Pulborough Brooks) hold good populations of the rare ramshorn snail *Anisus vorticulus*, which is otherwise mainly a broadland species.

One of the best reserves in the Arun Valley is Arundel (WWT; TQ 0208, OS 197). This is a super site at which to learn wildfowl identification, and it is one of the best wetland sites in Sussex. It is open all year and free to WWT members. A boardwalk takes visitors through one of Sussex's largest reedbeds, with bird hides at strategic points. For less active visitors, a comfortable viewing lounge gives good views of ducks and other waterbirds without the need to brave the elements.

The reserve occupies part of the Arun's floodplain, and is fed by clear spring water rising from the chalk hills nearby. Careful landscaping has channelled the water to create a variety of pools and wetland habitats. There is an excellent information building with educational displays. The walkways through the reserve provide good views of both tame and wild birds, predominantly waterfowl. In addition to the collections, Arundel attracts many wild birds, including Bewick's swans.

The old watercress beds and reedy fringes are a prime winter roosting site for many birds, including bearded tit, bittern, and water rail. Breeding birds here feature the local Cetti's warbler, water rail, and kingfisher, alongside the commoner reed and sedge warblers and reed buntings.

All three woodpeckers breed on the reserve, as do nuthatch, marsh tit, sparrowhawk, kestrel, tawny and barn owl, cuckoo, grey heron, mute swan, ruddy duck, and mandarin. Hides give good views of waders such as redshank, snipe, greenshank, and common and green sandpipers. The damp ground at the edges of the reeds has flowers such as hemp-agrimony, great willowherb, purple-loosestrife, and meadowsweet.

Pulborough Brooks (RSPB; TQ 0417) is just south of Pulborough, on a loop of the Arun. There is a car park and visitor centre, a circular footpath, and hides with views over the flooded meadows. In winter there may be Bewick's swans, white-fronted geese, gadwall, pintail, teal, and shoveler, alongside the large numbers of wigeon and mallard. Flowering-rush and frogbit (the latter a nationally declining aquatic) may be seen in the ditches, and the dragonflies include the rare club-tailed dragonfly, which breeds nearby on the Arun.

Nearby New Bridge Canal, Billingshurst (TQ 068260, OS 197) is a disused canal and river with good dragonflies (16 species): hairy and club-tailed dragonflies, white-legged damselfly, downy emerald, and scarce chaser.

SITE 152 Kingley Vale

A remarkable wood dominated by aged yew trees, in a superb hillside site with ancient burial mounds and commanding views.

Magical is not too fanciful an adjective to describe Kingley Vale NNR (SU 824088, OS 197; 150 ha), with its year-round dark, brooding canopy of dense yew foliage – cold and dank in winter and deliciously cool in the heat of the hottest summer's day. This site can justifiably be called unique, being the finest yew wood in Britain, and possibly in the whole of Europe. Although yew is a widespread tree or shrub, there are not many places where it forms entire woods as a canopy dominant, as here. More commonly, it appears sporadically in the shrub-layer of other woodland communities, as it does in some of the beech woods of central and western Europe. Although many of these trees are undoubtedly of great age, most are probably less than 200 years old, and ecologists now tend to regard the downland yew communities as stages in a succession towards a mixed woodland with beech and ash. The reserve is dominated by the yew wood, but also contains scrub and broadleaved woodland, as well as chalk grassland.

The scrub has hawthorn, blackthorn, juniper, spindle, wayfaring-tree, traveller's-joy, and white bryony.

The chalk grassland is very rich, with as many as 50 species of flowering plant in a single square metre. There are species such as horseshoe and kidney vetch, bird's-foot-trefoil, common rock-rose, harebell, clustered bellflower, and round-headed rampion, and the orchids include fly, bee, frog, fragrant, pyramidal, and autumn lady's-tresses. In some areas the upper layers are more acidic and here there are patches of species such as heather and tormentil that are not so well suited to calcareous soils.

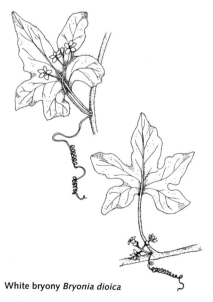

White bryony *Bryonia dioica*

Southern England

There is a nature trail from the field museum, which describes a circular route through the main habitats. The best time to visit Kingley Vale is in spring or summer, particularly on a warm day when the dry, open downs and the cool, shady wood provide the starkest of contrasts. This is also the best time to see butterflies, which include chalk-hill and Adonis blue, silver-washed fritillary, and purple emperor, as well as commoner species.

Botanically, some of the most interesting of the downland woods in the county are those which have been found to contain

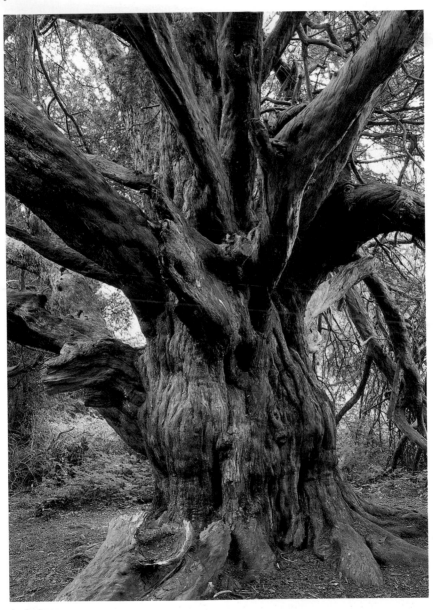

Ancient yew

large-leaved lime, a species whose main strongholds in Britain are the southern Pennines, north-east Yorkshire, and the Wye Valley. These sites are mostly in woods on the steeper scarp slopes or at the foot of the slopes, towards the western end of the Downs, in West Sussex and neighbouring Hampshire. One of the best of these is at Rook Clift, Treyford (SU 820182). The limes are mostly coppiced stools of considerable age, and the associated flora is typically ash, whitebeam, field maple, hazel, wych elm, and invading sycamore, with some beech, yew, pedunculate oak, and holly. Local ground flora species include twayblade, early purple orchid, gladdon, and spurge-laurel, and occasionally the fly honeysuckle and Italian lords-and-ladies, and the rare moss *Mnium stellare*. The invertebrates of these unusual communities include the rare cheese snail (*Helicodonta obvoluta*) and the leafhopper *Pediopsis tiliae*.

A selection of other important sites in the county

Adur Estuary (RSPB; TQ 212047), with its marshes and mudflats, is good for waders.

Black Down (NT; SU 9230) lies just south of Haslemere and rises to 280 m, the highest point in Sussex, with the eastern slopes carrying fine beech trees. Elsewhere there is mixed oak woodland, heath, and pasture.

Burton Pond Woodlands (WT; SU 978181, OS 197) is a varied reserve with woodland, heath, bog, and open water.

Cissbury Ring (NT; TQ 1409) is a good downland site.

Ebernoe Common (WT; SU 976278, OS 197). Ancient woodland with wild service-tree, wild daffodil, and bluebells. Also nightingales, purple emperor, and white admiral.

Park Corner Heath (TQ 511148). Mixed woodland with heathy grassland. Good for dragonflies and butterflies, the latter including silver-washed and both pearl-bordered fritillaries, grizzled skipper, and white admiral. Moths: cream-spot tiger, and eyed, elephant, pine, and broad-bordered bee hawk-moths. A good site for dormice.

Stedham Common (WT; SU 856218, OS 197) is mainly sandy heath, with some pine and birch woodland.

The Mens (WT; TQ 024237; 155 ha) is a wooded common and one of the richest wildlife sites in the region; a large remnant of the ancient Wealden Forest. Good for fungi, birds, and flowers.

Warnham NR (TQ 168323, OS 187) has a reed-fringed lake with woodland, scrub, and meadows. A total of 18 dragonflies and 23 butterflies are known from here, and these include the rare brilliant emerald and the local downy emerald, along with red-eyed damselfly and banded demoiselle.

East Sussex

153 Ashdown Forest

Former hunting forest with a rich heath, bog, and woodland flora and fauna.

Ashdown Forest (TQ 4332, OS 187), south-east of East Grinstead, is a classic Wealden site, consisting of a number of woods but also the largest area of lowland heath in south-east England. This was famously the landscape which inspired A. A. Milne to write his Winnie-the-Pooh stories.

Although forest by name, like the New Forest (p. 322), Ashdown Forest in fact consists of a mixture of woodland, scrub, and heath, both dry and wet, and so offers a wide range of habitats. Plants of the boggy sites include bog asphodel, cottongrass, bog-moss, and round-leaved sundew. The woods are interestingly mixed, with oak and birch, but also willow and Scots pine and tracts of carr with alder and alder buckthorn. Silver birch has spread out to cover parts of the heath, and there are also patches in which sweet chestnut is dominant.

The birds are typical of woodland and heath, with kestrel, sparrowhawk, hobby, tree pipit, stonechat, woodcock, nightjar, and nightingale. Hen harriers and great grey shrikes are occasional in winter. Mammals are well represented, with foxes, badgers, stoats, weasels, and wood

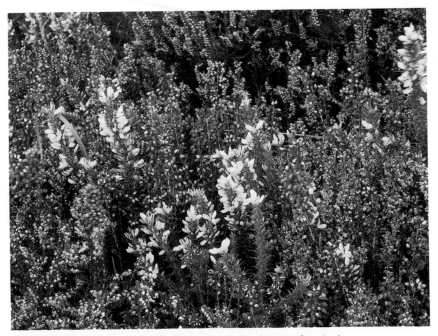

Heather (*Calluna vulgaris*), bell heather (*Erica cinerea*), dwarf gorse (*Ulex minor*)

mice. Deer are quite a feature, with roe, muntjac, and some sika in addition to the commoner fallow. The area is particularly rich in invertebrates as well; it has many dragonflies, and the butterflies include fritillaries (silver-washed, dark green, pearl-bordered, and small pearl-bordered), grayling, and silver-studded blue. The impressive emperor moth breeds on the heath, as does the bog bush-cricket.

In addition to the dry heath, there is also wet heath, grading into true bog. Heather, bell heather, gorse, and dwarf gorse are prominent in the dry heath, with cross-leaved heath in damper places. The bogs, with their bog-mosses, also have common cottongrass, bog asphodel, and sundew.

Fungi are much in evidence (best searched for in the autumn), with porcelain fungus (*Oudemansiella mucida*) and fly agaric (*Amanita muscaria*) particularly noteworthy. The former (also called slimy beech cap or poached egg fungus) is often found on beech branches while the latter is the unmistakable cartoon gnome fungus and tends to grow under birch.

Old Lodge SSSI (WT; TQ 460302, OS 198; 97 ha) preserves a representative portion of Ashdown Forest heathland, with its typical mix of woodland, heath, and bog.

SITE
154 South Downs

Fine walking country, with views over rolling countryside to the sea. Flowers and butterflies are the chief glories of the South Downs.

The South Downs, which stretch roughly from Winchester in the west to Eastbourne in the east, come closest to the coast in East Sussex, plunging steeply to the sea at Beachy Head. Although originally wooded, these rolling hills have been grazed for centuries by both sheep and rabbits, resulting in a very characteristic traditional habitat of chalk grassland, which quickly develops into scrub, and eventually woodland, if protected from grazing.

Viper's-bugloss
Echium vulgare

Downland plants include horseshoe vetch, bird's-foot-trefoil, greater knapweed, fairy flax, bugle, and wild thyme, with orchids such as bee, burnt, and early spider-orchid. In addition to common blue, there are also healthy populations of Adonis and chalk-hill blue, and the striking marbled white.

The river Cuckmere meanders through its broad floodplain in a series of wide loops and pools, before reaching the sea at Cuckmere Haven and the Seven Sisters Country Park (FC; TV 519995). This beautiful coastal site covers 280 ha of saltmarsh, chalk downland, and the coastal shingle and cliffs. In addition to more familiar plants such as carline and dwarf thistles, squinancywort, common centaury, autumn gentian, and common spotted-, early purple, and pyramidal orchids, there are rarer downland species including round-headed rampion, moon carrot, rock sea-lavender, small hare's-ear, and least lettuce.

The shingle has yellow horned-poppy, sea-kale, sea beet, mayweed, curled dock,

Seven Sisters

and viper's-bugloss, while the saltmarsh has sea-blite, sea aster, sea-purslane, sea wormwood, and glassworts. Ringed plovers and common terns nest in the area, and the lush meadows, water, and nearby scrub are a welcome first stop for migrants returning in the spring. On the cliffs there are fulmars and jackdaws. Regular passage birds are warblers, pied flycatcher, redstart, and ring ouzel, with rarer visits from bluethroat, red-breasted flycatcher, wryneck, and hoopoe.

Lullington Heath NNR (TQ 5502; 60 ha) contains one of the largest areas of chalk heath remaining in Britain. This is between the villages of Litlington and Jevington, west of Eastbourne and some 2 km north of the Seven Sisters Country Park. Here there is a rather unusual mix of plants of acid soils with those more usually associated with the chalk, resulting from the accumulation of a fine, slightly acid soil above the chalk. Acid indicators such as tormentil and heather grow alongside wild thyme and salad burnet.

Beachy Head (TV 595955) is an impressive cliff, reaching 150 m. It provides fine seawatching, especially productive during the migrations. Terns, scoters, and divers are frequent, with

occasional skuas, including pomarine. The butterflies include marbled white, chalk-hill blue, and grizzled skipper.

Birling Gap (NT; TV 554961) lies between Beachy Head and Cuckmere Haven. Access is by ladder to the shingle beach, which is backed by impressive chalk cliffs. Low tide reveals an array of sea creatures, and gulls and fulmars glide around the cliffs.

This whole area is good for passage migrants in spring and autumn, with firecrests and occasional even rarer species such as Pallas' and yellow-browed warbler.

The South Downs has recently been put forward as the next candidate NP (after the New Forest).

Wart-biter *Decticus verrucivorus*

Other sites nearby

Ditchling Beacon (NT; TQ 3313) also has excellent chalk downland, with glow-worms and marbled white.

Lewes Downs NNR (including Castle Hill and Mount Caburn) consists of a hill and valley with south-facing slopes, clothed in orchid-rich grassland with a little scattered scrub. It is part of the Lewes Downs SSSI, and Caburn is one of the most important of all the Bronze Age hill forts. This is the site of development of the famous South Down breed of sheep – now a rarity. The reserve is famous for its orchids, which include fragrant and pyramidal, and it has the largest British population of burnt orchid, with over 3000 plants in some years. There is also a rare rose here (small-leaved sweet-briar) which grows in the scrub. Invertebrates include Adonis and chalk-hill blue butterflies, and the scarce forester moth. Lewes Downs is 4 km south-east of Lewes. The best time to visit the site is between May and July, for wildflowers and invertebrates.

Castle Hill NNR (TQ 371070, OS 198; 50 ha; permit required) is a downland site with a very special flora and insect fauna. It is famous for its large numbers of early spider-orchid, and also boasts one of only a few British colonies of the wart-biter (a large bush-cricket).

Malling Down (WT; TQ 423107, OS 198), near Lewes, has a rich flora, with orchids and round-headed rampion; also Adonis and chalk-hill blues and marbled white.

155 Rye Harbour

Coastal reserve with shingle, saltmarsh, and gravel pits. A fine site for waders, especially in spring and autumn.

This site occupies a roughly triangular area between the rivers Brede and Rother and the shoreline. The shore is mostly protected by the Rye Harbour LNR (TQ 941188), while the flooded pit closest to Rye with its adjacent reedbeds, willow scrub, and wet grassland forms the reserve of Castle Water (WT; TQ 925185). The area is well served by a network of footpaths, and there are also hides close to some of the pools.

Botanically the site is rich, with five species of glasswort, and also the rare sea mouse-ear. Amongst the more showy plants are sea aster and the shingle specialities sea-kale, sea pea, and yellow horned-poppy.

Breeding birds here include common, Sandwich, and little terns, a few pairs of Mediterranean gull, redshank, lapwing, oystercatcher, and yellow wagtail. But the main bird interest is in the wintering and passage wildfowl and waders, with the latter coming in to roost at high tide. Regular waders of note include black-tailed and bar-tailed godwits, ruff, avocet, whimbrel, spotted redshank, greenshank, and (more rarely) Kentish plover and Temminck's stint. Black tern and little gull

Southern England

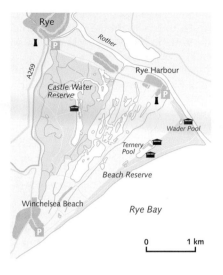

Rye

Rother

A259

Rye Harbour

Castle Water
Reserve

Wader Pool

Ternery
Pool

Beach Reserve

Winchelsea Beach

Rye Bay

0   1 km

are regular in spring, as is garganey. Marsh frogs thrive here, and there is an unusual invertebrate fauna, with medicinal leech, great silver diving beetle, bombardier beetle, grey bush-cricket, and wasp spider.

Not far to the west lies Pevensey Levels NNR (EN; TQ 670058, OS 199; 130 ha),

just north-east of Eastbourne, between Pevensey and Bexhill. It consists mainly of regularly flooded pasture with drainage ditches, and is part of a large area of grazed marshland covering over 4300 ha, much of which is designated an SSSI. This is a traditionally managed landscape and successful efforts are being made to encourage farming beneficial to the wildlife. The site was once a tidal lagoon, which was gradually cut off from the sea by banks of drifting shingle, forming a marsh. This was then drained in medieval times, and a regime of summer grazing and winter flooding developed.

One of the important practices here is regular ditch clearing, every few years. This keeps the drainage efficient and also benefits the special wildlife, which flourishes in the clear, relatively pollution-free water.

Some 110 species (about 70%) of Britain's aquatic flowering plants grow here, including more than a dozen species of pondweed and five species of duckweed. Of these, about 40 species are local or national rarities. The invertebrates are very diverse,

Stream on Pevensey Levels

too, with 21 species of dragonfly, great silver diving beetle, fen raft spider, and the leech *Placobdella costata*. This is also one of only a handful of British sites for the ramshorn snail *Anisus vorticulus*.

Wetland birds are well represented, with snipe, redshank, lapwing, and yellow wagtail amongst those breeding. The most notable amphibian is the marsh frog, which thrives in these southern coastal wetlands. In winter the flocks of wildfowl and waders are most impressive.

Access is restricted to prevent disturbance, but good views are possible from the minor roads, and car parks at Norman's Bay.

A selection of other important sites in the county

Fore Wood (RSPB; TQ 756126) is managed on a coppice system to provide a range of habitats of benefit to the ground flora (bluebells, wood anemones, early purple orchid) and birds (nightingales, garden warblers, blackcap) alike. Promotion of oak and hornbeam should increase numbers of birds, including hawfinch. White admiral.

Marline & Park Woods (WT; TQ 783123, OS 199; 40 ha) has woodland (with rare hornbeam coppice) and meadows.

Kent

156 Isle of Sheppey and Thames Estuary

Large island to the south of the Thames Estuary; largely low-lying and known mainly for its wildfowl and other waterbirds and waders.

The Isle of Sheppey lies between the mouth of the river Medway to the west and The Swale to the south. At its northern point lies the North Sea ferry port of Sheerness, but it is otherwise sparsely inhabited, except for some holiday home complexes, mainly used in the summer.

Much of the island consists of grazed marshy grassland, offering good feeding

Common razor shell *Ensis ensis*

grounds to many birds – over 240 species have been recorded here. Access is by the

A249 which crosses the narrow stretch of water (The Swale) separating the island from the mainland, just north of Sittingbourne. In winter it attracts huge, internationally important numbers of wildfowl and waders – thousands of Brent and white-fronted geese and tens of thousands of wigeon, along with curlew, oystercatcher, redshank, and grey plover.

There are two notable reserves here: Elmley Marshes (RSPB; TQ 926705), and Swale NNR (EN; TR 052682); both are well worth a visit.

Essex skipper *Thymelicus lineola*

At Elmley the water levels have been raised to recreate marsh conditions, with large patches of open water. Different grazing regimes are used to provide a mixture of grassland, which has increased the diversity of birds. In spring watch out for yellow wagtails and lapwings on the grazed meadows, and avocets on the flood, and listen for the loud croak of the marsh frog. Butterflies here include Essex skipper, and the dragonflies ruddy darter.

In winter these often chilly and rather bleak marshes attract several birds of prey – notably merlins, hen harriers, and peregrines – and you may spot short-eared owls quartering the fields and ditches as they hunt for small rodents. But be prepared for almost any raptor to turn up: buzzard, rough-legged buzzard, or possibly even a red kite. There are also thousands of wintering wildfowl, such as pintail and large flocks of wigeon, as well as Brent and white-fronted geese. Migrant waders include golden plover, whimbrel, black-tailed godwit, greenshank, ruff, green, wood, and curlew sandpipers and little stint, with spotted redshank in their black breeding plumage a speciality in June. Avocets now breed on the reserve, along with lapwing, redshank, oystercatcher, ringed plover, common and little tern, mallard, shoveler, gadwall, pochard, tufted duck, shelduck, and yellow wagtail.

Saltmarsh flowers to look for are sea-lavenders, sea aster, thrift, sea-purslane, glasswort, and golden-samphire, and there are grass snakes, slow-worms, and both common and marsh frogs on the reserve.

Elmley Marshes is reached by following the track sign-posted off the A249 for some 3 km to the car park. It is open daily (except Tuesdays, Christmas Day, and Boxing Day) from 9.00 am to 9.00 pm (or dusk). A walk of 2 km takes you to the first hide, with the furthest hide (at Spitend Point) being a similar distance further. Three hides surround a pool known as the flood, and a longer walk along the edge of The Swale takes you to Spitend Point at the tip of the promontory. This reserve is worth visiting at any time of year.

Swale NNR has tracks from the car park to a number of hides, one of which (tower hide) gives excellent views, and is a great place from which to scan the marshes. Alternatively, the sea wall is another vantage point. The beach at Shellness, which is well named, attracts flocks of shore larks and snow buntings in winter.

At Capel Fleet (TR 002682) there is a raptor watch point, from which the fields can be scanned. Sightings of birds of prey are most likely in the late afternoon in winter when the birds tend to congregate to roost (especially owls and harriers).

Other sites nearby

Cliffe Pools (OS 178; TQ 7277). This is one of the finest birdwatching sites in the region, the combination of coastal habitats and pools of varying depth proving irresistible to thousands of waders in particular. Autumn and winter are the best times to visit and, as well as commoner species, the following are pretty regular: both stints, spotted redshank, greenshank, grey plover, avocet, green sandpiper, little gull, Slavonian and black-necked grebes, goldeneye, hen harrier, and merlin.

Northward Hill (RSPB; TQ 784764, OS 178; 50 ha) (**High Halstow NNR**). Mixed woodland with woodpeckers, nightingales, warblers, Britain's largest heronry, and an impressive long-eared owl roost in winter (they sometimes breed). Also Essex skipper and purple and white-letter hairstreaks. The best time to see the herons (up to about 200 pairs), for which a permit is required, is February – they are early nesters and you will see more before the leaves appear. A later visit, in May, will probably be accompanied by songs of nightingale, blackcap, garden warbler, and turtle doves. In spring, the bluebells are impressive, and the butterflies

include white-letter hairstreak, a rather local species whose caterpillar feeds on the buds of elms. In winter the adjacent fields and marshes attract flocks of white-fronted geese, as well as hen harriers and merlins.

Nor Marsh & Motney Hill (RSPB; TQ 8270) may be viewed and visited from Riverside Country Park at Gillingham. The mudflats and saltmarshes are a favoured haunt of geese, sea ducks, and waders.

Oare Marshes (WT; OS 178) on The Swale Estuary has mudflats, saltmarsh, and pools, all ideal for waders. There is an information centre and car park, and good paths around the reserve along the edge of the mudflats and nearby Faversham Creek. Two hides, one overlooking one of the pools. Avocet and bearded tit are regular and may breed, but the best time to visit for the birds is autumn and winter. There are usually good numbers of black-tailed godwit, with frequent visits from common, green, wood, and curlew sandpiper, greenshank, and the occasional little egret. Other birds to expect are marsh harrier, short-eared owl, and merlin.

SITE
157 Blean Woods

One of the largest tracts of ancient broadleaved woodland in the whole of the region.

Blean Woods NNR (TR 109606, OS 179). This excellent woodland site preserves about 90 ha of mixed deciduous woodland, partly managed under a coppice-with-standards regime, to create good conditions for a rich ground flora and associated insects. The

Bluebell
Hyacinthoides non-scripta

main woodland type is sessile oak with hornbeam, a rather Continental community not well represented in the other regions of Britain. There are also sections in which sweet chestnut or beech are prominent, and there is the occasional wild service-tree.

Wood ants are common here – look out for their mounded nests. The undoubted star amongst the invertebrates here is the nationally rare heath fritillary. Blean is one of only two sites in Britain for this butterfly, which is best seen from late June to mid-July. The caterpillar feeds on common cow-wheat, which has been increased by regular coppicing. Estimates gave a total of some 10 000 of these pretty butterflies in 2000 – very impressive for a species which was almost extinct in Kent by the late 1980s. The woods hold many less familiar invertebrates, including rare beetles such as the orange and black *Acritus homeopathicus*, which is associated with burned patches in the woodland, and doubtless known to ancient charcoal burners.

The spring displays of bluebells and wood anemones can be quite spectacular, and the rides and glades also have familiar flowers such as common dog violet, cuckooflower, greater stitchwort, and bugle, as well as yellow archangel, wood spurge, common cow-wheat and lily-of-the-valley.

All the expected woodland birds are here: sparrowhawk, tawny owl, woodcock, the three woodpeckers, along with nuthatch, treecreepers, nightingales (about 30 pairs,

Heath fritillary *Mellicta athalia*

best heard in early May), marsh and willow tits, and also redpolls and siskins, mainly in the winter. Wood warblers and redstarts also usually breed here and with luck may be spotted, as may that hornbeam specialist the hawfinch. A patch of heath (rare in the county) has breeding nightjars and tree pipits, and it is worth watching out for woodcock. Listen, too, for the purring song of the turtle dove, a species which has declined markedly in recent years.

The RSPB reserve of Blean Woods is open from 7.00 am until an hour after sunset and includes a car park, picnic area, and a network of nature trails, one of which is wheelchair-friendly. It covers 310 ha, and includes oak–hornbean woodland, birch, and sweet chestnut. East Blean Wood is an adjacent reserve of the WT. It lies to the north-west of Canterbury, and can be reached from the A2 or A290, signposted from Rough Common. It has open access, and well-maintained footpaths.

SITE

158 Stodmarsh

Largest freshwater marsh south of the Thames, with a mixture of shallow lagoons, ditches, and extensive reedbeds; also wet woodland and meadows.

Stodmarsh NNR (EN; TR 221609; 163 ha) is a splendid wetland reserve, and undoubtedly one of the best examples of

this habitat in southern England. This wetland developed in a section of the Stour Valley subject to flooding, which by

Savi's warbler *Locustella luscinioides* (Mike Lane)

careful management has been turned into a perfect mix of woodland, scrub, reedbed, and open water – ideal for bird life and not without botanical and entomological interest as well.

In late spring listen for the booming call of the bittern – a rare sound these days. In addition to the expected reed and sedge warblers, you may hear the abrupt song of Cetti's warbler (a local speciality) or the seemingly endless reeling of a grasshopper warbler. The latter is worth double checking, however, especially if it comes from the reeds, as Savi's warbler is also possible here, and occasionally breeds. The numbers of Cetti's warbler vary, with population crashes following hard winters. Just for good measure, nightingales also breed here, mainly in the drier sites, so Stodmarsh is therefore a great place to get to grips with bird song. Small numbers of bearded tits are usually present in the reeds. The wet meadows are home to yellow wagtails, lapwing, snipe, redshank, shoveler, teal, and the occasional garganey. Other breeders here are marsh harrier and bearded tit, and hobbies regularly hunt over the reserve (as do noctule bats).

In winter, the reserve often has a great grey shrike in residence, as well as hen harriers, merlins, or the occasional rough-legged buzzard. There are often flocks of golden plovers, and water rails and bearded tits may be spotted in and around the reeds. The reserve is sometimes visited by Bewick's swans and white-fronted geese.

The plants include bogbean, greater spearwort, water forget-me-not, flowering-rush, marsh cinquefoil, marsh stitchwort, bladderwort, and frogbit. The ditches are also the haunt of grass snakes, water voles, and water shrews.

Access is easy along a flood barrier called the Lampen Wall, an embankment which crosses the reserve and gives good views over the nearby water and reedbeds. There is also a nature trail through the wet woodland. The reserve is east of Stodmarsh village, and west of Grove Ferry, about 500 m from the A28 Canterbury–Thanet road. There is a reserve car park in Stodmarsh. The reserve has two easy access trails and four hides, two of which are suitable for disabled access. There is also a nature trail, which is between 0.6 and 1.3 km, depending on the chosen route. There are leaflets available and panels for visitor information.

SITE 159 Kent downs

Rolling downland with species-rich chalk grassland – the haunt of butterflies and flowers, especially orchids.

The gently rolling grassland of the North Downs forms a superb habitat for many special flowers, and also for invertebrates, most notably butterflies. Like lowland heath, such places are managed and semi-natural, and most such sites would carry a climax broadleaved woodland if left to their own devices. The key factor responsi-

Southern England

Wild thyme *Thymus polytrichus*

ble for the creation and maintenance of downland is grazing, particularly by sheep, which have cropped the downland turf over many centuries, but also by rabbits, whose numbers have fluctuated over the years. Thus, again like heathland, chalk downland requires active management to retain its special richness, and to prevent succession through scrub to woodland. Although only scattered fragments remain in this area, there are some splendid downland reserves, such as those below.

Wye Downs NNR (TR 054469, OS 179; 130 ha) is mainly open chalk grassland, with patches of scrub and woodland, and has been an NNR for about 40 years. It is very rich in both plants and insects, with about 400 species of higher plant and about 2000 insect species. Orchids are a speciality here, with 19 recorded, amongst which are early and late spider-orchid, bee, fragrant, pyramidal, common spotted-orchid, lady, and greater butter-fly-orchid. The chalk grassland has horseshoe vetch, cowslips, autumn gentian, squinancywort, and both common and the rare dwarf milkworts. An impressive dry valley with rather steep sides, known as the Devil's Kneading Trough, lies at the centre of the reserve. This is a good site for the butterflies marbled white and Duke of Burgundy, and the rare black-veined moth breeds here at one of only a few British sites. Downland birds, such as meadow pipit, skylark, and kestrel thrive here, and there are more unusual species such as hawfinch (its favoured hornbeam is native in the woodland) and nightingale. The mammals include

common dormouse, which appreciates the hazel component of the woodland. Access is easy, with two parking areas and a clearly marked nature trail, which also helps to relieve public pressure from large areas of the reserve. The recommended time to visit (for maximum flowering) is May through early July.

Queendown Warren LNR (WT; TQ 827629, OS 178) is about 6 km south-east of Gillingham. This reserve is centred on an ancient area of chalk grassland which used to be a managed rabbit warren. Centuries of grazing have kept the grassland intact and has resulted in a rich community with a good chalk flora. In addition to typical chalk grassland species such as wild thyme, common milkwort, marjoram, common rock-rose, and bird's-foot-trefoil, there are horseshoe vetch and several orchids, including bee, fly, burnt, green-winged, man, and early spider-orchid. Both chalk-hill and Adonis blue can be seen here, and also stripe-winged grasshopper, a species characteristic of southern dry grassland. There are also interesting patches of scrub with

Bee orchid *Ophrys apifera*

Black-veined moth *Siona lineata*

hawthorn, elder, ash, dogwood, and hazel, and plenty of traveller's-joy clambering

amongst them – ideal cover for birds such as blackcap, whitethroat, and tits. Mature woodland is also represented here in the form of beech stands, mixed in places with oaks, hornbeam, birch, cherry, and sweet chestnut, and with bluebells, yellow archangel, honeysuckle, and both white and broad-leaved helleborines.

Lydden and Temple Ewell Downs (WT; TR 278453), just north-west of Dover, is one of Kent's best examples of chalk downland. It has rock-rose, horseshoe vetch, and orchids. There are several species of grasshopper and bush-cricket, and chalkhill blue and marbled white butterflies.

SITE 160 Dungeness

A highly unusual coastal region – the largest shingle formation in Europe – famous for its plants and invertebrates as much as for its seabirds.

The Dungeness Peninsula covers a large area to the south of Romney Marsh in southern Kent, mainly to the south of Lydd. This huge mass of over 2000 ha of shingle has built up gradually over thousands of years and a special flora is adapted to the vagaries of a shifting habitat. The nature sites to visit here include the splendid RSPB reserve, and the bird observatory.

Yellow horned-poppy
Glaucium flavum

Dungeness (TR 063196, OS 189), the RSPB's oldest reserve, is justly famous for its combination of shingle and extensive wetlands, which prove an irresistible combination for thousands of nesting seabirds. From the car park and nearby visitor centre, a series of footpaths afford good views of the wildlife, and several hides offer opportunities for observing the pools more closely.

Plants such as yellow horned-poppy and viper's-bugloss brighten up the shingle and the total flora stands at well over 430 species, including several rarities. The youngest shingle ridges have Babington's orache dominant, and the progressively older ridges have a more mixed flora, with species such as

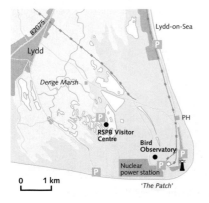

Southern England

Hawthorn, lichen heath

curled dock and sea-kale, then with false oat-grass, common cat's-ear, sea campion, mouse-ear hawkweed, hedge bedstraw, and the moss *Hypnum cupressiforme*. Still older ridges are dominated by broom, which reach a maximum age of about 20 years, with patches of lichens (notably *Cladonia*), the moss *Dicranum scoparium*, and English stonecrop. It is these older ridges where one might also find shepherd's cress, sheep's-bit, and the scarce Nottingham catchfly, the latter at one of its best sites in Britain. Common dodder is another interesting plant to look out for here.

The pools, scrapes, shingle banks, and islands provide ideal nesting sites for some 800 pairs of black-headed gulls, and birders here are well advised to check these carefully as this is one of very few places in Britain where the rare, but rather similar, Mediterranean gull breeds. There are also a few breeding common gulls. Another common breeder here (some 250 pairs) is the graceful Sandwich tern, originally named after the town of Sandwich further up the Kent coast.

Migration is an exciting period at Dungeness and many rare birds are seen, including pomarine skuas (often passing in early May), but the best areas to look for small migrants are the bushes around the observatory. Regular spring migrants include wheatear and ring ouzel, but there may also be rarer birds such as hoopoe, golden oriole, or subalpine warbler. Other migrants (more likely in autumn) are pied flycatcher, firecrest, red-backed shrike, wryneck, bluethroat, and tawny pipit. Black redstarts occasionally breed near the power station and it is always worth keeping an eye open for these charming birds.

One area of the reserve, known as Denge Marsh, has been managed to provide a rather different range of habitats, with shal-

Great crested newt *Triturus cristatus*

low pools and reedbeds. Here redshanks and lapwings breed, along with reed and sedge warblers. This is also where two rather special amphibians may be seen: marsh frog and great crested newt which breed in the ditches and ponds. Grass snakes and viviparous lizards are also found on the reserve. Burrowes Pit, the largest of the ponds in the reserve, is a good place to look for wildfowl, especially in winter when these may include smew. Watch out also for wintering grebes (including black-necked, red-necked, and Slavonian) and red-throated diver.

Opposite the RSPB reserve lies another large pit which may hold smew or ruddy duck in winter, but this can only be watched from the (at times busy) road. The coast to the east of Lydd is also worth visiting, especially for its waders which flock in to feed on the sandy flats. These include regular bar-tailed godwit, sander-ling, and grey plover, as well as more familiar species such as oystercatcher.

At the tip of the peninsula is the Dungeness lighthouse, which is open in summer and provides a spectacular view of the whole area.

Dungeness is one of the finest places for watching passing seabirds. A favoured spot is close to the outflow from the power station, called 'The Patch'. In spring, both little and Mediterranean gulls and roseate terns are regular visitors, while in autumn, gannets, great skuas, and little gulls may be seen, as well as Sandwich, Arctic, and black terns.

The southerly location makes Dungeness a good site for migrant butterflies such as painted lady and clouded yellow, and there are rare moths, too, including pygmy footman and Sussex emerald. A ground beetle new to Britain, *Bembidion coeruleum*, has recently been found here.

A selection of other sites in the county

Bough Beech Reservoir (WT; TQ 495489) is a good birdwatching site, with regular rarities, including night heron and little crake, passing ospreys, and autumn waders.

Ham Street Woods NNR (EN; TR 003337, OS 189; 97 ha): oak coppice with woodcock, redstart, hawfinch, and nightingale, and hoopoe regular in summer.

Hothfield Common SSSI (WT; TQ 969459, OS 189; 56 ha): bog and heath with heath spotted-orchid, keeled skimmer, and slow-worms.

Langdon Cliffs (NT; TR 335422) are part of the famous white cliffs, with a rich flora: bee, fragrant, and pyramidal orchids, meadow clary; butterflies include small blue.

Pegwell Bay (TR 340632, OS 179) is one of the best sites in the south for migrant birds, with a long list of unusual species such as black redstart, firecrest, golden oriole, and gull-billed tern.

Reculver Country Park SSSI (WT; TR 224693; 37 ha): cliffs and shore, with Roman fort remains; interesting fossils.

Sevenoaks Wildfowl Reserve (TQ 520565, OS 188) is a group of old gravel diggings, with good waterbirds.

Toy's Hill (NT; TQ 465517): woodland and heath on a greensand ridge; slopes have a fine show of spring bluebells.

Tudeley Woods (RSPB; TQ 616433): orchid-rich woods and heath, with tree pipit, woodlark, nightingale, willow tit, hawfinch, and nightjar.

Appendix
Organizations concerned with conservation and the environment

Principal government bodies

Countryside Agency
John Dower House
Crescent Place
Cheltenham
Gloucestershire GL50 3RA
Tel: 01242 521381
Fax: 01242 584270
Website: www.countryside.gov.uk

Countryside Council for Wales
Plas Penrhos
Fford Penrhos
Bangor
Gwynedd LL57 2LQ
Tel: 01248 385500
Fax: 01248 355782
Website: www.ccw.gov.uk

English Nature
Northminster House
Peterborough PE1 1UA
Tel: 01733 455000
Fax: 01733 568834
Email: enquiries@english-nature.org.uk
Website: www.english-nature.org.uk

Scottish Natural Heritage
12 Hope Terrace
Edinburgh EH9 2AS
Tel: 0131 4462201
Website: www.snh.org.uk

Joint Nature Conservation Committee (JNCC)
Monkstone House
City Road
Peterborough PE1 1JY
Tel: 01733 562626
Fax: 01733 555948
Email: feedback@jncc.gov.uk
Website: www.jncc.gov.uk

Forestry Commission
The general headquarters are in Edinburgh
231 Costorphine Road
Edinburgh EH12 7AT
Scotland
Tel: 0845 FORESTS (3673787)
Fax: 0131 3343047
Email: enquiries@forestry.gsi.gov.uk
Website: www.forestry.gov.uk

The Forestry Commission has three national offices
England
Great Eastern House
Tenison Road
Cambridge CB1 2DU
Tel: 01223 314546
Fax: 01223 460699
Email: fc.nat.off.eng@forestry.gsi.gov.uk

Scotland
231 Costorphine Road
Edinburgh EH12 7AT
Tel: 0131 3340303
Fax: 0131 314615
Email: fas.nat.office@forestry.gsi.gov.uk

Wales
Victoria Terrace
Aberystwyth
Ceredigion SY23 2DQ
Tel: 01970 625866
Fax: 01970 626177

Selected other organizations

Biological Records Centre
Monks Wood
Abbots Ripton
Huntingdon PE28 2LS
Tel: 01487 772400
Website: www.brc.ac.uk

British Dragonfly Society
The Haywain
Hollywater Road
Bordon
Hants GU35 0AD

British Trust for Ornithology (BTO)
The Nunnery
Thetford
Norfolk IP24 2PU
Tel: 01842 750050
Fax: 01842 750030
Email (magazine): btonews@bto.org

Butterfly Conservation
Manor Yard
East Lulworth
Wareham
Dorset BH20 5QP
Tel: 01929 400209
Website: www.butterfly-conservation.org

Field Studies Council
Cathy Preston
Preston Montford
Montford Bridge
Shrewsbury SY4 1HW
Tel: 01743 850674
Fax: 01743 850178
Email: fsc.headoffice@ukonline.co.uk

Mammals Trust UK
15 Cloisters House
8 Battersea Park Road
London SW8 4BG
Tel: 020 74985262
Fax: 020 74984459
Email: enquiries@mammalstrustuk.org
Website: www.mammalstrustuk.org

National Trust
36 Queen Anne's Gate
London SW1H 9AS
Tel: 020 72229251
Website: www.nationaltrust.org.uk

National Trust for Scotland
Wemyss House
28 Charlotte Square
Edinburgh EH2 4ET
Tel: 0131 2439300
Website: www.nts.org.uk

Plantlife – The Wild Plant Conservation Charity
21 Elizabeth Street
London SW1W 9RP
Tel: 020 78080100
Fax: 020 77308377
Email: enquiries@plantlife.org.uk
Website: www.plantlife.org.uk

Royal Society for the Protection of Birds (RSPB)
The Lodge
Sandy
Bedfordshire SG19 2DL
Tel: 01767 680551
Fax: 01767 692365
Website: www.rspb.org.uk

Wildfowl and Wetlands Trust
Slimbridge
Gloucestershire GL2 7BT
Tel: 01453 890333
Fax: 01453 890827
Email: enquiries@wwt.org.uk
Website: www.wwt.org.uk

Wildlife Trusts
Main office:
The Kiln
Waterside
Mather Road
Newark NG24 1WT
Tel: 0870 0367711
Fax: 0870 0360101
Email: info@wildlife-trusts.cix.co.uk
Website: www.wildlifetrust.org.uk

There are 46 local WTs, managing more than 2300 nature reserves

- *Avon*: (0117) 9268018; avonwt@cix.co.uk
- *Beds, Cambs, Northants, & P'boro*: (01223) 712400; northwt@cix.co.uk
- *Berks, Bucks, & Oxon*: (01865) 775476; bbowt@cix.co.uk
- *Birmingham & Black Country*: (0121) 4541199; urbanwt@cix.co.uk
- *Brecknock*: (01874) 625708; brecknockwt@cix.co.uk
- *Cheshire*: (01270) 610180; cheshirewt@cix.co.uk
- *Cornwall*: (01872) 273939; cornwt@cix.co.uk
- *Cumbria*: (01539) 448280; cumbriawt@cix.co.uk
- *Derbyshire*: (01332) 756610; derbywt@cix.co.uk
- *Devon*: (01392) 279244; devonwt@cix.co.uk
- *Dorset*: (01305) 264620; dorsetwt@cix.co.uk
- *Durham*: (0191) 5843112; durhamwt@cix.co.uk
- *Essex*: (01206) 729678; admin@essexwt.org.uk
- *Glamorgan*: (01656) 724100; glamorganwt@cix.co.uk
- *Gloucestershire*: (01452) 383333; info@gloucswt.cix.co.uk
- *Gwent*: (01600) 715501; gwentwildlife@cix.co.uk
- *Hampshire & Isle of Wight*: (02380) 613636; hampswt@cix.co.uk
- *Herefordshire*: (01432) 356872; herefordwt@cix.co.uk
- *Herts & Middlesex*: (01727) 858901; hertswt@cix.co.uk
- *Kent*: (01622) 662012; kentwildlife@cix.co.uk
- *Lancashire*: (01772) 324129; lancswt@cix.co.uk
- *Leicestershire & Rutland*: (0116) 2702999; leicswt@cix.co.uk
- *Lincolnshire*: (01507) 526667; lincstrust@cix.co.uk
- *London*: (0207) 2610447; londonwt@cix.co.uk
- *Manx*: (01624) 801985; manxwt@cix.co.uk
- *Montgomeryshire*: (01938) 555654; montwt@cix.co.uk
- *Norfolk*: (01603) 625540; nwt@cix.co.uk
- *Northumberland*: (0191) 2846884; northwildlife@cix.co.uk
- *North Wales*: (01248) 351541; nwwt@cix.co.uk
- *Nottinghamshire*: (0115) 9588242; nottswt@cix.co.uk
- *Radnorshire*: (01597) 823298; radnorshirewt@cix.co.uk
- *Scotland*: (0131) 3127765; scottishwt@swt.org.uk
- *Sheffield*: (0114) 2434335; sheffieldwt@cix.co.uk
- *Shropshire*: (01743) 241691; shropshirewt@cix.co.uk
- *Somerset*: (01823) 451587; somwt@cix.co.uk
- *Staffordshire*: (01889) 508534; staffswt@cix.co.uk
- *Suffolk*: (01473) 890089; suffolkwildlife@cix.co.uk
- *Surrey*: (01483) 488055; surreywt@cix.co.uk
- *Sussex*: (01273) 492630; enquiries@sussexwt.org.uk
- *Tees Valley*: (01642) 253716; clevelandwt@cix.co.uk
- *Ulster*: (01396) 830282; ulsterwt@cix.co.uk
- *Warwickshire*: (01203) 302912; warkswt@cix.co.uk
- *West Wales*: (01437) 765462; wildlife@wildlife-wales.org.uk
- *Wiltshire*: (01380) 725670; administrator@wiltshirewildlife.org
- *Worcestershire*: (01905) 754919; worcswt@cix.co.uk
- *Yorkshire*: (01904) 659570; yorkshirewt@cix.co.uk

Wildlife Trust (Scottish)
Cramond House
Cramond Glebe Road
Edinburgh EH4 6NS
Tel: 0131 3127765
Fax: 0131 3128705
Email: scottishwt@cix.co.uk

Woodland Trust
Autumn Park
Grantham
Lincolnshire NG31 6LL
Tel: 01476 581111
Fax: 01476 590808
Email: enquiries@woodland-trust.org.uk
Website: www.woodland-trust.org.uk

WWF-UK
Panda House
Weyside Park, Catteshall Lane
Godalming
Surrey GU7 1XR
Tel: 01483 426444
Fax: 01483 426409
Website: www.wwf-uk.org

Glossary

Blanket bog Extensive rain-fed peat mire covering flat or sloping land

Boulder-clay Clay-dominated soil with boulders; of glacial origin

Carr Scrub or low woodland developed in fen habitats, usually with alder and willow

Charophyte (stonewort) Member of a group of algae, with brittle, calcified tissues; found in clear, brackish waters

Clint Block in limestone pavement, resulting from dissection by grikes

Coombe Local name for a valley, mainly in the south-west of Britain

Corrie (cirque, cwm) Hollow, open at the lower edge, and with steep sides; a glacial feature found in mountains

Culm grassland Marshy grassland found in north Devon and adjacent parts of Cornwall, occurring over the Culm Measures – strata of Carboniferous slates and sandstones

Dune blow-out Section of a sand dune system eroded by wind

Dune slack Flat, marshy hollow within a sand dune system

Eutrophic Nutrient-rich; often applied to water bodies, which are typically well vegetated

Flush Wet area caused by surface seepage; typically in hilly locations and with characteristic vegetation

Grike Channels in limestone pavement, resulting from uneven erosion, and dividing the pavement into clints

Hydrosere Succession in vegetation from open water through aquatic and emergent plants to those of dry land

Karst Region with underlying limestone and features resulting from calcareous erosion

Limestone pavement Extensive area of exposed limestone, usually dissected by grikes and with characteristic vegetation

Machair coastal grassland over shell sand, typical of north-west Scotland; holds characteristic flora and fauna

Mire Wetland developed on peat, such as bog or fen habitats

Pingo An ice-cored mound developed in cold conditions; on melting may result in a hollow depression

Poor fen Nutrient-poor fen

Ramsar site Wetland site of international importance, listed under the convention signed in Ramsar, Iran, in 1971

Rich fen Nutrient-rich fen

Roding Display flight of woodcock, involving regular slow flight around territory at dusk, accompanied by croaking and whistling calls

Schist Medium-grained rock formed from slate

Schwingmoor Floating mire developed over water

Scree Coarse rock debris at the base of a cliff, usually on a steep slope

Stool The thickened base of a coppiced tree; tree stump from which shoots grow

Wildwood Original forest cover before the main impact of people and their associated livestock

Further reading

Asher, J., Warren, M., Fox, R., Harding, P., Jeffcoate, G., and Jeffcoate, S. (2001). *The Millennium Atlas of Butterflies in Britain and Ireland*. Oxford University Press.

Brooks, S. (1997). *Field guide to the dragonflies and damselflies of Great Britain and Ireland*. British Wildlife Publishing, Hampshire.

Chinery, M. (1993). *Insects of Britain and Northern Europe* (3rd edn). Harper Collins, London.

Cromack, D. (ed.) (2001 and annual). *The birdwatcher's yearbook and diary 2002*. Buckingham Press, Peterborough.

Gibson, R., Hextall, B., and Rogers, A. (2001). *Photographic guide to sea and shore life of Britain and North-west Europe*. Oxford University Press.

Greeves, L. and Trinick, M. (1996). *The National Trust guide* (revised edn). National Trust Enterprises, London.

Hill, P. and Twist, C. (1998). *Butterflies and dragonflies: a site guide* (2nd edn). Arlequin, Essex.

Holden, P. and Cleeves, T. (2002). *RSPB handbook of British birds*. A & C Black, London.

Marren, P. (1994). *England's National Nature Reserves*. Poyser, London.

Marren, P. (2002). *Nature conservation*. New Naturalist 91. Harper Collins, London.

Moss, B. (2001). *The Broads*. New Naturalist 89. Harper Collins, London.

Rackham, O. (1994). *The illustrated history of the countryside*. Phoenix Illustrated, London.

Snow, D. W. and Perrins, C. M. (ed.) (1998). *The birds of the Western Palearctic* (concise edn). Oxford University Press.

Stace, C. (1999). *Field flora of the British Isles*. Cambridge University Press.

Thomas, J. and Lewington, R. (1991). *The butterflies of Britain and Ireland*. Dorling Kindersley, London.

Tipling, D. (1996). *Top birding spots in Britain and Ireland*. Harper Collins, London.

Tolman, T. (2001). *Photographic guide to the butterflies of Britain and Europe*. Oxford University Press.

Young, G. (ed.) (1999). *The Wildlife Trust's nature reserves guide*. The Wildlife Trusts, Nottinghamshire. (Also published by Collins.)

Geographical Index

KEY TO SITE MAP SYMBOLS

National border	National Park or Forest Park
Site described in the text	Reserve or area of interest
River, stream or canal	Information point
Road	Parking
Dual carriageway	Hide or observation point
Path or track	High ground
Railway	Marsh
Ferry	Reedbed
Lighthouse	Dunes
Castle or tower	Sand or mudflats
Embankment	Shingle
Peak, height in metres	Woodland
Cliff or crag	Trees: deciduous / coniferous